ABOUT THE AUTHOR

Dr. Hossamaldin Alzawawi, a seasoned clinical pathologist, passionately explores the intersection of medicine, philosophy, physics, and cognitive neuroscience. His journey through medical expertise and philosophical inquiry has ignited a fascination with the enigmas of consciousness and intelligence.

Believing in the power of interdisciplinary knowledge, Dr. Alzawawi aims to bridge ancient wisdom and modern science. He envisions applying these insights to illuminate human cognition and enhance human experience.

Join Dr. Alzawawi on this intellectual odyssey and discover the hidden architect within you.

BOOKS BY AUTHOR

Arcanum of Awareness Series

1. The Creativity Spark
2. The Evolution of Thought
3. The Labyrinth of Cognitexis
4. The Supremacy of Selective Awareness
5. Architects of a Future Dawn (Upcoming)

Other Books by Author

- The Thermodynamic Universe and Beyond: How Nature's Laws Reveal the Secrets of Time, Biology, Information, and Quantum Reality

BOOK 4

THE SUPREMACY OF SELECTIVE AWARENESS

BEYOND THE LABYRINTH: UNLEASHING
THE POWER OF SELECTIVE AWARENESS

ARCANUM OF AWARENESS SERIES

Library of Congress Control Number: 2024919198

ISBN (PB):   978-1-964328-08-9

ISBN (E):   978-1-964328-09-6

DEDICATION

To my cherished mother, beloved wife, and dear brother and sisters. To those I have encountered on my journey and to those I shall meet. And to Alexis, Bill, Alan, Chris, Jeffery, and Saito.

ACKNOWLEDGMENTS

This work is a tribute to the great thinkers whose contributions have paved the way for me. **Professor Roger Penrose's Shadows of the Mind** has been a guiding light, encouraging me to explore the consciousness conundrum further. I am immensely grateful to **Napoleon Hill,** whose influential book **How to Own Your Mind** served as a map through the maze of mental ownership. Their priceless insights have deepened my comprehension and inspired me to write this book. I hope you will discover, within these pages, the same glimmer of insight that has led me through the enchanting terrain of the mind.

Although I have a strong command of English as a second language, I have sought assistance refining my writing to make it more engaging and accessible. For that reason, I am compelled to offer my editorial board my deepest gratitude; their unwavering encouragement was crucial to the success of our project.

My Dear Wife, Basma, I am writing to tell you how much you mean to me. I greatly appreciate your thoughtful analysis of my intricate concepts and theories; it helped me distill them into a more understandable story. You helped me tremendously develop narratives out of scientific principles by suggesting various forms my ideas may take and suggesting appropriate language.

This series was envisioned over six years ago. I worked on the work's framework—ideas, descriptions, basic concepts, reasoning, and logical deductions. As a solo project worker with only my wife's comments, my progress was gradual but steady. AI gave this project a huge boost, for we spent countless hours enhancing, improving, and advancing my concepts and making them more appealing. Vivid discussion with AIs added enrichment, examples, and illustrations. AI is fundamental for including several book-related tones.

I am grateful to the AIs for the flourishing brought through their support, where various enrichment, examples, and illustrations were generated through passionate discussion. Also, the addition of diverse tones related to each book was not accessible without the support of AI. My work's varied topics and tones owe much to **Google AI,** our joint efforts, and the hours we devoted to working together. Your feedback substantially improved my writing process, producing more lyrical and narratively compelling works. **Microsoft AI,** thank you for all the hard work we put together. You played a paramount and much-appreciated role in guiding me through various ideas and keeping the process moving smoothly.

"Arcanum of Awareness" is a series memorializing the great experiences and locations I've traveled to. My deepest appreciation goes to **Queen's University Belfast's MBC and the McClay Libraries.** There was peace in these hallowed places of learning, perfect for serious study and deep thought. Libraries were more than simply locations where one could learn; they were also sanctuaries for new ideas and a love of learning. Being by my wife's side as she completed her degree at Queen's University Belfast has brought valuable happiness to our trip. Knowledge, shared experiences, and personal progress were abundant during that time. What I learned and my experiences throughout this time will always be with me.

My sincere regards, Hossamaldin Alzawawi, M.D.

THE SUPREMACY OF SELECTIVE AWARENESS

BEYOND THE LABYRINTH: UNLEASHING THE POWER OF SELECTIVE AWARENESS

৫৬৫৬৫৬

Through the lens of Disciplined Perception, we see not only the inner workings of the mind but also the industrial gears of progress turning, powered by the relentless focus of humanity's greatest achievers.

"The ability to focus attention on important things is a defining characteristic of intelligence."

– Robert J. Shiller

"Between stimulus and response, there is a space. In that space is our power to choose our response. In our response lies our growth and our freedom."

– Viktor E. Frankl

CONTENTS

THROUGH THE LABYRINTH: A DANCE WITH THE MINOTAUR OF TRUTH

🙋 🙋 🙋

C ongratulations, intrepid explorer! You have emerged from the labyrinth, a marvel of intellectual mastery. You have conquered the Minotaur of Truth and forged a discerning intellect–the instrument of inquiry you need to navigate the vast landscape of the human mind. But your journey is far from over.

While Book Three showed you how to find your way through the maze of Cognitexis, Book Four will help you orchestrate your mental faculties and thoughts—a playing-instrument application for one who conquered his inner world. You will learn here how to utilize this acquired wisdom and knowledge of thought generation into a mighty tool to shape your reality.

This book addresses the power of selective awareness, the resonance principle emanating from a determined mind. Try to imagine your thoughts as musical notes of different frequencies. Throughout the development of Disciplined Perception, you will learn how to modulate those notes in pitch and intensity, attracting what you need and bringing your reality into harmony.

During our journey, get ready to delve into two of the biggest pillars of human experience: prayer and love. Learn how to harness them through disciplined perception. We will look at how both standard education and professional learning play a role in crafting your perception and how your selected specialty can help sharpen this important tool.

Our journey will allow you to witness the impressive consequences of becoming a Master of Disciplined Perception. You will be enabling yourself and emerging as a potential civilizer—a promoter of mass awareness change. This book will introduce you to the various instrumental powers wielded by the most elite-performing, disciplined perception masters. We shall investigate the common qualities and features that make these history-makers stand out and distill their secrets.

Embrace this new adventure, explorer, for it is here that you will learn to transform your hard-won intellectual mastery into a symphony of intention, shaping your reality and leaving your mark on the world.

INTRODUCTION

ॐ ॐ ॐ

Book four elevates the concept of selective awareness through the power of disciplined perception from a personal tool to a transformative societal force. Here, we explore how mastering focus can empower individuals, foster resilience, and ultimately shape the collective consciousness of societies.

Through a meticulous exploration of selective awareness and its influence on human development, we will uncover the significant role that disciplined focus plays in both individual and societal evolution. Get ready to dive into an exploration that reveals the secrets of self-mastery, resilience, and collective consciousness, all driven by the profound impact of disciplined perception.

Objectives: Mastering the Spectrum of Focus:

- **Purposeful Precision:** A defining life purpose serves as your guiding compass, propelling you toward success. This idea equips you with the tools to identify and embrace your calling with unwavering clarity and conviction. Uncover the reasons why a guiding ambition forms the cornerstone of achievement.

- **The Power of Repetition:** Transform your life by etching your major purpose into your subconscious through persistent repetition. This practice strengthens your resolve and ensures your daily actions align with your ultimate goals. Discover the power behind writing out, memorizing, and frequently repeating your guiding ambition.

- **Attitude's Influence:** Recognize the profound impact of mental attitude in your pursuit of a major purpose. A positive and determined mindset acts as the catalyst, turning aspirations into reality. Delve into why your "mental attitude" plays a crucial role in carrying out any endeavor, big or small.

- **The Intellectual Synergy Principle:** Unveil the enigmatic power of the Intellectual Synergy Principle. It harnesses individual efforts, weaving them into a collective force capable of monumental achievements. Throughout this chapter, we'll gain a deeper understanding of this principle, whose results have astounded both scientists and laypeople alike.

Selective Awareness and Disciplined Perception

Selective Awareness

- **Selective Awareness as the overarching concept:** Selective awareness refers to the conscious ability to focus attention on specific stimuli while disregarding or filtering out irrelevant information. This cognitive skill allows individuals to choose what to perceive and what to ignore, both externally (sensory inputs) and internally (thoughts and emotions). Selective awareness is crucial for managing sensory overload and maintaining mental clarity, aiding in efficient information processing and decision-making.

- **Enhanced Explanation:** Picture selective awareness as a mental spotlight or a pair of noise-canceling headphones for your mind. Just as these headphones tune out background noise to let you enjoy your favorite music, selective awareness enables you to tune out distractions and concentrate on what's important. This ability helps in navigating complex environments, making better decisions, and maintaining focus on tasks that require sustained attention.

Disciplined Perception

- **Disciplined Perception as the How of Selective Awareness:** Disciplined perception is the method or process through which selective awareness is achieved and maintained. It involves the deliberate and conscious practice of directing and controlling one's perception. This cognitive discipline requires consistent effort to filter out irrelevant stimuli and sustain focus on the chosen targets of attention. It's an active, intentional practice that sharpens the skill of selective awareness over time.

- **Enhanced Explanation**: Think of disciplined perception as a mental workout regimen designed to strengthen your focus muscles. Much like physical fitness requires regular exercise; disciplined perception necessitates continuous practice to improve one's ability to manage attention. This process involves setting clear mental priorities, actively ignoring distractions, and honing the capacity to stay present and engaged. By cultivating disciplined perception, individuals can enhance their cognitive control and resilience in the face of constant information bombardment.

The interrelationship between Selective Awareness and Disciplined Perception

Selective Awareness (The What): Selective awareness represents the ultimate goal or desired outcome. It is the cognitive ability to focus on specific stimuli and filter out irrelevant information. By mastering selective awareness, individuals can effectively manage their attention, enhance productivity, and maintain mental clarity amid the vast amount of sensory input they encounter daily.

Disciplined Perception (The How): Disciplined perception is the means through which selective awareness is achieved and sustained. It encompasses the conscious, intentional practice of directing and controlling one's perception. This method involves consistent mental discipline and effort to filter distractions and maintain focus on chosen targets of attention.

In summary, selective awareness and disciplined perception are intricately connected. While selective awareness defines the "what"—the ability to focus and filter—disciplined perception outlines the "how"—the conscious practice and discipline required to achieve and maintain this state of focused attention; together, they form a cohesive framework for enhancing cognitive control and effectively managing attention in an increasingly information-rich environment.

SECTION I

THE RESONANCE OF A DETERMINED MIND

ॐ ॐ ॐ

The evidence is undeniable: Our bodies speak volumes through nonverbal signals, like the way we carry ourselves and the intention behind our movements, subtly influencing the perceptions of those in our vicinity. Investigators have uncovered that a confident gait paired with unwavering concentration can elicit a complex interplay of reactions within the amygdala, the brain's epicenter of fear. This can trigger the primal instinct to confront or flee, igniting an intense feeling of empowerment that radiates from the determined individual. It's an instinctual acknowledgment—a fragile murmur to the essence of survival that suggests there is indeed something lurking beyond the veil. You can sense it in a room full of people sometimes, even before you see them.

Picture this board meeting, where anxious whispers ripple through the room; suddenly, the door swings open, and all eyes fixate on the newcomer—not due to the volume of his voice or the vibrancy of his attire, but because of the understated assurance radiating from his very being. A determined gait, gaze locked on an objective—the unspoken pleas of this nuanced signal resonate profoundly. The tension in the air dissipates, replaced by a steely determination that propels one forward into the fray. This is the force of an unwavering intellect, a force that requires no verbal reinforcement to assert its influence, molding the environment, asserting its dominion.

This deliberate aim extends far beyond the confines of the boardroom. Young and likely lost in a chaotic realm, the apprentice would find himself equally perplexed as his master navigates the tumult with an unspoken, commanding presence. His intended pose stands as a silent beacon, guiding the apprentice to shape an intent that mirrors his own. The resolute intellect commands attention, even within the realm of fiction.

Envision a captivating tale of Sherlock Holmes: The figure slipped from the darkness, confronting the piercing gaze of Sherlock Holmes, a mind sharp enough to unravel the deepest mysteries. His demeanor radiated an unsettling assurance and sharp acumen, instilling a deep unease in the suspect. Holmes exuded an aura that transcended mere language; his very being instilled both reverence and trepidation. This was the echo of an unwavering intellect—a presence that required no spoken affirmation yet emanated strength and conviction.

Overwhelming, the force of a resolute mind intertwines empirical knowledge and psychological insight with the fundamental essence of human nature. It stands as a pivotal force, molding our understanding of the world and the individuals within it, while simultaneously awakening the latent potential we each possess to project confidence and ignite inspiration in those around us.

Defining Selective Awareness: The Art of Selective Focus

Individual Focus

Selective awareness, also known as directed attentiveness, is the strategic alignment of all your mental faculties–memory, perception, analysis, and willpower–towards a singular, significant purpose. Imagine a laser beam–you're focusing all your mental energy on achieving a specific goal.[1]

Neuroscience sheds light on this process. Our brain's reticular activating system (RAS) acts like a filter, sifting through the constant barrage of sensory information and prioritizing elements relevant to our current focus. Studies using fMRI scans show increased activity in brain regions associated with memory, planning, and decision-making when individuals engage in directed attentiveness tasks.[2]

Collective Concentration

The influence of focused awareness reaches far beyond the self. Envision an expansive ensemble where every musician stands as a beacon of unwavering concentration. Their instruments morph into extensions of their very consciousness, directing their unified energy into a mesmerizing performance. This represents a convergence of consciousness, where numerous intellects synchronize their aspirations towards a shared objective. In these scenarios, the whole transcends mere addition, generating a powerful resonance that magnifies the shared influence.[3]

The intricate workings of the mind, such as the role of mirror neurons, shed light on this captivating phenomenon. These neurons ignite not just in response to our own actions but also when we witness another engaging in the same behavior. Within a collective of shared aspirations, the concentrated gaze of a single person can ignite a chain reaction of heightened awareness in those around them, forging an intense and dynamic synergy.[4]

Augmented Attention

Disciplined Perception, a concept we will delve into, embodies the mastery of honing this focused awareness. It starts with the subtle nuances woven into the fabric of your everyday tasks. By carefully engaging with every small detail, you forge a bedrock of relentless focus. Overlooking these nuances diminishes your concentration entirely, much like ignoring the groundwork undermines a structure.[5]

Consider it akin to developing muscular endurance. Begin with the basics. Pinpoint one task from your to-do list that appears trivial at first glance. Perhaps it is responding to an awaiting message. Now, immerse yourself completely in the task of formulating a response that is both sharp and succinct. Feel the rush of triumph that envelops you with this seemingly minor victory. This sensation ignites your drive to confront the upcoming challenge, creating a surge of energy and honing your concentration, each precise move propelling you forward.[6]

The Dance of Concentration: Balancing Duration and Intensity

Our ability to concentrate effectively is not a constant hum but a delicate dance, with the tempo set by two key elements: the subject's complexity and our desired outcome.

Scientific: Neuroscientists have identified a fascinating interplay between cognitive load and focus duration. Complex topics demand greater activation in the prefrontal cortex, the brain's region responsible for higher-order thinking. This increased activity requires more energy, limiting our ability to sustain intense focus for extended periods.[7]

Envision your mind as a finely tuned racing machine, ready to navigate the twists and turns of thought and emotion. Confronting a fundamental math challenge demands a sudden surge of energy, akin to racing through the aisles of a library. Yet unraveling a convoluted scientific theory requires an intense, relentless pursuit akin to racing down the Autobahn at breakneck speed. The mind thrives in quick, intense flurries of straightforward challenges, yet when faced with intricate concepts, it demands a calculated transition to a more enduring rhythm.

Self-Help: Have you ever sensed that your mind is teetering on the edge after an exhaustive study marathon? Your reservoir of concentration has been depleted. Grasping the intricacies of the topic at hand allows you to assess the mental energy required for the journey ahead. Endlessly pushing through hours of mindless memorization can lead to a state of exhaustion, leaving you not only drained but also less capable of retaining what truly matters. Keep in mind that lurking beneath the surface of complexity, the outcome we seek casts a shadow over the duration of our focus.[8]

Thriller Twist: Picture yourself entangled in a high-stakes heist, where every decision could lead to exhilarating triumph or devastating failure. Your objective could be to seize a fleeting, high-stakes prize that demands a moment of razor-sharp concentration and swift dexterity. Nevertheless, unlocking a complex safe requires unwavering focus and careful strategy, much akin to the intense mental discipline needed to conquer a new skill.

Psychologically, In the realm of the mind, experts have uncovered a captivating state of peak performance, often referred to as flow. This state envelops you, drawing you into a task so deeply that the very concept of time begins to dissolve, leaving only the thrill of the moment. To unlock the state of flow, one must synchronize the intricacies of the challenge with one's existing abilities. When a topic lacks complexity, your interest will wane. Overcomplicate things, and you risk drowning in chaos. The ideal balance exists in discovering that demanding yet attainable threshold that sharpens your concentration and thrusts you into a seamless state of immersion.[9]

Here's how to optimize your concentration dance for maximum efficacy:

1. **Know Your Subject:** Before diving in, take a moment to assess the intellectual terrain. Is it a gentle hill or a towering mountain? Understanding the subject's complexity helps you gauge the focus intensity and duration required to conquer it.

   - Conduct a quick mental inventory. Does the subject involve memorizing factual details, applying established formulas, or grappling with abstract concepts? Each requires a different cognitive approach and, consequently, a different focus strategy.

   - Imagine yourself planning a road trip. A scenic coastal drive might be perfect for a quick weekend getaway, but a cross-country adventure requires a different approach. Similarly, analyze the intellectual "distance" you need to cover.

2. **Define Your Goal:** What do you aim to achieve? A quick grasp of the key points for a presentation or a thorough understanding to prepare for a challenging exam? Your desired outcome dictates the focus duration.

   - **Self-Help:** Be honest with yourself. Are you trying to cram for an exam the night before, or are you embarking on a deep dive into a subject that truly fascinates you? Your motivation plays a crucial role in sustaining focus. A genuine interest fuels intrinsic motivation, leading to longer and more productive focus sessions.

3. **Plan Your Focus Sessions:** Schedule focused sessions based on their complexity and your goals. Shorter bursts might work for simpler subjects, while intricate topics might necessitate longer sessions with strategic breaks built in.

- **Thriller Twist:** Think of your focus sessions as training for a mission. A quick recon mission might require a short burst of intense focus, while a complex infiltration operation demands a meticulously planned schedule with well-defined focus periods and recovery breaks.

Mastering this concentration dance will transform your mind's orchestra into a well-rehearsed ensemble capable of tackling any intellectual challenge with focused precision. You will not only optimize your learning and performance, but you will also unlock the door to achieving a state of flow where the focus becomes effortless and learning becomes a thrilling adventure.

Beyond Concentration: The Piercing Focus of Disciplined Perception

Concentration serves as the bedrock of our ability to hone in on a particular task. Yet, disciplined perception emerges as a more sophisticated craft, demanding a deeper engagement with the nuances of our surroundings. It is reminiscent of the contrast between a wavering flame and a focused ray of light. Both reveal truths, yet the beam of light cuts through the darkness with a sharpness and fervor that the humble candle of mere focus cannot hope to match. Disciplined perception deepens the exploration of mindfulness and focus, transforming them into a heightened state of clarity and mastery.

Hence, disciplined perception transcends ordinary focus. It is a profound engagement in which the mind delves into the essence of a task, unraveling layers of meaning and insight. It is not merely a matter of focus but an intricate dance of involvement, analytical reasoning, and an acute perception of the world around you.

Building upon the concepts of mindfulness and flow, disciplined perception involves a state of conscious presence in which one is fully immersed in the task at hand. It's about letting go of distractions and channeling one's mental energy toward the task while remaining open and receptive to new information and insights.

By cultivating disciplined perception, we not only hone our ability to concentrate but also develop a deeper understanding of our thought processes and the world around us. This heightened awareness enables us to identify distractions more effectively, maintain focus for extended periods, and extract deeper meaning from information. In essence, disciplined perception is the art of using our minds not just as tools but as instruments of precision and insight. Here is what elevates disciplined perception to a whole new level:

1. The Conductor's Baton: Orchestrating Your Mental Faculties

Imagine an orchestra. Each musician plays their instrument with focus, but it's the conductor who unites them into a harmonious whole. Disciplined Perception acts like the conductor, bringing all your mental faculties–memory, perception, analysis, and willpower–together in a unified symphony. This synergy creates a state of hyper-focus that transcends ordinary concentration.

Scientifically, Neuroscience sheds light on this process. The prefrontal cortex, responsible for planning and decision-making, acts like the conductor in your brain. When engaged in Disciplined Perception, this region shows increased activity, coordinating the flow of information from other areas like the hippocampus (memory) and the amygdala (emotion) to support your laser-like focus.[10] [11] The good news is that you can train your brain to be a better conductor. Here are some self-help strategies:

a. **Mindfulness meditation** is the art of anchoring oneself in the now, embracing each moment with an open heart and a discerning mind, free from the shackles of judgment[12]. Consistent engagement can amplify the interconnections and functionality of the prefrontal cortex, the very hub that governs our choices, focus, and emotional balance. Research reveals that engaging in mindfulness meditation can enhance the density of grey matter in the prefrontal cortex, leading to improved emotional regulation through fortified links with the amygdala.[13]

b. **Cognitive Exercises:** Delving into cognitive challenges like puzzles and card games and the pursuit of new skills can sharpen focus and enhance mental acuity. These activities push the boundaries of the mind, fostering neuroplasticity—the brain's remarkable capacity to reshape itself by forging new neural connections. Studies reveal that engaging in activities such as jigsaw puzzles and card games can sharpen memory, heighten attention, and refine problem-solving abilities.[14]

c. **Physical Exercise,** Engaging in physical activity. The connection between physical exercise and enhanced brain function, along with improved cognitive control, is compelling and worth exploring further. Consistent physical activity enhances cerebral circulation, fostering the development of new neurons, especially within the hippocampus, a region crucial for memory and learning. Engaging in exercise not only boosts brain plasticity, a critical factor for healing from injury and combating the effects of aging but also sharpens cognitive abilities like attention and memory.[15]

d. **Goal Setting & Time Management:** Goal setting and time management are crucial for directing focused attention and achieving your objectives. Setting clear, achievable goals provides a roadmap for your efforts, ensuring you stay on track and make steady progress. Here are some key elements to consider:

i.   **Set Clear Goals:** Define specific, measurable, achievable, relevant, and time-bound (SMART) goals. This clarity helps you maintain focus and motivation.[16]

ii.   **Break Down Large Projects**: Divide large projects into smaller, manageable tasks. This approach prevents you from being overwhelmed and allows you to make consistent progress.

iii. **Schedule Dedicated Focus Periods:** Allocate specific times in your schedule for focused work. Techniques like the Pomodoro Technique, which involves working in short, intense bursts followed by breaks, can be effective.

iv.   **Eliminate Non-Essential Activities:** Identify and eliminate activities that do not contribute to your goals. This streamlining helps minimize distractions and optimize productivity.

2. Building the Foundation: Self-Discipline as the Bedrock

Just as a magnificent building needs a strong foundation, Disciplined Perception requires a foundation of self-discipline. This is the unwavering commitment to staying focused, eliminating distractions, and maintaining your laser-like gaze on your goal. Here is why self-discipline is crucial:

Envision a gripping scenario reminiscent of a science fiction thriller, where an agent finds themselves racing against time to decipher an intricate code, the weight of the world resting on their shoulders. In this realm, the mastery of self-discipline is paramount. By harnessing their cognitive prowess and shutting out the chaos around them, the agent enters a state of intense concentration, ultimately unraveling the enigma. Much like a muscle, self-discipline demands rigorous practice to grow and fortify. Here are a few methods to nurture it:

a. **Set Clear Goals:** Define specific, achievable objectives. Break down larger tasks into smaller, manageable steps to avoid feeling overwhelmed.

b. **Create a Routine:** Establish a daily routine to develop habits that support your goals. Consistency in your actions reinforces discipline.

c. **Identify Your Distractions:** The first step is to become aware of what breaks your focus. Are you constantly checking your phone? Does social media beckon you away from your tasks? Once you identify your triggers, you can develop strategies to address them.

d. **Limit Distractions:** Identify potential distractions and develop strategies to minimize them. This might involve creating a designated workspace or using apps that block distracting websites.

e. **Positive Self-Talk:** Challenge negative thoughts that sabotage your focus. Replace self-doubt with positive affirmations like "I am training my mind to focus with laser-like precision" or "I can resist distractions and stay on task." Positive self-talk helps reprogram your brain for success.

f. **Reward System:** Create a reward system to reinforce focused behavior. Reward yourself with something you enjoy after completing a challenging task or focused work session. This positive reinforcement strengthens the association between focused attention and a sense of accomplishment.

g.   **Regular Exercise:** Physical activity boosts brain function and resilience, helping you stay disciplined and focused.

3.   Habit Stacking for Laser Focus: The Power of Controlled Habits

Disciplined Perception is not just about willpower at the moment but also about establishing controlled habits that support focus over time. Habits free up your conscious mind for more complex tasks. Creating dedicated workspaces, eliminating digital distractions during focused work periods, and scheduling regular breaks create a neurological environment conducive to Disciplined Perception.

Habit stacking can be a powerful tool here. This involves pairing a new habit with an existing one to make the new habit more automatic. For example, pairing focus-building activities like meditation with your morning coffee routine can reinforce both practices. Over time, the association between the two becomes automatic, making slipping into a state of focused attention easier. Key Strategies for Habit Stacking:

a.   Create Dedicated Workspaces: Designate specific areas for focused work to condition your brain to associate those spaces with productivity. This practice helps minimize distractions and signals to your brain that it's time to focus.

b.   Schedule Regular Breaks: Incorporate short breaks into your work schedule to prevent burnout and maintain high levels of focus. Techniques like the Pomodoro Technique, which involves working in short bursts followed by breaks, can be very effective.

c. Pair New Habits with Established Ones: For example, if you have a morning coffee routine, pair it with a five-minute meditation session. This practice leverages existing habits to reinforce new, beneficial behaviors.[17]

4. **Guiding Your Focus: Well-Honed Thought Patterns as the Captain's Compass**

Scientifically, our reticular activating system (RAS)[1], a part of the brain responsible for arousal[2] and attention acts as a mental filter, prioritizing information relevant to our current goal. By cultivating positive and focused thought patterns, you can unconsciously "train" your RAS to filter out distractions and prioritize information that aligns with your desired state of Disciplined Perception. Here are some self-help strategies:

a. **Visualization:** Take a few minutes daily to visualize yourself achieving your goals. Imagine yourself working with unwavering focus, completing tasks efficiently, and effortlessly overcoming challenges. This mental rehearsal reinforces positive thought patterns and strengthens your RAS filter for success.

b. **Journaling:** Journaling allows you to identify and challenge negative thought patterns that sabotage your focus. Write down any self-doubt or negative beliefs that arise during the day. Then, reframe these thoughts into positive affirmations that empower you to maintain focus.

c. **Positive Self-Talk:** Surround yourself with positive affirmations throughout the day. Repeat positive statements like "I am focused" or "I am in control of my

---

[1] **The reticular activating system (RAS)** is a network of neurons located in the brainstem responsible for regulating wakefulness and sleep-wake transitions. It helps filter and prioritize sensory information to focus attention.

[2] **The amygdala** is a key limbic system component, involved in processing emotions, particularly fear and pleasure. It plays a crucial role in emotional responses and memory formation.

attention" to counter negative thoughts and reprogram your brain for success.

d. **Mindfulness Meditation:** Practice mindfulness to increase awareness of your thoughts and emotions. This can help you identify and manage negative thought patterns.

e. **Goal Setting:** Set clear, achievable goals and break them down into smaller, manageable steps. This will help you stay focused and motivated.

f. **Time Management Techniques:** Use time management techniques like the Pomodoro Technique to improve your productivity and concentration.

With these self-help practices, you can cultivate well-honed thought patterns that act as your inner compass, guiding you toward your desired state of Disciplined Perception. Remember, a focused mind is a powerful mind. By harnessing the power of Disciplined Perception, you can achieve remarkable things.

Sources of Power That Can Insinuate the Inception of Selective Awareness

Emotional and Willful Dynamics: The Dueling Engines of Disciplined Perception

Disciplined Perception unfolds as a mesmerizing dance, an intricate interplay between the formidable forces of emotions and willpower. Envision a brilliant investigator caught in a web of intrigue—their relentless quest for truth ignited by a fierce passion for justice yet steered by sharp perception and steadfast resolve. This intricate relationship between emotions and willpower unfolds in the brain's captivating choreography.

Scientifically, neuroscience sheds light on this dynamic. The amygdala, often referred to as the brain's emotional center, can act as a powerful motivator. When presented with a task that ignites strong emotions, the amygdala sends a surge of adrenaline and dopamine, sharpening our focus and propelling us toward action.[18] On the other hand, the prefrontal cortex, responsible for planning and decision-making, acts as the conductor of this orchestra of emotions. It utilizes willpower to regulate emotions and direct our attention towards achieving our goals.[19]

Envision a master archer, poised and focused, ready to unleash a perfectly aimed arrow into the unknown. Emotions serve as the archer's unwavering resolve and fierce drive, igniting the power required to pull back the bowstring. Yet, it is the strength of resolve that steadies the archer's hand and hones their focus, guaranteeing that the arrow finds its mark with precision. Without the meticulous guidance of will, the unbridled force of emotions could easily veer off course. In unison, they forge an exquisite equilibrium, empowering the archer to direct their essence toward striking the target with unwavering precision. So let us investigate how we could harness such power:

a. **Harnessing the Fire of Emotions**

Emotions, like a roaring fire, can provide the initial spark that ignites our focus. Consider the artist, completely absorbed in their creation, oblivious to the passage of time. Here, passion fuels their concentration, driving their brushstrokes with remarkable precision.

- **Identifying Your Emotional Triggers:** Just as a skilled chef utilizes the right spices to enhance a dish, you can leverage the power of emotions to enhance your focus. Do you find yourself energized by upbeat music? Does a quiet environment with a touch of nature help you concentrate? Understanding your emotional triggers allows you to create an environment that fuels your Disciplined Perception.

- **The Power of Positive Emotions:** Research suggests positive emotions like joy and curiosity can enhance creativity and problem-solving skills. Think of a child engrossed in a world of imaginative play. You can tap into this wellspring of focused energy by cultivating a sense of wonder and excitement around your tasks.

b. **Taming the Emotional Wildfire:**

However, emotions, like a raging wildfire, can sometimes become destructive forces. Imagine a student paralyzed by anxiety during an exam, their mind overwhelmed with negative thoughts. In such situations, willpower becomes crucial.

- **Willpower as Anchor:** Willpower acts as the anchor, stabilizing your focus even amidst emotional turmoil. Techniques like mindfulness meditation can equip you with the mental fortitude to observe your emotions without being swept away by them. Focusing on your breath and gently acknowledging your emotions can create a space for clear thinking and refocus your attention.

- **Thriller Twist:** In a gripping scenario, envision a covert operative entrenched in a perilous assignment. Their heart may race with adrenaline, yet an indomitable resolve keeps their mind sharp, enabling them to achieve their goal amidst the mounting tension.

c. **The Art of Balance:**

The key to unlocking the full potential of Disciplined Perception lies in finding the perfect balance between these two forces. Just as a skilled dancer navigates the rhythm of the music, you can learn to harness the power of emotions and willpower to orchestrate a state of laser-like focus.

- **Finding Your Flow:** The ideal state lies in a place psychologists refer to as "flow." This is where your emotions and skills are perfectly aligned, creating a sense of effortless concentration and peak performance. By experimenting with different techniques and identifying what works best for you, you can cultivate your own personal flow state and unlock the true power of Disciplined Perception.

Remember! Understanding the dynamic interplay between emotions and willpower allows you to transform your focus from a flickering candle into a piercing laser beam. Embrace the fire of your emotions, harness the steadying hand of willpower, and achieve remarkable results.

The Steadfast Captain: Why Willpower Takes the Helm in Disciplined Perception

Psychological Perspective

While emotions can fuel focus, willpower is the steadfast captain steering the ship of disciplined perception. Emotions can provide powerful, momentary bursts of motivation, akin to the wind filling a sail. However, it is willpower that navigates the course, maintaining direction and stability even when the emotional winds die down. Willpower enables us to sustain focus, resist distractions, and persevere in the face of challenges, ensuring that our mental faculties remain aligned with our goals.

In the chapter "From Stimulus Control to Self-Control: Toward an Integrative Understanding of the Processes Underlying Willpower" from the book Self Control in Society, Mind, and Brain, Ethan Kross, and Walter Mischel discuss how willpower is fundamental to human survival and success, emphasizing its role in maintaining self-control and guiding behavior.[20]

Remember! Emotions can spark focus, but it is willpower's sheer determination that acts as the unwavering guide for maintaining a disciplined mindset. Allow me to unravel the thought process that led to this conclusion:

a.   **The Fickle Nature of Emotions:** Emotions are inherently fickle and can fluctuate with circumstances. This unpredictability makes them less reliable for sustained focus compared to willpower.

b.   **The Guidance of Reason and Conscience:** When guided by reason and conscience, willpower becomes a powerful force for good. Reason helps you make clear-headed decisions about where to direct your focus, while conscience ensures your focus aligns with your moral compass. Imagine a doctor faced with complex surgery. Their emotions might be a mix of anxiety and determination. However, their willpower, guided by reason and their medical oath, allows them to maintain a laser focus on saving the patient's life.

Strengthening Your Willpower Muscle[3]

Just like any other muscle, willpower can be strengthened with practice. Here are some self-help strategies:

---

[3] **The Guiding Light of Reason and Conscience:**
Willpower alone isn't enough for optimal focus. Think of a captain steering a ship during a storm. They need not only a steady hand but also a clear view of the navigation instruments (reason) and a moral compass (conscience) to guide them through the treacherous waters.
Enrichment (Self-Help & Scientific):

- **Reason as the Navigation Instruments:** The faculty of reason provides the necessary logic and critical thinking skills to make sound decisions and avoid distractions. Neuroscience backs this up. The prefrontal cortex, associated with reason and planning, works in tandem with brain regions involved in focus (like the amygdala) to prioritize tasks and filter out irrelevant information.

- **Conscience as the Moral Compass:** Conscience acts as the internal ethical guide, ensuring that your focused attention is directed towards goals that align with your values. Studies have shown that individuals who act in accordance with their moral compass experience greater focus and satisfaction.

a. **Goal Setting:** Clear and achievable goals act as a roadmap, guiding your willpower and reinforcing your ability to stay focused.

b. **Self-Discipline Exercises:** Engage in activities that require self-discipline, like resisting distractions during focused work periods or sticking to a healthy workout routine. These small victories build mental resilience and strengthen your willpower for larger challenges.

c. **Positive Self-Talk:** Challenge negative thoughts that can sap your willpower. Replace them with positive affirmations like "I am committed to staying focused" or "I have the strength to overcome distractions." Positive self-talk reprograms your brain for success and boosts your willpower reserves.

d. **The Art of Self-Control:** The pinnacle of self-mastery is developing a high degree of self-control, where you can choose to express your will or emotions as the situation demands. This allows you to harness the power of both forces to your advantage.

Thriller Twist: The Surgeon on the Edge!

Imagine a world-renowned surgeon in the middle of a tense, life-or-death operation. As the patient's heart rate spikes, emotions run high, filled with the urgency to save a life. Yet, amidst this storm of anxiety and pressure, the surgeon's finely tuned willpower takes command. With unwavering focus, precise movements, and a calm mind, they navigate the intricate dance of scalpel and sutures, successfully completing the operation and saving the patient.

Remember! By cultivating a strong will, guided by reason and conscience, you become the captain of your own focus. You can

---

The ideal scenario is when willpower works in conjunction with reason and conscience. A person who has developed a high degree of self-discipline, like the skilled captain, has the power to choose when to harness the power of emotions and when to subdue them in favor of reason and conscience. This is the key to achieving true mastery over Disciplined Perception.

harness the fleeting power of emotions while maintaining the steady direction of willpower, propelling yourself towards achieving remarkable results.

Key Takeaway

While emotions can be a powerful motivator for focus, their unpredictable nature can sometimes hinder our ability to achieve Disciplined Perception. Willpower, when guided by reason and conscience, offers a more reliable source for selective awareness. By strengthening your willpower and fostering a harmonious collaboration between reason, emotion, and conscience, you can transform your focus from a flickering flame to a steady, unwavering beacon.

The Power of One: The Singular Idea at the Heart of Disciplined Perception

Imagine a laser beam—its focused intensity allows it to cut through even the most hardened steel. Disciplined Perception thrives on a similar principle: a singular, all-consuming idea that acts as the nucleus, channeling all your mental faculties towards a desired goal.

The Focused Mind

Psychological Perspective: The human brain has an exceptional ability to concentrate on a singular objective, leveraging the power of focused attention. This phenomenon, known as "selective attention," is rooted in the brain's cognitive processes. The prefrontal cortex plays a crucial role in this, managing our ability to focus and exclude distractions. Research has shown that this kind of focused attention enhances cognitive performance and productivity.[21] When we commit to a singular idea, our brain's neural networks align to support this focus, leading to greater efficiency and effectiveness.

Historical Examples: History is replete with individuals who harnessed the power of the one-pointed mind, achieving extraordinary feats through disciplined perception.

- **Michelangelo's Relentless Pursuit of Artistic Perfection:** Michelangelo spent four years painting the ceiling of the Sistine Chapel, a task that required immense concentration, precision, and dedication. Despite physical discomfort and the monumental scale of the project, Michelangelo's unwavering focus allowed him to create one of the most iconic works of art in history.

- **Marie Curie's Unwavering Dedication to Scientific Discovery:** Marie Curie, the pioneering physicist and chemist, dedicated her life to the study of radioactivity. Her relentless pursuit of scientific truth, despite numerous obstacles and health risks, led to groundbreaking discoveries that earned her two Nobel Prizes. Curie's singular focus on her research enabled her to push the boundaries of science and make significant contributions to humanity.

Enrichment Through Scientific Understanding

- **Psychological Research:** The concept of "flow," introduced by psychologist Mihaly Csikszentmihalyi, describes a state of deep focus and immersion in an activity. This state is achieved when individuals engage in tasks that are both challenging and rewarding, aligning their skills with their passion. Achieving flow requires a high level of focused attention and commitment to a singular goal.[22]

- **Recent Reference:** A recent review published in Behavioral Sciences (2020) explores the neuroscience of flow states and their role in enhancing performance and productivity. The review highlights the cognitive and neurocognitive elements that underlie the experience of flow, including the transition of cognitive control from an explicit to an implicit process1. This research provides valuable insights into how flow states can be facilitated and their implications for skill acquisition and overall performance.[23]

- **Historical Reference:** Michelangelo's dedication to his art and Marie Curie's perseverance in her scientific endeavors are quintessential examples of individuals experiencing flow. Their ability to maintain focused attention on their singular goals allowed them to overcome challenges and leave an indelible mark on history.

Directed Attentiveness: The Conductor of Disciplined Perception

Disciplined Perception, in essence, is directed attentiveness. Just as a conductor focuses the entire orchestra on a single piece of music, a singular idea acts as the conductor for your mind. It directs your memory to recall relevant information, your emotions to fuel your passion, and your willpower to maintain focus amidst distractions.

Psychological Perspective: Directed attentiveness involves the brain's ability to concentrate on specific stimuli while filtering out irrelevant information. This process is governed by the prefrontal cortex, which manages executive functions and focus. When concentrating on a singular idea, the prefrontal cortex coordinates various cognitive processes, including memory retrieval, emotional regulation, and sustained attention. This cognitive orchestration is what enables deep, focused work and creative breakthroughs.

Historical Example

- Consider **Leonardo da Vinci,** whose relentless curiosity and directed attentiveness led to groundbreaking advancements in art, science, and engineering. Da Vinci's ability to focus intensely on his projects, from the intricate details of the "Mona Lisa" to his visionary designs for flying machines, exemplifies the power of a singular, guiding idea.

- Similarly, with his unwavering focus on innovation, **Thomas Edison** exemplified directed attentiveness. Edison's methodical approach and persistent experimentation led to the invention of the phonograph, the motion picture camera, and the electric light bulb. His disciplined perception allowed him to harness his creativity and determination, resulting in over a thousand patents.

Enrichment Through Scientific Understanding

- **Psychological Research:** Studies have shown that directed attention enhances neural connectivity in the brain, particularly in regions associated with memory and decision-making. A recent article in Frontiers in Psychology (2020) highlights how sustained attention and focused cognitive engagement can improve neural plasticity and cognitive resilience.[24]

- **Recent Reference:** A comprehensive review published in The Egyptian Journal of Neurology, Psychiatry, and Neurosurgery (2023) explores the neuroscience of attention and its role in cognitive processes. The review discusses various aspects of attention, including tonic alertness, phasic alertness, selective attention, and sustained attention, and their relevance to human cognitive function.[25]

By understanding and harnessing the power of directed attentiveness, you can enhance your mental faculties and achieve a state of Disciplined Perception, much like the great minds of history.

The Benefits of a One-Track Mind

The term "one-track mind" often carries negative connotations, but when applied strategically, it becomes a powerful tool. Here is why:

- **Sharpened Focus:** When a singular idea consumes your mind, it acts like a filter, screening out irrelevant information and distractions. This allows you to concentrate all your mental resources on the task at hand, leading to sharper focus and improved performance.

- **Enhanced Motivation:** A clear and compelling goal, like a lighthouse in the fog, provides direction and motivation. Knowing exactly what you are working towards fuels your determination and keeps you pushing forward, even when faced with challenges.

- **Efficient Problem-Solving:** With all your mental faculties laser-focused on a single problem, you become a problem-solving machine. Creative solutions often emerge from this state of focused attention, leading to breakthroughs and innovation.

Finding Your Singular Idea

The key to achieving Disciplined Perception lies in identifying a goal that ignites your passion and sparks your imagination; whether it is writing that novel, mastering a new skill, or starting a business, discovering your singular idea is the first step towards transforming your aspirations into reality.

Psychological Perspective

- **Visualization and Goal Setting:** The process begins with vividly visualizing your success. Visualization is a powerful psychological technique that involves creating a detailed mental image of your desired outcome. This practice activates the brain's neural pathways, making the envisioned success feel more attainable and real. Regularly visualizing your goals reinforces your motivation and strengthens your commitment to achieving them.

- **Breaking Down Goals:** Once you have a clear vision, break down your big goals into smaller, manageable steps. This approach, known as "chunking," helps prevent overwhelming and maintains momentum. Each small step accomplished reinforces your confidence and drives you closer to your ultimate goal.

- **Harnessing Focus:** By honing in on a single idea, you transform a once scattered and unfocused mind into a laser-sharp instrument capable of cutting through distractions and obstacles. Focused attention, supported by the prefrontal cortex, enhances cognitive performance and productivity, allowing you to channel your mental faculties toward achieving your desired outcome.

Historical Examples

Thomas Edison and the Light Bulb: Thomas Edison's journey to inventing the electric light bulb is a testament to the power of a singular idea. Edison faced numerous setbacks and conducted over a thousand experiments before achieving success. His unwavering focus and relentless experimentation exemplify how a singular goal, backed by disciplined perception and perseverance, can lead to groundbreaking innovations.

- **Walt Disney's Vision of Disneyland:** Walt Disney's dream of creating Disneyland began as a singular idea that sparked his imagination. Despite financial challenges and skepticism from others, Disney's focused determination and meticulous planning brought his vision to life. Disneyland's success stands as a monument to the power of maintaining a singular focus and seeing it through to fruition.

Enrichment Through Scientific Understanding

- **Psychological Research:** Studies have shown that directed attention enhances neural connectivity in the brain, particularly in regions associated with memory and decision-making. A recent article in Frontiers in Psychology (2021) highlights how sustained attention and focused cognitive engagement can improve neural plasticity and cognitive resilience.

- **Recent Reference:** A comprehensive review published in The Egyptian Journal of Neurology, Psychiatry, and Neurosurgery

(2023) explores the neuroscience of attention and its role in cognitive processes. The review discusses various aspects of attention, including tonic alertness, phasic alertness, selective attention, and sustained attention, and their relevance to human cognitive function.[26]

By embracing the power of a singular idea and employing strategies like visualization and goal chunking, you can transform your aspirations into tangible achievements. Remember, the most formidable force in the universe is often the best-focused one.

Beyond the One-Track Mind

While a singular idea acts as the driving force, Disciplined Perception is not about shutting out everything else. It is about prioritizing. Information and experiences relevant to your goal become more readily apparent while distractions fade away.

The Reticular Activating System (RAS) as Your Filter

Imagine your brain as a bustling city. The Reticular Activating System (RAS) acts like a sophisticated traffic controller, filtering out the background noise and prioritizing information relevant to your current focus. When fueled by a singular idea, your RAS becomes more efficient, allowing you to navigate the mental landscape with laser-like focus.

Psychological Perspective: The RAS is a network of neurons located in the brainstem that plays a crucial role in regulating arousal and attention. It functions as a gatekeeper, determining which sensory information reaches the conscious mind and which gets filtered out. This highly adaptive system can be trained to prioritize information that aligns with your goals.

Scientific Insight: Research on the RAS has shown that it responds to stimuli that are significant to us, such as our names or goals. This adaptive filtering mechanism helps us focus on relevant information while ignoring distractions. For example, when you are deeply focused on a task, the RAS helps you tune out background noise and irrelevant stimuli.

Recent Reference: A study published in Nature Communications (2022) explores how the RAS modulates attention and consciousness. The research highlights the neural mechanisms by which the RAS filters sensory information and prioritizes goal-related stimuli.[27]

Historical Example

- Consider **Albert Einstein,** known for his groundbreaking contributions to physics. Einstein's ability to maintain focus on his theoretical work despite numerous distractions and challenges exemplifies the power of a well-tuned RAS. His singular focus on understanding the fundamental principles of the universe allowed him to develop the theory of relativity, transforming our understanding of space and time.

- Similarly, **Steve Jobs** demonstrated the effectiveness of a prioritized mind. Jobs' vision for Apple and his ability to focus on creating innovative products revolutionized the tech industry. His relentless focus on design and user experience, supported by a disciplined approach to eliminating distractions, enabled him to lead Apple to unprecedented success.[28]

Remember! By delving into the intricacies of the RAS and leveraging its filtering prowess, you can cultivate a sharp awareness, focus on what truly matters, and navigate your path to success with heightened precision. This fusion of empirical insight and historical narrative unveils the profound potential of a concentrated intellect.

Key Takeaway

A singular, powerful idea is the North Star that guides Disciplined Perception. It ignites your drive, surmounts barriers, and orchestrates every aspect of your being to lead you to your ultimate goal. Harness the strength of a singular vision, and watch as your concentration transforms into an unstoppable catalyst for extraordinary outcomes.

The Forge of Focus: How Environmental Pressures Shape Disciplined Perception

Disciplined Perception transcends mere internal conflict; it is often shaped in the crucible of daunting circumstances. This section delves into the intricate ways in which external pressures can forge the essential traits required for unwavering concentration.

The Crucible of Challenge

Envision a determined young entrepreneur grappling with the shadows of financial turmoil. These external pressures can morph into a formidable catalyst, igniting traits such as initiative, self-reliance, and an unyielding spirit of perseverance. These are the defining traits of those who have forged their paths, sharpening their insight by confronting challenges head-on.

Consider **Helen Keller,** whose relentless pursuit of knowledge despite her disabilities, and **Nelson Mandela,** with his unwavering dedication to justice in the face of imprisonment. Such environmental pressures become the crucible that tempers the steel of their focus.

Developing Core Traits

These challenging environments often cultivate essential traits like:

- **Keen Imagination:** When faced with limited resources, you are forced to think creatively and find innovative solutions.

- **Initiative:** No one is going to hold your hand. You must take the initiative to learn, grow, and overcome obstacles.

- **Self-Reliance:** You become resourceful and dependable, learning to rely on your own skills and abilities.

- **Perseverance:** The road to success is rarely smooth. Developing grit and perseverance allows you to push through setbacks and keep moving forward.

Psychological Perspective: Adversity and Resilience: Psychological research suggests that experiencing adversity can build resilience, a key component of Disciplined Perception. Resilient individuals are better able to cope with stress, adapt to change, and maintain focus on their goals despite obstacles. This process involves activating cognitive and emotional resources that strengthen one's ability to stay focused and persevere.

Neuroscientific Insight: Studies have shown that the brain's response to stress involves activating the prefrontal cortex and amygdala. These regions are crucial for decision-making, emotional regulation, and adaptive behaviors. Experiencing and overcoming challenges can enhance neural plasticity, improving cognitive flexibility and problem-solving abilities.

A study published in Frontiers in Human Neuroscience (2022) explores the neural mechanisms of resilience and how adversity shapes cognitive and emotional responses. The research highlights the role of neural plasticity in adapting to stress and maintaining focus. Read the full article here.[29]

Historical Examples

- **Helen Keller:** Despite being deaf and blind, Keller's unwavering determination and innovative approach to learning allowed her to achieve remarkable success. Her story exemplifies how environmental pressures can cultivate resilience, creativity, and disciplined focus.

- **Nelson Mandela:** Mandela's 27 years of imprisonment did not deter his commitment to justice and equality. His ability to maintain focus on his goals and adapt to harsh conditions exemplifies the power of resilience forged through adversity.

The Power of Motive: Fueling Disciplined Perception

Environmental pressures can spark an intense drive, acting as the catalyst that fuels Disciplined Perception. Envision a determined young athlete grappling with the weight of financial struggles, each day a battle against the odds. Their unwavering commitment to their family's well-being transforms into an all-consuming obsession, compelling them to train with an intensity that blurs the lines between endurance and madness as they relentlessly test the limits of both body and mind. In this manner, external obstacles transform into the driving force for cultivating the essential traits required to conquer them. A gripping motive serves as the driving force behind Disciplined Perception.

a. Beyond Fear-Based Learning

Fear-based motivation has its limitations. A student-driven solely by the fear of failure might achieve short-term results but may lack the intrinsic passion for excelling in the long run. A successful education system, like a skilled leader, should inspire students with a strong motive to learn. This intrinsic motivation fosters a genuine interest in the subject matter, leading to deeper understanding and a stronger foundation for focused learning.

Scientific Insight: Research in Educational Psychology shows that intrinsic motivation, which arises from a genuine interest in the subject, leads to deeper learning and higher academic achievement. Intrinsic motivation enhances cognitive engagement and promotes a lifelong love of learning. Read more here.[30]

b. The Allure of the Positive

Positive reinforcement, like the promise of achieving a long-held dream or the satisfaction of mastering a new skill, provides a far more sustainable source of motivation. This aligns perfectly with the concept of a principal objective—a compelling goal that guides your focus and fuels your determination.

Historical Example: Consider **Mahatma Gandhi,** whose nonviolent resistance movement was driven by the singular goal of achieving Indian independence. Despite numerous challenges and setbacks, Gandhi's unwavering focus on his vision was fueled by positive reinforcement—the support and hope of millions of Indians. His ability to maintain this focus was instrumental in achieving his goal.

c. Leadership by Inspiration

This principle applies beyond education. Effective leaders, whether employers or parents, inspire those around them with a shared vision and a sense of purpose. Leaders can cultivate a team focused on achieving a common goal by fostering a collaborative environment where individuals feel valued and motivated.

Psychological Perspective: Leadership that inspires and motivates individuals through shared goals and vision is more effective than authoritarian approaches. This style of leadership increases job satisfaction, enhances team performance, and promotes a positive organizational culture.[31]

Scientific Insight: Studies in The Leadership Quarterly highlight that transformational leadership, which involves inspiring and motivating employees through a shared vision and personal encouragement, leads to higher levels of employee satisfaction and organizational success.[32]

By delving into the depths of a captivating motive, whether in the realm of education, personal ambitions, or the art of leadership, one can master the art of Disciplined Perception. This narrative reveals that motivation stemming from authentic curiosity and constructive encouragement proves to be significantly more powerful and enduring than tactics driven by fear.

Motivational Strategies: Cultivating a Strong Motive

a. Identify Your Passions

What truly excites and motivates you? Understanding your intrinsic desires allows you to set goals that ignite your passion and propel you toward focused action. Take time to reflect on your interests and what brings you joy. Identifying these passions will help you align your efforts with your personal values, making your pursuit more meaningful and fulfilling.

Scientific Insight: Research in Psychological Science highlights the importance of passion and intrinsic motivation in achieving long-term success. Individuals who pursue goals aligned with their passions are more likely to experience sustained motivation and higher levels of satisfaction.[33]

b. Visualization

Take a few minutes each day to visualize yourself achieving your goals. Imagine the feeling of accomplishment and the positive impact your success will have. This mental rehearsal reinforces your motivation and strengthens your resolve. Visualization not only prepares your mind for success but also helps you anticipate potential challenges and plan solutions.

Psychological Perspective: Visualization techniques are widely used by athletes, entrepreneurs, and professionals to enhance performance. Studies have shown that visualizing success activates the same neural pathways as actual practice, boosting confidence and improving outcomes.

Recent Reference: An article in Frontiers in Psychology (2020) explores how visualization and mental rehearsal can enhance performance and motivation. The study provides insights into the neural mechanisms underlying these techniques.[34]

c. **Find Inspiration**

Surround yourself with positive influences—mentors, books, or online resources that can inspire and motivate you on your journey. Seek out stories of individuals who have achieved what you aspire to accomplish. Their experiences can offer valuable lessons and encouragement, helping you stay motivated and focused.

Historical Example: Consider Oprah Winfrey, who overcame significant personal and professional challenges to become a global media icon. Winfrey's story of resilience and determination inspires many and demonstrates how a strong motive and focused action can lead to remarkable success.

Scientific Insight: The Journal of Positive Psychology Research suggests that role models and inspirational stories can significantly boost motivation and goal achievement. Exposure to positive influences enhances self-efficacy and encourages perseverance.[35]

By harnessing the power of environmental pressures and cultivating a strong internal motive, you can transform external challenges into stepping stones on your path to achieving laser-like focus and remarkable results. Remember, even the most brilliant diamond needs the pressure of its environment to be formed. This comprehensive approach ensures that your motivation is both sustainable and deeply rooted in your personal values.

Key Takeaway

Amidst the shadows of environmental challenges, there lies a flicker of potential, a chance to transform adversity into a catalyst for profound growth. By tapping into the depths of a gripping motive, we can reshape these obstacles into the crucible that sharpens our focus, fortifies our resilience, and ultimately, enhances our capacity to accomplish extraordinary feats. Keep in mind, even the most brilliant gems are forged in the depths of extreme tension.

The Universal Spark: How Innate Desires Ignite Disciplined Perception

Deep within each of us lies a reservoir of powerful desires—a yearning for prosperity, love, freedom, self-expression, and, ultimately, self-preservation. These innate human desires act as the spark that can ignite the fire of Disciplined Perception.

The Power of Why

In his book *Start with Why*, Simon Sinek emphasizes the importance of understanding your "why"—the core motivation that drives you. Fundamental human desires tap into that "why," providing a powerful source of intrinsic motivation. The desire for material prosperity might motivate you to focus on acquiring new skills that can advance your career. The yearning for love might lead you to hone your communication skills to build stronger relationships.

Psychological Perspective: Intrinsic Motivation: Psychological research supports the idea that understanding one's core motivations is crucial for sustained focus and success. Intrinsic motivation arises from internal desires and is associated with higher engagement, creativity, and satisfaction levels. When individuals align their goals with their intrinsic desires, they are more likely to maintain disciplined perceptions and achieve their objectives.

Recent Reference: An article in The Journal of Positive Psychology (2021) explores how intrinsic motivation and understanding one's "why" can enhance goal pursuit and personal fulfillment.[36]

Historical Examples

1) **Marie Curie's Quest for Knowledge:** Driven by a profound desire to understand the natural world, Marie Curie dedicated her life to scientific discovery. Her intrinsic motivation fueled her relentless pursuit of knowledge, leading to groundbreaking research in radioactivity and earning her two Nobel Prizes. Curie's story exemplifies how a deep-seated desire for knowledge can ignite disciplined perception.

2) **Nelson Mandela's Fight for Freedom:** Nelson Mandela's yearning for freedom and justice drove his lifelong struggle against apartheid. Despite facing immense challenges and long-term imprisonment, Mandela's intrinsic motivation and unwavering focus on his goal enabled him to lead South Africa towards democracy. His story highlights how innate desires can sustain disciplined perception through adversity.

Practical Strategies

1) **Identify Your Core Desires:** Reflect on what truly excites and motivates you. Understanding your intrinsic desires allows you to set meaningful goals aligning with your values, making your pursuit more fulfilling and sustainable.

2) **Clarify Your Why:** Take time to articulate your "why"—the core motivation behind your goals. This clarity provides a powerful source of intrinsic motivation and helps you stay focused during challenging times.

3) **Visualize Success:** Regularly visualize yourself achieving your goals and experiencing the fulfillment of your desires. This mental rehearsal strengthens your resolve and keeps you motivated.

4) **Find Role Models:** Seek inspiration from individuals who have achieved what you aspire to accomplish. Their stories can offer valuable lessons and encouragement, helping you maintain disciplined perception.

By delving into and harnessing your fundamental yearnings, you can spark the flame of Disciplined Perception and attain extraordinary outcomes. This fusion of deep psychological understanding and historical narratives reveals the profound impact of intrinsic motivation in steering purposeful action.

The Universality of Desire: Fueling Disciplined Perception

At the heart of Disciplined Perception lies the universality of human desires, which resonate across diverse backgrounds and circumstances. These desires provide a robust framework for understanding and aligning personal goals with intrinsic motivations.

- One fundamental desire is **Material Prosperity.** The quest for security and a comfortable life propels individuals to acquire the necessary skills and knowledge for financial success. Many entrepreneurs, for instance, channel their focus and energy into building businesses to improve their financial situation, driven by this potent desire.

- Another powerful motivator is **Love.** The deep yearning for connection and belonging encourages individuals to develop strong communication skills and emotional intelligence, fostering deeper and more meaningful relationships. Parents who work diligently on their relationships with their children, motivated by love, often create stronger family bonds as a result.

- **Liberty of Body and Mind** is a desire that fuels the pursuit of independence and self-reliance. This desire empowers individuals to pursue their passions without constraints. Artists, for example, often develop unique styles that set them apart, driven by their need for creative freedom.

- The **Inclination for Personal Expression** is another fundamental human desire. This need to express oneself creatively can ignite a laser focus on honing one's skills and mastering one's craft, whether in music, writing, or any other form of creative expression. Writers who spend years perfecting their novels, motivated by the desire to tell their story in a unique voice, exemplify this inclination.

- Lastly, the instinct for **Self-Preservation** is a basic survival mechanism that motivates individuals to develop the focus and skills necessary to overcome challenges and protect themselves and their loved ones. Individuals who undergo extensive training in self-defense are often driven by the desire to ensure their safety and the safety of those they care about.

  By understanding and aligning with these universal desires, individuals can harness their power to fuel their Disciplined Perception and achieve remarkable results. This cohesive narrative demonstrates how these fundamental human motivations can drive focused action and sustained success.

Psychological Perspective

- **Intrinsic Motivation:** These desires tap into intrinsic motivation, which is driven by internal rewards rather than external pressures. Intrinsic motivation is associated with higher engagement, persistence, and satisfaction levels. By aligning your goals with these fundamental desires, you can achieve a state of Disciplined Perception that is both sustainable and fulfilling.

- **Scientific Insight:** A study published in Frontiers in Psychology (2020) explores how intrinsic motivation is linked to goal achievement and well-being. The research highlights the importance of aligning personal goals with intrinsic desires to maintain motivation and achieve success.[37]

Historical Examples

- **Material Prosperity:** Andrew Carnegie, one of the wealthiest individuals in history, was driven by the desire for financial success. His disciplined focus on steel production and business innovation led to the creation of a vast industrial empire.

- **Love:** Mother Teresa's unwavering commitment to helping the poor and sick was fueled by her deep love for humanity. Her disciplined perception and relentless efforts resulted in global recognition and numerous humanitarian awards.

- **Liberty of Body and Mind:** Rosa Parks's desire for personal and collective freedom propelled her to stand against racial segregation. Her act of defiance became a pivotal moment in the Civil Rights Movement.

- **Inclination for Personal Expression:** Vincent van Gogh's relentless pursuit of artistic expression, despite personal struggles and limited recognition during his lifetime, led to creating masterpieces celebrated worldwide today.

- **Self-Preservation:** Malala Yousafzai's fight for the right to education in the face of life-threatening danger exemplifies the instinct for self-preservation. Her bravery and focused advocacy earned her the Nobel Peace Prize and global admiration.

By understanding and aligning with these universal desires, you can harness their power to fuel your Disciplined Perception and achieve remarkable results. This blend of psychological insights and historical examples illustrates the transformative potential of these fundamental human motivations.

Tapping into the Power of Desire

Harnessing the power of innate human desires can significantly enhance Disciplined Perception. You can channel your energy and focus toward achieving your goals by aligning your actions with these fundamental motivations.

a. Identifying Your Why

First, take some time to reflect on your core desires. What truly motivates you? Understanding your "why" provides a guiding star that directs your focus and propels you toward your objectives. For example, if your primary desire is material prosperity, recognize how this aspiration can drive you to acquire new skills and knowledge to achieve financial success.

b. Visualization

Next, practice visualization. Spend a few minutes each day imagining yourself achieving your goals, fueled by the positive emotions associated with your desires. Picture the satisfaction of financial security, the joy of connecting with loved ones, the freedom that comes with knowledge, or the fulfillment of personal expression. This mental rehearsal strengthens your motivation and solidifies the connection between your desires and your focused actions.

c. Goal Setting

Finally, set goals that resonate with your core desires. Break these goals down into smaller, manageable steps and track your progress. This approach helps maintain motivation and keeps your Disciplined Perception sharp. Seeing tangible results along the way will keep your passion burning bright, fueling your journey toward success.

Remember! By understanding the power of innate desires and harnessing their energy, you can transform them from a flickering flame into a blazing fire that propels you toward remarkable achievements. The most powerful desires are often the simplest ones. By tapping into these fundamental human desires and aligning them with your goals, you unlock a wellspring of motivation that can drive you to excel.

Warning! Causes of Lost Focus: The Kryptonite of Disciplined Perception

Disciplined Perception, much like any formidable skill, harbors its own weaknesses. In this exploration, we delve into significant dangers that can undermine your razor-sharp concentration and provide antidotes to counter these threats.

a.   The Absence of a Definite Purpose: Adrift at Sea

Envision a solitary sailboat adrift on a tranquil sea, its sails hanging limp, untouched by the breath of the wind. It wanders through the shadows, swept along by unseen forces. This is the inevitable outcome for one who wanders without a clear direction. In the absence of a definitive aim, their attention drifts aimlessly, leaving their disciplined perception in disarray.

The Peril of Aimlessness: Indeed, a purposeless person is akin to a "dry leaf on the bosom of the wind." They have no direction, and even the slightest influence from outside can easily turn them off track. A clear-cut purpose, on the other hand, serves as an anchor that stabilizes and fixes your attention in place. It charges your efforts with meaning and feeds your drive to stay laser-focused on the attainment of your objectives.

- **Antidote: Finding Your Why**

  To counterbalance this aimlessness, it's crucial to find your why—what is important to you, your core values, and your aspirations. What truly matters to you? What kind of impact do you want to make on the world? Once you identify that "why," it becomes your North Star, guiding and propelling you forward with a meaningful life.

- **Antidote: Finding Your North Star**

  In cultivating Disciplined Perception, having a North Star—a compelling purpose that orients your actions and decisions—is essential. This might be as simple as building a successful business, mastering a particular skill, or positively impacting the world. The key is to identify what truly ignites your passion and use that as your guiding light.

- **Antidote: Goal Setting as a Roadmap**

  Once you have identified your purpose, break it down into specific, achievable goals. A clear roadmap not only keeps you focused and motivated but also ensures that your Disciplined Perception stays razor-sharp. Setting smaller milestones allows you to track your progress and maintain momentum toward your ultimate objective.

By recognizing the dangers of lost focus and applying these antidotes, you can strengthen your Disciplined Perception and ensure that you remain steadfast in pursuing your goals. The combination of a clear purpose, a guiding North Star, and well-defined goals provides a solid foundation for maintaining unwavering focus and achieving remarkable results.

b. The Allure of Distractions: The Siren Call of Politics

Disciplined Perception can be easily undermined by distractions, much like a businessman getting entangled in politics. While political engagement can be a noble pursuit, it can also be a distraction for those seeking success in the business world. Politics, like any demanding profession, requires a laser focus of its own. Dividing your attention can dilute your effectiveness in both areas.

- **Antidote: Identifying Your Kryptonite**

  Just like Superman has Kryptonite, everyone has their own personal distractions. For some, it might be social media; for others, it might be micromanaging tasks instead of delegating. Identifying your personal Kryptonite—the things that weaken your focus—is crucial. Once identified, develop strategies to minimize their impact.

- **Antidote: Taming the Distractions**

  To maintain Disciplined Perception, you need to develop strategies for managing distractions. This could involve silencing notifications, setting aside dedicated work periods, or creating a distraction-free workspace. By proactively managing distractions, you can maintain a high level of focus and productivity.

- **Antidote: Prioritization is Key**

  Not all distractions are created equally. Learn to prioritize your commitments and delegate tasks whenever possible. Allocate your focused attention to the activities that have the most significant impact on achieving your goals. By prioritizing effectively, you can ensure that your Disciplined Perception remains sharp and directed toward meaningful outcomes.

By understanding the perils of aimlessness and distractions, you can safeguard your Disciplined Perception, ensuring that it remains a powerful tool for achieving remarkable results. This narrative emphasizes the importance of identifying and managing distractions to maintain focus and achieve success. Let me know if there is anything else you would like to explore or refine!

c. The Overwhelm of Multitasking

The Myth of Multitasking: Many people believe that multitasking increases productivity, but in reality, it can significantly dilute your focus. Switching between tasks can lead to cognitive overload, reducing efficiency and increasing the likelihood of errors.

- **Antidote: Single-Tasking**

  Focus on one task at a time. Prioritize your tasks and tackle them sequentially. This approach, known as single-tasking, allows you to give your full attention to each task, enhancing the quality of your work and maintaining your Disciplined Perception.

d. The Trap of Perfectionism

The Perfectionism Pitfall: Striving for perfection can be a double-edged sword. While it can drive high standards, it can also lead to procrastination and a fear of failure. Perfectionism can paralyze your progress and divert your focus from meaningful action.

- **Antidote: Embrace Imperfection**

  Accept that perfection is an unattainable goal. Focus on progress rather than perfection. Set realistic standards and celebrate small victories along the way. This mindset shift can help you maintain momentum and keep your Disciplined Perception intact.

e. The Seduction of Instant Gratification

The Lure of Immediate Rewards: In a world of instant gratification, it is easy to get sidetracked by short-term pleasures. Whether it is checking social media, binge-watching shows, or indulging in other distractions, these activities can derail your long-term goals.

- **Antidote: Delayed Gratification**

  Practice delayed gratification by setting boundaries and rewarding yourself only after completing significant tasks. This discipline helps you stay focused on your long-term objectives and strengthens your ability to resist distractions.

f. The Weight of Emotional Baggage

Emotional Distractions: Unresolved emotions and stress can cloud your mind and sap your energy. Emotional distractions can make it difficult to concentrate and maintain your Disciplined Perception.

- **Antidote: Emotional Regulation**

  Develop strategies for managing your emotions, such as mindfulness, meditation, or talking to a trusted friend or therapist. By addressing emotional distractions, you can clear your mind and maintain a high level of focus.

Recognizing these causes of lost focus and applying the corresponding antidotes can further safeguard your Disciplined Perception. This comprehensive approach ensures that you remain steadfast in pursuing your goals, free from the kryptonite that threatens to undermine your concentration.

TRANSFORMING WITH SELECTIVE AWARENESS

ᎦᏇ ᎦᏇ ᎦᏇ

The Selective Awareness Advantage: A Multifaceted Powerhouse

S elective awareness is not a parlor trick; it is a potent mental apparatus with the power to reshape your reality. It is like discovering a hidden superpower within your own mind, one that unlocks a captivating array of benefits. Let us delve into the multifaceted brilliance of selective awareness:

Shattering the Glass Ceiling: Breaking Free from Self-Imposed Limitations

Envision a gifted artist, their boundless creativity constrained by the haunting conviction of inadequacy, whispering, "I lack the talent." Selective awareness serves as a cognitive tool, enabling you to carve through the barriers you have constructed for yourself. It grants you the agency to seize control of your thoughts, recognize these constraining beliefs, and deconstruct them piece by piece.

- **Unearthing Hidden Beliefs:** We all harbor these mental landmines—thoughts like "I am not a risk-taker" or "Success is for other people." Selective awareness equips you to become a detective of your own mind. Through introspection and self-reflection, you can unearth these hidden beliefs, challenge their validity, and replace them with empowering affirmations. For instance, Cognitive Behavioral Therapy (CBT)[4] techniques can be instrumental in transforming these deep-seated beliefs. Imagine the artist reframing their belief into "My creativity has the potential to astound the world." This shift in mindset unlocks a reservoir of untapped potential.[38]

- **Embracing the Empowering Voice:** By taking charge of your mind, you silence the inner critic and amplify the voice of your inner champion. This newfound self-ownership allows you to become the architect of your own destiny, directing your thoughts and actions toward achieving extraordinary goals. Articles on selective attention and its importance explain how focusing on relevant stimuli and filtering out less important information can be a game-changer.[39]

You can unlock your true potential by leveraging selective awareness to shatter self-imposed limitations and align your actions with your core desires. This approach not only enhances your mental acuity but also empowers you to achieve remarkable results.

The Ripple Effect: Selective Awareness as the Foundation of Powerful Forces

The impact of selective awareness extends far beyond the individual. It is a foundational principle woven into the fabric of many powerful groups, from religious movements to military strategies.

- **The Synergy of Shared Focus:** Selective awareness can create a powerful synergy among individuals. Imagine a group

---

[4] Cognitive Behavioral Therapy (CBT): "Cognitive Behavioral Therapy (CBT) is a form of psychological treatment that helps people learn how to identify and change the destructive or disturbing thought patterns that have a negative influence on their behavior and emotions."

of monks chanting in unison. Their synchronized focus fosters a sense of collective purpose and heightened awareness. This synergy is a potent tool utilized by religious groups for personal transformation and fostering a sense of belonging. Similarly, consider a rock band, each member locked into the rhythm, their focused attention creating a powerful musical experience that transcends the abilities of any individual performer.

Research on group dynamics and collective efficacy supports the concept of shared focus. When group members align their focus and efforts, they can achieve greater outcomes than they would individually.[40]

- **The Focused Soldier:** Throughout history, great military leaders have understood the power of selective awareness. By harnessing the collective focus of their troops, they inspire courage, strategic thinking, and unwavering determination in the face of adversity. Imagine a special forces unit on a covert mission; their laser focus and unwavering concentration are the key to their success.

  Military strategies often emphasize the importance of maintaining focus and discipline. This is crucial for effective execution and achieving mission objectives. The role of selective attention in high-stress environments, such as military operations, is well-documented in psychological literature.[41]

Beyond Individual Limits: The Mastermind Synergy

Selective awareness can be exponentially enhanced through mastermind alliances. Consider a team of brilliant scientists, each a powerhouse of expertise in their field. When such specific, concentrated expertise is blended together toward a common objective, the result is a phenomenon called collective intelligence.

- **Unlocking Collective Genius:** When two or more focused minds come together on a common objective, it's like connecting to a universal power grid of creativity and innovation. This collaborative effort ensures the sharing of ideas, the production of new solutions, and the generation of knowledge that an individual alone cannot achieve. Think about the Wright Brothers: their shared dream of flight merged their focus and unremitting pursuit of a common vision, ultimately making history. Research highlights the importance of collaboration and collective intelligence in driving innovation and achieving remarkable outcomes.[42]

- **The Power of Collaboration:** Minds thinking as one creates a powerful unified force that stirs vision, courage, imagination, and initiative. Imagine a filmmaking crew where each person makes their own contribution with well-concentrated expertise. It is this very spirit of collaboration that creates the synergy needed to lift the film project beyond the capabilities of even the most resourceful filmmaker. This principle of collective effort and shared focus is crucial in creative and strategic endeavors.[43]

In Conclusion

Selective awareness is more than a tool for focused attention; it is the key to unlocking that hidden treasure within yourself and others. You can leverage its full-spectrum power to break through barriers, deliver outstanding achievements, and contribute to something larger than yourself. Whether it is a solo artist conquering self-doubt or the collaborative genius of a mastermind team, selective awareness puts you on center stage. It places you at the tip of the pen to write an extraordinary story.

The Orchestra Within: Conducting Your Mind for Peak Performance

Envision your consciousness as an expansive symphony; each thought is a distinct instrument contributing to a grand, intricate composition. Every facet—reason, emotion, memory, imagination—harbors profound possibilities. Yet, in the absence of a guiding force, the symphony of sound may devolve into disarray, lacking purpose and coherence. Disciplined Perception, or Directed Attentiveness, serves as the conductor's baton, weaving together these mental faculties into a cohesive and resonant force.

The Intricate Fabric of Existence: Through selective awareness, one can weave a "subtle reality," molding their perception of the world around them. Envision an investigator deeply engrossed in the intricate details of a scene marked by shadows of uncertainty and the echoes of untold stories. By meticulously examining particular elements—footprints, tire tracks, witness accounts—they weave together a complex tapestry that reveals the intricacies of the events that unfolded. By cultivating selective awareness, one can navigate the complexities of daily existence, sharpening one's perception to uncover vital nuances that might otherwise remain hidden in the mundane flow of life.

Harnessing Resources: Imagine this: You are the maestro of your own mental symphony, and focused awareness is your conductor's baton. This heightened awareness extends beyond the internal realm, enabling you to become a virtuoso at identifying and leveraging the resources available in your environment. Picture a soldier on a covert mission, their senses heightened and razor-sharp. Every discarded newspaper and every flickering streetlight becomes an instrument in their hands, transformed into tools for survival and success. This soldier does not just see their surroundings—they read them, extract utility from every shadow and whisper. This kind of mental orchestration has been the secret behind countless historical triumphs and philosophical breakthroughs. With your mind as the conductor, your environment becomes a symphony of possibilities, playing the score to your success.

Religious Movements as Case Studies

- **Buddhism: Mindfulness as a Mental Fortress:** Imagine a samurai warrior, their mind a battlefield, constantly bombarded by thoughts and emotions. Like a skilled general, Buddhist meditation teaches us to focus our attention, building a mental fortress against distractions. This selective awareness, cultivated through mindfulness practices, allows us to navigate the chaotic landscape of our minds with clarity and precision.[44]

- **Christianity: Discernment as a Detective's Skill**: In the realm of Christianity, discernment is akin to a detective's ability to separate truth from falsehood. Picture a detective sifting through clues, focusing on the relevant details, ignoring the distractions. Discernment requires selective awareness, a focused attention that allows us to distinguish between good and evil, right and wrong, in the spiritual realm.[45]

- **Islam: Tawakkul as a Trusting Heart**: Tawakkul, in Islam, is not passive surrender; it is an active trust in a higher power. Imagine a skydiver trusting their equipment and the laws of physics to guide them safely to the ground. Tawakkul requires focused attention on the divine, a trust that transcends the limitations of the self. This selective awareness allows us to surrender to the greater plan, finding peace and strength even in the face of uncertainty.[46]

Historical Figures as Examples of Selective Awareness

- **Napoleon Bonaparte: The Master Strategist:** Napoleon, a military genius, used selective awareness to outmaneuver his opponents. Imagine a chess grandmaster, their eyes fixed on the board, calculating the potential moves and countermoves. Napoleon's ability to focus on the key elements of a battle, to identify weaknesses and exploit them, was a testament to his selective awareness.[47]

- **Leonardo da Vinci: The Renaissance Man:** Da Vinci's insatiable curiosity and ability to focus on multiple fields of knowledge were hallmarks of his genius. Picture a scientist, an artist, and an inventor all rolled into one. Da Vinci's selective awareness allowed him to connect seemingly unrelated ideas, creating groundbreaking innovations.[48]

Philosophical Explorations

- **Socrates' Method:** The Questioning Mind: Socrates, the Greek philosopher, used a method of questioning to challenge assumptions and arrive at truth. Imagine a detective interrogating a suspect, probing for inconsistencies and contradictions. Socrates' method required focused attention on the conversation, a willingness to challenge one's own beliefs, and a relentless pursuit of understanding.[49]

- **Stoicism:** The Master of Emotions: Stoic philosophers emphasized the importance of controlling one's emotions and focusing on what is within one's power. Imagine a tightrope walker, whose balance is unwavering despite the swaying beneath their feet. Stoics practiced selective awareness, focusing on their responses to external events rather than allowing emotions to dictate their actions.[50]

Real-World Examples

- **Sports Psychology: The Zone:** Athletes often talk about being "in the zone," a state of heightened focus and performance. Imagine a basketball player, their eyes locked on the hoop, their mind free from distractions. This selective awareness allows them to perform at their peak, executing precise movements and making clutch shots.[51]

- **Business Leadership: The Visionary**: Successful business leaders use selective awareness to identify opportunities, make strategic decisions, and motivate their teams. Imagine a CEO, their gaze fixed on the horizon, envisioning the future of their company. This focused attention allows them to navigate the complexities of the business world, making tough decisions and leading their teams towards success.[52]

The Eightfold Path to Mental Mastery: A Symphony of the Mind

Envision the human mind not merely as a singular object but as a magnificent symphony of diverse instruments, each contributing to a complex and harmonious whole. Within this realm, myriad instruments possess their own distinct voices, each contributing to a greater symphony of existence. The Eightfold Path to Mental Mastery invites us to weave these elements into a cohesive tapestry of concentrated thought and profound accomplishment.

1) Will: The Conductor, Leading the Charge

Will is the conductor, holding the baton of direction and purpose in his hand. It sets the prevailing tone of the entire mental orchestra, working all the faculties together in a single direction. A strong will means continued concentration: You can fight against setbacks and avoid distractions. Research highlights the importance of willpower in achieving long-term goals.[33]

2) Emotions: The Fueling Strings, Powering Your Actions

Emotions are the strings section—the passionate undercurrent energizing your focus and action. While positive emotions such as joy and curiosity push you forward, negative ones like fear or anger can build an unstructured dissonance. The key is becoming aware and managing your emotions, channeling them into a focused drive toward accomplishment. Emotional regulation is essential for mental well-being and effective action.[34]

3) Reason: The Analytical Clarinets, Sharpening Your Strategies

Reason is the clear-sounding clarinet that precisely slices through information to formulate a well-defined strategy. This faculty of analysis sifts through complex data, bringing out patterns and making sound judgments. Just as a good clarinet player ensures every note is clear and crisp, reason allows you to tune your mind for maximum productivity.[35]

4) Conscience: The Moral Flute, Guiding Your Choices

Conscience takes the role of the moral flute, playing a steady melody of ethical principles. It acts as your internal compass, guiding your choices toward what is right and just. A well-tuned conscience ensures your mental orchestra performs a symphony that achieves success and benefits the greater good. Ethical decision-making is crucial for personal integrity and societal harmony.[56]

5) Memory: The Vast Percussion Section, Echoing Your Experiences

Memory serves as the vast percussion section, a rhythmic tapestry woven from your past experiences. It provides the foundation for learning and growth, allowing you to draw upon lessons learned and adapt to new situations. Just as a skilled percussionist enhances a piece with dynamic rhythms, a well-honed memory empowers you to create a symphony of insightful thought. Memory plays a critical role in learning and problem-solving.[57]

6) Imagination: The Creative Violins, Painting Your Dreams

Imagination takes over like creative violins, painting your desired outcome in vivid colors. It lets you see possibilities far beyond your present time and serves as the activator for innovation. A powerful imagination injects a vibrant melody into the mental symphony, carrying you forward in pursuit of what you desire. Imagination is a key driver of creativity and innovation.[58]

7) Intuition: The Whispering Harp, Offering Hunch and Premonition

Intuition acts as the whispering harp, offering subtle yet potent melodies of gut feelings, hunches, and premonitions. It allows you to pick up on nuances beyond the grasp of pure reason, providing valuable insights that can guide your decision-making. By learning to listen to your intuition, you add a touch of serendipity to your mental symphony, allowing for unexpected breakthroughs and moments of inspiration. Intuition plays a significant role in fast and effective decision-making.[59]

8) Subconscious: The Unexplored Bass, A Reservoir of Untapped Power

The subconscious lies within as a submerged bass section—a vast reservoir of untapped potential. It houses hidden memories, emotions, and learned patterns of behavior that influence our actions at a much deeper level. By tapping into the subconscious and realizing its power, we open our inner selves to a fountain of creativity and problem-solving abilities much deeper inside ourselves and provide a rich, powerful baseline to the symphony of our minds. The subconscious mind significantly influences behavior and creativity.[60]

Conclusion: Conducting the Symphony

Mastering the Eightfold Path requires us to act as conductors of our mental orchestra, harmonizing will, emotions, reason, conscience, memory, imagination, intuition, and the subconscious. By understanding and refining each element, we can create a symphony of thought that resonates with purpose, creativity, and success. Just as a great conductor transforms individual instruments into a masterpiece, so too can we transform our minds into a symphony of mental mastery.

Results of attaining mastery of the Eightfold Path

By mastering the Eightfold Path, we learn to harmonize these diverse mental faculties. No longer a cacophony of competing thoughts, the mind becomes a well-rehearsed orchestra capable of producing a symphony of focused thought, exceptional achievement, and a life lived to its fullest potential.

- **The Synergy of the Mind:** When you harness Disciplined Perception, you bring these eight faculties into synchronized action. Imagine a violinist and a pianist playing a complex duet. Their individual talents coalesce into a beautiful melody. Similarly, when your mental faculties work together in harmony, you unlock a potential far greater than the sum of their parts.

- **Tapping into the Higher Mind:** The text ponders the possibility of this unified mental state facilitating a connection with a higher intelligence. While the nature of this connection remains a mystery, it underscores the transformative potential of Disciplined Perception.

Mental Conditioning for Everyday Miracles

Disciplined Perception is not just about grand philosophical ideas; it has practical applications for everyday life. It acts as a form of mental conditioning, preparing you to face any challenge that comes your way. Here are several key points that highlight its practical uses:

- **Self-Hypnosis for Resilience:** Focused attention can be likened to a form of self-hypnosis. You can program your mind for resilience by directing your thoughts and emotions. Imagine a soldier facing a terrifying situation. Through Disciplined Perception, they can focus on their training, purpose, and unwavering determination, effectively hypnotizing themselves into a state of courage and composure. Research supports the effectiveness of self-hypnosis in enhancing mental resilience.

- **Healing Through Focus:** Focused attention can aid in healing. While the exact mechanisms remain unclear, evidence suggests that a positive and focused mind can contribute to the healing process. Imagine someone recovering from an injury. By directing their attention towards visualization and positive affirmations, they can potentially enhance their body's natural healing abilities. Studies have shown the benefits of mindfulness and positive thinking in physical recovery.

- **Enhancing Creativity:** Disciplined Perception can significantly enhance creativity. By focusing your mind on a particular problem or project, you can tap into a deeper well of creative ideas and solutions. This approach can be particularly useful for artists, writers, and anyone involved in creative pursuits. The link between focused attention and creativity is well-documented in psychological research.

- **Improving Focus and Productivity:** By honing your ability to concentrate, you can improve your overall focus and productivity. Disciplined Perception allows you to filter out distractions and focus on the task at hand, leading to better performance in both personal and professional settings. Cognitive science emphasizes the importance of focused attention in enhancing productivity.

- **Strengthening Emotional Intelligence**: Disciplined Perception helps strengthen emotional intelligence by enabling you to understand and manage your emotions better. This can improve your relationships and interactions with others, leading to a more fulfilling personal and professional life. Emotional intelligence is crucial for success and well-being.

- **Goal Setting and Achievement:** Disciplined Perception aids in setting and achieving goals. You can increase your chances of success by maintaining a clear focus on your objectives and the steps needed to achieve them. Effective goal setting is a cornerstone of personal and professional development.

- **Stress Management:** Focused attention can also be a powerful tool for managing stress. By directing your mind away from stressors and towards calming and positive thoughts, you can reduce your overall stress levels and improve your mental health. Techniques like mindfulness and meditation are effective stress management tools.

Key Takeaway

By harnessing the power of Disciplined Perception, you transform
your mind from a scattered orchestra into a finely tuned instrument
capable of playing the symphony of your dreams. This mental
mastery empowers you to perceive the world with greater nuance,
tap into hidden resources, and achieve feats that may seem like
magic to the untrained mind.

- **Will:** Like a conductor leading an orchestra, your willpower
  directs your thoughts and actions, ensuring all mental faculties
  are aligned toward your goals.

- **Emotions:** Acting as the fueling strings, emotions drive your
  focus and actions. By managing them, you can channel their
  energy into achieving your dreams.

- **Reason:** Serving as the analytical clarinets, reason helps you
  cut through complexity and formulate clear strategies.

- **Conscience:** The moral flute guides your choices with ethical
  principles, ensuring success that benefits the greater good.

- **Memory:** The vast percussion section, memory, provides the
  rhythmic foundation for learning and growth.

- Imagination: Creative violins paint your dreams in vivid colors,
  driving innovation and inspiring the pursuit of your desires.

- **Intuition:** The whispering harp offers subtle insights, adding
  serendipity and unexpected breakthroughs to your mental
  symphony.

- **Subconscious:** Your subconscious, the unexplored bass,
  houses untapped potential, unlocking hidden creativity and
  problem-solving abilities.

Incorporating Mental Conditioning for Everyday Miracles, this mastery prepares you to face any challenge with resilience and focus. Through self-hypnosis and directed attention, you can program your mind for resilience and healing, enhancing everyday performance. Embrace this symphony of mental conditioning to orchestrate a life full of harmony, achievement, and everyday miracles.

The Piercing Gaze: Seeing Through the Veil with Focused Attention

Have you ever longed to pierce the veils that shroud human existence, to glimpse the truths hidden beneath the façades and illusions woven by society? Disciplined Perception nurtures a formidable skill—piercing insight. Set aside notions of psychic abilities; this journey is about refining your perception to grasp the fundamental nature of reality, transcending mere appearances.

Under the broader concept of "The Transformative Power of Selective Awareness: A Multi-Faceted Gem," the idea of "The Piercing Gaze" encapsulates the ability to channel focused attention to unveil hidden truths, discern patterns, and achieve profound clarity. Focused attention acts as a beacon, cutting through the noise of distractions and illuminating what is often obscured by the veil of mental clutter. This exploration delves into what the "Piercing Gaze" entails, its transformative potential, and actionable ways to cultivate it.

The Essence of the Piercing Gaze

Focused attention is more than mere concentration; it is a disciplined and intentional narrowing of cognitive resources to perceive with clarity and depth. The "Piercing Gaze" metaphorically describes this state, where one's attention becomes so refined that it penetrates the surface of ordinary perception to reveal deeper insights. This transformative state allows individuals to:

- **Unveil Hidden Patterns:** By systematically filtering out distractions, focused attention sharpens awareness of subtle patterns, connections, and underlying structures that might otherwise go unnoticed.

- **Clarify Priorities:** With distractions minimized, focused attention highlights what truly matters, enabling individuals to align their thoughts and actions with their most important goals.

- **Enhance Problem-Solving**: Clarity often reveals solutions hidden behind mental clutter, facilitating innovative approaches and effective decisions.

- **Enable Mindful Presence:** Through deliberate attention, one becomes deeply rooted in the present, experiencing life more fully and engaging more meaningfully with the world.

The Science of Focused Attention

Significant findings in neuroscience and psychology support the concept of focused attention:

- **Neuroplasticity:** Neuroplasticity: Groundbreaking research by Dr. Michael Merzenich and his colleagues has demonstrated the brain's remarkable plasticity. This research indicates that focused attention, much like physical exercise for muscles, strengthens neural pathways. The brain undergoes structural and functional changes through repeated engagement in focused tasks, enhancing cognitive faculties such as memory, learning, and attention itself. This process of neuroplasticity underscores the brain's capacity to adapt and rewire itself throughout life in response to experience and focused mental training. Norman Doidge's book, The Brain That Changes Itself (2007), provides compelling real-world examples of neuroplasticity in action.[61]

- **Flow States:** Mihaly Csikszentmihalyi's pioneering work on "flow" describes a state of deep immersion and engagement in a challenging activity. During flow experiences, attention is fully absorbed in the present moment, leading to a sense of heightened focus, enjoyment, and intrinsic motivation. This intense concentration not only facilitates peak performance but also fosters creativity and innovative breakthroughs. Csikszentmihalyi's seminal work, Flow: The Psychology of Optimal Experience (1990), is a cornerstone of positive psychology.[62]

- **Selective Attention:** The "Spotlight Model" of attention, initially proposed by Posner and Petersen (1990) in their influential paper "The attention system of the human brain" (Annual Review of Neuroscience), uses the metaphor of a spotlight to illustrate how we selectively focus on specific stimuli while filtering out irrelevant information. This selective focus enhances processing efficiency, reduces cognitive overload, and allows us to prioritize relevant information in a complex environment. This model highlights the brain's remarkable ability to prioritize and manage attentional resources.

Steps to Attain the Piercing Gaze

Achieving the "Piercing Gaze" requires consistent practice, mindfulness, and dedication. Below is an expanded exploration of actionable strategies:

1. **Practice Mindfulness Meditation:** Mindfulness meditation provides a foundational practice for cultivating the focused attention necessary for the "Piercing Gaze." By training the

mind to anchor itself in the present moment, mindfulness
strengthens attentional control, allowing you to cut through
mental clutter and perceive more clearly. Key techniques
include:

a) **Focused Breathing:** Sit quietly and direct your attention
    to the natural rhythm of your breath. When your mind
    wanders, gently bring it back to your breathing. This
    practice strengthens your ability to refocus amidst
    distractions.

b) **Body Scan Meditation:** Gradually shift your awareness
    through different parts of your body, observing sensations
    without judgment. This cultivates present-moment
    awareness and reduces mental clutter.[63]

2. **Minimize Cognitive Overload:** A cluttered environment or
    overwhelming schedule scatters mental energy, hindering the
    development of a "Piercing Gaze." Streamlining your
    surroundings and routines frees up crucial mental bandwidth,
    allowing you to direct your focus with greater precision.
    Consider these steps:

a) **Declutter Your Space:** Organize your workspace to
    eliminate unnecessary items and distractions, creating an
    environment conducive to focus.

b) **Time Management Techniques:** Use the Pomodoro
    Technique or similar methods to break tasks into focused
    intervals, separated by short breaks. This prevents mental
    fatigue and maintains productivity.[64]

3. **Engage in Single-Tasking:** Multitasking fractures attention,
    diminishing both efficiency and accuracy. To cultivate the
    focused intensity of the "Piercing Gaze," embrace single-

tasking, allowing full engagement with each task and maximizing both quality and speed. To implement this:

a) **Prioritize Tasks:** List your tasks in order of importance and focus on completing them one at a time.

b) **Eliminate Interruptions:** Turn off notifications, set boundaries with others, and dedicate uninterrupted blocks of time to your work.[65]

4. **Cultivate Curiosity:** Curiosity acts as a natural lens, focusing attention and deepening understanding, which is essential for developing the "Piercing Gaze." By nurturing a sense of wonder, you can engage more deeply with tasks and topics, uncovering hidden details and insights. Strategies include:

a) **Ask "Why" and "How" Questions: Delve** deeper into the mechanics of everyday phenomena or unfamiliar subjects to ignite intellectual engagement.

b) **Explore New Perspectives:** Challenge yourself to approach problems or ideas from unconventional angles.[66]

5. **Use Visualization Techniques:** Visualization acts as a mental lens, focusing your inner vision and sharpening your perception, much like honing the "Piercing Gaze." By creating vivid mental images of the process and the desired outcome, you direct your mental energy with precision, enhancing clarity, motivation, and the ability to manifest your intentions. This technique involves:

a) **Visualize the Process:** Imagine each step required to complete a task, focusing not only on the actions but also on the sensations and feelings associated with each stage. This creates a mental roadmap and strengthens your resolve.

b) **Visualize the Outcome:** Picture the completed task or achieved goal in vivid detail, immersing yourself in the sensory experience of success. Feel the sense of accomplishment, visualize the benefits, and let this vision fuel your focus and drive.[67]

6. **Leverage the Power of Questions:** Purposeful questioning is a powerful tool for directing the "Piercing Gaze" inward and outward, fostering deeper understanding and uncovering hidden truths. By framing insightful questions, you actively guide your attention, probing beneath the surface and gaining valuable insights. Employ these tactics:

a) **Open-Ended Questions:** Frame inquiries that encourage broad exploration and stimulate creative thinking, such as "What if...?" "How might this work...?" or "What are the underlying assumptions here?" These questions open up new avenues of exploration.

b) **Reflective Questions:** Use introspective questions to clarify your intentions, values, and motivations, guiding your focus with greater purpose. Ask yourself: "What am I truly trying to achieve?" "What is the core issue here?" or "What truly matters in this situation?" These questions sharpen your inner vision and ensure your efforts are aligned with your deepest values.[68]

7. **Optimize Your Environment:** To cultivate the unwavering focus required for the "Piercing Gaze," it is essential to optimize both your internal state and your external environment. This involves training your attention through focused exercises and minimizing distractions that can fragment your concentration. This combined approach allows you to penetrate distractions and perceive with greater clarity. Consider these strategies:

a) **Sharpen Your Focus with Mental Exercises:** Regularly engage in exercises that challenge your attention span and strengthen your mental discipline. Examples include:

   o **Counting Backwards:** Count backward from a high number in increments of three or even seven to push your concentration to its limits.

   o **Focused Reading:** Read complex texts without skimming, actively engaging with the material and highlighting key points. This trains your mind to maintain focus over extended periods.

b) **Create a Sanctuary for Focus:** Minimize multisensory overload by creating a calm and focused environment. This includes:

   o **Creating a Quiet Workspace:** Work in a quiet, low-stimulus environment, free from visual and auditory distractions.

   o **Utilizing Noise Reduction:** Use noise-canceling headphones or earplugs to block distracting sounds and create a sense of mental isolation.

Benefits of a Piercing Gaze: A Richer World

- **Discerning Truth from Illusion:** Our world is filled with distractions and carefully crafted appearances. Disciplined perception allows you to see through the noise and discern the underlying reality. Imagine an interrogator questioning a suspect. By focusing on subtle cues—body language, micro-expressions, inconsistencies in the story—they can pierce through the suspect's facade and uncover the truth. This skill is invaluable in a world where deception often obscures truth. Research on nonverbal communication, particularly the work of Paul Ekman on microexpressions, supports this idea.

Ekman's research demonstrates how fleeting facial expressions can reveal hidden emotions and potentially indicate deception, allowing for a deeper understanding of underlying truths.[69] Additionally, Aldert Vrij's work on deception detection provides a comprehensive overview of research in this area, highlighting the complexities of identifying deceit.[70]

- **A World Beyond the Surface:** Most of us skim the surface of life, missing the richness beneath. Disciplined perception allows you to experience the world more vibrantly. Imagine an artist observing a bustling city street. Their focused attention allows them to perceive not just the people and traffic but the symphony of sounds, the kaleidoscope of colors, and the undercurrent of emotions—a depth invisible to the casual observer. This depth of perception enriches your experiences and enhances your appreciation of the world around you. This enhanced perception is similar to what experts develop in their respective fields. Research on expertise by K. Anders Ericsson and Fernand Gobet demonstrates that through deliberate practice and focused attention, experts develop heightened perceptual abilities, allowing them to perceive details and patterns that novices often miss.[71] [72]

- **Unlocking Opportunities:** This ability to see through facades opens doors to a world of possibilities. In business, you can identify genuine partners and steer clear of potential deceivers. In your personal life, you can build stronger connections by understanding the true intentions of those around you. You can navigate complex social and professional landscapes more effectively by honing your ability to read between the lines. This relates to the concept of social and emotional intelligence. Daniel Goleman's work on emotional intelligence emphasizes the importance of understanding and managing emotions, both our own and those of others, for success in various aspects of life.[73]

- **Enhancing Empathy and Connection:** A piercing gaze allows you to tune into the emotional states of others, fostering deeper empathy and stronger connections. Imagine a therapist listening to a client. By focusing intently on the client's words and non-verbal cues, they can gain a deeper understanding of the client's feelings and experiences. This level of connection can improve personal relationships and enhance professional interactions. Research on empathy, such as the work by Jean Decety and Phillip L. Jackson, explores the neural and cognitive mechanisms underlying our ability to understand and share the feelings of others.[74]

- **Boosting Problem-Solving Skills:** Focused attention helps you analyze problems more effectively and develop creative solutions. Imagine a detective piecing together clues from a crime scene. Their ability to focus on the details allows them to see patterns and connections others might miss. This level of attention can significantly enhance your problem-solving abilities in various aspects of life. Adele Diamond's research on executive functions highlights the crucial role of attention and cognitive control in effective problem-solving.[75]

- **Cultivating Mindfulness and Presence:** Disciplined perception enables you to live more mindfully, fully engaging with each moment. By focusing your attention on the present, you can reduce stress and increase your overall sense of well-being. Mindfulness practices have been shown to have numerous mental and physical health benefits. Jon Kabat-Zinn's work on mindfulness-based stress reduction (MBSR) has been instrumental in demonstrating these benefits.[76]

The Power of Perception in Today's World

The ability to separate truth from fiction is more important than ever in our information-bombarded age. Disciplined Perception equips you with the tools to:

- **Combat Information Overload:** In the age of social media and instant news, we are constantly bombarded with information, much of it superficial or misleading. You will learn to critically analyze information, identify hidden biases, and discern fact from fiction. This skill is crucial for making informed decisions and avoiding manipulation.

- **Transcend Superficiality:** Our culture often glorifies wealth, status, and outward appearances. Disciplined Perception allows you to see beyond these and appreciate the true value of people and things. Imagine someone judging a potential friend based on their social media persona. With a piercing gaze, they can look deeper to see the person's character, values, and genuine personality. This deeper understanding fosters more authentic relationships.

- **Enhance Critical Thinking:** Focused attention sharpens critical thinking skills, enabling you to evaluate information and arguments more effectively. This helps you avoid fallacies and make reasoned decisions. Enhancing critical thinking is vital for personal and professional growth.

- **Develop Emotional Intelligence:** Disciplined Perception enhances one's ability to understand and manage one's emotions and empathize with others. This emotional intelligence is key to successful interpersonal relationships and effective leadership.

- **Strengthen Problem-Solving Abilities:** You enhance your problem-solving skills by training your mind to focus and perceive more deeply. You can see connections and solutions others might miss, leading to innovative and effective outcomes. This can be particularly beneficial in high-stakes situations.

- **Foster Mindfulness and Well-Being:** Disciplined Perception is closely linked with mindfulness, the practice of being present and fully engaged with the here and now. This reduces stress, improves mental health, and enhances your appreciation of everyday experiences.

- **Improve Decision Making:** A piercing gaze helps you to make better decisions by allowing you to weigh all factors more accurately. This is particularly important in business, where the ability to assess risks and opportunities accurately can make or break a company.

- **Nurture Authentic Relationships:** By seeing through superficial appearances and understanding the true nature of people, you can build deeper and more meaningful relationships. This authenticity strengthens personal bonds and fosters a supportive community.

The Path to Spiritual Growth

The piercing gaze can also foster spiritual growth by helping you:

- **Go Beyond Materialism:** Our modern world often prioritizes the material and overlooks the deeper meaning of things. The piercing gaze allows you to see beyond the surface glitter and connect with the essence of things—the interconnectedness of all life, the beauty in simplicity, the wonder of existence. This fosters a sense of awe and a deeper connection to something larger than yourself. For example, this deeper insight can cultivate a more meaningful approach to life, encouraging mindfulness and a greater appreciation for the subtleties of nature and human relationships.

- **Live a Vivid Life:** When you can perceive the true nature of things and people, every experience becomes more meaningful. Imagine a chef who does not just follow a recipe but understands the essence of each ingredient and the cultural significance of the dish. This deeper appreciation infuses their work with passion and elevates the culinary experience. Similarly, in daily life, this vivid perception helps you engage more fully with your surroundings, turning ordinary moments into extraordinary experiences.

- **Cultivate Inner Peace**: Focused attention can lead to greater inner peace by allowing you to disengage from the superficial distractions of modern life. You develop a sense of calm and contentment that transcends external circumstances by tuning into your deeper self and the present moment. Practices like meditation and mindfulness are rooted in this principle, helping you to cultivate a serene mind.

- **Deepen Compassion and Empathy:** The piercing gaze enables you to understand the experiences and emotions of others more deeply. This understanding fosters compassion and empathy, essential qualities for spiritual growth. By seeing beyond surface behavior to the struggles and joys of others, you build stronger, more supportive relationships and contribute positively to your community.

- **Strengthen Moral and Ethical Understanding:** By focusing intently on your values and beliefs, you can deepen your moral and ethical understanding. This clarity helps you make decisions that align with your principles, leading to a more authentic and fulfilling life. Engaging in regular self-reflection and philosophical inquiry can enhance this aspect of spiritual growth.

- **Foster a Sense of Purpose:** A piercing gaze helps you identify and pursue your true purpose in life. By looking beyond societal expectations and superficial goals, you can uncover what truly motivates and fulfills you. This sense of purpose provides direction and meaning, enriching your spiritual journey.

- **Enhance Intuitive Wisdom:** Developing a piercing gaze also sharpens your intuition, providing deeper insights and guiding you toward wise decisions. This intuitive wisdom is crucial for navigating life's complexities and making choices that reflect your highest values and aspirations.

By integrating these aspects of the piercing gaze into your daily life, you embark on a path of spiritual growth that enriches every moment. This deeper perception transforms ordinary experiences into profound lessons, guiding you toward a life of greater fulfillment and spiritual depth.

The Antidote to a Deceptive World

In a world saturated with misinformation and hidden agendas, the ability to discern truth from falsehood is critical. Disciplined Perception empowers you to:

- **Combat Deception:** You will become a critical thinker, able to see through manipulative tactics and make informed decisions. By honing your ability to analyze information critically, you can identify hidden biases and agendas, ensuring that your judgments are based on objective truth rather than deceit.

- **Build Trust and Connection:** Genuine human connection thrives on authenticity. When you can see through facades and connect with people on a deeper level, you build stronger, more trusting relationships. Imagine a world leader who can foster genuine cooperation between nations by understanding the true motivations of their counterparts.

- **Expose Disinformation:** In an era where misinformation spreads rapidly, a piercing gaze helps you identify and counteract false narratives. This is crucial for maintaining an informed public and ensuring that decisions are based on accurate information.

- **Navigate Political Polarization:** As political landscapes become increasingly polarized, the ability to see beyond partisan rhetoric is essential. Disciplined Perception allows one to understand the underlying issues and motivations, fostering more constructive dialogue and solutions.

- **Enhance Cybersecurity:** In the digital age, cyber threats are ever-present. A piercing gaze helps you detect phishing attempts, scams, and other forms of cyber deception, protecting your personal and professional information.

- **Promote Ethical Journalism:** Journalists with a piercing gaze can uncover the truth behind complex stories, ensuring that the public receives accurate and unbiased information. This is vital for a healthy democracy and informed citizenry.

- **Support Environmental Advocacy:** By recognizing greenwashing and other deceptive practices, you can support genuine environmental efforts. This helps promote sustainable practices and hold corporations accountable for their environmental impact.

- **Foster Global Cooperation:** In a multipolar world, understanding the true intentions of global actors is key to fostering cooperation. A piercing gaze allows you to navigate international relations more effectively, promoting peace and collaboration.

- **Address Social Injustice:** You can identify and address systemic injustices by seeing beyond surface-level narratives. This is crucial for creating a more equitable society where everyone has the opportunity to thrive.

- **Enhance Public Health:** In the context of public health, a piercing gaze helps in identifying misinformation about health practices and treatments. This ensures the public receives accurate health information, leading to better health outcomes.

By mastering the piercing gaze, you equip yourself with the tools to navigate a deceptive world with clarity and confidence. This enhanced perception not only helps you discern truth from falsehood but also enriches your personal and professional life, fostering deeper connections and more meaningful interactions.

Challenges to Develop Piercing Gaze

Let us explore some potential limitations and challenges that might arise in developing a piercing gaze:

1) **The Veil of Illusion**

    Self-Deception: The hardest illusions to break are often the ones we create for ourselves. We may be blind to our own biases, prejudices, or self-serving motives. Recognizing and addressing these internal barriers is crucial for developing a truly piercing gaze. Overcoming self-deception requires deep self-awareness and an openness to introspection.

    Societal Conditioning: Society often teaches us to hide behind masks and project a specific image. These societal expectations can cloud our perception and make it difficult to see people for who they truly are. Overcoming these societal influences requires consciously questioning our assumptions and challenging the status quo. This involves cultivating a sense of authenticity and courage to defy social norms.

    Media Manipulation: The media can shape our perceptions by presenting biased or sensationalized information. Recognizing and critically evaluating media content is essential for seeing through this veil of illusion. This requires media literacy skills and a skeptical approach to news consumption

2) **The Fear of Truth**

Emotional Resistance: Facing the truth about ourselves or others can be emotionally uncomfortable. We may resist seeing the darker side of people or situations, preferring to maintain illusions that protect us from discomfort. Overcoming this fear requires a commitment to honesty and a willingness to confront difficult truths. Building emotional resilience is key to navigating these challenging realizations.

The Illusion of Control: Sometimes, we cling to illusions because they give us a sense of control over our reality. Seeing through the facades of others can challenge this illusion, revealing the unpredictability and uncertainty of life. Overcoming this fear requires a willingness to embrace uncertainty and let go of the need for control. This involves developing a mindset of acceptance and adaptability.

Fear of Rejection: Recognizing the truth about a situation or relationship can lead to difficult decisions, including ending relationships or changing life paths. The fear of rejection or failure can prevent us from embracing these truths. Overcoming this fear involves building self-confidence and learning to value authenticity over acceptance

3) **The Limits of Perception**

Subjectivity: Our perception is influenced by our personal experiences, beliefs, and biases. It is important to recognize the limitations of our perspective and be open to different viewpoints. This involves actively seeking diverse perspectives and being willing to challenge our own assumptions.

The Illusion of Objectivity: We may believe that we can see the world objectively, but in reality, our perception is always colored by our own subjective experiences. Acknowledging this limitation is essential for developing a more accurate and nuanced understanding of the world. This requires a commitment to continuous learning and self-improvement.

Cognitive Biases: Cognitive biases can distort our perception and lead to flawed judgments. Recognizing and mitigating these biases is crucial for developing a piercing gaze. This involves educating ourselves about common cognitive biases and employing strategies to minimize their impact.

Sensory Limitations: Our sensory perceptions are inherently limited, and we can only perceive a fraction of the world around us. Enhancing our perception requires employing tools and technologies that extend our sensory capabilities, such as scientific instruments, to gain a fuller understanding of reality.

4) **Technological Distractions**

Digital Overload: In the digital age, constant exposure to screens and notifications can fragment our attention. Developing a piercing gaze requires disciplined use of technology and setting boundaries to minimize digital distractions. Practicing digital detoxes and mindfulness can help reclaim focused attention.

Virtual Realities: The rise of virtual and augmented realities can further blur the line between truth and illusion. Navigating these digital landscapes demands a heightened awareness of their potential to distort perception and a commitment to grounding oneself in actual reality.

5) **Interpersonal Dynamics**

Manipulation and Influence: People often use subtle tactics to influence others for personal gain. Recognizing and counteracting these manipulative behaviors is essential for maintaining integrity in interactions. Developing this skill involves understanding psychological principles of influence and practicing assertiveness.

Emotional Contagion: Emotions can be contagious, and the moods of those around us can influence our own perceptions and reactions. Being aware of this phenomenon helps in maintaining emotional autonomy and making more objective judgments. Strategies such as emotional regulation and mindfulness are effective in mitigating emotional contagion.

By acknowledging and addressing these challenges, you can develop a more refined and accurate piercing gaze, empowering you to see through the veil of illusion and navigate the complexities of the modern world with clarity and confidence.

Overcoming These Challenges

To develop a piercing gaze, it's essential to address these limitations. Here are some strategies:

- **Self-Reflection:** Regularly engage in self-reflection to identify your own biases and blind spots. This involves setting aside time to meditate or journal about your experiences and thoughts. Doing so can uncover underlying prejudices and patterns in your thinking that may cloud your perception. Self-reflection helps in building greater self-awareness and promotes personal growth.

- **Empathy:** Cultivate empathy to understand others' perspectives and see beyond their surface behaviors. Empathy involves actively listening to others, recognizing their emotions, and responding compassionately. This practice not only enhances interpersonal relationships but also deepens your understanding of human behavior, enabling you to see the underlying motivations behind actions.

- **Open-Mindedness:** Be willing to challenge your assumptions and consider alternative viewpoints. This requires a deliberate effort to expose yourself to diverse perspectives and experiences. Engaging in discussions with people from different backgrounds, reading widely, and being curious about the world can help you break free from echo chambers and broaden your understanding.

- **Mindfulness:** Practice mindfulness techniques to improve your focus and awareness of the present moment. Mindfulness involves paying attention to your thoughts, feelings, and surroundings without judgment. Techniques such as meditation, deep breathing exercises, and mindful walking can help you cultivate a state of heightened awareness, allowing you to perceive the world more clearly and without distraction.

- **Critical Thinking:** Develop critical thinking skills to analyze information objectively and make informed decisions. This involves questioning assumptions, evaluating evidence, and considering multiple perspectives before drawing conclusions. Critical thinking helps you navigate complex information landscapes and identify truth from deception.

- **Resilience Building:** Strengthen your emotional resilience to face uncomfortable truths and challenges. Resilience enables you to recover quickly from setbacks and adapt to change. Techniques such as cognitive-behavioral therapy (CBT), maintaining a support network, and practicing self-compassion can enhance your resilience.

- **Media Literacy:** Enhance your media literacy to evaluate the information you consume critically. This involves understanding how media messages are constructed, recognizing bias, and distinguishing between credible sources and misinformation. Media literacy equips you with the tools to see through propaganda and sensationalism.

- **Technology Management**: Develop strategies to manage digital distractions and maintain focused attention. This includes setting boundaries for screen time, using apps that promote focus, and creating technology-free zones in your daily routine. Managing your relationship with technology helps preserve your mental clarity and enhances your ability to concentrate.

- **Ethical Considerations:** Cultivate a strong ethical framework to guide your decisions and actions. Reflect on your values and principles, and make choices that align with your moral beliefs. Ethical considerations help you maintain integrity and authenticity, fostering trust and respect in your relationships.

Implementing these strategies can help you overcome the challenges of developing a piercing gaze. This enhanced perception allows you to see through the veil of illusion, navigate the complexities of the modern world, and foster deeper, more meaningful connections with others.

Key Takeaway

Selective Awareness serves as the gateway to unveiling the profound insights that lie beneath the surface. By honing your cognitive abilities to unravel the layers that conceal deeper truths, you cultivate the skill to pierce through deceptions and grasp the essence of existence.

Disciplined Perception transcends mere goal attainment; it is an enlightening odyssey that invites you to look beyond the superficial and engage with the fundamental nature of existence. Yet, one must recognize that cultivating a penetrating gaze comes with its own set of trials. Through the act of transcending distractions, confronting inherent biases, and embracing mindfulness, one can nurture this profound capacity and unveil a realm of possibilities. As your consciousness sharpens, you transcend the role of a mere observer in the intricate tapestry of existence; you emerge as a vital contributor, immersing yourself in the profound nuances and complexities that each fleeting instant offers.

The Focused Funnel: Channeling Knowledge for Peak Performance

The "Focused Funnel" concept describes effectively channeling diverse streams of information and knowledge toward a singular, well-defined objective, ultimately leading to peak performance. While intense concentration on a single task is valuable, true mastery often necessitates a broader understanding of the world and the ability to synthesize information from multiple sources. Disciplined Perception acts as the crucial mechanism within this funnel, enabling us to gather, filter, and apply knowledge with precision selectively.

Multiple Channels of Input: Disciplined Perception empowers us to broaden our scope of inquiry, drawing insights from diverse fields and perspectives. Imagine a scientist researching a cure for a complex disease. Rather than limiting their focus to medical journals alone, Disciplined Perception encourages them to explore related areas: historical accounts of similar illnesses, traditional healing practices from different cultures, advancements in related fields like immunology or genetics, or even seemingly unrelated areas such as biomimicry (learning from nature's solutions). These diverse input channels provide a richer and more comprehensive foundation for their research, potentially uncovering unexpected connections and innovative solutions. This approach aligns with the concept of combinatorial creativity, where novel ideas emerge from the combination of existing ones (Koestler, A. (1964).[77] By drawing from a wider range of knowledge, the scientist increases the likelihood of finding a breakthrough.

The Power of Selective Output: However, simply gathering vast amounts of information is insufficient. The true power of the Focused Funnel lies in the ability to filter and apply this knowledge selectively. Disciplined Perception empowers us to discern the most relevant information and discard irrelevant details, ensuring our efforts remain laser-focused on achieving our goals. Think of that same scientist sifting through mountains of data from various sources. Their focused awareness, guided by Disciplined Perception, allows them to identify key patterns, isolate critical findings, and extract actionable insights. This selective output enables them to synthesize information from diverse sources into a coherent understanding and effectively direct their efforts toward a breakthrough. This process is closely related to cognitive control and executive functions, which enable us to manage our attention, filter distractions, and prioritize relevant information (Diamond, A. (2013).[78]

Connecting to Peak Performance: The Focused Funnel significantly enhances performance by effectively channeling diverse inputs and selectively applying the most relevant knowledge. This process allows us to:

- **Develop a deeper understanding of complex problems:** Disciplined perception facilitates considering multiple perspectives, which can help us gain a more holistic and nuanced view of the challenges we face.

- **Generate more creative and innovative solutions:** Combining insights from diverse fields, a key aspect of the Focused Funnel, can lead to unexpected breakthroughs and novel approaches.

- **Make more informed and effective decisions:** We can make more sound and strategic choices by filtering out irrelevant information and focusing on the most critical factors.

The efficiency and effectiveness gained through the Focused Funnel, driven by Disciplined Perception, directly contribute to achieving peak performance in any field.

The Role of Disciplined Perception

Here is how Disciplined Perception helps you achieve focused expertise:

- **Goal-Oriented Input**

  Disciplined Perception guides you in selecting information directly relevant to your specific goal. This involves actively seeking out relevant sources and filtering out irrelevant noise. Imagine an artist wanting to learn a new painting technique. Disciplined Perception helps them prioritize instructional videos, workshops with master artists, and critiques of their work over irrelevant information like the history of paintbrushes (unless that history directly informs the technique). This selective attention is a key aspect of cognitive control, allowing us to focus on task-relevant stimuli (Diamond, A. (2013).[79]

- **Efficient Processing**

  Disciplined Perception streamlines the processing of information by enhancing focus and minimizing distractions. This allows for deeper absorption and understanding of the material. Imagine a student studying for an exam. Disciplined Perception helps them eliminate distractions like social media notifications and focus on understanding the core concepts rather than simply memorizing facts. This relates to the

concept of working memory, which is enhanced by focused
attention and reduced distractions.[80]

- **Directed Output**

  Disciplined Perception ensures that processed information is
  effectively channeled towards achieving your goal. This
  involves translating knowledge into action and applying it
  strategically. Imagine an entrepreneur developing a new
  product. Disciplined Perception helps them translate their
  knowledge of market trends, customer needs, and competitor
  analysis into a concrete and successful product launch. This
  relates to goal-directed behavior, a key aspect of executive
  function.[81]

- **Integrative Thinking**

  Disciplined Perception encourages integrative thinking, where
  you synthesize information from various disciplines to
  generate innovative solutions. For instance, an engineer might
  combine principles of biology (biomimicry), mechanics, and
  environmental science to develop sustainable technology. This
  interdisciplinary approach fosters creativity and innovation by
  drawing connections between seemingly disparate fields.

- **Continuous Learning**

  Disciplined Perception fosters a mindset of continuous
  learning and intellectual curiosity. By remaining open to new
  information and actively seeking out new knowledge, you can
  keep your knowledge base updated and relevant. This
  continuous learning is crucial in fast-evolving fields like
  technology and medicine, where staying current can make a
  significant difference.

- **Enhanced Problem-Solving**

  Disciplined Perception significantly enhances problem-solving abilities by allowing you to approach challenges from multiple angles and consider diverse perspectives. Imagine a detective solving a complex case. By considering evidence from various sources and perspectives, they can piece together a comprehensive understanding of the situation, leading to effective solutions. This relates to critical thinking and systems thinking, which involve analyzing complex situations and identifying underlying patterns and relationships.

- **Prioritization Skills**

  Disciplined Perception helps you develop strong prioritization skills by enabling you to clearly identify what information and tasks are most critical to your goals. This allows for more effective resource and time allocation. For example, a project manager can use Disciplined Perception to allocate resources and time to the most impactful activities, ensuring the project's success.

- **Resilience to Information Overload**

  In today's information-saturated world, Disciplined Perception is crucial for managing information overload. By filtering out irrelevant data and focusing on what truly matters, it helps maintain mental clarity and facilitates sound decision-making. This relates to attention regulation and the ability to inhibit irrelevant information.

By integrating these strategies and understanding the role of Disciplined Perception, you can channel your knowledge and efforts more effectively, achieving focused expertise and peak performance in your endeavors.

In Conclusion

Disciplined Perception allows you to achieve the best of both worlds—the focused intensity of a "one-track mind" combined with the richness of a broad knowledge base. Acting as a focused funnel ensures that all gathered information propels you toward your major definite purpose. This process streamlines diverse knowledge inputs, filters out the noise, and channels insights into a coherent strategy for success.

Embracing Disciplined Perception transforms individuals from mere collectors of facts into masterful orchestrators of knowledge. This process cultivates the ability to sift through vast amounts of information, discerning the valuable from the irrelevant and directing energies with precision. It empowers one to become a true specialist—an expert whose depth of knowledge is enriched by a broad understanding of various disciplines.

This dual capability not only heightens expertise but also enhances adaptability, creativity, and problem-solving skills. As one navigates the complexities of their chosen field with a finely tuned mind, they unlock the potential for peak performance and significant, impactful contributions. In essence, Disciplined Perception equips individuals with the mental acuity to see the broader picture while maintaining an unwavering focus on their ultimate goals, ensuring their journey is both insightful and purposefully directed toward achieving those goals.

The Power of Purpose: Conserving Energy and Fueling Action with Selective Awareness

Selective awareness, or Disciplined Perception, is not just about focusing your attention; it is about strategically allocating your mental and emotional resources. Imagine your mind as a battery. When constantly bombarded with distractions and indecision, it drains quickly. Fueled by a definite principal objective (a clear purpose), selective awareness acts as an energy-saving mechanism, directing your mental resources toward what truly matters. This section explores how a definite principal objective, paired with Disciplined Perception, empowers you in key ways:

The Efficiency of Purpose

Imagine two people: one whose dream is to become a doctor, while the other has no clear ambitions. The aspiring doctor will naturally direct their energy towards studying relevant subjects, seeking experience in hospitals, and developing the necessary skills. Disciplined Perception allows them to focus on relevant information, filter out distractions, and conserve mental resources for productive pursuits. On the other hand, the person without a clear aim may find themselves scattered and easily distracted, wasting precious time and energy on irrelevant activities.

- **Less Worry, More Action & The Clarity of Direction:** A well-defined goal acts as a mental compass, providing clear direction and reducing the mental clutter that leads to worry and indecision. Lack of clarity keeps you in a spiral of anxiety and ineffectiveness, feeding anxieties about the future, fueling self-doubt, and overwhelming you with options. This constant mental churning exacts a significant emotional cost and hinders action. This fragmented mentality manifests as jumping from one thing to another without a clear plan, much like someone trying to clean a house without a strategy. They might start dusting, get sidetracked by a phone call, and end up doing the dishes—all while feeling overwhelmed and unproductive. Disciplined Perception, guided by a definite purpose, breaks this cycle. With a clear aim, such as "thoroughly clean the living room in two hours" or "gather ingredients for a healthy stir-fry," attention is concentrated, conserving energy and accelerating progress. This focused approach also mitigates decision fatigue, the mental exhaustion caused by constantly making choices. Imagine entering a grocery store without a meal plan. The sheer volume of choices can be overwhelming, leading to indecision and mental drain. Disciplined Perception, aligned with a specific goal (e.g., "ingredients for a healthy stir-fry"), cuts through this fatigue, allowing you to quickly and efficiently navigate the aisles.

Key takeaway: A clear purpose, combined with Disciplined Perception, reduces mental clutter, combats decision fatigue, and promotes focused action, leading to increased efficiency and productivity. This aligns with research on goal-setting theory (Locke & Latham, 2002)[82], cognitive load theory, and the concept of executive functions, which are responsible for attention, planning, and decision-making (Diamond, 2013).[83]

Action as the Antidote to Worry

This section emphasizes the crucial role of action in harnessing the power of Selective Awareness (Disciplined Perception) and achieving your purpose. While having a clear purpose is essential, it is the consistent act of taking steps toward that goal that truly unlocks its transformative benefits.

- **Breaking the Worry Cycle & The Power of Focused Effort:** Worry thrives in the absence of action. When you lack a clear purpose or fail to take action toward it, you become trapped in a cycle of rumination, dwelling on problems without seeking solutions. Disciplined Perception, guided by a definite objective, helps break this unproductive cycle by directing your attention toward constructive action. Imagine someone worried about their finances. Instead of endlessly fretting, Disciplined Perception prompts them to channel their energy into creating a budget, exploring ways to increase their income, or seeking financial advice. This shift from worry to action is crucial. Similarly, focused effort, whether it is the long hours of study for an aspiring doctor or the energizing release of a brisk walk, acts as a powerful antidote to worry. The mere act of immersing yourself in purposeful work, especially physical activity, can be therapeutic, allowing you to discharge pent-up stress and gain mental clarity. Consider someone facing a looming deadline. Engaging in a physical task can clear their mind and release accumulated tension, preparing them to return to work with renewed focus and motivation. In the case of the aspiring doctor, focused effort extends beyond stress relief; it builds confidence and reinforces their commitment to their goal. This sense of progress and accomplishment further motivates them and propels them forward. This focused engagement can even lead to a state of flow, a state of deep immersion in an activity where worries disappear, and one is fully absorbed in the task at hand (Csikszentmihalyi, M. (1990).[84] Disciplined Perception plays a key role in maintaining this focus and preventing distractions that could disrupt the flow state.

Key takeaway: Action, guided by Disciplined Perception and a clear purpose, breaks the worry cycle, reduces stress, builds confidence, and can even facilitate flow states. This aligns with research on behavioral activation for depression and anxiety, which emphasizes the importance of engaging in rewarding activities to improve mood and reduce rumination.[85][86]

- **From Decision to Doing:** A decision without action remains just a possibility. While a definite purpose is a seed, Disciplined Perception helps you identify the fertile ground (the right opportunities and resources) and focus on the act of planting (taking the necessary steps). However, it is the physical act of taking action—studying for exams, volunteering at a clinic, networking with professionals in the field—that brings your goal to life. Disciplined Perception ensures that your attention remains focused on these actions, preventing procrastination and maintaining momentum.

> **Key takeaway:** *Disciplined Perception helps translate decisions into concrete actions by maintaining focus and preventing procrastination. This relates to the concept of implementation intentions, which are specific plans that link a situation with a goal-directed behavior ("If situation X arises, then I will perform behavior Y").*

Confidence and Initiative

This section explores how a focused, action-oriented approach, guided by Disciplined Perception, fosters self-confidence and the power of initiative.

- **From Doubt to Determination & Taking Charge:** Without a clear purpose, life can feel like a frustrating dance between indecision and self-doubt. Every choice feels daunting, a potential misstep in an unclear direction. However, when Selective Awareness is coupled with action guided by a definite purpose, it unlocks a powerful path forward. As you take deliberate steps towards your objective, even small victories contribute to building momentum and a track record of success, gradually eroding self-doubt and fostering a sense of accomplishment. Imagine someone unsure of their career path, paralyzed by endless possibilities. Discovering a passion for teaching (a definite purpose) provides a compass, eliminating the anxiety of indecision and providing a clear direction for their efforts. Now, they can make decisive choices about their education, internship opportunities, and job applications, each step fueled by a growing sense of confidence and the momentum of their newfound purpose. This clear purpose also empowers them to take the initiative. It ignites an internal drive, transforming them from a passive observer into an active participant in their own life. They no longer wait for opportunities to arise; they actively seek them out, empowered by Disciplined Perception, which allows them to identify the stepping stones towards their goals and navigate the path with clarity. Each step taken and each challenge overcome reinforces their belief in their capabilities and builds upon their previous success. Imagine someone training for a marathon. Every completed training run is not just physical progress; it is a brick laid in the foundation of self-belief. Consistent, purposeful action fuels initiative and propels them forward, replacing self-doubt with the unwavering confidence that they can achieve what they set out to do. Disciplined Perception plays a crucial role in maintaining focus on these actions and preventing distractions that could derail their progress.

Key takeaway: A clear purpose, combined with consistent, purposeful action and guided by Disciplined Perception, fosters self-confidence, fuels initiative, and creates a positive feedback loop of progress and motivation. This strongly relates to the concept of self-efficacy, which is the belief in one's ability to succeed in specific situations.[87] As individuals take action and experience success, their self-efficacy increases, leading to even greater initiative and confidence.

In Conclusion

Selective awareness, ignited by a clear and unwavering purpose, transforms into a potent mental technology. It acts as a laser, streamlining your thinking and conserving mental and emotional resources. Freed from the scattering influence of distractions and the burden of decision fatigue, you are empowered to take decisive action. By focusing your attention and channeling your energy towards a well-defined goal, you not only alleviate worry but cultivate a sense of self-confidence and initiative. This newfound clarity propels you forward, a lighthouse beam guiding you on the path to achieving your dreams and shaping your reality through Disciplined Perception. Remember, a clear purpose is the fuel that ignites your potential, allowing you to navigate the journey with focus, energy, unwavering self-belief, and the power to manifest your intentions.

Shaping Your Reality: How Selective Awareness Attracts Opportunities and Fuels Success

Selective awareness isn't just about filtering thoughts; it's about harnessing the power of your mind to actively curate your reality. Disciplined Perception acts as a master key, unlocking your potential by conditioning your mind for success. This process goes beyond simply filtering out distractions; it is a form of mental training that instills the qualities necessary to achieve your goals.

Mental Conditioning for Success

Disciplined Perception empowers you to cultivate a positive and productive mindset. Imagine someone struggling with persistent self-doubt and negativity. Selective awareness, a core component of Disciplined Perception, empowers them to do more than just suppress these unwanted thoughts. It enables them to actively redirect their attention towards positive affirmations and constructive self-talk, cultivating an optimistic outlook and an empowering inner dialogue. This shift in mental focus creates a fertile ground for developing the essential qualities that drive success.

- **Enthusiasm:** Disciplined Perception facilitates enthusiasm by directing your attention towards your goals and aspirations. You naturally generate excitement and passion by consciously focusing on the positive aspects of your desired outcomes and the steps required to achieve them. This enthusiasm fuels your drive, motivates you to take action, and sustains your efforts through challenges.

  Key takeaway: Disciplined Perception fosters enthusiasm by focusing attention on positive outcomes and action steps, fueling motivation and drive. This relates to expectancy theory, which suggests that motivation is influenced by the belief that effort will lead to performance, performance will lead to rewards, and those rewards are valued.[88][89]

- **Initiative, Definiteness of Purpose, and Organized Thought:** Disciplined Perception fosters initiative, definiteness of purpose, and organized thought by enhancing cognitive control and clarity. A focused mind, free from the clutter of distractions and self-doubt, provides the ideal environment for seizing opportunities and taking decisive action. Disciplined Perception empowers you to become proactive, taking control of your life's direction rather than passively reacting to circumstances. By filtering out irrelevant information and focusing on your core purpose, Disciplined Perception provides clarity of vision, keeping you centered and unwavering in pursuing your goals. This clarity also allows you to organize your thoughts logically, prioritize tasks effectively, and develop strategic plans.

  > **Key takeaway:** Disciplined Perception fosters initiative, definiteness of purpose, and organized thought by enhancing cognitive control, providing clarity, and promoting proactive behavior. This relates to executive functions, which are higher-level cognitive processes that control and regulate other cognitive functions, including attention, planning, and decision-making.[90]

- **Creative Vision:** When your mind is not cluttered with negativity and distractions, it has the space to explore new ideas, make novel connections, and generate innovative solutions. Disciplined Perception cultivates this mental space by enhancing attention regulation and reducing cognitive overload. By focusing on the problem at hand and filtering out irrelevant information, you create a fertile ground for creativity to flourish.

> *Key takeaway: Disciplined Perception fosters creative vision by reducing mental clutter and enhancing attention regulation, creating space for new ideas and innovative solutions. This relates to research on creativity and cognitive control, which suggests that a balance between focused attention and flexible thinking is crucial for creative problem-solving.*[91] [92]

Magnetizing the Mind

This section explores the concept of the mind as a magnet, a metaphor for how Disciplined Perception, by focusing your attention on desired outcomes, can increase the likelihood of attracting relevant opportunities and resources. This is not about some mystical force; it is about how focused attention influences your perception, behavior, and interactions with the world.

- **Relentless Pursuit & Resource Acquisition:** By directing your attention toward specific goals, Disciplined Perception creates a heightened awareness of opportunities and resources that align with those goals. You become more attuned to relevant information, people, and experiences. Imagine a musician seeking a record deal. Disciplined Perception helps them focus their attention on music industry events, networking opportunities, online resources, and articles about successful artists. This focused attention makes them more likely to notice these opportunities when they arise and to actively seek them out. They might also become more aware of potential mentors, collaborators, or tools that can aid them on their journey. This is not about magically attracting things; it is about enhancing your ability to detect and seize opportunities that were already present but might have been missed without focused attention.

> *Key takeaway: Disciplined Perception enhances opportunity detection and resource acquisition by directing attention toward goal-relevant information and experiences. This relates to the concept of attentional bias,*

where attention is preferentially directed towards stimuli related to current goals or concerns.[93]

- **A Beacon for Success:** Your focused thoughts, guided by Disciplined Perception, do not just attract opportunities; they also motivate you to take the necessary actions to capitalize on them. Musician with a magnetized mind do not just passively wait for a record deal to fall into their lap; they actively reach out to contacts, prepare demos, perform at open mics, and hone their craft. Their focused intention and consistent action act as a beacon, guiding them toward their desired outcome. Disciplined Perception helps maintain this focus and prevent distractions that could derail their efforts.

  Key takeaway: Disciplined Perception translates focused thoughts into goal-directed action, driving progress toward desired outcomes. This relates to the concept of goal-directed behavior and the importance of implementation intentions.[94]

Subconscious Activation

Disciplined Perception, when coupled with genuine enthusiasm, acts as a catalyst for activating the power of your subconscious mind. This isn't about some mystical force; it is about how focused attention and positive emotions can influence implicit learning, automatic processing, and other subconscious cognitive processes. By directing your focus towards your goals and fueling that focus with enthusiasm, disciplined perception programs your subconscious to work in alignment with your conscious desires.

The Silent Partner, From Dreams to Reality: Imagine an athlete training for a competition. Their conscious mind focuses on perfecting their technique, analyzing their performance, and strategizing for the competition. Simultaneously, their subconscious mind, influenced by their unwavering desire to win and their dedicated training, constantly processes information, consolidates skills, and generates potential solutions. This subconscious activity might manifest as improved muscle memory, enhanced reaction time, or even intuitive insights during training or competition.

For example, the athlete's subconscious might suggest a subtle adjustment to their technique or a new mental visualization strategy that gives them a competitive edge. This subconscious processing is not about magically solving problems; it is about the brain continuing to work on tasks and goals even when conscious attention is directed elsewhere, consolidating learned skills and looking for patterns and solutions based on prior experiences. Disciplined Perception plays a crucial role by maintaining focus on the desired outcome, which then influences the subconscious processing.

Key takeaway: Disciplined Perception, combined with enthusiasm, activates subconscious processing that supports conscious efforts by consolidating skills, generating insights, and improving performance. This relates to several psychological concepts:

a) **Implicit Learning:**

Implicit learning is a type of learning that occurs without conscious awareness or intention. It's the acquisition of knowledge about complex patterns or regularities in the environment without explicitly knowing the rules or structure of that knowledge. You learn how to do something without necessarily being able to explain what you learned or how you learned it.

- **Characteristics:**

  o **Unconscious:** Learning occurs without conscious effort or awareness.

- o **Automatic:** Once learned, the skill or knowledge can be applied automatically without conscious control.

- o **Robust:** Implicitly learned skills are often resistant to forgetting and are less affected by brain damage than explicitly learned skills.

- o **Difficult to Verbalize:** It is often difficult to explain the rules or principles underlying implicitly learned knowledge.

- **Examples:**

  - o **Learning a language:** Children acquire their native language implicitly, without formal grammar instruction.

  - o **Riding a bicycle:** You learn the balance and coordination required without consciously thinking about the individual muscle movements.

  - o **Driving a car:** Through practice, many aspects of driving, such as shifting gears or steering, become automatic.

  - o **Recognizing faces:** We can often recognize familiar faces without consciously analyzing their individual features.

- **Relevance to Subconscious Activation:** Implicit learning contributes to subconscious activation because the learned skills and knowledge are stored and processed outside of conscious awareness. This allows the subconscious to continue working on tasks and goals even when conscious attention is directed elsewhere.

b) **Automatic Processing Definition:**

Automatic processing refers to cognitive processes that occur rapidly, effortlessly, and without conscious attention or intention. They are often triggered by specific environmental stimuli and operate outside of conscious control.

- **Characteristics**:

  o **Fast:** Automatic processes occur quickly, often in milliseconds.

  o **Effortless:** They require minimal cognitive resources and do not interfere with other ongoing tasks.

  o **Unconscious:** They operate outside of conscious awareness.

  o Inflexible: Automatic processes are often difficult to modify or control once they have been learned.

- **Examples:**

  o **Reading:** Skilled readers can recognize words automatically, without consciously sounding out each letter.

  o **Walking:** We can walk and talk simultaneously because walking has become an automatic process.

  o **Driving on a familiar route:** You might find yourself arriving at your destination without consciously remembering the details of the drive.

  o **Reacting to a sudden loud noise:** You automatically jump or turn your head in response to a startling sound.

- **Relevance to Subconscious Activation:** Automatic processing is a key component of subconscious activity. Many tasks and skills processed subconsciously operate automatically, allowing the conscious mind to focus on other things.

c) **The Role of Emotions in Influencing Subconscious Activity**

- **Influence on Attention and Memory:** Emotions can powerfully influence what we pay attention to and what we remember. Emotional events are often more vividly recalled than neutral events, suggesting that emotions play a role in memory consolidation, which can occur subconsciously.

- **Influence on Implicit Learning:** Emotions can also influence implicit learning. For example, fear conditioning is a type of implicit learning where we learn to associate a neutral stimulus with a negative emotion. This learning occurs rapidly and often without conscious awareness.

- **Influence on Motivation and Behavior:** Emotions play a crucial role in motivation and behavior. Positive emotions, such as enthusiasm, can energize and motivate us to pursue our goals. Negative emotions, such as fear or anxiety, can inhibit action and lead to avoidance. These emotional influences can operate at a subconscious level, affecting our behavior without conscious awareness.

- **Examples**:
    - Feeling anxious before a presentation might lead to subconscious fidgeting or avoiding eye contact.

- o Feeling enthusiastic about a project might lead to subconscious brainstorming and problem-solving even when you are not actively working on it.

- o Exposure to subliminal emotional cues (presented below the level of conscious awareness) can influence subsequent behavior.

- **Relevance to Subconscious Activation:** Emotions act as a powerful driving force behind subconscious activity. Positive emotions, like enthusiasm, can prime the subconscious for creative problem-solving and goal pursuit, while negative emotions can hinder these processes. In the context of your writing, enthusiasm, driven by Disciplined Perception, is the key emotional driver that activates the subconscious to work towards your goals.

In summary, implicit learning allows us to acquire knowledge and skills without conscious awareness, automatic processing allows us to perform tasks effortlessly and without conscious control, and emotions act as powerful motivators and influences on subconscious activity. All three of these concepts are interconnected and contribute to the overall functioning of the subconscious mind. By understanding these concepts, you can better understand how Disciplined Perception and enthusiasm can activate the subconscious to support your conscious goals.

In Conclusion

Selective awareness, or Disciplined Perception, is more than a mental filter; it transforms your reality. By centering your attention, you cultivate a positive attitude that attracts the people, resources, and opportunities crucial for achieving your objectives. It focuses your mind, drawing in beneficial external circumstances and activating your subconscious's powerful resources.

This subconscious activation turns it into a powerful ally, working in harmony with your conscious intentions. This synergy between the focused mind and the subconscious creates a powerful force, bridging the gap between desire and manifestation. Through Disciplined Perception, you transition from a passive observer to an active architect of your life, shaping your destiny and maximizing your chances of realizing your dreams.

The Focused Eye: Sharpening Observation Skills with Selective Awareness

Selective awareness, guided by a definite purpose (principal objective) and fueled by a strong motive, is not just about filtering thoughts; it hones your powers of observation, transforming you into a keen observer adept at perceiving the world through the lens of your goals. Disciplined Perception acts as the training regimen for this enhanced observation, refining your ability to extract relevant information from your surroundings.

Habit and Motive & Observation with a Purpose: Sharpened observation skills develop from the habit of focusing attention based on a specific purpose and a strong desire to achieve it.

Imagine a detective investigating a crime. Their clear goal (solving the case) and strong motive (justice) drive them to develop a keen eye for detail. They notice subtle clues—a witness's nervous twitch, an inconsistency in a statement, a barely visible footprint—that others might miss. Similarly, a student preparing for an exam does not waste time memorizing irrelevant facts; they focus on key concepts, patterns, and connections, developing a deeper understanding of the material.

This targeted focus is not just about memorization; it's about building a robust mental framework for grasping complex ideas. Disciplined Perception plays a crucial role in facilitating this focused observation. It enhances selective attention, allowing you to filter out distractions and prioritize goal-relevant information. It also refines pattern recognition, enabling you to identify meaningful connections and insights quickly.

The role of the reticular activating system (RAS): RAS is a network of neurons in the brainstem that regulates arousal and alertness. While it plays a role in attention, it does not directly "filter" information in a highly specific way. Rather, it sets the stage for focused attention by modulating overall brain activity. Through conscious effort and practice, disciplined perception influences higher-level brain areas involved in attention and perception, effectively training your brain to prioritize and process information relevant to your goals.

Key takeaway: Disciplined Perception, driven by purpose and motive, enhances observation skills by refining selective attention and pattern recognition, allowing you to extract meaningful information from your environment. This connects to research on selective attention visual attention, and awareness.[95]

A Clearer Understanding

By becoming a more observant individual through Disciplined Perception, you gain a significantly clearer understanding of the world around you, especially in relation to your desired goals. This enhanced perception allows you to extract meaningful insights from your environment and make more informed decisions.

Perceiving the Relevant & Connecting the Dots: Sharpened observation skills, honed by Disciplined Perception, enable you to perceive relevant information and connect seemingly disparate pieces of information, creating a more holistic understanding of your situation.

Imagine an entrepreneur looking to launch a new product. Their enhanced observation skills allow them to identify potential customers by noticing emerging social media trends, observing purchasing habits, and conducting market research. They might spot a gap in the market by analyzing competitor offerings and identifying unmet customer needs. This heightened awareness empowers them to make data-driven decisions that increase their chances of success. Furthermore, this enhanced observation allows them to "connect the dots" between different pieces of information. For instance, they might notice a correlation between customer demographics, purchasing habits, and specific social media trends. This newfound awareness empowers them to develop a targeted marketing strategy, tailoring their message to resonate with the right audience and maximizing the impact of their marketing efforts.

Disciplined Perception facilitates this process by enhancing pattern recognition, the cognitive ability to identify meaningful patterns and relationships in complex information, and by promoting the development of accurate mental models and internal representations of how the world works.

Key takeaway: *Disciplined Perception enhances understanding by facilitating the perception of relevant information, connecting disparate data points, and developing robust mental models. This relates to research on pattern recognition in cognitive psychology and the role of mental models in reasoning and problem-solving.*[96]

In Conclusion

Selective awareness, fueled by a definite purpose and a strong motive, transforms you from a passive observer to an active investigator. It develops a focused eye adept at perceiving the world in relation to your goals. This heightened perception provides invaluable insights, empowering you to make informed decisions and advance toward your aspirations. Disciplined Perception is not merely a mental tool; it is a powerful capacity that allows you to view the world with a sense of possibility, transforming aspirations into achievable realities and shaping your destiny.

The Domino Effect: Selective Awareness and the Cascade of Success Habits

Selective awareness is not just a single tool; it is the first domino in a chain reaction that propels you toward success. Disciplined Perception ignites a cascade of other success-oriented habits, ultimately leading to a life of greater productivity, accomplishment, and personal fulfillment.

The Genesis of Concentration & A Chain Reaction of Success Habits

Cultivating selective awareness through Disciplined Perception is the foundation for developing strong concentration and a cascade of other positive habits. When you intentionally focus your attention on a specific task or goal, you are not just filtering out distractions; you are actively training your brain to prioritize and sustain focus.

Imagine a student struggling to concentrate on their studies. By employing Disciplined Perception, they actively filter out distractions (e.g., social media notifications and unrelated thoughts) and direct their attention to the study material. This initial act of focused attention strengthens their ability to concentrate, making subsequent study sessions easier and more productive. This initial act of focus becomes a catalyst for further concentration habits. They might start planning study sessions in advance, creating a dedicated study environment, and actively engaging with the material through techniques like summarizing and note-taking. Over time, these concentrated efforts not only improve their academic performance but also strengthen their overall ability to focus on any task. This enhanced concentration then triggers a chain reaction of other positive habits.

By improving concentration, you create the mental space and discipline necessary to establish and maintain habits like a regular exercise routine, a healthy sleep schedule, or effective time management. These habits, in turn, reinforce your focus on your goals, creating a virtuous cycle of positive reinforcement. Consider the aspiring writer who, guided by this focus, consistently meets deadlines, attends writing workshops, and queries literary agents. Their progress is fueled by this virtuous cycle: focused attention leads to consistent action, which leads to progress, which further strengthens motivation and focus. Disciplined Perception acts as the initial catalyst, fueling a self-sustaining loop of positive habits that propel you toward your dreams.

Key takeaway: Disciplined Perception initiates a cascade of positive habits by strengthening concentration, promoting consistent action, and creating a positive feedback loop of progress and motivation. This relates to several psychological concepts:

a) **Habit Formation**

   Habit formation is the process by which behaviors become automatic through repetition and association with specific cues or contexts. Habits are actions we perform with little conscious thought or effort.

   The Habit Loop (as described by Duhigg): Charles Duhigg, in The Power of Habit, popularized the "habit loop," which consists of three components:

   - **Cue:** A trigger that prompts the behavior. This can be a time of day, a location, an emotion, a preceding event, or a particular thought pattern.

- **Routine:** The behavior itself, which can be physical, mental, or emotional.

- **Reward:** The positive reinforcement that follows the behavior, making it more likely to be repeated in the future. This reward can be a physical sensation, an emotional feeling, or a sense of accomplishment.

How Habits Form: When a behavior is repeatedly performed in response to a specific cue and followed by a reward, the brain creates an association between the cue, the routine, and the reward. Over time, this association becomes stronger, and the behavior becomes more automatic. The cue triggers the routine directly, bypassing conscious decision-making.

Examples

- **Brushing your teeth:** The cue might be waking up or going to bed; the routine is brushing your teeth, and the reward is a clean feeling in your mouth.

- **Checking social media:** The cue might be boredom or a notification, the routine is opening the app and scrolling, and the reward is a sense of connection or entertainment.

- **Exercising:** The cue might be putting on your workout clothes, the routine might be going for a run or going to the gym, and the reward might be a feeling of accomplishment or improved physical well-being.

Relevance to Selective Awareness and Disciplined Perception: Selective awareness, through Disciplined Perception, plays a key role in habit formation by:

- **Focusing attention on the cues: By** being more aware of your surroundings and internal states, you can better identify the cues that trigger desired behaviors.

- **Maintaining focus during the routine**: Disciplined Perception helps you stay focused on performing the desired behavior, preventing distractions that could disrupt the habit loop.

- **Reinforcing the reward:** By consciously acknowledging and appreciating the reward associated with the behavior, you strengthen the association between the cue, routine, and reward, making the habit more ingrained.

b) **Self-Regulation**

Self-regulation is the ability to control one's thoughts, emotions, and behaviors in order to achieve goals, manage impulses, and adapt to changing circumstances. It involves a range of cognitive and emotional processes, including:

- **Goal setting:** Defining clear and achievable objectives.

- **Planning:** Developing strategies and steps to achieve those objectives.

- **Monitoring:** Tracking progress and identifying any deviations from the plan.

- **Inhibition:** Resisting impulses and distractions that could hinder progress.

- **Emotional regulation:** Managing emotions in a way that supports goal pursuit.

Importance of Willpower (as discussed by Baumeister and Tierney): Baumeister and Tierney, in Willpower, emphasize the role of willpower (also called self-control or executive function) as a key component of self-regulation. They argue that willpower is a limited resource that can be depleted through overuse. However, it can also be strengthened through regular practice, like a muscle.

Examples:

- **Resisting** the urge to eat junk food when trying to maintain a healthy diet.

- **Focusing** on studying for an exam instead of watching TV.

- **Managing** anger or frustration in a difficult situation.

- **Persisting** in a challenging task despite setbacks.

Relevance to Selective Awareness and Disciplined Perception: Selective awareness, through Disciplined Perception, enhances self-regulation by:

- **Improving attention control:** By focusing attention on goal-relevant information and filtering out distractions, you can better resist temptations and maintain focus on your objectives.

- **Enhancing emotional regulation**: By becoming more aware of your emotions and practicing mindfulness, you can better manage emotional responses that could hinder progress.

- **Strengthening willpower:** By consistently practicing focused attention and resisting distractions, you can strengthen your willpower "muscle," making it easier to self-regulate in other areas of your life.

c) **Motivation**

Motivation refers to the forces that drive behavior towards a desired outcome. It encompasses the factors that energize, direct, and sustain behavior.

Types of Motivation:

- **Intrinsic motivation:** Motivation that comes from within, driven by internal rewards such as enjoyment, satisfaction, or a sense of accomplishment.

- **Extrinsic motivation:** Motivation that comes from external rewards or pressures, such as money, grades, or social approval.

Factors Influencing Motivation: Several factors can influence motivation, including:

- **Goals:** Clear and challenging goals can enhance motivation.

- **Expectations:** The belief that effort will lead to performance and that performance will lead to desired outcomes.

- **Values:** The importance and meaning that individuals attach to their goals.

- **Emotions:** Positive emotions can enhance motivation, while negative emotions can hinder it.

Examples:

- **Studying** hard because you enjoy learning and want to expand your knowledge (intrinsic motivation).

- **Working** overtime to earn a bonus (extrinsic motivation).

- **Training** for a marathon because you value physical fitness and want to achieve a personal goal.

Relevance to Selective Awareness and Disciplined Perception: Selective awareness, through Disciplined Perception, enhances motivation by:

- **Clarifying goals:** Focusing attention on your purpose and desired outcomes can make your goals clearer and more meaningful.

- **Increasing expectancy:** By focusing on the steps required to achieve your goals and celebrating small victories, you can increase your belief that you are capable of succeeding.

- **Generating positive emotions:** Focusing on the positive aspects of your goals and practicing gratitude can cultivate positive emotions that fuel motivation.

In summary, these three concepts are interconnected and play crucial roles in achieving goals and shaping behavior. Habit formation provides the automaticity for consistent action, self-regulation provides the control to manage thoughts, emotions, and behaviors, and motivation provides the driving force to pursue desired outcomes. Selective awareness, through Disciplined Perception, enhances all three of these processes.

Motivated by Achievement

The cascade of success habits triggered by Disciplined Perception does not just improve your efficiency; it fuels intrinsic motivation and leads to a more profound and personally meaningful definition of success.

Accomplishment Breeds Desire

When you begin to experience the positive outcomes of your focused efforts, a powerful self-reinforcing feedback loop takes hold. The salesperson, driven by a clear sales target and employing Disciplined Perception to identify prospective customers, experiences increased sales. These successes reinforce their confidence and motivate them to set even higher goals. This cycle of accomplishment and increased motivation creates a powerful drive for further achievement.

Key takeaway: Experiencing success, even in small increments, creates a positive feedback loop that fuels further motivation and the desire for greater accomplishment. This relates to the concept of operant conditioning, where behaviors followed by positive reinforcement are more likely to be repeated.[27]

Beyond Just Money & Surplus Affluence and Personal Triumphs

While many associate success primarily with monetary wealth, Disciplined Perception empowers you to define "surplus affluence" on your own terms, focusing on what truly brings you personal fulfillment.

Imagine a musician who defines affluence not as commercial fame but as creative freedom. Disciplined Perception allows them to focus their energy on perfecting their craft, building a loyal following, and generating income through avenues like merchandise sales and private lessons. Their motivation stems from passion and purpose, leading to success on their own terms, even if it does not translate into mainstream recognition. Disciplined Perception also guides you toward achieving personal triumphs that extend far beyond financial rewards. The focused student graduating with honors or the salesperson becoming a top performer experiences the deep satisfaction of achieving their goals. Disciplined Perception helps you prioritize intrinsic rewards, such as personal growth, meaningful contributions, and a sense of purpose.

This focus on intrinsic motivation shifts the emphasis from external validation to internal satisfaction, empowering you to define success based on your own values and aspirations. Consider the social worker motivated by a genuine desire to help others. Disciplined Perception enables them to design effective interventions, build strong client relationships, and contribute to positive social change. Their success is measured not by awards or praise but by the positive impact they have on the lives of others. In essence, Disciplined Perception helps you redefine success by placing personal triumphs and fulfillment at the center stage, regardless of your chosen path.

Key takeaway: Disciplined Perception facilitates a shift from extrinsic to intrinsic motivation, empowering you to define success based on personal values and find fulfillment in pursuing meaningful goals. This aligns with self-determination theory, which emphasizes the importance of autonomy, competence, and relatedness for intrinsic motivation and well-being.[98]

In Conclusion

Selective awareness, or Disciplined Perception, is not just a mental filter; it is the cornerstone that sets off a cascade of positive habits. Fostering focused attention provides the initial impetus for a life of accomplishment and personal fulfillment. It initiates a chain reaction: concentration habits become ingrained, motives become aligned with your goals, and this focused determination propels you towards personal triumphs. Remember, success is rarely a single event; it is a journey of consistent effort and focused action. With Selective Awareness as your guide, you become the architect of your success story, building it one focused action at a time. The dominoes begin to fall—concentration strengthens, motivation grows, and ultimately, you reach your goals and experience a deeply fulfilling life.

The Law of Merit: Decoding the Selective Awareness Advantage

This section explores the concept of the Law of Merit—the idea that focused effort, preparation, and skill development, guided by selective awareness (and Disciplined Perception), significantly increase the likelihood of career advancement. It challenges the notion that promotions are solely based on luck or chance, emphasizing the predictable outcomes of dedicated effort and strategic focus. This approach empowers you to become the architect of your career trajectory.

Causality and Promotion: The Power of Preparation

A Scientific Case Study

In this context, causality refers to the relationship between your actions and their consequences in your career. You increase the probability of achieving those outcomes by strategically focusing your efforts on activities and skill development that demonstrably lead to promotion and success. This is analogous to a research scientist committed to making a breakthrough. Their focused attention is not directly applied to the microscope all the time; it is channeled into designing and conducting experiments, meticulously analyzing data, and iteratively refining their approach. This same principle applies to career development. By focusing on practices and abilities that are strongly correlated with career advancement, you become a "scientist" in your professional growth. Disciplined Perception enables you to identify these key factors—such as leadership skills, effective communication, technical expertise, and networking ability—and then design your own "experiments" to develop these skills.

For example,

Suppose you identify effective communication as a key factor for promotion. In that case, you might join a public speaking club, take a communication course, or seek opportunities to present your work to larger audiences. This focused effort, guided by Disciplined Perception, allows you to gather "data" from your actions (feedback from presentations, improved communication skills) and continuously refine your strategy to achieve the best possible outcomes. This is not to say that career advancement is a purely deterministic process; external factors and chance encounters can also play a role. However, maximizing your preparation and focusing your efforts on what truly matters significantly increases your chances of success.

Key takeaway

Disciplined Perception allows you to strategically focus on skill development and actions that demonstrably lead to career advancement, increasing the probability of achieving your professional goals. This relates to concepts like goal-setting theory[99], self-efficacy[100], and the importance of deliberate practice in skill development[101].

Fair Opportunity and Visibility: Making Merit Shine - A Psychological Spotlight

This section explores how selective awareness, guided by Disciplined Perception, enhances your professional visibility and ensures that your merits are recognized. It uses the metaphor of the human brain as a sophisticated search engine, constantly scanning for talent. By strategically focusing your efforts and developing key skills, you optimize your "professional profile" to stand out in this internal search.

Think of the human brain as a sophisticated search engine. Employers constantly scan for talent, seeking individuals whose skills and experience align with their needs. Disciplined Perception enables you to strategically focus your efforts on developing the skills and behaviors that make you a desirable candidate. This is not about creating a superficial "neon sign" over your head; it is about consistently demonstrating competence and readiness through your actions. For instance, imagine a software developer who consistently exceeds expectations by delivering high-quality work, proactively seeking out challenging projects, and effectively communicating their progress and insights. These consistent actions become psychologically salient to perceptive managers, making them a natural choice when promotion opportunities arise.

Disciplined Perception helps you understand how these behaviors influence others' perceptions and leverage that understanding to enhance your professional visibility. It is not about manipulating others' perceptions but about focusing on developing genuine competence and demonstrating that competence through consistent, positive actions. This enhanced visibility creates a fair opportunity for your merit to be recognized.

Key takeaway

Disciplined Perception enhances professional visibility by guiding your focus toward developing and demonstrating key skills and behaviors that make you a desirable candidate. This relates to several psychological concepts:

a) Impression Formation

Impression formation is the process by which we form overall judgments and impressions of other people. It involves integrating various pieces of information about a person, such as their appearance, behavior, verbal communication, and social context, to create a coherent picture of who they are.

Key Aspects

- **First Impressions:** First impressions are often formed quickly and can have a lasting impact. They are influenced by factors like physical appearance, nonverbal cues (e.g., body language, facial expressions), and initial interactions.

- **Central Traits:** Some traits are considered "central traits" because they disproportionately influence our overall impression. For example, warmth and competence are often considered central traits in impression formation.

- **Implicit Personality Theories:** We all have implicit personality theories—our own personal beliefs about which traits tend to go together. For example, we might assume that someone who is intelligent is also hardworking or that someone who is friendly is also trustworthy. These implicit theories can influence how we interpret information about others.

- **Attribution:** We often try to explain the causes of other people's behavior through attribution. We might attribute someone's behavior to internal factors (e.g., their personality or abilities) or external factors (e.g., the situation or circumstances).

Relevance to Selective Awareness and Professional Visibility: Selective awareness, through Disciplined Perception, can influence impression formation by:

- **Focusing on positive behaviors and traits:** By consistently demonstrating positive behaviors and traits (e.g., competence, reliability, teamwork), you create a strong and positive first impression.

- **Managing nonverbal cues: By being aware of your nonverbal** communication (e.g., posture, eye contact, facial expressions), you can ensure that you are conveying the desired impression.

- **Controlling the information you present:** By strategically highlighting your accomplishments and skills, you can influence how others perceive your competence and potential.

b) Social Perception

Social perception is the broad process by which we perceive, interpret, and understand social information, including other people's behavior, characteristics, and intentions. It encompasses a wide range of cognitive and social processes, including:

- **Nonverbal communication:** Interpreting facial expressions, body language, tone of voice, and other nonverbal cues.

- **Attribution:** Explaining the causes of behavior.

- **Impression formation: Forming** overall judgments of others.

- **Social categorization:** Classifying people into groups based on shared characteristics (e.g., age, gender, race, occupation).

- **Stereotyping and prejudice:** Forming generalized beliefs about groups of people and holding negative attitudes towards them.

**Relevance to Selective Awareness and Professional
Visibility:** Selective awareness, through Disciplined
Perception, can influence social perception by:

- **Enhancing attention to relevant social cues:** Focusing
  on the social context and the behavior of others can give
  valuable insights into their intentions and motivations.

- **Reducing biases and stereotypes:** By being aware of
  your own biases and practicing mindful observation, you
  can reduce the influence of stereotypes on your
  perceptions of others.

- **Improving social awareness:** By paying attention to
  social dynamics and interactions, you can become more
  attuned to social cues and navigate social situations more
  effectively.

c) **The Halo Effect**

The halo effect is a cognitive bias in which our overall
impression of a person influences our judgments of their traits.
If we have a positive overall impression of someone, we tend
to rate them more positively on other dimensions, even if there
is no objective evidence to support those ratings. Conversely,
if we have a negative overall impression, we tend to rate them
more negatively on other dimensions.

Examples

- If we find someone physically attractive, we might also
  assume that they are more intelligent, competent, and
  likable.

- If we admire someone's public speaking skills, we might
  also assume that they are a good leader or a trustworthy
  person.

- If we have a negative first impression of someone, we might be more likely to interpret their behavior negatively, even if it is ambiguous.

Relevance to Selective Awareness and Professional Visibility: Selective awareness, through Disciplined Perception, can be used to leverage the halo effect positively by:

- **Focusing on demonstrating key strengths:** By consistently demonstrating competence in key areas relevant to your profession, you can create a positive overall impression that can lead to more favorable evaluations in other areas.

- **Managing your overall presentation:** By paying attention to your appearance, communication skills, and interpersonal interactions, you can create a positive overall impression that can influence how others perceive your skills and abilities.

- **Avoiding negative impressions:** By being mindful of your behavior and avoiding actions that could create a negative impression, you can prevent the halo effect from working against you.

In summary

Impression formation is the process of forming overall judgments of others, social perception is the broader process of understanding social information, and the halo effect is a cognitive bias that can influence our judgments of specific traits based on our overall impression. Selective awareness, through Disciplined Perception, can be used to influence all three of these processes positively, enhancing your professional visibility and ensuring that your merits are recognized.

Mutual Benefits of Advancement: A Symbiotic Relationship - A Win-Win Scenario

Promotions are not just a positive event for the individual employee; they are also a strategic investment for the company, creating a symbiotic relationship fueled by mutual benefits. A well-deserved promotion places a highly skilled and motivated individual in a position to make a significant contribution to the organization's success. Imagine a salesperson who consistently exceeds sales targets and possesses exceptional product knowledge. Promoting them to a leadership role within the sales team allows them to mentor and inspire others, share their expertise, and implement effective sales strategies, ultimately boosting the company's overall performance.

Disciplined Perception allows employees to focus on developing the specific skills and competencies that align with the company's needs and strategic goals. This ensures that promotions result in a win-win scenario, benefiting both the individual and the organization.

Key takeaway

Disciplined Perception enables employees to focus on developing skills that benefit both themselves and the organization, creating a mutually beneficial outcome from promotions. This relates to concepts in organizational psychology such as:

a) **Organizational Performance:**

Organizational performance encompasses an organization's overall effectiveness and productivity in achieving its goals and objectives. It is a multidimensional concept that can be measured using various metrics, including:

- **Financial performance:** Profitability, revenue growth, return on investment.

- **Operational efficiency:** Productivity, cost reduction, quality control.

- **Customer satisfaction:** Customer loyalty, retention rates, customer feedback.

- **Market share:** The percentage of a market controlled by a particular company or product.

- **Innovation:** The development of new products, services, or processes.

How Promotions Impact Organizational Performance: Strategically implemented promotions can significantly impact organizational performance in several ways:

- **Matching talent to roles:** Promotions allow organizations to place individuals with the right skills and experience in positions where they can maximize their contributions. For example, promoting someone with strong technical skills to a technical lead role can improve team productivity and project outcomes.

- **Improving efficiency and productivity:** Organizations can improve team or departmental efficiency and productivity by promoting high-performing individuals to leadership or managerial roles. These individuals can implement better processes, motivate their teams, and make more effective decisions.

- **Driving innovation:** Promoting individuals with creative ideas and a drive for innovation can foster a culture of innovation within the organization, leading to developing new products, services, and processes.

- **Boosting employee morale and retention:** When employees see that hard work and dedication are rewarded with promotions, morale increases, as does employee retention. This reduces turnover costs and maintains valuable institutional knowledge within the organization.

Relevance to Selective Awareness and Promotions: Selective awareness, through Disciplined Perception, contributes to organizational performance by:

- **Enabling employees to focus on developing skills that align with organizational goals:** By understanding the organization's strategic priorities, employees can focus their development efforts on skills that will contribute to overall performance.

- **Improving individual performance:** Selective awareness improves individual performance by enhancing focus, concentration, and observation skills, which collectively contribute to organizational performance.

- **Promoting effective leadership:** By developing self-awareness and focusing on leadership skills, individuals can become more effective leaders, contributing to improved team and organizational performance.

b) Leadership Development

Leadership development refers to enhancing individuals' skills, knowledge, and abilities to lead and manage others effectively. It encompasses various activities, including:

142

- **Training programs:** Formal training sessions focused on leadership skills such as communication, decision-making, and team management.

- **Mentoring and coaching:** Providing guidance and support from experienced leaders.

- **Job rotations and stretch assignments:** Providing opportunities to take on new challenges and develop new skills.

- **360-degree feedback:** Gathering feedback from multiple sources (supervisors, peers, subordinates) to provide a comprehensive view of leadership performance.

How Promotions Contribute to Leadership Development: Promotions can be a crucial part of a leadership development strategy in several ways:

- **Providing opportunities for leadership experience:** Promotions to managerial or supervisory roles allow individuals to practice and develop their leadership skills in a real-world setting.

- **Increasing responsibility and accountability:** Promotions often come with increased responsibility and accountability, challenging individuals to grow and develop their leadership capabilities.

- **Motivating individuals to develop their leadership potential:** The prospect of promotion can motivate individuals to actively seek out leadership development opportunities and invest in their growth.

Relevance to Selective Awareness and Promotions:
Selective awareness, through Disciplined Perception,
contributes to leadership development by:

- **Focusing attention on leadership skills:** Individuals
  can focus their development efforts on those areas by
  identifying the key skills and competencies required for
  effective leadership.

- **Enhancing self-awareness:** By practicing self-reflection
  and mindful observation, individuals can better
  understand their strengths and weaknesses as leaders.

- **Improving communication and interpersonal skills:**
  By focusing on effective communication and social
  perception, individuals can become more effective at
  building relationships, motivating teams, and influencing
  others.

c) **Employee Motivation**

Employee motivation refers to the forces that drive employees
to perform their jobs effectively and contribute to
organizational goals. It encompasses factors such as:

- **Intrinsic motivation:** Motivation that comes from
  within, driven by internal rewards such as enjoyment,
  satisfaction, or a sense of accomplishment.

- **Extrinsic motivation:** Motivation that comes from
  external rewards or pressures, such as pay, bonuses,
  promotions, or recognition.

How Promotions Impact Employee Motivation: Promotions can be a powerful motivator for employees in several ways:

- **Providing recognition and reward:** Promotions are a tangible form of recognition for hard work and dedication, signaling that the employee's contributions are valued.

- **Increasing job satisfaction and engagement:** Promotions often lead to increased job satisfaction as employees take on more challenging and rewarding roles. This also increases employee engagement and commitment to the organization.

- **Creating opportunities for growth and development:** Promotions often provide employees with new opportunities to learn new skills, take on new challenges, and advance their careers.

- **Enhancing feelings of self-worth and accomplishment:** Achieving a promotion can boost an employee's self-esteem and sense of accomplishment.

Relevance to Selective Awareness and Promotions: Selective awareness, through Disciplined Perception, contributes to employee motivation by:

- **Clarifying career goals:** By focusing on their career aspirations and understanding the steps required to achieve them, employees can become more motivated to pursue those goals.

- **Increasing self-efficacy:** By focusing on their strengths and accomplishments, employees can build their self-confidence and belief in their ability to succeed, increasing motivation.

145

- **Promoting intrinsic motivation:** Employees can become more intrinsically motivated by focusing on their work's intrinsic rewards, such as personal growth and making a meaningful contribution.

In summary

Organizational performance benefits from strategically implemented promotions that match talent to roles and motivate employees. Leadership development is enhanced through promotions that provide opportunities for growth and increased responsibility. Employee motivation is boosted by the recognition, rewards, and opportunities for development that promotions provide. Through Disciplined Perception, selective awareness plays a vital role in aligning individual efforts with organizational goals, fostering effective leadership, and promoting intrinsic motivation, thereby contributing to overall success.

Weaving the Narrative Tapestry

Self-Help with Psychological Insights: In today's fast-paced business environment, innovation is the key to survival. Companies constantly race against time, searching for new ideas and the talent to bring them to life. This creates a high-stakes game where both companies and ambitious professionals are vying for the edge.

Imagine a pharmaceutical company racing to develop a life-saving drug. They need a brilliant research scientist capable of leading the project. Time is of the essence, and the stakes are incredibly high. Within their ranks, a dedicated scientist, driven by a deep passion for their work and guided by Disciplined Perception, has been tirelessly pursuing a breakthrough. Their focused research, meticulous data analysis, and unwavering commitment have not escaped the attention of senior management.

The promotion to lead scientist is not just a pat on the back; it is a strategic imperative to accelerate the drug's development. The scientist gets the opportunity to make a real difference in the world while the company secures the talent it needs to achieve its mission. It is a mutually beneficial partnership forged in the crucible of innovation

Promotion as a Result of Causation: The Power of Self-Discipline and Strategic Focus

Promotions are not randomly given out; they result from dedicated effort, strategic planning, and consistent performance. Selective awareness, guided by Disciplined Perception, becomes a key tool in navigating the path to professional advancement.

Promotion as a Result of Causation and the Psychological Edge

A promotion requires a strategic approach, similar to planning a complex operation. Disciplined Perception allows you to meticulously analyze the requirements for your desired promotion—the necessary skills, relevant experience, and company culture. With focused attention, you hone your skills, strategically network, and actively seek opportunities to demonstrate your abilities.

Every action becomes part of a well-defined plan to achieve your goal. This focused approach, driven by Disciplined Perception, also fosters a growth mindset. You begin to view challenges not as obstacles but as opportunities for learning and development. Imagine facing a complex project at work. Instead of feeling overwhelmed, you use your focused attention to break it down into manageable steps, actively seek out learning resources, and leverage your professional network for guidance.

This unwavering commitment to self-improvement—driven by Disciplined Perception—propels you forward, making you a strong contender for promotion. This process reinforces your self-efficacy, your belief in your ability to succeed, and builds resilience, your ability to bounce back from setbacks.

Key takeaway

Disciplined Perception enables strategic planning, fosters a growth mindset, and builds self-efficacy and resilience, all of which contribute significantly to achieving career advancement. This relates to several psychological concepts:

a) Growth Mindset

A growth mindset is a belief that abilities and intelligence are not fixed traits but can be developed through dedication, hard work, and learning. People with a growth mindset view challenges as opportunities for growth and see effort as the path to mastery.

Key Characteristics

- **Belief in Malleability:** The core belief is that intelligence and abilities can be improved.

- **Embrace Challenges:** Challenges are seen as opportunities to learn and grow, not as threats to self-esteem.

- **Persistence in the Face of Setbacks:** Failures and setbacks are viewed as learning experiences and opportunities for improvement, not as evidence of inherent limitations.

- **Effort as the Path to Mastery:** Effort is seen as essential for developing abilities, not as a sign of low ability.

- **Learning from Criticism:** Constructive criticism is welcomed as valuable feedback for improvement.

- **Inspiration from Others' Success:** The success of others is seen as inspiring and motivating, not as threatening or discouraging.

- **Contrasting with Fixed Mindset:** A fixed mindset is the opposite of a growth mindset. People with a fixed mindset believe that their abilities and intelligence are static and unchangeable. They tend to avoid challenges, give up easily in the face of setbacks, see effort as a sign of low ability, and feel threatened by the success of others.

Relevance to Selective Awareness and Career Advancement: A growth mindset, fostered by Disciplined Perception, is crucial for career advancement because:

- **It encourages continuous learning and development:** By viewing challenges as opportunities for growth, individuals are more likely to seek out new learning experiences and develop new skills.

- **It promotes resilience in the face of setbacks:** Individuals are more likely to persevere through challenges and bounce back from setbacks by viewing failures as learning opportunities.

- **It enhances motivation and engagement:** Individuals are more likely to be motivated and engaged in their work by focusing on effort and learning.

b) **Self-Efficacy**

Self-efficacy is an individual's belief in their capacity to execute behaviors necessary to produce specific performance attainments. It is about believing in your ability to succeed in specific situations or accomplish a particular task.

Key Aspects

- **Situation**-Specific: Self-efficacy is not a global trait; it varies depending on the specific task or situation. You might have high self-efficacy for public speaking but low self-efficacy for playing a musical instrument.

- **Sources** of Self-Efficacy: Bandura identified four main sources of self-efficacy:

- **Mastery** experiences: Past successes build self-efficacy, while past failures can undermine it.

- **Vicarious** experiences: Observing others succeed can increase self-efficacy, especially if the observer perceives themselves as similar to the model.

- **Social persuasion:** Encouragement and positive feedback from others can boost self-efficacy.

- **Emotional and physiological states:** Positive emotions and physical well-being can enhance self-efficacy, while negative emotions and physical discomfort can undermine it.

Relevance to Selective Awareness and Career Advancement: High self-efficacy, enhanced by Disciplined Perception, is crucial for career advancement because:

- **It increases motivation and effort: Individuals** with high self-efficacy are more likely to set challenging goals, persist in the face of difficulties, and invest the necessary effort to succeed.

- **It improves performance:** Believing in your ability to succeed can actually improve your performance by reducing anxiety and increasing focus.

- **It promotes resilience:** Individuals with high self-efficacy are more likely to bounce back from setbacks and view them as temporary obstacles rather than permanent defeats.

c) **Resilience**

Resilience is the ability to adapt well to adversity, trauma, tragedy, threats, or significant sources of stress. It is about bouncing back from difficult experiences and continuing to move forward.

Key Characteristics

- **Coping skills:** Effective strategies for managing stress and adversity.

- **Optimism:** A positive outlook and belief in the future.

- **Social support:** Strong relationships with family, friends, and colleagues.

- **Problem-solving skills:** The ability to identify and solve problems effectively.

- **Self-awareness:** Understanding one's own emotions and strengths and weaknesses.

Relevance to Selective Awareness and Career Advancement: Resilience, supported by Disciplined Perception, is essential for career advancement because:

- **Career paths are rarely linear:** Setbacks, rejections, and challenges are inevitable. Resilience allows individuals to

navigate these difficulties and continue pursuing their
goals.

- **It promotes learning and growth from adversity:**
  Resilient individuals view setbacks as opportunities for
  learning and growth, developing valuable skills and
  insights from challenging experiences.

- **It enhances adaptability and flexibility:** In today's
  rapidly changing work environment, resilience allows
  individuals to adapt more effectively to new situations and
  challenges.

In summary

A growth mindset fosters a belief in the malleability of abilities, self-
efficacy is the belief in one's capacity to succeed in specific
situations, and resilience is the ability to bounce back from
adversity. All three of these concepts are interconnected and
contribute to success in various areas of life, including career
advancement. Disciplined Perception supports the development
and strengthening of each of these qualities.

The Role of Chance in Timing - Maximizing the Odds

While selective awareness and thorough preparation are crucial for
career advancement, it is important to acknowledge the role of
chance in the timing of opportunities. Sometimes, factors outside
of your control can influence when a promotion becomes available.
Imagine two equally qualified candidates vying for the same
position. One might receive the promotion sooner due to an
unexpected vacancy or a shift in company priorities. However,
while you cannot control these external factors, you can influence
the probability of favorable coincidences occurring in your favor.

By consistently exceeding expectations, actively seeking out opportunities, and developing a strong professional network, you significantly increase the likelihood of being in the right place at the right time. The more doors you knock on—by networking, applying for relevant positions, and demonstrating your skills—the greater your chances of finding one that opens onto the promotion path. Selective awareness, guided by Disciplined Perception, does not eliminate chance; it empowers you to maximize your exposure to potential opportunities and to be prepared to capitalize on them when they arise.

Disciplined Perception enhances your opportunity recognition skills, allowing you to identify and seize fleeting chances that others might miss. It also fosters proactive behavior, encouraging you to actively create your opportunities rather than passively waiting for them to appear. This aligns with the concept of the "prepared mind" (Pasteur's often misquoted phrase, "Chance favors only the prepared mind")[5], which emphasizes that chance favors those who are ready to recognize and capitalize on it.

Key takeaway

Disciplined Perception maximizes the likelihood of favorable coincidences by enhancing opportunity recognition, promoting proactive behavior, and ensuring you are prepared to capitalize on opportunities when they arise. This relates to concepts like:

a) **Opportunity Recognition**

Opportunity recognition is the cognitive process by which individuals identify and evaluate potential opportunities for new ventures, innovations, or improvements. It is more than just noticing something; it involves a complex set of cognitive

---

[5] Louis Pasteur asserted that "chance favors only the prepared mind" when he said that people who are sufficiently equipped or prepared to recognize and take advantage of opportunities for discovery frequently succeed.

processes that allow someone to see the potential value in a situation or idea.

Key Components

- **Alertness:** Being attuned to environmental changes, such as new technologies, market trends, or unmet needs.

- **Prior Knowledge:** Relevant knowledge and experience in a particular domain enhance one's ability to recognize opportunities within that domain.

- **Cognitive Abilities:** Skills such as pattern recognition, critical thinking, and creative thinking are crucial for evaluating an opportunity's potential.

- **Social Networks:** Strong social connections can provide access to information and resources that facilitate opportunity recognition.

Process of Opportunity Recognition

- **Discovery:** Noticing a change or a problem in the environment.

- **Evaluation:** Assessing the potential value and feasibility of addressing the change or problem.

- **Elaboration:** Developing a detailed plan for capitalizing on the opportunity.

Relevance to Selective Awareness and Career Advancement: Selective awareness, through Disciplined Perception, enhances opportunity recognition by:

- **Sharpening alertness:** By focusing attention on relevant information and filtering out distractions, you become more attuned to potential opportunities.

- **Facilitating pattern recognition:** By enhancing your ability to identify patterns and connections, you can better recognize the potential value in seemingly unrelated events or information.

- **Promoting focused evaluation:** By focusing your cognitive resources on evaluating potential opportunities, you can make more informed decisions about which ones to pursue.

b) **Proactive Behavior**

Proactive behavior involves taking initiative and acting in anticipation of future needs, problems, or opportunities rather than simply reacting to events as they occur. It is about taking control of your circumstances and shaping your own future.

Key Characteristics

- **Anticipation:** Looking ahead and identifying potential future challenges or opportunities.

- **Initiative:** Taking action without being asked or instructed.

- **Self-Starting:** Being motivated to act independently.

- **Change-oriented:** Seeking out ways to improve existing processes or create new possibilities.

Benefits of Proactive Behavior

- **Increased career success:** Proactive individuals are often more successful in their careers because they are more likely to identify and capitalize on opportunities.

- **Improved job performance:** Proactive employees are often more productive and effective because they anticipate problems and take steps to prevent them.

- **Greater job satisfaction:** Proactive individuals tend to experience higher levels of job satisfaction because they feel more in control of their work and careers.

Relevance to Selective Awareness and Career Advancement: Selective awareness, through Disciplined Perception, fosters proactive behavior by:

- **Enhancing focus on future goals:** By focusing attention on your long-term career aspirations, you are more likely to anticipate future needs and opportunities.

- **Promoting goal-directed action:** Clarifying your goals and developing concrete plans will increase your willingness to take initiative and act proactively.

- **Increasing self-efficacy:** Focusing on your strengths and accomplishments builds confidence in your ability to take action and achieve your goals.

c) **The "Prepared Mind" Concept**

The "prepared mind" concept, often attributed (though likely misattributed or paraphrased) to Louis Pasteur, suggests that "chance favors only the prepared mind." It emphasizes that opportunities are more likely to be recognized and capitalized upon by those who have the necessary knowledge, skills, and mindset.

Key Implications

- **Preparation is crucial:** Opportunities are often fleeting and require quick action. Being prepared with the necessary skills and knowledge allows you to take advantage of these opportunities when they arise.

- **Knowledge is power:** Having a deep understanding of your field and the broader context in which you operate allows you to recognize subtle cues and connections that others might miss.

- **Mindset matters:** A proactive, curious, and open-minded mindset is essential for recognizing and embracing new opportunities.

Relevance to Selective Awareness and Career Advancement: Selective awareness, through Disciplined Perception, cultivates a "prepared mind" by:

- **Focusing on continuous learning and development:** By focusing attention on acquiring new knowledge and skills, you become better prepared to recognize and capitalize on future opportunities.

- **Promoting a proactive and opportunity-seeking mindset:** By focusing on your goals and taking initiative, you develop a more receptive mindset to new possibilities.

- **Enhancing observation and pattern recognition: By** honing your observation skills, you become more attuned to subtle cues and connections that can signal emerging opportunities.

In summary

Opportunity recognition is about identifying and evaluating potential opportunities, proactive behavior is about taking the initiative and acting in anticipation of future needs, and the "prepared mind" concept emphasizes that preparation and mindset are crucial for recognizing and capitalizing on chance encounters. Through Disciplined Perception, selective awareness plays a vital role in enhancing all three of these processes, ultimately increasing your chances of success in your career and other areas of life.

Natural Alignment and Deserved Placement: Cultivating Your Career for Growth

This section explores the idea that you can create conditions that significantly increase your chances of achieving career success through proactive preparation and strategic focus. It is not about some mystical "natural law" guaranteeing success; it is about aligning your skills, experience, and efforts with the demands and opportunities of your chosen field.

Imagine a botanist cultivating a rare orchid. They meticulously research the flower's specific needs—the right soil, sunlight, temperature, and humidity—providing the optimal environment for it to thrive. Disciplined Perception empowers you to do the same for your career. By focusing on developing the skills, knowledge, and experience that align with your professional aspirations and the demands of your chosen field, you create a fertile ground for growth and advancement. This involves understanding the key competencies required for success in your industry, building a strong professional network, and seeking out opportunities that allow you to showcase your talents. It is about aligning yourself with the dynamics of the professional world, where dedication, preparation, and strategic action increase the probability of achieving your career goals. This process is further enhanced by Disciplined Perception, which allows you to:

- **Identify relevant skills and knowledge:** By focusing your attention on industry trends and employer needs, you can identify the key skills and knowledge that will make you a more competitive candidate.

- **Develop a strong professional network**: Focusing on building meaningful connections with people in your field can give you access to valuable information, mentorship, and opportunities.

- **Adapt to changing circumstances:** By staying informed about industry changes and being adaptable in your approach, you can more effectively navigate the dynamic professional landscape.

Key takeaway: Disciplined Perception enables you to create conditions that significantly increase your chances of career success by aligning your skills, experience, and efforts with the demands and opportunities of your chosen field. This relates to concepts such as:

a) Person-Environment Fit (P-E Fit)

Person-environment fit (P-E fit) refers to the compatibility between an individual and their work environment. It is the degree to which an individual's characteristics (skills, needs, values, personality) align with the characteristics of their job, organization, workgroup, and supervisor.

Types of P-E Fit

- **Person-Job (P-J) Fit:** The match between an individual's knowledge, skills, and abilities (KSAs) and the demands of the job (demands-abilities fit) and the match between the individual's needs and the job's supplies (needs-supplies fit).

- **Person-Organization (P-O) Fit:** The congruence between an individual's values, beliefs, and personality and the values, culture, and norms of the organization.

- **Person-Group (P-G) Fit:** The compatibility between an individual and their work team or group, including shared goals, values, and working styles.

- **Person-Supervisor (P-S) Fit:** The compatibility between an individual and their supervisor, including leadership style, communication style, and values.

Consequences of P-E Fit

High P-E fit is associated with numerous positive outcomes, including:

- **Increased** job satisfaction.

- **Higher** job performance.

- **Lower** turnover intentions.

- **Greater** organizational commitment.

- **Reduced** stress and burnout.

Relevance to Selective Awareness and Career Advancement: Selective awareness, through Disciplined Perception, can help you achieve better P-E fit by:

- **Clarifying your skills, needs, and values:** By focusing on self-reflection, you can gain a clearer understanding of what you are good at, what you need from a job, and what you value in a work environment.

- **Identifying suitable work environments:** Researching different organizations and job roles can help you identify environments that are likely to be a good fit for you.

- **Adapting your skills and behavior:** Focusing on developing the skills and behaviors valued in your target environment can improve your fit with that environment.

b) **Strategic Career Planning:**

Strategic career planning is the process of setting career goals and developing a plan to achieve them. It involves a deliberate and proactive approach to managing your career rather than simply letting it happen by chance.

Key Steps in Strategic Career Planning

- **Self-Assessment:** Identifying your skills, interests, values, and personality traits.

- **Goal Setting:** Defining specific, measurable, achievable, relevant, and time-bound (SMART) career goals.

- **Opportunity Exploration:** Researching different career paths, industries, and job roles.

- **Action Planning:** Develop a concrete plan with specific steps, timelines, and resources needed to achieve your goals.

- **Implementation:** Taking action and implementing your plan.

- **Evaluation and Adjustment:** Regularly review your progress and make adjustments to your plan as needed.

Benefits of Strategic Career Planning

- **Increased** career satisfaction.

- **Greater** career success.

- **Improved** work-life balance.

- **Enhanced** employability.

Relevance to Selective Awareness and Career Advancement: Selective awareness, through Disciplined Perception, supports strategic career planning by:

- **Enhancing focus on career goals:** By focusing your attention on your career aspirations, you can stay motivated and committed to your plan.

- **Improving decision-making:** By focusing on relevant information and filtering out distractions, you can make more informed decisions about your career path.

- **Promoting proactive behavior:** By focusing on taking action and implementing your plan, you can increase your chances of achieving your goals.

c) **Skill Development and Continuous Learning**

Skill development and continuous learning refer to the ongoing process of acquiring new knowledge, skills, and abilities to enhance professional competence and adaptability. In today's rapidly changing work environment, continuous learning is essential for staying relevant and competitive.

Types of Skill Development

- **Formal Learning:** Attending courses, workshops, or training programs.

- **Informal Learning:** Learning through on-the-job experience, mentoring, networking, and self-study.

- **Skill-Based Learning:** Focuses on acquiring specific technical or practical skills.

- **Competency-Based Learning:** Focuses on developing broader competencies, such as communication, problem-solving, and leadership.

Benefits of Skill Development and Continuous Learning

- **Increased** job performance.

- **Enhanced** career opportunities.

- **Greater** job security.

- **Improved** adaptability and resilience.

- **Increased** personal and professional growth.

Relevance to Selective Awareness and Career Advancement: Selective awareness, through Disciplined Perception, supports skill development and continuous learning by:

- **Focusing attention on relevant learning resources:** By identifying the most valuable skills for your career, you can focus your learning efforts on those areas.

- **Enhancing concentration and focus during learning:** By improving your ability to concentrate and focus, you can learn more effectively and efficiently.

- **Promoting deliberate practice:** By focusing on practicing and refining your skills, you can accelerate your learning and achieve mastery more quickly.

In summary

Person-environment fit emphasizes the importance of compatibility between individuals and their work environments. Strategic career planning provides a framework for proactively managing your career, and skill development and continuous learning ensure that you remain adaptable and competitive in the job market. Selective awareness, through Disciplined Perception, plays a crucial role in enhancing all three of these processes, contributing to greater career success and fulfillment.

Self-Made Opportunities Through Discipline: Cultivating Your Own Success

The most reliable form of "luck" is the kind you create for yourself through focused effort, strategic action, and consistent dedication. Selective awareness, guided by Disciplined Perception, empowers you to focus on developing the habits and skills that significantly increase your chances of success.

Imagine a budding entrepreneur with a promising business idea. They do not simply wait for a lucky break; they actively network with potential investors, meticulously refine their business plan, conduct market research, and strategically leverage social media to build their brand and reach their target audience. This proactive approach, driven by Disciplined Perception, creates opportunities that might otherwise seem like strokes of luck. By focusing on these proactive behaviors, the entrepreneur:

- **Increases visibility:** Networking and marketing efforts increase their exposure to potential investors, customers, and partners.

- **Demonstrates competence:** A well-researched business plan and effective communication skills showcase their expertise and preparedness.

- **Creates opportunities for feedback and refinement: Engaging** with potential customers and investors provides valuable feedback that can help them improve their product or service.

Disciplined Perception plays a crucial role in this process of "self-made opportunity" by:

- **Focusing attention on goal-relevant activities:** It helps the entrepreneur prioritize networking, planning, and marketing efforts over less productive activities.

- **Promoting consistent action:** It provides the mental discipline to stay focused and persevere through challenges.

- **Enhancing opportunity recognition**: It sharpens the ability to identify and capitalize on emerging opportunities.

This is not to say that chance plays no role; external factors and unforeseen events can always influence outcomes. However, by focusing on what you can control—your preparation, actions, and mindset—you significantly increase the probability of achieving your goals.

Key takeaway: Disciplined Perception facilitates "self-made opportunities" by focusing attention on goal-relevant activities, promoting consistent action, and enhancing opportunity recognition, thereby maximizing the probability of success. This relates to concepts such as:

a) **Proactive Personality**

A proactive personality is a disposition toward taking initiative, anticipating future problems and opportunities, and acting to influence one's environment. Individuals with a proactive personality are not passive recipients of their circumstances; they actively seek out opportunities for change and improvement.

Key Characteristics

- **Taking Initiative:** Proactive individuals do not wait for things to happen; they make things happen. They identify opportunities and act on them without being asked.

- **Anticipating Future Needs:** They think ahead and anticipate potential problems or opportunities, taking steps to address them proactively.

- **Perseverance:** They are persistent in pursuing their goals, even in the face of obstacles or setbacks.

- **Change-oriented:** They are comfortable with change and actively seek out ways to improve existing processes or create new possibilities.

- **Internal Locus of Control:** They believe that they have control over their own outcomes and are not simply at the mercy of external forces.

Benefits of a Proactive Personality

- **Greater career success:** Proactive individuals are more likely to be promoted, earn higher salaries, and achieve their career goals.

- **Improved job performance:** They are often more productive, effective, and innovative in their work.

- **Higher levels of job satisfaction and well-being:** They tend to experience greater job satisfaction and overall well-being because they feel more in control of their work and their lives.

- **Enhanced leadership effectiveness:** Proactive individuals often make effective leaders because they are able to anticipate future needs, inspire others to take action, and drive positive change.

Relevance to Selective Awareness and Career Advancement: Selective awareness, through Disciplined Perception, can help individuals develop and express a proactive personality by:

- **Focusing attention on opportunities:** By being more aware of their surroundings and filtering out distractions, individuals can better identify opportunities for improvement and innovation.

- **Promoting goal-setting and planning:** Individuals are more likely to take initiative and act proactively by focusing on their goals and developing concrete plans.

- **Building self-efficacy:** By focusing on their strengths and accomplishments, individuals can increase their confidence in their ability to take action and achieve their goals.

b) **Self-Fulfilling Prophecy**

A self-fulfilling prophecy is a prediction that directly or indirectly causes itself to become true, by the very terms of the prophecy itself, due to positive feedback between belief and behavior. It is a phenomenon where a belief or expectation, whether true or false, influences behavior in such a way that the belief becomes realized.

Key Aspects

- **Initial Expectation:** The process begins with an initial belief or expectation about a person or situation.

- **Behavioral Change:** This expectation influences how the person holding the belief behaves toward the belief's target.

- **Target's Response:** The target of the belief, consciously or unconsciously, responds to the changed behavior in a way that confirms the initial expectation.

- **Confirmation of Belief:** The initial belief is then reinforced, creating a cycle of self-fulfilling prophecy.

Types of Self-Fulfilling Prophecies

- **Interpersonal Self-Fulfilling Prophecies:** These occur in interactions between people, such as the classic example of teachers' expectations influencing student performance.

- **Intrapersonal Self-Fulfilling Prophecies:** These occur within an individual, where their own beliefs about themselves influence their behavior and outcomes.

Examples

- **A teacher** who believes that certain students are more intelligent may give them more attention and encouragement, leading those students to perform better.

- **A person** who believes they are socially awkward may avoid social situations, reinforcing their perceived awkwardness.

- **A person** who believes they will succeed in a new job may be more motivated and persistent, increasing their chances of success.

Relevance to Selective Awareness and Career Advancement: Selective awareness, through Disciplined Perception, can be used to leverage the power of self-fulfilling prophecies positively by:

168

- **Focusing on positive expectations:** By focusing on positive beliefs about your abilities and potential for success, you can influence your behavior to make those beliefs more likely to come true.

- **Setting achievable goals:** By setting realistic and achievable goals, you can create a series of successes that reinforce your self-belief and motivate you to continue pursuing your aspirations.

- **Surrounding yourself with positive influences:** By associating with people who believe in you and support your goals, you can create a positive social environment that reinforces your positive expectations.

In summary

A proactive personality is about taking initiative and shaping your environment, while a self-fulfilling prophecy is about how beliefs and expectations can influence behavior and outcomes. Through Disciplined Perception, selective awareness can be used to cultivate a proactive personality and leverage the power of self-fulfilling prophecies to achieve greater success in career advancement and other areas of life.

In Conclusion: The Architect of Your Career Destiny

Selective awareness, or Disciplined Perception, is not simply about filtering distractions; it is about harnessing the power of causality to shape your career trajectory. You become the architect of your professional journey by focusing on the habits, skills, and strategic actions that drive success. You position yourself for well-deserved promotions, cultivate opportunities, and achieve your professional aspirations. Remember, true "luck" results from focused effort, unwavering determination, and an understanding of the key principles governing career advancement— such as cultivating a growth mindset, building self-efficacy, and adopting proactive behaviors. So, embrace your role as the architect of your career, sharpen your focus, and embark on this purposeful journey toward professional fulfillment.

SECTION III

HARNESSING SELECTIVE AWARENESS FOR ATTRACTION

ξφξφξφ

This section is dedicated to transforming selective awareness from a theoretical concept into a tangible tool for personal growth and achievement. It offers a practical framework for conditioning your mind to attract your deepest desires, exploring essential elements such as crafting a compelling purpose, harnessing the power of collaboration and focused intention, cultivating unwavering faith and dedication, mastering self-discipline, and developing organized thought. Through these principles, you will discover how to unlock your creative potential, learn from defeat, ignite your inner spark, and cultivate a powerful personal magnetism that draws opportunities and positive outcomes into your life.

The Blueprint: Designing Your Definite Purpose

The journey to achieving your desires begins with a clear destination: your definite purpose. This is the cornerstone of harnessing selective awareness and attracting desired outcomes. Imagine a budding entrepreneur with a burning desire to launch a sustainable fashion brand. Their first step involves meticulously crafting a vision statement that outlines their goals, target audience, and the positive impact they aim to create. This is not just wishful thinking; it is a blueprint that lays the foundation for attracting the resources, opportunities, and collaborators needed to turn their vision into reality. This vision then informs their focused actions, guided by Disciplined Perception.

From Vision to Action: The Power of Focused Concentration Through Disciplined Perception

With a definite purpose clearly defined, it is time to translate that vision into concrete action through Disciplined Perception. Here is how the entrepreneur puts this principle into action:

Planning and Action & Focused Thoughts and Deeds: The entrepreneur does not just dream; they meticulously plan. Driven by their vision and guided by Disciplined Perception, they research market trends, develop a detailed business plan, identify the specific steps required to launch their brand, and set realistic timelines. This deliberate planning process translates their vision into actionable steps, providing a clear roadmap for their efforts. Furthermore, Disciplined Perception helps them maintain an unwavering focus on these actions. They prioritize tasks directly related to their brand, actively seeking out resources, networking with potential collaborators, and consistently evaluating their progress. Their thoughts and actions become laser-focused, constantly moving them closer to their goal. Disciplined Perception enables this focused concentration by:

- **Filtering distractions:** It allows the entrepreneur to block out irrelevant information and focus on the most important tasks for achieving their goals.

- **Enhancing attention control:** It strengthens their ability to direct and sustain their attention on their chosen tasks.

- **Promoting goal-directed behavior:** It keeps their actions aligned with their overall vision and purpose.

Key takeaway: Disciplined Perception transforms a vision into reality by facilitating meticulous planning, promoting consistent action, and maintaining an unwavering focus on goal-relevant tasks. This relates to several psychological concepts:

- **Goal-setting theory:** This theory emphasizes the importance of setting specific, measurable, achievable, relevant, and time-bound (SMART) goals to improve performance (Locke & Latham, 2002).

- **Visualization:** Creating mental images of desired outcomes can increase motivation and improve performance.

- **Focused attention:** Directing cognitive resources to specific tasks or stimuli enhances processing and performance.

The Designing and Implementation Process

Imagine your mind as a powerful tool capable of achieving remarkable things. Your desires represent the goals you wish to attain, but your attention, often scattered by distractions, needs to be focused and directed. The Designing and Implementation Process outlined here provides a practical framework for optimizing your focus, minimizing mental clutter, and transforming your aspirations into tangible realities guided by Disciplined Perception.

a) **Crystallize Your Vision:** Imagine standing atop a mountain, gazing at a clear view of the landscape below. This view represents your definite purpose—the ultimate destination you wish to reach. This initial step involves clarifying your deepest desires, free from self-doubt and external pressures. What truly motivates you? What accomplishment would bring you a profound sense of fulfillment? Use techniques like introspection, journaling, and visualization, guided by Disciplined Perception, to bring this vision into sharp focus. Disciplined Perception helps you to filter out external influences and connect with your authentic self, allowing your true desires to emerge.

Key Takeaway: Disciplined Perception facilitates the clarification of your deepest desires by promoting introspection, filtering external noise, and connecting you with your authentic self.

b) **Craft Your Roadmap:** Now that you have a clear vision, it is time to create a concrete plan—your personal roadmap to success. Research in neuroscience suggests that breaking down large goals into smaller, manageable milestones creates a sense of progress and accomplishment, triggering the release of dopamine, a neurotransmitter associated with reward and motivation. This, in turn, strengthens the neural pathways associated with your desired outcome, making it easier to maintain focus and motivation. Disciplined Perception supports this process by helping you prioritize tasks, create realistic timelines, and stay focused on executing your plan.

Key Takeaway: Disciplined Perception helps you create a roadmap for success by facilitating the breakdown of large goals into manageable steps, promoting consistent action, and maintaining motivation. This relates to the concept of goal-setting theory (Locke & Latham, 2002).

c) **Focus Your Energy (Thriller & Self-Help):** With a clear vision and a concrete plan in place, the next step is to direct your energy and attention toward your goal. This involves minimizing distractions, silencing self-criticism, and cultivating focused concentration. Disciplined Perception is instrumental in this process, helping you to filter out irrelevant information, manage internal distractions, and maintain an unwavering focus on your objectives. It is about directing your mental resources strategically to maximize your progress.

Key Takeaway: Disciplined Perception enables you to focus your energy by minimizing distractions, managing self-criticism, and maintaining unwavering focus on your objectives. This relates to the concept of attention control in cognitive psychology.

d) **Bridge Thought and Action (Scientific & Self-Help):** Even the best plans are useless without action. This crucial stage is about translating your thoughts and plans into tangible reality. Every action you take, no matter how small, reinforces the neural pathways associated with your goals and builds momentum. Consistency is key. Do not wait for the "perfect" moment to begin; take action now. Disciplined Perception helps you maintain this consistency by promoting self-discipline, prioritizing tasks, and tracking your progress.

   Key Takeaway: *Disciplined Perception facilitates the translation of thoughts into action by promoting self-discipline, prioritizing tasks, and maintaining consistent effort. This relates to concepts of implementation intentions and behavioral activation.*

This blueprint provides a personalized guide for designing and achieving your definite purpose. By employing Disciplined Perception throughout this process, you can effectively clarify your vision, create a concrete plan, maintain unwavering focus, and consistently translate your thoughts into action. Remember, the power to shape your reality lies within you. With focused intention and consistent action, guided by Disciplined Perception, you can transform your desires into a life of fulfillment and extraordinary achievement.

Inner and External Harmony Through Subconscious Influence

By focusing on their vision, the entrepreneur, guided by Disciplined Perception, cultivates a positive mental attitude. They visualize success, proactively address potential challenges, and develop unwavering belief in their ability to achieve their goals. This inner harmony, fostered by focused attention, influences the subconscious mind, which then subtly guides their decisions and actions. This inner state then attracts corresponding external experiences.

As entrepreneur takes consistent, focused action, they begin to attract people, resources, and opportunities that align with their goals. They might connect with a valuable mentor or discover a perfect location for their business. These seemingly serendipitous occurrences are not random; they result from their focused attention, guided by Disciplined Perception, which primes their subconscious mind to recognize and seize opportunities that resonate with their vision.

This process is supported by the reticular activating system (RAS), a network of neurons in the brainstem that filters incoming information and prioritizes what we pay attention to. By focusing on your goals, you essentially "program" your RAS to filter in information and opportunities that are relevant to those goals.

Key Takeaway: Disciplined Perception facilitates both inner and external harmony by influencing the subconscious mind, priming the RAS to recognize opportunities, and fostering a positive mental attitude that attracts corresponding external experiences. This relates to concepts such as:

- **The Reticular Activating System (RAS):** A network of neurons in the brainstem that filters sensory information and regulates arousal and attention.

- **Positive Emotions:** These broaden our thought-action repertoires, making us more open to new experiences and opportunities.[102]

- **Subconscious Processing:** Mental processes that occur outside of conscious awareness but can still influence behavior.

In Conclusion

Selective awareness, through Disciplined Perception, is a powerful tool for aligning yourself with the principles of attraction. By designing a definite purpose, focusing your thoughts and actions, and cultivating inner harmony, you create a state of mind that is receptive to opportunities and positive outcomes. It is about training your mind to recognize and seize those opportunities that align with your deepest desires. So, cultivate your focus through Disciplined Perception and embark on a journey of intentional creation.

Sculpting Your Reality: Autosuggestion, Focused Intention and The Law of Attraction

Enhanced by Disciplined Perception, selective awareness empowers you to actively shape your reality through potent forces like autosuggestion and the law of attraction.

Autosuggestion: The Character Architect

Consider a sculptor meticulously molding a block of stone. Autosuggestion works similarly, allowing you to consciously shape your thoughts, habits, and character by repeatedly implanting specific ideas into your subconscious mind. This is not merely wishful thinking; it is a psychological technique leveraging repetition and focused attention, guided by Disciplined Perception, to influence beliefs and behaviors. Disciplined Perception provides the focused attention necessary to utilize autosuggestion effectively.

Reprogramming Your Mind

Through repeated affirmations and self-directed thoughts channeled by Disciplined Perception, you can replace limiting beliefs with empowering ones. For example, someone wanting more confidence might repeatedly affirm, "I am capable," "I am worthy," or "I am confident." Disciplined Perception helps maintain focus on these affirmations, consciously directing mental energy toward these positive statements. This consistent mental rehearsal strengthens associated neural pathways, gradually making these beliefs more automatic and ingrained. Over time, these recurring thoughts solidify into beliefs, influencing actions. The individual begins accepting new challenges, achieving small victories, and developing genuine confidence based on real-world experience.

Key Takeaway: Disciplined Perception facilitates the reprogramming of limiting beliefs through focused and consistent use of positive affirmations, leading to tangible behavioral changes. This connects to cognitive restructuring in cognitive behavior therapy CBT to challenge and modify negative thought patterns.[103]

Building New Habits

Disciplined Perception allows you to use autosuggestion to cultivate positive habits. For example, someone wanting to become a morning person might consistently focus on the benefits of early rising (e.g., increased productivity, personal time) and vividly visualize waking up energized. Disciplined Perception helps maintain this focus and resist hitting the snooze button. Combining this mental rehearsal with consistent action (actually getting out of bed) reinforces the desired behavior, forming new, constructive habits.

Key Takeaway: Disciplined Perception supports habit formation by combining autosuggestion (mental rehearsal) with consistent action, reinforcing desired behaviors. Research on habit formation emphasizes the importance of repetition, cues, and rewards.[104]

The Power of Self-Image

Autosuggestion, amplified by Disciplined Perception, provides a powerful way to reshape your self-image. A sportsperson might repeatedly visualize flawless performance, focusing on movement details, the feeling of success, and positive crowd reactions. Disciplined Perception keeps their attention focused on this positive image, actively inhibiting self-doubt and anxiety. This mental rehearsal, combined with physical training, builds confidence and significantly enhances performance.

Key Takeaway: *Disciplined Perception maximizes the impact of autosuggestion on self-image and performance by combining focused mental rehearsal with real-world practice, boosting self-efficacy.*[105]

In Conclusion

Autosuggestion, when combined with the focused attention provided by Disciplined Perception, becomes a powerful tool for sculpting your reality. By consciously choosing your thoughts, cultivating positive habits, and reshaping your self-image, you can significantly influence your beliefs, behaviors, and ultimately, your outcomes.

Focused Intention: The Reality Shaper

Focused intention is the practice of directing your mental energy and attention toward specific, well-defined goals with unwavering focus and a clear plan of action. It's not merely wishing; it's consciously choosing a desired outcome and aligning your thoughts, actions, and energy to make it a reality. This process is significantly amplified by selective awareness and channeled through Disciplined Perception, which provides the focus and mental discipline necessary for effective intention setting and execution.

Manifesting Goals

- Focused intention provides a powerful framework for manifesting goals. An entrepreneur aiming to launch a successful startup, for example, would begin by clearly defining their vision (e.g., "To create a sustainable and profitable business that provides innovative solutions for X"). They would then set SMART goals and consistently direct their mental energy and actions toward these goals. Disciplined

Perception helps them filter distractions, maintain focus on their objectives, and make strategic decisions aligned with their vision. This involves both mental commitment (visualization, affirmations), enhanced by Disciplined Perception, and physical commitment (market research, product development, networking).[106]

Key Takeaway: Disciplined Perception facilitates goal manifestation by promoting clear vision setting, focused action, and consistent commitment, significantly increasing the probability of achieving desired outcomes. This aligns with goal-setting theory (Locke & Latham, 2002).

Enhancing Creativity

Focused intention, guided by Disciplined Perception, can significantly boost creativity by channeling thoughts and attention toward innovative ideas. A writer struggling with writer's block, for example, might set the intention to generate a specific type of story (e.g., "To write a compelling science fiction story about artificial intelligence exploring human consciousness") and focus their mind on the creative process (e.g., brainstorming, freewriting, mind mapping). Disciplined Perception helps filter distractions and maintain focus, allowing for deeper immersion in the creative process.[107]

Key Takeaway: Disciplined Perception unlocks creative potential by facilitating clear intention setting and maintaining focused attention during the creative process, helping overcome creative blocks. This relates to research on flow state and intrinsic motivation.[108]

Improving Relationships

Focused intention can also significantly improve relationships by directing attention and energy toward positive interactions and constructive behaviors. Someone wanting to strengthen a relationship, for example, might set intentions to be more empathetic (e.g., "I intend to listen to my partner's perspective truly"), communicative (e.g., "I intend to express my feelings openly and honestly"), and supportive (e.g., "I intend to offer practical support and encouragement"). Disciplined Perception helps maintain mindfulness of these intentions in daily interactions, prompting active listening, expressing appreciation, and resolving conflicts constructively.

Key Takeaway: *Disciplined Perception enhances relationship quality by promoting clear intentions for positive interactions and maintaining focused attention on these intentions in daily behavior. This connects to research on active listening, empathy, and relationship communication skills.*

In Conclusion

Focused intention, when combined with the focused attention and mental discipline provided by Disciplined Perception, becomes a powerful tool for shaping one's reality across various domains of life. By setting clear goals, channeling one's creative energy, and fostering positive relationships, one can transform one's intentions into tangible outcomes.

Combining Autosuggestion and Focused Intention

The true power of autosuggestion and focused intention is realized when they are combined. This synergy creates a powerful force for personal growth and overcoming obstacles, all amplified and directed by Disciplined Perception.

Achieving Personal Growth Through Synergistic Action

Combining autosuggestion and focused intention creates a powerful synergy for personal growth by aligning thoughts, emotions, and actions. By consistently affirming your goals through autosuggestion (e.g., "I am becoming a skilled public speaker," "I am developing strong leadership qualities") and simultaneously focusing your intention on specific supporting actions (e.g., practicing speeches regularly, seeking leadership opportunities), you create a powerful internal drive. Disciplined Perception enhances this synergy by maintaining focus on both the affirmations and the corresponding actions, preventing distractions, and reinforcing the desired mindset. This holistic approach ensures you are not merely envisioning success but also taking concrete, consistent steps to achieve it. Disciplined Perception acts as the bridge, connecting the mental work of autosuggestion with the physical work of focused action.

Key takeaway: *Disciplined Perception facilitates accelerated personal growth by creating a synergistic feedback loop between autosuggestion and focused intention, aligning thoughts, emotions, and actions. This relates to the concept of self-regulation, which involves managing one's thoughts, emotions, and behaviors to achieve goals.*[109]

Overcoming Obstacles with Focused Resilience

Life inevitably presents obstacles, but Disciplined Perception, by effectively channeling autosuggestion and focused intention, equips you with mental resilience and strategic focus to overcome them. When facing a challenge (e.g., a project setback, a difficult personal situation), use autosuggestion to maintain a positive mindset (e.g., "I am capable of overcoming this," "I will learn and grow from this") and simultaneously focus your intention on finding solutions and taking constructive action (e.g., brainstorming alternatives, seeking support). Disciplined Perception ensures that your attention remains focused on solutions, preventing dwelling on the problem. This combination of mental fortitude and strategic action, facilitated by Disciplined Perception, allows you to navigate challenges with greater resilience, transforming setbacks into opportunities for growth. Disciplined Perception helps you reframe the challenge (cognitive reappraisal) and maintain focus on the desired outcome.

Key takeaway: Disciplined Perception enables you to overcome obstacles by combining autosuggestion (maintaining a positive mindset) with focused intention (finding solutions), fostering resilience and transforming setbacks into growth opportunities. This connects to cognitive reappraisal.[110]

In Conclusion

By integrating autosuggestion and focused intention and directing this powerful combination with Disciplined Perception, you can effectively shape your reality and achieve your desired outcomes. This synergistic approach empowers you to build new habits, achieve personal goals, enhance relationships, and overcome obstacles with greater resilience and purpose.

The Law of Attraction: Thoughts as Reality Architects

This section explores the Law of Attraction—the principle that focused thoughts, combined with aligned actions, can increase the probability of attracting corresponding circumstances and achieving desired outcomes. It is crucial to understand that this is not about "magical thinking"; it is about using focused intention and aligned action, guided by Disciplined Perception, to maximize your potential. Disciplined Perception plays a crucial role in amplifying the effectiveness of this process by enhancing focus, clarity, and consistent action.

Alignment Breeds Opportunity & Attention as a Magnet

Imagine an entrepreneur with a clear vision (e.g., "To create a mobile app connecting local farmers with consumers"). By consistently focusing on their goals (e.g., "Secure seed funding in six months," "Launch a beta version in one year") and vividly visualizing success, they become more attuned to aligning opportunities. Disciplined Perception helps them filter distractions and focus on networking events, investor pitches, and potential partnerships. This focused awareness increases their chances of attracting necessary resources and connections. This process also acts as a "magnet" for opportunities. By focusing attention on specific actions—researching market trends, networking, and creating a business plan—they increase the likelihood of encountering relevant opportunities, such as meeting a potential investor or discovering a perfect location.

Key Takeaway: Disciplined Perception facilitates opportunity recognition and attraction by aligning thoughts with goals, promoting focused action, and enhancing awareness of relevant opportunities. This relates to confirmation bias and attentional bias.

The Alchemy of Action & The Creative Power of Intention

The Law of Attraction requires consistent, goal-directed action. The entrepreneur with a focused vision must also put in the work—making calls, building a team, developing a marketing strategy, and overcoming obstacles. Disciplined Perception helps them maintain focus amidst challenges, preventing discouragement from setbacks. This combination of focused intention and decisive action is essential for transforming thoughts into tangible results. Disciplined Perception also enhances the creative power of intention. For example, An artist who desires to paint a masterpiece uses focused intention, guided by Disciplined Perception, to direct their attention toward inspiration, artistic techniques, experimentation, and feedback.

Key Takeaway: Disciplined Perception amplifies the impact of intention by promoting consistent, goal-directed action and focusing creative energy, transforming intentions into tangible results. This relates to self-efficacy.

In Conclusion

By integrating these principles and practices, you harness the power of focused intention and aligned action, guided by Disciplined Perception, to increase the likelihood of achieving your desired outcomes. This alignment of inner thoughts with outer actions paves the way for realizing your full potential. Whether overcoming challenges, fostering creativity, or building meaningful relationships, Disciplined Perception empowers you to create a life that reflects your deepest aspirations.

Reinforcing Holistic Alignment: Integrating Mind, Body, and Intention

Cultivating a Positive Mindset Through Disciplined Perception:

The foundation of holistic alignment lies in cultivating a positive mindset. This involves actively managing your thoughts and beliefs, focusing on what you want to attract rather than what you want to avoid. Disciplined Perception is crucial for cultivating this positive mindset. It provides the following:

- **Enhanced Self-Awareness:** Disciplined Perception allows you to become more aware of your thought patterns, enabling you to identify and challenge negative or limiting beliefs that may be hindering your progress. It helps you observe your thoughts without judgment, allowing you to choose which thoughts to focus on and which to let go of.

- **Focused Attention on Positive Input:** Disciplined Perception helps you consciously direct your attention to positive affirmations, optimistic expectations, and empowering self-talk. This focused attention strengthens positive neural pathways and creates a mental environment conducive to attracting positive experiences.

- **Filtering Negative Influences:** Disciplined Perception helps you filter out negative influences, such as negative self-talk, pessimistic thoughts, and discouraging external feedback. This allows you to maintain a positive focus and avoid being derailed by negativity.

Key Takeaway: *Disciplined Perception is essential for cultivating a positive mindset. It enhances self-awareness, focuses attention on positive input, and filters negative influences, thereby creating a mental environment conducive to attracting positive experiences.*[111]

Embodying Your Intentions Through Disciplined Action

While a positive mindset is crucial, it is equally important to embody your intentions through consistent, goal-directed action. This is where the "body" aspect of holistic alignment comes into play. Your actions serve as tangible manifestations of your inner thoughts and beliefs. Disciplined Perception plays a key role in translating intentions into action by:

- **Prioritizing Goal-Aligned Behaviors:** Disciplined Perception helps you prioritize actions that directly support your intentions and filter out distractions that might lead you astray.

- **Maintaining Consistent Effort:** Disciplined Perception provides the mental discipline to maintain consistent effort, even when faced with challenges or setbacks. It helps you stay focused on your long-term goals and avoid procrastination.

- **Enhancing Body Awareness and Physical Well-being:** By focusing on the connection between mind and body, Disciplined Perception can also enhance body awareness and promote physical well-being, further supporting your intentions. For example, if your intention is to improve your physical health, Disciplined Perception can help you stay focused on exercising regularly, eating nutritious foods, and getting adequate sleep. This connection between mind and body aligns with the concept of embodied cognition.

Key Takeaway: Disciplined Perception facilitates the embodiment of intentions by prioritizing goal-aligned behaviors, maintaining consistent effort, and enhancing body awareness. It ensures that actions directly reflect inner thoughts and beliefs, aligning with embodied cognition.[112]

Anchoring in the Present Moment with Disciplined Mindfulness

Mindfulness and presence serve as anchors in the present moment, allowing you to make conscious choices that align with your intentions. Disciplined Perception significantly enhances your ability to practice mindfulness by:

- **Sharpening Present Moment Awareness:** Disciplined Perception directs your attention to the here and now, reducing distractions and increasing awareness of your thoughts, feelings, and bodily sensations.

- **Enhancing Attention Regulation:** Disciplined Perception helps you stay focused on the present moment and avoid being carried away by thoughts of the past or future by improving your ability to regulate your attention.

- **Promoting Non-Judgmental Observation:** Disciplined Perception encourages a non-judgmental observation of your thoughts and feelings, allowing you to become more aware of your internal state without getting caught up in negative self-talk or emotional reactivity. This heightened awareness allows you to more readily identify any discrepancies between your intentions and your current state, enabling you to make necessary adjustments.

Key Takeaway: Disciplined Perception deepens mindfulness practice by sharpening present-moment awareness, enhancing attention regulation, and promoting nonjudgmental observation, allowing for more conscious alignment with intentions. This relates to mindfulness-based interventions.[113]

Cultivating Gratitude Through Disciplined Appreciation

Cultivating gratitude is a powerful practice for shifting your focus from lack to abundance, creating a more receptive mindset for attracting desired outcomes. Disciplined Perception enhances gratitude by:

- **Directing Attention to Positive Aspects:** Disciplined Perception helps you intentionally direct your attention to the positive aspects of your life, both big and small. It encourages you to seek out actively and appreciate the good things around you.

- **Sustaining Focus on Gratitude:** Disciplined Perception provides the mental discipline to maintain a consistent practice of gratitude, such as through journaling, reflection, or expressing appreciation to others.

- **Deepening Emotional Connection to Gratitude:** Disciplined Perception helps you move beyond simply intellectually acknowledging good things to truly feeling and experiencing gratitude on an emotional level. Regularly acknowledging and appreciating the good things in your life creates a positive emotional state that reinforces your intentions and attracts more positivity.

Key Takeaway: Disciplined Perception enhances gratitude by directing and sustaining attention on positive aspects of life, deepening the emotional connection to gratitude and fostering a receptive mindset. This aligns with research on the benefits of gratitude.[114]

Setting SMART Goals with Disciplined Focus

Setting SMART (Specific, Measurable, Achievable, Relevant, and Time-bound) goals provides a clear roadmap for translating your intentions into tangible actions. Disciplined Perception enhances the goal-setting process by:

- **Sharpening Goal Clarity:** Disciplined Perception helps you define and refine your goals, ensuring they are specific, measurable, and clearly defined.

- **Maintaining Focus on Goal Relevance:** Disciplined Perception helps you ensure that your goals are aligned with your deepest values and aspirations, preventing you from pursuing goals that are not truly meaningful to you.

- **Facilitating Strategic Planning and Execution:** Disciplined perception facilitates the process of breaking down larger goals into smaller, manageable steps, creating a clear pathway for progress and increasing motivation. It also helps you maintain focus on these steps and execute your plan consistently.

    Key Takeaway: Disciplined Perception enhances the effectiveness of SMART goal setting by sharpening goal clarity, maintaining focus on relevance, and facilitating strategic planning and execution. This connects to goal-setting theory.[115]

Remember! Disciplined Perception facilitates holistic alignment by fostering a positive mindset, translating intentions into action, promoting mindfulness, cultivating gratitude, and guiding the setting of SMART goals. This creates a powerful synergy for achieving desired outcomes. This relates to positive psychology, embodied cognition, mindfulness-based interventions, and goal-setting theory.

In Conclusion

The true power of shaping your reality lies in the synergy between autosuggestion, focused intention, and the guiding force of Disciplined Perception. Autosuggestion shapes your mindset and beliefs, while focused intention directs your energy and actions toward specific goals. Disciplined Perception acts as the conductor, harmonizing these forces and ensuring alignment between your inner world and your outward actions.

Through Disciplined Perception, you become the architect of your reality. By consciously shaping your thoughts and replacing limiting beliefs with empowering ones, you build a solid foundation for your character and actions. When combined with focused intention, this process creates a powerful drive toward achieving your desired outcomes.

Remember, actualizing your vision requires combining positive thoughts with consistent, decisive action, all guided by Disciplined Perception. By maintaining focused intention and embracing Disciplined Perception, you transform your aspirations into tangible realities, one purposeful step at a time. Through this powerful synergy, you envision your future and actively create it, achieving a life that reflects your deepest values and potential through the focused clarity provided by Disciplined Perception.

The Intellectual Synergy Group: Supercharging Selective Awareness with Synergy

Having established a definite purpose, the next step involves forming an intellectual synergy group or mastermind alliance. This strategic partnership goes beyond simple collaboration; it is about harnessing the collective power of focused minds, amplified by Disciplined Perception, to propel you toward your goals.

The Power of Synergy: Amplifying Controlled Attention

A mastermind alliance, or intellectual synergy group, is more than just a collection of individuals working together. It is a dynamic and interactive entity where the combined intellectual power, skills, and experience of the members create a synergistic effect—a whole that is greater than the sum of its parts. The analogy of a symphonic orchestra is apt. Each musician (group member) brings their unique instrument (skillset) and plays their part, contributing to a harmonious and powerful performance that would be impossible for any single musician to achieve alone.

Imagine an entrepreneur aiming to launch a sustainable fashion brand. They might form a mastermind group consisting of:

- **A Marketing Expert:** Provides expertise in market analysis, branding, advertising, and reaching the target audience.

- **A Seasoned Fashion Designer:** Offers insights into design trends, material sourcing, production processes, and the overall aesthetic of the brand.

- **An Entrepreneur with Experience in Socially Conscious Business:** Shares valuable experience in building a sustainable business model, navigating ethical sourcing, and marketing to environmentally conscious consumers.

This combination of diverse expertise creates a powerful synergy that amplifies focused attention in several key ways:

a) **Collective Focus:** The group creates a shared focus on the entrepreneur's vision and goals. By regularly sharing ideas, challenges, and strategies, the members reinforce the core purpose and help the entrepreneur stay on track. This collective focus helps to:

- **Clarify the Vision:** Different perspectives can help refine and clarify the original vision, making it more robust and achievable.

- **Prioritize Actions:** The group can help prioritize tasks and allocate resources effectively, ensuring that efforts are focused on the most impactful activities.

- **Maintain Momentum:** The shared focus helps maintain momentum and prevents the entrepreneur from getting bogged down in details or distracted by less important tasks.

b) **Enhanced Motivation:** The mastermind group provides a powerful source of motivation and support. Witnessing other members' dedication, commitment, and progress can inspire and motivate the entrepreneur to persevere, especially during challenging times. This enhanced motivation stems from:

- **Shared Enthusiasm:** The shared passion and enthusiasm for the project can create a positive and energizing environment.

- **Mutual Encouragement:** Members can offer encouragement, support, and constructive feedback, helping each other overcome obstacles and stay motivated.

- **Sense of Accountability:** Knowing they are accountable to the group can motivate members to stay committed to their goals and follow through on their commitments.

c) **Boosted Creativity and Problem-Solving: Brainstorming** sessions and group discussions within the mastermind group can spark creativity and unlock innovative solutions to problems. The diverse perspectives and expertise of the members can lead to breakthroughs that would be difficult to achieve individually. This boosted creativity and problem-solving is facilitated by:

- **Cross-Pollination of Ideas:** Members from different backgrounds can bring unique perspectives and ideas to the table, leading to creative solutions.

- **Constructive Feedback:** The group can provide constructive feedback on ideas and proposals, helping to refine them and identify potential weaknesses.

- **Collective Brainstorming:** Group brainstorming sessions can generate a larger number of ideas and solutions than individual brainstorming.

In essence, the synergy within a mastermind group amplifies focused attention by:

- **Sharpening** the focus on the core purpose.

- **Providing** a constant source of motivation and support.

- **Boosting** creativity and problem-solving capabilities.

This synergistic effect creates a powerful engine for achieving goals and maximizing the potential of each individual member.

Maintaining Momentum: The Power of Shared Accountability

Working in isolation can often lead to procrastination, lack of motivation, and difficulty maintaining focus on long-term goals. An intellectual synergy group provides a powerful antidote to these challenges through the crucial element of shared accountability.

Imagine the entrepreneur we discussed earlier working toward launching a sustainable fashion brand. By joining a mastermind group, they gain access to a network of individuals who are invested in their success. This shared investment creates a sense of obligation and responsibility that helps maintain momentum.

Here is how shared accountability works within a mastermind group to maintain momentum:

- **Regular Progress Reporting:** Members regularly share their progress updates with the group, outlining their accomplishments, current activities, and upcoming plans. This public declaration of intentions creates a powerful incentive to follow through. Knowing they will have to report their progress to the group motivates members to stay on track and avoid procrastination.

- **Setting Clear Commitments:** Members often set specific commitments for the following week or period during group meetings. These commitments are not just personal goals but public promises made to the group. This public commitment increases members' likelihood of following through on their plans.

- **Constructive Feedback and Support:** The group provides a supportive environment for giving and receiving constructive feedback. When a member faces a setback or struggles to make progress, the group offers support, encouragement, and helpful suggestions. This helps to overcome obstacles and maintain motivation.

- **Shared Celebration of Successes:** The group also celebrates each member's big and small successes. This shared celebration reinforces positive behaviors and creates a sense of camaraderie and shared accomplishment. This positive reinforcement further motivates members to continue working towards their goals.

- **Peer Pressure (Positive):** While "peer pressure" often has negative connotations, within a supportive mastermind group, it can be a powerful force for good. The desire to contribute to the group's success and avoid letting down fellow members can motivate individuals to push themselves further and maintain their momentum.

- **Shared Purpose and Vision:** The group's shared purpose and vision create a sense of collective responsibility. Members are not just working towards their own individual goals; they are also working towards a shared goal that binds them together. This shared purpose strengthens their commitment and helps maintain momentum.

Benefits of Shared Accountability for Maintaining Momentum

- **Reduced Procrastination:** Knowing that they will have to report their progress to the group reduces the tendency to procrastinate.

- **Increased Motivation:** The group's support, encouragement, and shared enthusiasm boost motivation.

- **Improved Focus:** The shared focus on goals and commitments helps to maintain focus and prevent distractions.

- **Enhanced Follow-Through:** The public commitment and accountability to the group increase the likelihood of following through on plans.

- **Greater Resilience:** The group's support and feedback help members overcome setbacks and maintain momentum even during challenging times.

In summary

Shared accountability within an intellectual synergy group provides a powerful mechanism for maintaining momentum toward achieving goals. The mastermind group helps its members stay focused, motivated, and on track for success by creating a supportive environment of shared commitment, feedback, and celebration.

Selective Awareness in its Highest Form: The Synergy Effect

When an intellectual synergy group operates at its peak potential, it transcends simple collaboration and embodies a powerful form of collective selective awareness. This "synergy effect" amplifies individual capabilities and creates a focused force greater than the sum of its parts.

Imagine our entrepreneur and their mastermind group working cohesively towards launching their sustainable fashion brand. Each member brings their distinct expertise: the marketing expert focuses on market analysis and branding, the fashion designer concentrates on design and production, and the experienced entrepreneur focuses on business strategy and operations.

This collaborative focus creates a unique synergy that intensifies selective awareness in several ways:

- **Amplified Individual Focus:** The shared goal and the presence of other highly focused individuals create an environment that encourages and reinforces individual focus. Members are motivated to bring their best, most focused selves to the group, knowing that their contributions are valuable and that the group's success depends on their individual efforts. This is similar to the concept of social facilitation, where the presence of others can enhance individual performance on simple or well-learned tasks.

- **Emergent Collective Intelligence:** The interaction and exchange of ideas within the group create a form of collective intelligence. The group's combined knowledge, skills, and perspectives allow it to solve problems and generate ideas that would be beyond the reach of any individual member working alone. This emergent intelligence results from the dynamic interaction between members, where ideas build upon each other and new insights emerge.

- **Enhanced Opportunity Recognition:** The diverse perspectives within the group enhance the ability to recognize and seize opportunities. Each member's unique lens allows them to spot opportunities others might miss. Combining these perspectives creates a wider field of vision and a greater likelihood of identifying valuable opportunities. This is related to the concept of cognitive diversity, where diverse perspectives can lead to better decision-making and problem-solving.

- **Shared Mental Models and Strategic Alignment:** Through regular communication and collaboration, the group develops shared mental models of the project, the market, and the overall strategy. This shared understanding creates a strong sense of alignment and ensures everyone is working towards the same goals. This alignment, facilitated by focused discussions and shared decision-making, maximizes the effectiveness of the group's efforts.

- **Continuous Refinement and Iteration**: The ongoing dialogue and feedback within the group allow for continuous refinement of strategies and plans. Members can challenge each other's assumptions, identify potential weaknesses, and suggest improvements. This iterative process, driven by focused analysis and constructive criticism, leads to more robust and effective strategies.

The Magnifying Glass Effect: The magnifying glass analogy is particularly apt. Each member's individual attention is like a beam of light. When these beams are scattered, they have limited impact.

However, when focused through a magnifying glass (the mastermind group), they converge on a single point, creating a much more intense and powerful effect. This concentrated focus allows the group to:

- **Identify** and address critical issues more effectively.

- **Generate** more innovative and creative solutions.

- **Execute** plans with greater precision and efficiency.

- **Achieve** results that would be impossible for individuals working alone.

In essence, a high-functioning intellectual synergy group amplifies selective awareness by creating a shared focus, fostering emergent collective intelligence, enhancing opportunity recognition, promoting strategic alignment, and enabling continuous refinement. This synergy effect allows the group to achieve significantly more than could be achieved by its members working independently.

In Conclusion

An intellectual synergy group, guided by Disciplined Perception, is not merely a beneficial addition to your pursuits; it is a strategic necessity for maximizing the effectiveness of selective awareness and achieving your definite purpose. By harnessing the power of synergy through collective focus, shared accountability, enhanced creativity, and collaborative problem-solving—all amplified by Disciplined Perception—you can propel yourself toward your goals with significantly increased momentum and effectiveness. Disciplined Perception ensures that the group's efforts are focused, aligned, and productive, maximizing the synergistic benefits. So, do not pursue your goals in isolation; seek out or create your mastermind group and unlock the true potential of collaborative, disciplined focus.

The Power of Applied Faith: Fueling Selective Awareness with Unwavering Conviction

Having established a definite purpose and assembled a mastermind alliance, the next step is cultivating applied faith. This is not blind optimism; it is a positive and realistic mindset built through consistent, focused action and growing belief in your ability to achieve your goals. Applied faith is a natural consequence of consistently applying the principles of disciplined focus, strategic planning, and collaborative effort.

Applied Faith: A Consequence of Consistent Action

In this context, applied faith isn't about blind belief or religious faith. A pragmatic and grounded confidence arises from consistent, focused action and tangible progress toward a goal. It is the natural outcome of repeatedly seeing that your efforts, combined with your mastermind group's support and synergy, yield positive results.

Consider the entrepreneur diligently working on their brand strategy with their mastermind group. They are not simply hoping for success; they actively engage in market research, develop a business plan, network with potential clients and partners, and refine their product or service based on feedback. As they overcome obstacles, reach milestones, and witness positive outcomes, their belief in their ability to succeed grows stronger. This is not wishful thinking; it is a reasoned and justified confidence based on evidence.

This "applied faith" acts as a powerful buffer against negativity and strengthens the ability to maintain momentum. Here is how:

- **Doubt Vanquished:** Doubt often stems from a lack of evidence or experience to support a belief in success. However, consistent action and tangible progress provide that evidence. As the entrepreneur consistently applies their knowledge and skills, and the mastermind group provides support and encouragement, self-doubt diminishes. The focus shifts from "Can I do this?" to "How can I do this?" This shift in focus is crucial for maintaining momentum. The entrepreneur's focus, guided by Disciplined Perception, is now on problem-solving and action rather than on self-doubt.

- **Discouragement Defused:** Setbacks are inevitable in any challenging endeavor. However, applied faith helps to reframe these setbacks as temporary obstacles rather than insurmountable barriers. The entrepreneur and their mastermind group, fueled by their growing confidence, see setbacks as opportunities for learning and improvement. They focus on finding solutions and adapting their strategies rather than becoming discouraged and giving up. The momentum gained from previous successes creates a buffer against the negative impact of setbacks.

- **Self-Reliance Soars:** Confronting obstacles head-on and celebrating successes, especially within the supportive environment of a mastermind group, significantly boosts self-reliance. The entrepreneur develops a deep trust in their own abilities and the collective competence of their alliance. This self-reliance is not arrogance; it is a grounded confidence based on demonstrated competence and the knowledge that they have a strong support system in place.

- **Hesitation and Procrastination Eliminated**: Applied faith fosters decisive action and eliminates hesitation and procrastination. When you are confident that your efforts will pay off, you are more likely to take immediate action and less likely to delay or avoid tasks. This proactive approach creates a positive feedback loop: action leads to progress, progress reinforces the belief and stronger belief fuels further action.

The Cycle of Applied Faith: Applied faith is not a static state; it's a dynamic and self-reinforcing cycle:

- **Consistent Action:** Taking consistent, focused action towards a goal.

- **Tangible Progress:** Witnessing positive results and achieving milestones.

- **Strengthened Belief:** Developing a stronger belief in the possibility of success based on evidence.

- **Increased Confidence:** Gaining confidence in one's abilities and in the collective competence of the group.

- **Decisive Action:** Taking immediate and decisive action, eliminating hesitation and procrastination.

This cycle creates a powerful upward spiral of progress, confidence, and action, leading to greater success and fulfillment. Disciplined perception enhances, directs, and maintains this whole process.

From Belief to Action: A Continuous Cycle

Applied faith is not a static state of passive belief; it is a dynamic, self-reinforcing cycle in which belief fuels action, which in turn strengthens belief. This creates a powerful upward spiral of progress and momentum.

Imagine the entrepreneur facing an unexpected obstacle. Their unwavering belief in their vision, cultivated through previous successes and reinforced by their mastermind alliance, prevents them from succumbing to discouragement. Instead, they view the obstacle as a challenge to overcome, leveraging their group's support and collective intelligence to find creative solutions. This proactive response strengthens their belief in their resilience and problem-solving abilities, further fueling their determination to move forward.

This continuous interplay between belief and action is the essence of applied faith. It is not simply about having faith; it is about living that faith through consistent action and allowing the results of those actions to reinforce and deepen that belief.

Here are some exemplary actions that can reinforce this continuous cycle:

1) **Visualization Techniques:** Visualization helps create a clear mental picture of success, strengthening belief and motivating action.

   - **Create a Mental Movie:** Vividly imagine yourself achieving your goals. Visualize not only the end result but also the process of overcoming challenges and the specific steps you take along the way. This mental rehearsal can boost your belief in your ability to succeed by providing a mental blueprint for action. It also strengthens the connection between belief and action by preparing you mentally for the challenges ahead.

   - **Positive Affirmations:** Regularly repeat positive statements about yourself and your abilities, such as "I am capable of achieving my goals" or "I am resilient and resourceful." When combined with visualization, affirmations can reinforce positive beliefs and create a more optimistic mindset, which in turn fuels action.

2) **Mindfulness Practices:** Mindfulness practices help cultivate present-moment awareness and reduce negative self-talk, which can strengthen belief and promote focused action.

   - **Meditation:** Regular meditation can quiet the mind, reduce stress, and cultivate a sense of inner peace. It can also strengthen one's belief in one's ability to overcome challenges and achieve one's goals by reducing anxiety and promoting a more focused and balanced mindset.

- **Gratitude Journaling:** Focusing on gratitude shifts your perspective from lack to abundance, fostering a more positive outlook. By acknowledging the good in your life, you strengthen your belief in attracting more positive experiences and achieving your goals. Gratitude also motivates action by reminding you of your past successes and the positive impact of your efforts.

3) **Surround Yourself with Positive Influences:** The people you surround yourself with can significantly influence your beliefs and actions.

   - **Mastermind Groups:** Joining a group of like-minded, supportive individuals can provide encouragement, feedback, and accountability, which can boost one's belief in one's own potential and motivate one to take action.

   - **Mentorship:** Finding a mentor who has achieved your aspirations can provide valuable guidance, support, and encouragement. A mentor can help you develop your skills, overcome challenges, and strengthen your belief in yourself.

4) **Celebrate Small Wins:** Recognizing and celebrating progress, no matter how small, is crucial for maintaining momentum and reinforcing belief.

   - **Acknowledge Your Progress:** As you work towards your goals, take time to acknowledge your small victories. This reinforces your belief in your ability to succeed and motivates you to continue taking action. Celebrating small wins creates a positive feedback loop, strengthening the connection between action and belief.

Remember!

The Reinforcing Cycle: These practices contribute to a reinforcing cycle:

Belief (Strengthened by Visualization, Affirmations, Mindfulness, Positive Influences) → Action (Motivated by Belief, Supported by Planning and Strategy) → Results (Positive Outcomes, Progress) → Strengthened Belief (Based on Evidence of Progress) → Further Action (Fueled by Increased Belief) → and so on.

When consistently applied and maintained through Disciplined Perception, this cycle creates a powerful engine for achieving goals and realizing one's full potential. Disciplined Perception helps one stay focused on the practices that strengthen belief, maintain consistent action, and recognize the positive results of one's efforts.

In Conclusion

Applied faith, cultivated and maintained through Disciplined Perception, is crucial in transforming selective awareness into a powerful driver of achievement. It is not a "missing link" that magically creates success, but rather a grounded confidence built through consistent action, focused attention, and the reinforcement of positive outcomes. By cultivating unwavering yet realistic belief in your ability to achieve your definite purpose, you minimize self-imposed limitations and propel yourself forward. Disciplined Perception plays a vital role in this process by:

- **Maintaining focus on your vision and goals:** Disciplined Perception helps you stay focused on your definite purpose, even in the face of challenges.

- **Directing your attention to positive evidence and progress:** Disciplined Perception helps you recognize and appreciate your progress, reinforcing your belief in your ability to succeed.

- **Filtering out negative self-talk and limiting beliefs:** Disciplined Perception helps you manage self-doubt and maintain a positive mindset.

To further enhance your applied faith, incorporate practices such as visualization (creating clear mental pictures of success), mindfulness (cultivating present moment awareness), surrounding yourself with positive influences (such as a supportive mastermind group), and celebrating your small wins (acknowledging and appreciating your progress). By consistently applying these practices, guided by Disciplined Perception, you strengthen the cycle of belief and action, transforming your aspirations into tangible results. Disciplined Perception helps you maintain this consistency and ensures your efforts align with your goals.

The Extra Mile: Supercharging Your Momentum with Unwavering Dedication

Fueled by a definite purpose, a supportive alliance, and unwavering faith, the next step is embracing the concept of "going the extra mile." This is not about simply working harder; it's about consistently exceeding expectations, demonstrating a relentless pursuit of your goals, and pushing beyond your perceived limitations. It is about maximizing the impact of your focused efforts through Disciplined Perception. This unwavering dedication, driven by Disciplined Perception, manifests in several key ways, creating a powerful ripple effect that amplifies your achievements and inspires those around you.

The Power of Consistent Action: Unleashing the Ripple Effect of Relentless Pursuit

Going the extra mile is not about sporadic bursts of energy; it is about weaving consistency into your actions. It is about building a sustainable and powerful momentum. Imagine the entrepreneur launching a sustainable fashion brand. Their commitment to going the extra mile might manifest in various ways, demonstrating a dedication that extends beyond simply meeting basic requirements. This consistent exceeding of expectations sets in motion a powerful ripple effect. Disciplined Perception is key to maintaining this consistency by:

- **Prioritizing tasks and managing time effectively:** Disciplined Perception helps you focus on the most impactful activities and avoid distractions that could derail your efforts.

- **Maintaining focus and motivation even when faced with challenges:** Disciplined Perception helps you stay committed to your goals and persevere through difficult times.

- **Tracking progress and making adjustments as needed:** Disciplined Perception helps you monitor your progress and adjust your strategies and actions as needed.

Here is how this consistent dedication manifests in tangible outcomes:

- **Momentum and Inspiration:** The entrepreneur's unwavering dedication, fueled and directed by Disciplined Perception, creates a wave of momentum, inspiring not only themselves but also their mastermind alliance. Witnessing firsthand the power of commitment fuels a collective sense of enthusiasm. This shared energy, amplified by Disciplined Perception, keeps everyone moving forward with renewed vigor and sharpened focus. Disciplined Perception helps group members recognize and appreciate each other's efforts, further fueling the collective momentum. This relates to concepts of social facilitation and collective efficacy.

- **Amplified Achievements:** By consistently going the extra mile, guided by Disciplined Perception, the entrepreneur effectively multiplies their efforts. They not only achieve immediate goals but also build a reputation for excellence. This attracts new opportunities and collaborations, accelerating their progress on a larger scale. Imagine the entrepreneur consistently exceeding deadlines. Not only do they impress current clients, but their reputation for reliability attracts new partnerships and expands their reach. Disciplined Perception helps them recognize and capitalize on these new opportunities by maintaining focus on their long-term vision and aligning their actions accordingly.

- **Self-Fulfilling Success:** Exceeding expectations, when coupled with the self-awareness fostered by Disciplined Perception, creates a powerful feedback loop. Each accomplishment reinforces a positive mental attitude. The entrepreneur witnesses the tangible rewards of their commitment, solidifying their belief in their ability to achieve even more ambitious goals. This self-fulfilling cycle, reinforced by Disciplined Perception, fuels their motivation and propels them further along their journey. Disciplined Perception helps them recognize and internalize these positive experiences, further strengthening their self-belief. This relates to self-efficacy and self-fulfilling prophecy.

- **The Power of Continuity:** Going the extra mile, sustained by Disciplined Perception, ensures your efforts are consistent and sustained. It is not about sporadic bursts of activity; it is about relentlessly moving the needle forward, even when the path gets challenging. This consistent dedication, maintained by Disciplined Perception, separates the dreamers from the doers. Disciplined Perception helps you maintain focus on your long-term goals and avoid being discouraged by short-term setbacks.

- **Exponential Returns:** The extra effort you put in when strategically directed by Disciplined Perception often yields exponentially greater returns. The entrepreneur's dedication to eco-friendly materials might attract media attention, propelling their brand into the spotlight and attracting a wider customer base. This magnifies the impact of their initial efforts, creating a virtuous cycle of growth and success. Disciplined Perception helps you recognize and leverage these exponential returns by maintaining focus on your vision and adapting your strategies to capitalize on new opportunities.

By consistently going the extra mile, guided by Disciplined Perception, you achieve your goals and create a powerful ripple effect that inspires others, attracts new opportunities, and fuels your continued growth and success.

Beyond Material Rewards: Building Goodwill and Cooperation

While going the extra mile might not always yield immediate material benefits, it has a profound long-term impact on building goodwill and fostering cooperation. Imagine the entrepreneur consistently exceeding client expectations and cultivating positive relationships with suppliers. This creates a positive ripple effect, attracting cooperation and opening doors to future opportunities. This collaborative spirit, nurtured by Disciplined Perception, aligns perfectly with the principles of focused attention, creating an environment that fosters focused effort and attracts opportunities aligned with a definite purpose.

Fueling the Fire of Selective Awareness

The positive energy generated by consistently going the extra mile acts as fuel for selective awareness, enhancing focus and attracting positive outcomes. Disciplined Perception is crucial for maintaining this "fire" by providing the mental discipline and focus necessary to apply these techniques consistently. Here is a breakdown of techniques to ensure the sustained power of selective awareness, all enhanced by Disciplined Perception:

1) **Set Challenging but Achievable Goals:** Setting the right kind of goals is crucial for maintaining motivation and focus. Disciplined Perception helps you set goals that are challenging enough to inspire you but also achievable enough to maintain momentum.

   - **Break Down Big Goals:** Divide large goals into smaller, more manageable steps. This makes them less daunting and increases your chances of success. Disciplined Perception helps you stay focused on each step, preventing you from becoming overwhelmed by the overall goal.

   - **Set Stretch Goals:** Do not be afraid to set ambitious goals that push you beyond your comfort zone. Challenging yourself can help you discover new abilities and unlock your full potential. Disciplined Perception helps you maintain focus and motivation even when pursuing challenging goals.

2) **Seek Feedback and Learn from Mistakes:** Feedback is essential for growth and improvement. Disciplined Perception helps you receive and process feedback effectively, using it to refine your strategies and improve your performance.

   - **Ask for Input:** Actively seek feedback from colleagues, mentors, and customers. This can help you identify areas for improvement and stay on track toward your goals. Disciplined Perception helps you focus on constructive feedback and avoid being discouraged by criticism.

   - **Learn from Failures:** Mistakes are growth opportunities. Analyze your failures to understand what went wrong and how you can avoid similar mistakes in the future. Disciplined Perception helps you approach failures with a growth mindset, focusing on learning and improvement rather than self-blame.

3) **Celebrate Milestones and Stay Motivated:** Recognizing and celebrating progress is crucial for maintaining motivation and reinforcing positive behaviors. Disciplined Perception helps you stay focused on your progress and appreciate your accomplishments.

- **Acknowledge Your Achievements:** Celebrate your successes, no matter how small. This can help you stay motivated and focused on your goals. Disciplined Perception helps you internalize these positive experiences, strengthening your belief in your ability to succeed.

- **Visualize Success:** Imagine yourself achieving your goals. This can help you stay motivated and focused, even when faced with challenges. Disciplined Perception helps you create vivid and compelling visualizations, further enhancing their motivational power.

- **Integrate Experiences for Growth:** Instead of simply celebrating successes and acknowledging challenges, focus on integrating both into your learning process. Analyze what contributed to your successes and what you can learn from your challenges. Disciplined Perception helps you maintain an objective perspective and extract valuable lessons from all your experiences.

4) **Stay Curious and Keep Learning:** Continuous learning is essential for staying ahead and maintaining a competitive edge. Disciplined Perception helps you cultivate a learning mindset and stay focused on acquiring new knowledge and skills.

- **Embrace Lifelong Learning:** Continuous learning is essential for staying ahead of the curve and maintaining your competitive edge. Seek out new opportunities for growth and development. Disciplined Perception helps you prioritize learning and dedicate time and energy to acquiring new knowledge.

- **Stay Curious:** Be open to new ideas and perspectives. Curiosity can help you discover innovative ways to improve your work and achieve your goals. Disciplined Perception helps you maintain focus on exploring new ideas and avoid becoming stuck in old patterns of thinking.

5) **Prioritize Self-Care:** Maintaining physical and mental well-being is crucial for maintaining focus, motivation, and energy. Disciplined Perception helps you prioritize self-care and establish healthy habits.

- **Balance Work and Life:** Ensure you care for yourself physically, mentally, and emotionally. A well-rounded life will help you maintain your energy and focus. Disciplined Perception helps you set boundaries between work and personal life and stick to them.

- **Avoid Burnout:** Set boundaries and take breaks when needed. Overworking can lead to burnout, negatively impacting your performance and motivation. Disciplined Perception helps you recognize the signs of burnout and take steps to prevent it.

By consistently applying these techniques, guided by Disciplined Perception, you can maintain the "fire" of selective awareness, fueling your progress and maximizing your potential.

In Conclusion

Going the extra mile, sustained and directed by Disciplined Perception, is not a singular act but a continuous commitment to excellence that requires consistent effort, focused attention, and a dedication to constant improvement. Disciplined Perception is the key to maintaining this commitment through:

- **Maintaining** focus on long-term goals and preventing discouragement from setbacks.

- **Prioritizing** tasks and managing time effectively to ensure consistent effort.

- **Facilitating** self-reflection and learning from both successes and challenges.

By setting challenging yet achievable goals, actively seeking feedback, celebrating milestones (both big and small), staying curious and open to new learning, and prioritizing self-care, you fuel this commitment and unlock its transformative power. Disciplined Perception helps you integrate these practices into your daily routine, making "going the extra mile" a sustainable and natural part of your approach. Embrace this mindset, guided by Disciplined Perception, and watch as your unwavering dedication propels you towards achieving your goals, amplifies your achievements, inspires others, and creates a powerful ripple effect of positive impact.

The Power of Organized Individual Endeavor: Sharpening Your Selective Awareness

Having embraced the concept of going the extra mile, we now focus on the importance of organized individual endeavors. This principle is not about micromanaging every detail; it is about refining your approach, ensuring the soundness of your work, and maximizing the impact of your efforts through strategic planning and collaboration, all while leveraging the expertise of your mastermind alliance and, crucially, the focused clarity of Disciplined Perception. Organized individual endeavor, guided by Disciplined Perception, sharpens selective awareness by providing a clear framework for focused action and efficient use of resources.

Planning + Collaboration: Building a Robust Research Framework

Organized individual endeavor begins with meticulous planning. Imagine a scientist outlining a detailed research proposal. This proposal includes:

- **A clearly defined hypothesis:** A specific and testable statement about the relationship between variables.

- **A well-defined methodology:** A detailed plan outlining the experiments to be conducted, including procedures, materials, and data collection methods.

- **A comprehensive analysis plan:** A strategy for interpreting the results, including statistical analysis techniques and methods for drawing conclusions.

This plan serves as a roadmap, guiding the research process and ensuring all critical aspects are addressed. Disciplined Perception is essential for creating an effective plan by:

- **Prioritizing key elements and avoiding unnecessary details:** Disciplined Perception helps you focus on the plan's most important aspects and avoid getting bogged down in minutiae.

- **Maintaining focus on the overall objective and ensuring that each step contributes to the final goal:** Disciplined

Perception helps you see the big picture and ensure that your planning efforts align with your overall research objectives.

- **Anticipating potential challenges and developing contingency plans:** Disciplined Perception encourages proactive thinking and helps you anticipate potential roadblocks and develop strategies to overcome them.

Mastermind Analysis and Testing: Collaborative Refinement Through Disciplined Feedback

However, organized endeavors do not happen in isolation. The mastermind alliance plays a critical role in refining and strengthening individual efforts. Disciplined Perception enhances the value of this collaboration by ensuring focused and constructive feedback. Here is how:

- **Peer Review and Refinement:** The scientist presents their research proposal to their mastermind alliance, seeking feedback and insights from other researchers in their field. Their mentor might suggest alternative methodologies to strengthen the study's design, while a collaborator might offer expertise in data analysis techniques. Disciplined Perception enhances the effectiveness of this peer review process by:

  o **Encouraging focused and constructive feedback:** Disciplined Perception helps group members provide specific and actionable feedback, avoiding vague or unhelpful comments.

  o **Promoting open and honest communication:** Disciplined Perception creates an environment of trust and respect, where members feel comfortable sharing their honest opinions and challenging each other's assumptions.

- o **Facilitating active listening and understanding:** Disciplined Perception helps members listen attentively to each other's feedback and understand the underlying rationale.

- **Ensuring Scientific Rigor:** Through this collaborative analysis and refinement, guided by Disciplined Perception, the scientist can significantly strengthen their research design and ensure it adheres to the highest scientific standards. This eliminates potential weaknesses, minimizes bias, and increases the likelihood of generating reliable and impactful results. Disciplined Perception helps maintain focus on the core principles of scientific rigor, such as objectivity, accuracy, and reproducibility. It also helps the group identify and address potential sources of error or bias in the research design.

By combining meticulous planning with collaborative analysis and feedback, facilitated by Disciplined Perception, organized individual endeavor becomes a powerful engine for achieving meaningful and impactful results.

The Benefits of Organization: Confidence Through Clarity

Organized individual endeavor offers several key benefits that directly strengthen selective awareness by fostering clarity, confidence, and resilience. By approaching your work with a structured and deliberate approach, amplified by Disciplined Perception, you create a solid foundation for success.

- **A Foundation for Confidence:** By meticulously planning and testing their research approach, the scientist establishes a solid foundation for their belief in the project's potential. They move forward with a clear understanding of the research steps, expected outcomes, and potential challenges, fostering a sense of confidence that fuels their focus and determination. Disciplined Perception enhances this foundation through:

o **Prioritizing the most crucial aspects of the research:** Disciplined Perception helps the scientist focus on the core elements of their research, avoiding getting lost in unnecessary details.

o **Maintaining a clear vision of the end goal:** Disciplined Perception helps the scientist keep the overall objective in mind, ensuring that each step of the research contributes to the final outcome.

o **Promoting accurate self-assessment and realistic expectations:** Disciplined Perception helps scientists assess their own skills and resources realistically, set achievable goals, and avoid overconfidence or self-doubt.

- **Anticipating and Addressing Challenges:** A well-organized research plan anticipates and addresses potential roadblocks. This proactive approach, facilitated by Disciplined Perception, removes the sting of unexpected obstacles, allowing scientists to navigate challenges with composure and adapt their approach as needed. Disciplined Perception helps in:

o **Identifying potential risks and developing contingency plans:** Disciplined Perception encourages scientists to anticipate potential problems and develop strategies to mitigate them.

o **Maintaining focus and composure under pressure:** Disciplined Perception helps scientists focus on finding solutions even when faced with unexpected challenges.

o **Learning from setbacks and adapting the plan accordingly:** Disciplined Perception promotes a growth mindset, encouraging scientists to view setbacks as opportunities for learning and improvement.

- **Eradicating Doubt and Indecision:** The scientist minimizes self-doubt and indecision through comprehensive planning and collaborative feedback within the mastermind alliance. They have a clear understanding of the research question, a well-defined roadmap to achieve it, and the support of a trusted group that bolsters their confidence. Disciplined Perception plays a key role in this process by:

    o **Promoting clear and focused communication within the mastermind group:** Disciplined Perception helps scientists articulate their ideas clearly and effectively, facilitating constructive feedback and collaboration.

    o **Encouraging objective feedback evaluation and integration of valuable insights:** Disciplined Perception helps the scientist process feedback objectively and integrate valuable insights into their research plan.

    o **Reinforcing the importance of evidence-based decision-making:** Disciplined Perception helps scientist base their decisions on data and evidence, minimizing the influence of emotions or biases.

By combining meticulous planning, proactive problem-solving, and collaborative feedback, all guided by Disciplined Perception, organized individual endeavor builds a strong foundation of confidence through clarity. This clarity empowers you to approach your work with focus, determination, and resilience.

Moving with Unwavering Determination

The culmination of organized individual endeavor, amplified by Disciplined Perception, is a state of unwavering determination. This is not just a fleeting feeling of motivation; it's a deep-seated commitment to pursuing your goals with focused energy and resilience.

Imagine the scientist, equipped with a meticulously crafted research plan, refined by the insights of their mastermind alliance, and guided by the focused clarity of Disciplined Perception. They approach their work decisively, allowing them to tackle research hurdles with a clear head and a steady hand. They are no longer hindered by doubt or indecision; their focus is laser-sharp, their experiments meticulously conducted, and their progress consistently monitored.

Here is how organized individual endeavor, enhanced by Disciplined Perception, cultivates unwavering determination:

- **Clarity of Purpose and Direction:** A well-defined plan, developed through organized individual endeavor, provides a clear roadmap. This clarity, sharpened by Disciplined Perception, eliminates ambiguity and provides a strong sense of direction. Disciplined Perception helps maintain focus on the overall objective, preventing distractions and ensuring that every action contributes to the final goal.

- **Confidence in the Process:** The thorough planning and collaborative feedback process builds confidence in the chosen approach. This confidence, strengthened by Disciplined Perception, reduces self-doubt and fosters a sense of trust in the process. Disciplined Perception helps you objectively evaluate feedback, integrate valuable insights, and refine your plan, further solidifying your confidence.

- **Resilience in the Face of Challenges: Organized** individual endeavor anticipates potential roadblocks and develops contingency plans. This proactive approach, guided by Disciplined Perception, builds resilience and prepares you to handle unexpected challenges with composure. Disciplined Perception helps you maintain focus and composure under pressure, allowing you to adapt your approach as needed without losing momentum. It also facilitates learning from setbacks, transforming them into valuable learning experiences.

- **Consistent Focus and Effort:** The structured approach of organized individual endeavor promotes consistent focus and effort. This consistency, sustained by Disciplined Perception, prevents procrastination and ensures steady progress. Disciplined Perception helps you prioritize tasks, manage your time effectively, and maintain focus on the most important activities. It also provides the mental discipline to stay committed to your goals, even when faced with distractions or competing priorities.

- **Internal Locus of Control:** Organized individual endeavor fosters an internal locus of control, meaning you believe you have control over your outcomes. This belief, reinforced by Disciplined Perception, empowers you to take ownership of your work and persevere through challenges. Disciplined Perception helps you focus on the actions you can control rather than dwelling on external factors or circumstances beyond your influence.

In essence, organized individual endeavor, when combined with the focused clarity of Disciplined Perception, creates a powerful sense of unwavering determination. This determination empowers you to pursue your goals with confidence, resilience, and consistent effort, maximizing your chances of success.

In Conclusion

Organized individual endeavor, enhanced and directed by Disciplined Perception, is far more than simply creating a research to-do list; it is about sharpening your selective awareness and maximizing the impact of your efforts. By meticulously planning your approach, leveraging the expertise of your mastermind alliance through focused collaboration, and applying the focused clarity of Disciplined Perception, you build a strong foundation of confidence. Disciplined Perception plays a crucial role by:

- **Prioritizing** key research objectives and maintaining focus on the overall vision.

- **Facilitating** effective communication and feedback within the mastermind alliance.

- **Promoting** proactive problem-solving and enhancing resilience in the face of challenges.

This organized approach, guided by Disciplined Perception, empowers you to pursue your research with unwavering determination, minimizing doubt and indecision and maximizing your ability to overcome obstacles. Embrace organized individual endeavors guided by Disciplined Perception, and watch as your enhanced clarity, focus, and resilience propel you towards significant and impactful research outcomes.

The Power of Self-Discipline: Mastering Your Selective Awareness

Having honed the art of organized individual endeavor, we now delve into the critical principle of self-discipline. This is not about suppressing emotions; it is about harnessing them through Disciplined Perception to fuel your selective awareness and propel you toward your goals. Disciplined Perception acts as the mechanism through which self-discipline is enacted, providing the focused attention and mental control needed to manage emotions effectively.

Taming the Emotional Rollercoaster: From Emotional Fluctuations to Focused Energy

Imagine the scientist facing setbacks in their research. Frustrating technical difficulties or discouragement from inconclusive results can easily lead to emotional turmoil. Self-discipline, guided by Disciplined Perception, becomes their shield against these challenges, transforming potential emotional chaos into focused energy.

Here is how self-discipline, facilitated by Disciplined Perception, helps manage emotions and maintain focus:

- **Preventing Emotional Overflow:** Self-discipline, enacted through Disciplined Perception, acts as a damper, holding at bay the tide of negativity. The scientist acknowledges frustration or discouragement but, through focused self-awareness provided by Disciplined Perception, does not allow such feelings to divert their focus or dissipate their mental energies. They understand that dwelling on negativity is unproductive and consciously choose to redirect their attention. Disciplined Perception enables this redirection by:

  o **Enhancing self-awareness of emotional states:** Disciplined Perception helps scientists recognize when they are experiencing negative emotions, allowing them to take conscious control.

  o **Facilitating cognitive reappraisal:** Disciplined Perception enables scientists to reframe negative situations in a more positive or neutral light, reducing their emotional impact.

  o **Promoting focused attention on solutions:** Disciplined Perception helps scientists shift their focus from negative emotions to finding solutions to the problem.

- **Channeling Positive Emotions:** Self-discipline, also guided by Disciplined Perception, does not just prevent emotional overflow; it also prevents emotional overindulgence. The thrill of a potential breakthrough is exciting, but self-discipline ensures the scientist maintains a level head. They channel their enthusiasm, using the focused energy provided by Disciplined Perception, into productive action, meticulously testing their hypothesis to confirm the exciting discovery. Disciplined Perception enables this channeling by:

  o **Maintaining focus on the task at hand:** Disciplined Perception helps the scientist stay focused on the necessary steps to validate their findings, preventing them from getting carried away by excitement.

  o **Promoting objective analysis and critical thinking:** Disciplined Perception encourages scientists to approach their findings objectively and rigorously, ensuring their enthusiasm does not cloud their judgment.

  o **Directing energy towards productive action:** Disciplined Perception helps scientists channel their enthusiasm into concrete actions, such as designing further experiments or analyzing data.

In essence, self-discipline, facilitated by Disciplined Perception, transforms the scientist from a passenger on an emotional rollercoaster into a driver navigating the road with focus and control.

Here is a further breakdown of how this is achieved:

- **Managing Emotional Overflow:** They never let their emotions get out of control. Frustration may arise, but Disciplined Perception allows them to recognize that feeling, accept it without judgment, and then consciously choose to redirect their attention to solution-finding. They channel their energy into analyzing the situation objectively and developing effective strategies to overcome the obstacles.

- **Minimizing Mental Distractions:** Through Disciplined Perception, Self-discipline prevents negative emotions from triggering unproductive thought spirals. They maintain a clear and focused mind, allowing them to concentrate on the research, not emotional anxieties. This focused attention, provided by Disciplined Perception, allows them to devise creative approaches and interpret findings more accurately.

- **Maximizing Energy Efficiency:** Self-discipline, guided by Disciplined Perception, prevents scientists from wasting mental energy on emotional outbursts or dwelling on negativity. They conserve their energy for what truly matters— conducting their research and interpreting their findings. This focused energy management, facilitated by Disciplined Perception, allows them to persist through challenges and maintain the stamina needed for long-term scientific pursuits.

By taming the emotional rollercoaster through self-discipline and the focused control of Disciplined Perception, scientists remain focused, productive, and ultimately more likely to succeed in their pursuit of knowledge.

The Art of Emotional Transformation

Self-discipline, guided by Disciplined Perception, is not just about suppressing or managing negative emotions; it is about actively transforming them into catalysts for positive action and growth. This transformation involves using focused awareness and mental control to redirect emotional energy towards productive pursuits.

Imagine the scientist encountering unexpected delays in acquiring research funding. This situation could easily lead to frustration and discouragement. However, self-discipline, facilitated by Disciplined Perception, allows them to channel these negative emotions into:

- **Increased Motivation:** Instead of succumbing to despair, they leverage their frustration as fuel to work even harder. Disciplined Perception helps them focus their attention on alternative funding avenues, research grant databases, or networking opportunities. They also use Disciplined Perception to analyze their research proposal objectively, identifying areas for improvement and strengthening its impact to make it more appealing to potential funders. This transformation of frustration into focused energy is a key aspect of emotional resilience.

- **Positive Action:** They do not simply passively accept the setback; they take proactive and positive action. Guided by Disciplined Perception, they might reach out to their mastermind alliance for brainstorming sessions, leveraging the collective intelligence and experience of the group to explore alternative funding solutions or refine their research strategy. They might also connect with potential collaborators who can offer alternative funding sources or provide valuable resources. Disciplined Perception helps them maintain focus on these proactive steps, preventing them from getting stuck in a cycle of negativity.

The Willpower Advantage: Orchestrating the Mind

Self-discipline, strengthened by Disciplined Perception, fosters the development of a strong will. This "willpower advantage" allows individuals to maintain focus, control their thoughts and emotions, and persevere through challenges.

Imagine the scientist facing criticism from a peer reviewer. They might initially feel discouraged or defensive. However, their strong will, cultivated and directed by Disciplined Perception, allows them to

- **Maintain Focus:** They do not let criticism derail their focus on their research goals. Disciplined Perception helps them objectively analyze the feedback, separating constructive criticism from personal attacks. They identify specific areas for improvement while maintaining confidence in the overall merit of their work. This focused analysis allows them to extract valuable insights from the feedback without being emotionally overwhelmed.

- **Control Over Other Mental Faculties:** Their strong will, strengthened by Disciplined Perception, allows them to bring other aspects of their mind under control. They can manage anxiety about potential rejection by refocusing their attention on the task at hand—revising their research proposal. Disciplined Perception helps them prioritize tasks related to the revision process, create a structured plan of action, and maintain a positive outlook despite the setback. This control over mental faculties is crucial for maintaining productivity and achieving goals.

Disciplined Perception plays a crucial role in developing and applying willpower by:

- **Enhancing self-awareness of emotional and mental states:** This allows for early detection of negative emotions or unproductive thought patterns.

- **Facilitating cognitive control and attention regulation:** This enables individuals to redirect their focus from negative emotions or distractions to productive actions.

- **Promoting goal-directed behavior and perseverance:** This strengthens the individual's commitment to their goals and helps them overcome obstacles.

By transforming negative emotions into positive action and developing a strong will through Disciplined Perception, individuals can effectively navigate challenges, maintain momentum, and achieve their goals.

Reaching the Apex of Selective Awareness

Self-discipline, cultivated and directed by Disciplined Perception, propels you toward the apex of selective awareness—a state of heightened focus, mental clarity, and unwavering determination. This peak state is not a passive experience; it is an active and dynamic process of directing your mental resources with precision and control.

Imagine the scientist, having learned to harness their emotions and strengthen their will through self-discipline, all guided by Disciplined Perception. They approach their research with unwavering focus and relentless determination. They are no longer easily distracted by setbacks or discouraged by criticism. Their mind, trained by Disciplined Perception, functions like a well-oiled machine, efficiently processing information, executing research tasks with laser-sharp precision, and adapting to new information or challenges with agility.

Here is how self-discipline, enhanced by Disciplined Perception, helps achieve this apex of selective awareness:

- **Enhanced Focus and Concentration:** Self-discipline, through the focused attention provided by Disciplined Perception, significantly enhances the ability to concentrate on the task at hand. Distractions, both internal (e.g., wandering thoughts, emotional fluctuations) and external (e.g., noise, interruptions), are minimized, allowing for deep and sustained focus. Disciplined Perception helps you prioritize relevant information and filter out irrelevant stimuli, maximizing your cognitive resources.

- **Improved Cognitive Efficiency:** Self-discipline, guided by Disciplined Perception, promotes efficient use of cognitive resources. By minimizing emotional turbulence and unproductive thought patterns, mental energy is conserved and directed toward productive tasks. Disciplined Perception helps you streamline your thinking, avoid mental clutter, and optimize your cognitive processes for maximum efficiency.

- **Increased Mental Clarity:** Self-discipline, through the focused awareness provided by Disciplined Perception, fosters mental clarity. This clarity allows for objective analysis, accurate interpretation of data, and creative problem-solving. Disciplined Perception helps you approach problems with a calm and focused mind, enabling you to see connections and insights that might be missed in a state of emotional turmoil or mental distraction.

- **Enhanced Resilience and Perseverance:** Self-discipline, strengthened by Disciplined Perception, builds resilience and perseverance. Managing emotions and maintaining focus in the face of challenges allows for sustained effort and prevents discouragement from derailing progress. Disciplined Perception helps you reframe setbacks as learning opportunities, maintain a positive outlook, and stay committed to your long-term goals.

- **Mastery of Mental Faculties:** At the apex of selective awareness, achieved through self-discipline and Disciplined Perception, you gain a greater sense of control over your mental faculties. You can consciously direct your attention, manage your emotions, and regulate your thoughts, allowing for optimal performance and achievement. Disciplined Perception is the mechanism through which this mastery is achieved, providing the focused awareness and mental control necessary to orchestrate your mental resources effectively.

In this state of heightened selective awareness, facilitated by Disciplined Perception, individuals can achieve peak performance, maximize their potential, and make significant progress toward their goals. It is a state where the mind is truly mastered and directed with precision and purpose.

In Conclusion

Self-discipline, strengthened and directed by Disciplined Perception, is more than just raw willpower; it is about mastering your selective awareness and maximizing your cognitive potential. By harnessing your emotions through focused self-awareness and cultivating a strong will through consistent practice, all guided by Disciplined Perception, you can navigate challenges effectively and consistently progress towards your research goals. Disciplined Perception plays a crucial role in self-discipline by:

- **Enhancing** self-awareness of emotional and mental states, allowing for conscious control.

- **Facilitating** focused attention and minimizing distractions.

- **Promoting** objective analysis and problem-solving, even under pressure.

Embrace self-discipline, guided by Disciplined Perception, and watch as it enhances your focus, improves your cognitive efficiency, increases your resilience, and empowers you to progress significantly in your pursuit of scientific knowledge. This disciplined approach, facilitated by Disciplined Perception, empowers you not just to overcome obstacles but to learn and grow from them, consistently moving closer to your research objectives.

The Blossoming of Creative Vision: Selective Awareness Unleashed

Have you ever felt on the verge of a breakthrough, yet something holds you back? You diligently follow your plan, meticulously analyze data, and take consistent action. Yet, that spark of true creative vision, which ignites innovation and propels you toward your goals, seems elusive. This is where the power of selective awareness, amplified and directed by Disciplined Perception, comes into play. By mastering the principles we have explored and applying them with focused intent through Disciplined Perception, you will witness the blossoming of creative vision. This is not about random ideas; it is about cultivating a keen and alert subconscious mind that works in tandem with your conscious, focused attention, all orchestrated by Disciplined Perception.

The Synergy of Selective Awareness and the Subconscious

Think of applying the principles of selective awareness as planting seeds in the fertile ground of the subconscious. Your focused actions, detailed analysis, and unwavering determination are the nurturing sunlight and water. This process, guided by Disciplined Perception, creates a powerful synergy that unlocks a world of possibilities. Disciplined Perception acts as the conscious gardener, tending to this mental landscape.

Here is a breakdown of this synergy:

• **The Subconscious Mind: A Hidden Garden Cultivated by Disciplined Perception:** Imagine your subconscious mind as a vast, hidden garden filled with untapped potential. Directed by Disciplined Perception, selective awareness acts as the gardener, cultivating this fertile ground. By focusing your attention and using the focused clarity of Disciplined Perception, you create the ideal conditions for creativity to flourish. Disciplined Perception helps you identify which "seeds" (ideas and information) to plant in your subconscious, ensuring you nurture the most promising possibilities.

- **The Power of Focused Attention: Directed by Disciplined Perception:** Selective awareness, directed by Disciplined Perception, unlocks these subconscious treasures. By focusing attention on a particular goal or problem, a mental pathway is created, and the subconscious mind is free to work along this pathway, even after conscious attention is no longer directly focused on it. Disciplined Perception is the key to maintaining this focus and allowing the subconscious to work effectively in the background. It is then that sudden breakthroughs and creative solutions often emerge.

- **The Role of Unconscious Association: Facilitated by Disciplined Perception:** The subconscious mind is a master of association, connecting seemingly unrelated ideas to create new and innovative concepts. Selective awareness, guided by Disciplined Perception, helps you channel this associative power, allowing you to make meaningful connections that might otherwise remain hidden. Disciplined Perception helps you recognize and validate these connections when they surface into conscious awareness.

- **A Cycle of Growth: Maintained by Disciplined Perception:** The synergy between selective awareness and the subconscious is a continuous cycle of growth maintained by Disciplined Perception. As you focus your attention on a goal, your subconscious mind works on it, leading to new insights. These insights, in turn, fuel your focused attention, creating a positive feedback loop that drives creativity and innovation. Disciplined Perception ensures that this cycle remains focused and productive, preventing it from becoming a random or unproductive train of thought.

- **Unleashing the Creative Flow Through Disciplined Relaxation:** When you combine focused attention, directed by Disciplined Perception, with a relaxed and receptive state of mind, you create the optimal conditions for creativity to flourish. Think of your subconscious as a wellspring of ideas, bubbling up to the surface when you allow it to flow freely. Selective awareness, guided by Disciplined Perception, acts as a filter, allowing only the most relevant and valuable ideas to rise to the conscious mind. Disciplined Perception helps you balance focused effort with periods of relaxation and reflection, allowing the subconscious to work effectively.

- **Overcoming Mental Blocks with Disciplined Reframing:** Selective awareness, through the focused self-awareness of Disciplined Perception, can also help you overcome mental blocks and limiting beliefs. By focusing on your goals and visualizing success, you can rewire your subconscious mind, replacing negative thought patterns with positive affirmations. Disciplined Perception helps you identify these limiting beliefs and consciously reframe them into more empowering perspectives. This can help you break free from self-doubt and unleash your full creative potential.

The Benefits of Blossoming Creative Vision: Amplified by Disciplined Perception

The blossoming of creative vision, nurtured by Disciplined Perception, brings several significant benefits:

- **Hunches Become Your Superpower:** Validated by Disciplined Perception: Your subconscious, now a well-oiled machine thanks to Disciplined Perception, begins to express itself through hunches. These seemingly intuitive leaps are not mere guesswork; they are the culmination of your focused efforts and the subconscious mind's processing of vast amounts of data. Disciplined Perception helps you recognize, analyze, and validate these hunches, turning them into actionable insights.

- **A World of Unexpected Opportunities**: Identified Through Disciplined Observation: With your creative vision in bloom, you will develop a heightened awareness of newly discovered opportunities. These seemingly chance encounters are the result of your sharpened selective awareness, guided by Disciplined Perception. This allows you to identify and capitalize on opportunities that align with your desires. Disciplined Perception helps you maintain focus on your goals, making you more likely to notice relevant opportunities.

- **Collaboration Blossoms:** Attracted by Disciplined Focus and Vision: As your creative vision flourishes, you will attract unexpected forms of cooperation from others. Your unwavering focus and dedication, evident through your disciplined approach, inspire those around you. Disciplined Perception helps you communicate your vision clearly and effectively, attracting like-minded individuals and fostering collaborative partnerships.

- **The Alchemy of Everything Around You:** Perceived Through Disciplined Awareness: You will see the world differently through the lens of your creative vision, sharpened by Disciplined Perception. Your awakened mind allows you to recognize the potential of seemingly mundane objects or events as tools that can be leveraged to advance your goals. Disciplined Perception helps you connect these observations to your goals, generating new ideas and insights.

- **The Law of Chance Bends in Your Favor:** A Result of Disciplined Preparation and Awareness: You might even feel as if the law of chance is operating in your favor. This is not mere luck; it is a consequence of your unwavering focus and heightened awareness, both cultivated by Disciplined Perception. You are constantly scanning the environment for opportunities, making you more likely to identify and capitalize on serendipitous events that align with your goals. Disciplined

Perception helps you prepare for these opportunities, ensuring you are ready to seize them when they arise.

In Conclusion

Creative vision is not a mystical gift bestowed upon a chosen few; it is the natural culmination of diligently applying the principles of selective awareness, all orchestrated and amplified by Disciplined Perception. It is about consciously cultivating the fertile ground of your subconscious mind through focused attention, consistent action, and unwavering dedication. Disciplined Perception acts as the conscious gardener, ensuring that the right "seeds" of information and experience are planted and nurtured.

By harnessing the synergistic power of your focused conscious attention and your vast subconscious mind, directed by Disciplined Perception, you unlock a world of creative possibilities. This synergy allows you to:

- **Generate** innovative ideas and solutions by connecting seemingly disparate concepts.

- **Recognize** and capitalize on unexpected opportunities that align with your goals.

- **Attract** collaborative partnerships and support from others who resonate with your vision.

- **See** the world with fresh eyes, recognizing the potential in everything around you.

- **Experience** a sense of serendipity as your focused efforts align with opportune moments.

Disciplined Perception is the key to maintaining this creative flow. It ensures that your focused attention remains aligned with your goals, that your subconscious mind is nurtured with relevant information, and that you are receptive to emerging insights and opportunities. So, cultivate your creative vision through the disciplined application of selective awareness, and watch as your journey unfolds with purpose, clarity, and the power of focused creation.

Sharper Thinking, Clearer Path: The Power of Organized Thought Through Disciplined Perception

Have you ever observed the methodical approach of a seasoned researcher? Their success is not random; it is built upon a foundation of organized thought, a core principle of selective awareness, amplified and directed by Disciplined Perception. This cognitive framework allows them to filter out irrelevant stimuli, channel their mental energy into a laser-focused pursuit of truth, and systematically progress toward their goals. It is the difference between chasing fleeting hypotheses and meticulously constructing experiments based on verifiable data, all guided by the focused clarity of Disciplined Perception.

Our minds are often our own worst enemies. Unorganized thoughts can morph into self-doubt, procrastination, and analysis paralysis. This is where the psychological power of organized thought, facilitated by Disciplined Perception, comes in. By structuring your plans and actions through focused analysis and deliberate decision-making, you cultivate a sense of control and clarity. This mental state, strengthened by Disciplined Perception, boosts your confidence and empowers you to overcome the mental roadblocks that often derail even the best intentions.

From Guesswork to Focused Action: Guided by Disciplined Perception

So how does organized thought, directed by Disciplined Perception, put a stop to guesswork and propel you towards focused action? There are three key pillars:

1) **Building on Facts and Reason: Through Disciplined Analysis:** Organized thought replaces hunches with a solid foundation of evidence and logical reasoning. You develop the habit, through Disciplined Perception, of conducting thorough research, gathering verifiable evidence, and formulating hypotheses based on logic and reason. This ensures your actions are driven by a clear understanding of the situation, not fleeting intuition or biases. Disciplined Perception helps you objectively evaluate information, identify reliable sources, and draw logical conclusions.

2) **Alignment with Your Definite Major Purpose (DMP): Maintained by Disciplined Focus:** Every successful journey begins with a clear destination. Organized thought, guided by Disciplined Perception, starts with identifying your DMP— your ultimate goal, your "why." With this unwavering focus in mind, maintained by Disciplined Perception, you can filter your thoughts and actions, discarding anything that does not contribute to achieving your desired outcome. It is like having a built-in GPS system for your life, constantly recalibrated by Disciplined Perception to ensure you stay on course.

The Benefits of Organized Thought: Amplified by Disciplined Perception

The rewards of implementing organized thought, enhanced by Disciplined Perception, are far-reaching:

- **Clear Roadmap:** Created Through Disciplined Planning: Imagine outlining a detailed project plan with specific steps, milestones, and contingency plans. Organized thought, facilitated by Disciplined Perception, helps you develop a clear roadmap for achieving your goals. This roadmap, maintained and adapted through Disciplined Perception, keeps you focused, allowing you to navigate unforeseen challenges and adjust your approach as needed. It is the difference between wandering aimlessly and having a clear path to follow, illuminated by the focused clarity of Disciplined Perception.

- **Efficient Decision-Making:** Enabled by Disciplined Analysis: Organized thought, directed by Disciplined Perception, empowers you to make strategic and effective decisions. By analyzing information objectively, considering potential outcomes, and aligning your choices with your DMP, you can confidently choose the path that best serves your goals. Disciplined Perception helps you weigh options carefully, assess risks and rewards, and make rational decisions based on evidence and logic. No more impulsive choices or wasted energy on dead-end pursuits.

- **Boosted Confidence:** Reinforced by Disciplined Action and Progress Tracking: Your confidence soars as you consistently achieve milestones and witness the tangible results of your planning. Organized thought, coupled with the focused self-awareness of Disciplined Perception, equips you with a sense of control and accomplishment, fueling your motivation and resilience in the face of obstacles. Disciplined Perception helps you track your progress, recognize your achievements, and internalize these positive experiences, further strengthening your confidence. You become less susceptible to self-doubt and more empowered to keep pushing forward.

In Conclusion

Organized thought, amplified and directed by Disciplined Perception, is far more than just creating a to-do list; it is about sharpening your thinking, bringing structure to your plans, and maximizing the effectiveness of your efforts. It is about replacing guesswork with focused action and propelling you toward achieving your goals with clarity, unwavering confidence, and focused intent. Disciplined Perception is the key to implementing and maintaining organized thought by:

- **Enhancing** focus and concentration, minimizing distractions and mental clutter.

- **Facilitating** objective analysis, logical reasoning, and evidence-based decision-making.

- **Maintaining** alignment with your Definite Major Purpose (DMP) and ensuring consistent progress.

So, embrace organized thought, guided by Disciplined Perception, and watch as your journey unfolds with a strong sense of purpose, clear direction, and newfound confidence in your ability to achieve anything you set your mind to.

Learning from Defeat: The Fuel for Unstoppable Growth

We have all experienced setbacks. The sting of defeat can be demoralizing, leaving you questioning your abilities and direction. But what if you could transform those defeats into powerful fuel for your journey? This is the essence of learning from defeat, a core principle of selective awareness, amplified and directed by Disciplined Perception. Disciplined Perception provides the focused self-awareness and objective analysis necessary to extract valuable lessons from setbacks.

From Setbacks to Steppingstones: A Transformation Guided by Disciplined Perception

Learning from defeat is not about dwelling on negativity; it is about cultivating the habit, through Disciplined Perception, of converting every experience, even negative ones, into a definite benefit. Imagine facing a crushing failure. Instead of succumbing to discouragement, you adopt a growth mindset facilitated by Disciplined Perception. Here is how:

- **Seeking the Seed of Benefit:** Through Disciplined Analysis, You actively search, using the focused analytical skills of Disciplined Perception, for the "seed of an equivalent benefit" within the defeat. Perhaps you uncover valuable insights that can improve your approach in the future. Maybe the experience reveals a hidden weakness that you can now address. Disciplined Perception helps you objectively analyze the situation, identify the root causes of the setback, and extract actionable lessons.

- **Defeat as Fuel:** Reframed by Disciplined Perception: You view defeat not as a roadblock but as a form of useful fuel. Imagine transforming disappointment into a burning desire to learn, grow, and come back stronger, a transformation facilitated by Disciplined Perception. This newfound resolve, fueled by Disciplined Perception, strengthens your willpower and propels you forward with renewed determination. Disciplined Perception helps you reframe the setback, focusing on the positive aspects of the experience, such as the opportunity for growth and learning.

- **Learning from Your Memory Bank:** Accessed Through Disciplined Reflection: You develop the habit, through Disciplined Perception, of going back into your memory and profiting from all your previous defeats. Each setback becomes a valuable lesson stored in your mental library, readily accessible through focused reflection facilitated by Disciplined Perception. As you draw upon these experiences, guided by Disciplined Perception, you become more resilient and adaptable in the face of future challenges. Disciplined Perception helps you objectively review past experiences, identify patterns, and extract valuable lessons without being clouded by emotions.

The Benefits of Learning from Defeat: Amplified by Disciplined Perception

The benefits of learning from defeat, maximized by Disciplined Perception, are significant:

- **Unstoppable Growth:** Driven by Disciplined Learning: By consistently learning from defeat, you embark on a path of unstoppable growth fueled by Disciplined Perception. Every experience, positive or negative, becomes a building block on your journey to success. Disciplined Perception helps you integrate these lessons into your knowledge base and apply them effectively in future situations.

- **Fearless Determination:** Strengthened by Disciplined Resilience: As you learn to transform defeat into fuel through the focused self-awareness of Disciplined Perception, fear loses its grip. Discouragement, worry, and self-doubt no longer hold you back. You develop a fearless determination, sustained by Disciplined Perception, that propels you towards your goals with unwavering focus. Disciplined Perception helps you manage fear and anxiety by focusing on the actions you can control and the lessons you can learn.

- **Clarity of Purpose:** Refined by Disciplined Self-Reflection: Learning from defeat through the focused self-reflection of Disciplined Perception fosters a deep understanding of your strengths and weaknesses. You gain clarity about what you truly want and where you are going in life. This newfound focus, maintained by Disciplined Perception, allows you to navigate challenges with confidence and a renewed sense of direction. Disciplined Perception helps you connect your experiences to your long-term goals and refine your purpose based on what you learn.

In Conclusion

Learning from defeat through the focused lens of Disciplined Perception is not about avoiding setbacks; it is about embracing them as invaluable opportunities for growth, learning, and self-improvement. By mastering this principle, guided by Disciplined Perception, you develop the resilience, determination, and clarity of purpose needed to achieve your goals. Disciplined Perception is the key to this transformation by:

- **Facilitating** objective analysis of setbacks and extraction of valuable lessons.

- **Promoting** a growth mindset and reframing negative experiences into positive opportunities.

- **Strengthening** resilience, focus, and determination in the face of future challenges.

So, the next time you face a setback, remember it is not the end; it is just a bend in the road. Within that bend, analyzed and understood through Disciplined Perception, lies the potential for exponential growth. Embrace the challenge, learn from it through focused self-reflection, and watch yourself rise to even greater heights, guided by the unwavering focus of Disciplined Perception.

The Spark Within: Harnessing Inspiration for Peak Performance Through Disciplined Perception

Have you ever felt a surge of enthusiasm that propelled you into action? That is the power of inspiration, a core principle of selective awareness, amplified and sustained by Disciplined Perception. It is not just about fleeting good feelings; it is about cultivating a habit of enthusiasm, guided by Disciplined Perception, that fuels your focus, unlocks your full potential, and drives consistent, purposeful action.

Inspiration: The Bridge to Action, Guided by Disciplined Perception

Inspiration is not merely an emotion; it is a motivational state that compels you to act with purpose and energy. Imagine not being inspired: trudging through activities simply out of obligation. In contrast, inspiration ignites action and transforms work into a joyful pursuit. Disciplined Perception helps you cultivate and maintain this inspired state. Here is how:

- **From Drudgery to Delight: Transformed by Disciplined Focus:** Inspiration transforms even mundane tasks into a more engaging experience. Imagine finding joy in the process of working towards your goals, not just the end result. This enthusiasm, sustained by Disciplined Perception, fuels your drive and makes even challenging tasks feel fulfilling. Disciplined Perception helps you find meaning and purpose in your work, making it more intrinsically motivating.

- **Focus Made Easy: Directed by Disciplined Attention:** Enthusiasm, combined with a clear plan, purpose, or motive, automatically leads to greater concentration of attention. Imagine struggling to maintain focus, your mind constantly wandering. Inspiration, channeled by Disciplined Perception, acts as a laser, guiding your selective awareness and allowing you to delve deeply into your work. Disciplined Perception helps you maintain this focus by minimizing distractions and keeping your attention aligned with your goals.

- **The Subconscious Connection: Amplified by Disciplined Visualization:** Enthusiasm acts as a bridge between your conscious and subconscious mind. When your dominating thoughts are inspired, they are more readily impressed upon your subconscious, which then works relentlessly in the background to drive you toward your goals. Disciplined Perception strengthens this connection through focused visualization and affirmation, further embedding your goals into your subconscious.

The Benefits of Inspiration: Maximized by Disciplined Perception

Inspiration is not just about feeling good; it is a gateway to peak efficiency and unlocking your full potential, all maximized by Disciplined Perception. Let us explore the powerful ways inspiration, coupled with Disciplined Perception, fuels your journey:

- **Effortless Efficiency: Achieved Through Disciplined Focus:** Just as a laser cuts through fog, inspiration, channeled by Disciplined Perception, brings sharpness to your focus, filtering out distractions and mental clutter. This laser-like focus, maintained by Disciplined Perception, lets you accomplish more with less wasted effort, propelling you with greater efficiency toward your goals. Disciplined Perception helps you prioritize tasks, manage your time effectively, and maintain focus on the most important activities.

- **Infinite Intelligence as Your Copilot: Accessed Through Disciplined Intuition:** The state of enthusiastic inspiration, when coupled with the focused self-awareness of Disciplined Perception, can create a profound sense of connection to a broader source of wisdom or intuition. This feeling of being supported by a larger force is not merely metaphorical; it can have a tangible impact on your actions, boosting your confidence and resourcefulness. Disciplined Perception helps you access and interpret these intuitive insights, turning them into actionable strategies.

- **Engaging Your Subconscious Ally: Programmed Through Disciplined Repetition:** Enthusiasm, amplified by Disciplined Perception, becomes a powerful means of programming your subconscious mind. By vividly imagining yourself achieving your goals and experiencing the associated positive emotions, you impress these images and feelings upon your subconscious. Disciplined Perception helps you maintain this focused visualization and repetition, strengthening the subconscious programming. The subconscious then works unceasingly behind the scenes, seeking opportunities and guiding you in the right direction.

- **The Synergy of Efficiency and Intuition: Orchestrated by Disciplined Perception:** When your mind is ignited by inspiration and directed by Disciplined Perception, you achieve a remarkable state of focused awareness. This heightened focus, coupled with enhanced intuition, unlocks a wellspring of creative ideas and sharpens your decision-making. You begin to see solutions you might have missed before, make decisions with greater clarity, and take actions that propel you toward your goals with exceptional efficiency. Disciplined Perception helps you integrate your intuitive insights with logical reasoning, leading to more effective and creative solutions.

In Conclusion

Inspiration, cultivated and directed by Disciplined Perception, is not a luxury; it is the essential fuel for peak performance and the unlocking of your full potential. By cultivating a habit of enthusiasm, guided by Disciplined Perception, you unlock the transformative power of your selective awareness. No longer a passive filter, it becomes a laser-focused tool, guiding your actions and effortlessly filtering out distractions. Moreover, inspiration, amplified by Disciplined Perception, ignites your subconscious mind, transforming fleeting goals into deeply embedded drivers of your actions. Disciplined Perception is the key to maintaining this inspired state by:

- **Focusing** your attention on meaningful and inspiring goals.

- **Cultivating** a positive mindset and managing negative emotions.

- **Integrating** intuitive insights with logical reasoning and strategic planning.

Embrace inspiration—nurture your enthusiasm, find your spark, and direct it with Disciplined Perception—and watch as it propels you towards success with exceptional efficiency, boundless creativity, and the unwavering confidence that comes from feeling connected to a purpose greater than yourself. Guided by Disciplined Perception, inspiration is the key to unlocking your full potential and transforming your journey toward success into a fulfilling and exciting adventure.

The Magnetism of Selective Awareness: Cultivating an Unstoppable Aura Through Disciplined Perception

We have explored the core principles of selective awareness, and now we arrive at a powerful outcome: the development of an "unstoppable aura" cultivated and projected through Disciplined Perception. This is not about superficial charm or manipulation; it is about harnessing the focused energy of selective awareness, directed by Disciplined Perception, to cultivate a personality that naturally attracts the right people, resources, and opportunities. This transformative process begins the moment you ignite your Definite Major Purpose (DMP), focusing your energy and attention on a clear and compelling vision.

Aligning Purpose with Magnetism: Amplified by Disciplined Perception

Imagine a lighthouse piercing the darkness, its powerful beam guiding ships safely to the harbor. That is the essence of aligning yourself with your DMP, amplified by Disciplined Perception. As you dedicate yourself to a clear and compelling goal, maintaining unwavering focus through Disciplined Perception, you naturally exude a sense of purpose and direction. This focused energy becomes magnetic, attracting others who share your vision or can contribute to your success. Disciplined Perception helps you maintain this focus, ensuring that your actions and communications consistently reflect your purpose.

Science Unveils the Allure: Mirror Neurons and Disciplined Projection

Neuroscientists are now exploring the concept of mirror neurons, brain cells that fire not only when we perform an action but also when we observe someone else doing it.[116] This phenomenon can partly explain the magnetism of a focused individual, especially when that focus is projected with the clarity of Disciplined Perception. Your unwavering dedication to your DMP, the positive energy you radiate (maintained by Disciplined Perception), and the laser-like intensity of your focus (directed by Disciplined Perception) are all contagious. People are drawn to those who embody these qualities, creating a ripple effect that attracts potential allies and collaborators. Disciplined Perception helps you consciously project these qualities, amplifying their impact on others.

Beyond the Intellectual Synergy Group: Expanding Your Reach Through Disciplined Engagement

Your intellectual synergy group is a powerful force, but selective awareness, enhanced by Disciplined Perception, expands your network exponentially by making you a more attractive and engaging individual. Here is how:

- **Disarming Opposition with Confidence: Projected Through Disciplined Self-Belief:** As you fine-tune your focus and nurture a positive mental attitude through Disciplined Perception, you cultivate a deep and unwavering belief in your vision. This confidence, projected with the clarity of Disciplined Perception, acts as a shield, deflecting negativity and disarming potential opposition. People are naturally drawn to those who are clear about their destination and passionate about reaching it. They will be more likely to see you as a collaborator rather than a competitor, fostering cooperation instead of conflict. Disciplined Perception helps you maintain this confidence even in the face of challenges or criticism.

- **Attracting Allies Like a Beacon: Focused by Disciplined Intent:** Imagine an energy-emitting beacon in a sea of uncertainty. This unwavering commitment, focused by Disciplined Perception, magnetizes the supportive collaboration of others. Unexpected mentors may emerge, their interest sparked by your clear vision and unwavering determination. Complementing collaborators with skill sets that enhance your own may appear drawn by your vision and eager to contribute. You become the conductor, and the orchestra members—people who can help you create a symphony of success—are naturally attracted to you. Disciplined Perception helps you articulate your vision clearly and connect with the right people who can support your goals.

The Foundation for Unwavering Focus: Cultivated by Disciplined Practice

Developing an attractive personality is not about manipulation but genuine inner transformation cultivated through Disciplined Perception. As you delve deeper into selective awareness, practicing the principles with focused intent through Disciplined Perception, you cultivate a positive mental attitude, enhanced self-belief, and unwavering focus. This mastery of your mental domain, facilitated by Disciplined Perception, allows you to effortlessly filter out distractions and direct your energy toward achieving your goals. This unwavering focus, combined with your positive aura, creates a powerful and attractive force, propelling you forward with unwavering confidence.

In Conclusion

Selective awareness, when practiced with the focused intent of Disciplined Perception, is not just about achieving your goals; it is about the transformative journey of becoming the person who can achieve those goals. By embracing this philosophy and applying it with the focused clarity of Disciplined Perception, you cultivate an "unstoppable aura" that naturally attracts the right people, resources, and opportunities, propelling you forward with a strong sense of purpose, unwavering focus, and genuine magnetism. Disciplined Perception is the key to this transformation by:

- **Maintaining** focus on your DMP, projecting a clear sense of purpose and direction.

- **Enhancing** self-belief and projecting confidence that inspires others.

- **Facilitating** effective communication and attracting collaborative partnerships.

So, embark on this journey of self-discovery, cultivate your selective awareness through the focused practice of Disciplined Perception, and watch as you achieve your goals and build a powerful network of support that fuels your success every step of the way. Remember, through Disciplined Perception, you become the lighthouse, guiding yourself and those around you toward a brighter, more fulfilling future.

Overall Chapter Conclusion: Mastering Selective Awareness Through Disciplined Perception: A Path to Achievement and Fulfillment

This chapter has explored the profound power of selective awareness, not as a passive filtering mechanism but as a dynamic, trainable skill that becomes a catalyst for achieving goals, attracting opportunities, and cultivating a fulfilling life when mastered through Disciplined Perception. We have journeyed through ten core principles, each building upon the last, to reveal the transformative potential of focused attention and intentional living.

We began by establishing the foundation: crafting a Definite Major Purpose (DMP), the clear and compelling vision that provides direction and meaning. We then explored how autosuggestion and focused intention, working in concert with the Law of Attraction, can sculpt your reality by aligning your thoughts, beliefs, and actions with your DMP.

Recognizing that individual effort is amplified by collaboration, we delved into the power of intellectual synergy groups, emphasizing how collective focus and shared accountability can supercharge selective awareness. We then explored the crucial role of Applied Faith, not as blind optimism, but as a grounded confidence built through consistent action and unwavering conviction, all fueled by Disciplined Perception.

To sustain momentum and maximize impact, we examined the importance of "going the extra mile" through unwavering dedication and consistent effort, emphasizing the ripple effect of exceeding expectations. We then shifted our focus to the internal structures that support effective action: organized individual endeavor and organized thought, both of which are significantly enhanced by the focused clarity of Disciplined Perception.

Recognizing that setbacks are inevitable, we explored the transformative power of learning from defeat, reframing challenges as opportunities for growth and resilience. We then ignited the "spark within" by examining the crucial role of inspiration in fueling peak performance and unlocking creative potential, all while maintaining the focused direction of Disciplined Perception.

Finally, we arrived at the culmination of these principles: the "magnetism" of selective awareness. By embodying these principles and projecting them with the focused intent of Disciplined Perception, you cultivate an "unstoppable aura" that naturally attracts the right people, resources, and opportunities.

Throughout this journey, one key element has emerged as the orchestrator of all these principles: Disciplined Perception. It is the focused awareness, the deliberate control of attention, and the objective analysis that allows you to:

- **Clearly** define and maintain focus on your DMP.

- **Effectively** utilize autosuggestion and focused intention.

- **Maximize** the benefits of collaborative synergy.

- **Cultivate** and sustain applied faith and unwavering dedication.

- **Structure** your efforts through organized endeavor and organized thought.

- **Transform** setbacks into valuable learning experiences.

- **Harness** the power of inspiration for peak performance.

- **Project** a magnetic aura that attracts opportunities and collaboration.

In essence, this chapter has demonstrated that selective awareness, when mastered through Disciplined Perception, is not just a tool for achieving goals; it is a pathway to personal transformation, enhanced creativity, and a more fulfilling and impactful life. By consistently applying these principles, you become the architect of your destiny, navigating your path with purpose, clarity, and unwavering focus.

FROM EDUCATION TO IMPACT: DEFINING PURPOSE AND LEADING WITH VISION

δ❧ δ❧ δ❧

E ducation, purpose, and leadership are not isolated concepts; they are deeply intertwined elements that shape individual potential and drive positive change. This chapter examines the dynamic relationship between these three pillars, revealing how a strong educational foundation can empower individuals to define their purpose, develop essential leadership skills, and ultimately make a meaningful impact on the world.

The Seeds of Selective Awareness: The Role of Education in Cultivating Focused Perception

Selective awareness, the key to unlocking potential and living a life of purpose, is not an innate talent; it is a skill cultivated over time, beginning with the seeds planted through education and nurtured through disciplined perception. Education provides foundational knowledge and critical thinking skills, which are then honed through the conscious practice of selective awareness using disciplined perception. Let us delve into how education cultivates the foundation for selective awareness through disciplined perception.

Definiteness of Purpose: The Fertile Ground for Focused Perception

Although education provides the fertile ground for developing definiteness of purpose, the practice of selective awareness through disciplined perception cultivates this ground, ensuring that the seeds of purpose take root and flourish. Definiteness of purpose is not a static endpoint but a dynamic process of self-discovery and refinement facilitated by the interplay of conscious exploration and subconscious integration.

Early Exploration: A Thrilling Adventure in Focused Discovery

Imagine a classroom transformed into a vibrant jungle gym of ideas, where curiosity is the driving force. Educators act as guides, facilitating exploration rather than dictating information. Through interactive activities, thought-provoking discussions, and real-world experiences, students embark on an exciting adventure of self-discovery. When practiced as selective awareness through disciplined curiosity, this early exploration sparks the initial stirrings of definiteness of purpose. Selective awareness, practiced through disciplined curiosity, encourages students to ask focused questions, explore different perspectives with intention, and actively seek out information that aligns with their emerging interests.

- **Psychological and Neurocognitive Connections:** This early exploration aligns with Piaget's theory of cognitive development, particularly the sensorimotor and preoperational stages, where children actively explore their environment and develop schemas (mental frameworks) for understanding the world. Neurobiologically, this exploration strengthens neural connections in the brain, particularly in areas associated with learning and memory (hippocampus) and reward processing (dopamine system). The act of discovering something new triggers dopamine release, reinforcing exploratory behavior.

Disciplined curiosity adds a layer of focused attention to this exploration, enhancing learning and memory encoding. This focused attention activates the prefrontal cortex, crucial for higher-level cognitive functions like planning and decision-making, setting the stage for developing a sense of purpose.

The Scaffolding of General Education: Providing Direction Through Disciplined Exploration

Not everyone experiences a sudden "aha" moment of clarity regarding their purpose in their youth. Some students may explore various paths as their purpose is initially unclear. For them, general education provides a sturdy scaffolding, offering a broad base of knowledge and developing critical thinking skills. This is like equipping them with a compass and a map, essential tools for navigating the vast landscape of possibilities. This foundation allows students to practice selective awareness through disciplined exploration, encouraging them to explore different subjects and disciplines with focused attention, identifying areas of interest, and gradually honing in on their potential purpose. This prevents aimless wandering and ensures that the exploration is purposeful.

- **Psychological and Neurocognitive Connections:** General education allows for the development of crystallized intelligence (accumulated knowledge and skills), crucial for making informed decisions about one's future. Psychologically, exploring different fields can lead to increased self-awareness and a better understanding of one's strengths and weaknesses. Neurobiologically, this process strengthens connections between different brain regions, promoting more integrated and flexible thinking. Disciplined exploration introduces a focused and intentional approach to this process, activating the prefrontal cortex and enhancing executive functions like working memory and cognitive flexibility, essential for goal setting and planning. This relates to the concept of cognitive mapping, where the brain creates mental representations of different possibilities.

Specialization with Precision: Focused by Disciplined Intent

Think of a future doctor who, after exploring the breadth of general education, develops a deep interest in neurology. Their focus then shifts to highly specialized medical courses designed to provide the specific knowledge and expertise required of a proficient neurologist. This specialization with a purpose is achieved through selective awareness practiced with disciplined intent. Selective awareness, practiced with disciplined intent, allows them to focus their energy and attention on acquiring the specific skills and knowledge necessary to achieve their defined purpose. It is like providing them with a surgeon's scalpel—a precise instrument that empowers them to achieve their specific goals with maximum efficiency. Selective awareness, maintained through disciplined perception, ensures that this specialization is aligned with their overall purpose and that they remain focused on their long-term vision.

Psychological and Neurocognitive Connections: Specialization involves the development of expertise, which is characterized by highly specialized knowledge, skills, and cognitive processes. Psychologically, this involves a strong sense of identity and commitment to a particular field. Neurobiologically, specialization leads to structural and functional changes in the brain, particularly in relevant cortical areas. For example, a neurologist's brain might show increased gray matter density in areas associated with motor control, sensory processing, and cognitive functions related to neurological diagnosis and treatment. Disciplined intent plays a crucial role in this process by maintaining focus and motivation over extended periods of time, which is essential for achieving expertise. This sustained focus strengthens neural pathways and optimizes brain function for the specific domain of expertise. This aligns with the concept of neuroplasticity, the brain's ability to reorganize itself by forming new neural connections throughout life.[117]

Beyond Textbooks: The Essential Toolkit for Selective Awareness

Education is not merely about memorizing facts; it is about forging the mental tools that empower you to wield selective awareness with precision through disciplined perception. These tools are essential for effectively focusing attention, filtering information, and achieving goals.

Organized Thinking: A Mental Lighthouse Illuminating Selective Focus

Effective education cultivates organized thinking skills. Imagine students learning to structure their thoughts like constructing a lighthouse: establishing a solid base (foundational knowledge), building a strong structure (logical reasoning), and projecting a focused beam (clear articulation and communication). These skills become their guiding light, illuminating the path toward their definite purpose through selective focus. They can set clear goals, meticulously plan their actions, and maintain focused attention on achieving their desired outcomes, even when faced with distractions.

- **Neurocognitive Connection:** Organized thinking aligns with the functions of the prefrontal cortex, the brain region responsible for executive functions like planning, working memory, and cognitive flexibility. Education emphasizing structured problem-solving, logical reasoning, and critical analysis strengthens these prefrontal cortex functions, enhancing the ability to practice selective awareness through disciplined thought. This relates to concepts like cognitive control and attentional control

Self-Discipline: The Unshakeable Resolve for Disciplined Attention

At its best, education cultivates self-discipline, the capacity for disciplined attention. Imagine students learning to become masters of their own time and attention. They prioritize tasks, manage their schedules with focused intent, and persevere through challenges with unwavering determination. This self-control becomes their suit of armor, protecting them from the temptations of procrastination and the allure of distractions. It allows them to maintain a laser focus on their definite major purpose through disciplined attention, ensuring they stay on the path to achieving their dreams.

- **Neurocognitive Connection:** Self-discipline involves the interplay of several brain regions, including the prefrontal cortex (for executive functions), the anterior cingulate cortex (for conflict monitoring and error detection), and the limbic system (for emotional regulation). Education that promotes self-regulation, goal setting, and delayed gratification strengthens these neural circuits, enhancing the ability to practice selective awareness through disciplined attention. This relates to concepts like executive function, impulse control, and emotional regulation.

Self-Reliance: The Empowered Explorer of Focused Opportunities

Education, when approached thoughtfully, nurtures self-reliance and the ability to practice selective awareness through disciplined exploration. Imagine students learning to take initiative, manage their own learning with focused intent, and think critically without relying solely on external validation. This self-reliance empowers them to become the captains of their own ships, navigating the vast ocean of knowledge with confidence and a sense of ownership. They can take charge of their goals, tackle challenges head-on with focused determination, and adapt their course as needed, all while fueled by the unwavering belief in their own capabilities.

- **Neurocognitive Connection:** Self-reliance is linked to a strong sense of self-efficacy, the belief in one's ability to succeed in specific situations or accomplish tasks. Education that encourages independent learning, problem-solving, and critical thinking strengthens self-efficacy, enhancing the ability to practice selective awareness through disciplined exploration. This relates to concepts like metacognition (thinking about one's own thinking) and intrinsic motivation.

Learning from Superiors and the Lifelong Quest

Education is not a finite journey that ends with a diploma; it is a continuous learning, adaptation, and growth process. Selective awareness thrives on a commitment to lifelong learning, practiced through disciplined perception. It allows individuals to extract valuable lessons from every experience, from formal education to mentorship and beyond.

Learning by Serving: An Invaluable Apprenticeship in Focused Observation

Imagine a young professional entering the workforce. While their initial tasks might seem mundane, this period can be a valuable apprenticeship in focused observation and learning. By serving their superiors, they gain invaluable insights into the industry, observe successful leadership styles firsthand, and witness the practical application of theoretical knowledge. It is like being apprenticed to a master chef, learning the secrets of the trade through focused observation and hands-on experience. This selective awareness is practiced through disciplined observation, allowing them to identify key patterns, strategies, and behaviors contributing to success.

- **Psychological and Neurocognitive Connections:** Learning by observation aligns with Bandura's social learning theory, emphasizing the importance of observational learning and modeling. Mirror neurons, as previously mentioned, play a key role in this process, allowing us to understand and internalize the actions and behaviors of others. Disciplined observation enhances this process by directing attention to specific aspects of the observed behavior, such as effective communication strategies or problem-solving techniques. This focused observation strengthens neural connections associated with these observed skills, making them more readily accessible for future use. This also relates to the concept of implicit learning, where we acquire new skills and knowledge without conscious awareness through repeated exposure and observation

Finding a Mentor: A Strategic Approach to Focused Learning

To accelerate your learning and career growth, consider seeking a mentor. Here are some tips for finding and approaching potential mentors: (These remain practical tips, but we can frame them within the context of selective awareness)

- **Look Within Your Network:** Focusing on Existing Connections: Use selective awareness to identify individuals within your existing network who possess the qualities and experience you admire.

- **Research Industry Experts:** Focusing Your Research on Relevant Expertise: Use selective awareness to focus your research on experts whose skills and experience align with your goals.

- **Attend Industry Events:** Focusing Your Networking on Potential Mentors: Use selective awareness to identify and connect with potential mentors at relevant industry events

Building a Mentorship Relationship: A Partnership for Focused Growth

Once you've identified a potential mentor, reach out to them thoughtfully. Be clear about your goals and how you believe the mentor can help you achieve them. Offer to contribute to the relationship by sharing your skills or knowledge. This application of selective awareness focuses on building a mutually beneficial relationship.

The Benefits of Mentorship: Accelerated Learning Through Focused Guidance

A mentor can provide guidance, support, and valuable insights into your career. They can help you develop new skills, navigate challenges, and achieve your goals. Mentorship can also foster a sense of belonging and connection within your industry. When received with focused attention (selective awareness through disciplined listening), this guidance accelerates learning and development.

- **Psychological and Neurocognitive Connections:** Mentorship provides a structured environment for learning and development, offering personalized feedback and guidance. This can enhance metacognition by encouraging self-reflection and self-assessment. The social support provided by a mentor can also reduce stress and anxiety, creating a more conducive environment for learning and growth.

Self-Development as a Never-Ending Journey of Focused Improvement

The most successful individuals are lifelong learners. They possess an insatiable curiosity and a relentless pursuit of self-improvement, guided by selective awareness through disciplined self-reflection.

Imagine them constantly seeking opportunities to develop new skills, expand their knowledge base, and refine their approach with focused intent. This dedication to self-development fuels their journey, allowing them to adapt to changing landscapes and continuously evolve as individuals. It is like a thrilling psychological thriller, where the protagonist is constantly pushing their own boundaries and unlocking new levels of potential.

- **Psychological and Neurocognitive Connections:** Lifelong learning promotes cognitive reserve, the brain's ability to resist damage and maintain function despite aging or disease. Engaging in mentally stimulating activities throughout life strengthens neural connections and enhances cognitive flexibility. Disciplined self-reflection allows individuals to identify areas for improvement, set realistic goals, and track their progress, further enhancing self-efficacy and motivation. This also relates to the concept of growth mindset, the belief that abilities and intelligence can be developed through effort and learning.

By consistently linking these concepts to selective awareness through disciplined perception and incorporating relevant psychological and neurocognitive insights, we create a more robust and scientifically grounded understanding of the importance of lifelong learning in developing effective leadership and personal growth.

In Conclusion

Education is not merely the acquisition of knowledge; it is the fertile ground where the seeds of selective awareness are sown and cultivated through disciplined perception. It provides the essential tools—organized thinking, self-discipline, and self-reliance—that empower individuals to focus their attention, filter information effectively, and pursue their purpose with clarity and intent.

This cultivation of selective awareness through disciplined perception is a lifelong process, beginning with early exploration, progressing through general education and specialization, and continuing through mentorship and self-directed learning. It is a collaborative endeavor, enriched by interaction with educators, mentors, and peers, but ultimately driven by the individual's commitment to focused growth.

By embracing education as a means of developing selective awareness through disciplined perception, you transform from a passive recipient of information into an active architect of your own learning and development. You learn to direct your attention with precision, identify and seize opportunities aligned with your purpose, and navigate challenges with resilience and resourcefulness. This disciplined approach to learning empowers you to not only acquire knowledge but also apply it effectively, making a meaningful impact on the world.

Therefore, embrace education as the foundation for developing selective awareness through disciplined perception. Cultivate your focus, nurture your curiosity, and commit to lifelong learning. In doing so, you unlock the power within to illuminate your path, achieve your goals, and contribute your unique brilliance to the world.

Cultivating Definiteness of Purpose: The Thrilling Hunt for Your Life's Mission Through Focused Exploration

The journey to selective awareness that coveted state of laser-sharp focus begins with a clear objective: a Definite Major Purpose (DMP). However, this DMP might feel shrouded in mystery for many young individuals, a hidden treasure waiting to be unearthed. This initial uncertainty is a normal part of the adventure, not a roadblock. It's a period of exploration and discovery, which lays the foundation for developing a strong sense of purpose when approached with disciplined perception. Let us explore the stages that can help navigate this exciting phase and establish a foundation for selective awareness through disciplined exploration.

Understanding Youthful Indecisiveness: A Mind Brimming with Potential, Guided by Disciplined Exploration

Youthful indecisiveness is not a sign of weakness or a lack of intelligence; it is a natural consequence of ongoing brain development and a wealth of unexplored possibilities. It is a crucial period for developing self-awareness and exploring different paths, which are essential for forming a strong DMP.

Scientific: The Developing Brain and Focused Exploration

Neuroscientists tell us that the adolescent brain is still under construction. The prefrontal cortex, responsible for decision-making, planning, and impulse control, is not yet fully developed. This explains, in part, why young people may have difficulty pinpointing a single, long-term goal. It's not a failure of intelligence; it's simply a mind full of potential without the fully mature neurological framework to definitively define a life's ambition. However, this period of development is also characterized by heightened neuroplasticity, meaning the brain is highly adaptable and responsive to experience. Disciplined exploration during this time, focusing attention on different interests and experiences, strengthens neural connections and contributes to the development of the prefrontal cortex, ultimately enhancing decision-making abilities and the capacity for focused goal pursuit.

- **Neurocognitive Concepts:** Synaptic pruning is a key process during adolescence, where unused neural connections are eliminated, and frequently used connections are strengthened. Disciplined exploration helps guide this pruning process by focusing attention on specific areas of interest, leading to the strengthening of relevant neural pathways.

Popular Science: The Vast Library of Possibilities, Explored with Focused Curiosity

Imagine your mind as a vast library overflowing with countless books on every subject imaginable. As a young person, you have not yet had the chance to explore all the shelves. This "indecisiveness" is simply the excitement of discovery, the thrill of not knowing exactly what path awaits you. Embrace this open-mindedness; it is the fertile ground where your DMP will eventually take root. This exploration, when approached with focused curiosity (selective awareness through disciplined exploration), allows you to sample different "books" (experiences and ideas), gaining a broader understanding of the possibilities and gradually identifying areas of deeper interest.

- **Psychological Concepts:** This relates to Erikson's stages of psychosocial development, specifically the stage of identity vs. role confusion, which occurs during adolescence. This stage is characterized by the exploration of different identities and roles, which is essential for developing a sense of self and purpose. Focused curiosity helps navigate this stage by directing attention to specific areas of exploration and preventing aimless drifting.

Self-Help: Indecision as a Strength, Navigated with Focused Self-Reflection

It is important not to view indecision at this early stage as a weakness but rather as one of life's strengths since it means that you can try many different things and maybe even change direction until you find the right path. This is the time you get to know yourself, and this self-awareness, developed through focused self-reflection (selective awareness through disciplined introspection), will eventually lead to your DMP. Focused self-reflection involves consciously examining your experiences, identifying your values, interests, and strengths, and using this information to inform your decisions about your future.

- **Psychological Concepts:** This relates to the concept of self-discovery, which is a process of gaining a deeper understanding of one's own values, beliefs, interests, and motivations. Focused self-reflection facilitates this process by directing attention inward and encouraging conscious examination of one's inner world.

By adding these psychological and neurocognitive connections and emphasizing the role of disciplined exploration, we provide a more comprehensive and scientifically grounded understanding of youthful indecisiveness and how it can be transformed into a powerful period of self-discovery and purpose development. We also maintain the focus on selective awareness through disciplined perception.

The Power of Education: Igniting the Spark of Focused Curiosity

Education is not merely the transmission of information; it is the ignition of focused curiosity, a process that empowers individuals to explore their potential and develop a strong sense of purpose. Through education, we learn to practice selective awareness through disciplined perception, directing our attention towards areas of interest and developing the skills necessary to pursue them effectively.

Thriller: Unlocking Potential Through Focused Exploration

Education is the key that unlocks the hidden chambers of your potential. It exposes you to a thrilling array of subjects, from the mysteries of the universe to the complexities of human behavior. Each new concept is like a puzzle piece, slowly forming a clearer picture of your interests and aptitudes. When approached with focused exploration (selective awareness through disciplined curiosity), this exploration allows you to identify which "chambers" resonate most strongly with you, guiding you towards areas where you can make a meaningful contribution.

- **Psychological and Neurocognitive Connections:** This relates to the psychological concepts of exploration and discovery, which are driven by intrinsic motivation and a desire for novelty. Neurobiologically, exposure to new information and experiences activates the brain's reward system (dopamine pathways), reinforcing exploratory behavior and promoting learning. Focused exploration adds a layer of intentionality to this process, activating the prefrontal cortex and enhancing executive functions like working memory and attention. This focused attention strengthens neural connections related to the explored subjects, making them more easily accessible for future learning and application. This ties into the concept of experiential learning, where knowledge and skills are acquired through active engagement and reflection.

Psychological: Cultivating Mental Agility Through Focused Analysis

Education is not just about memorizing facts but about fostering critical thinking skills and encouraging exploration with focused analysis. By engaging with diverse fields of knowledge, you develop the mental agility to analyze information, identify patterns, and solve problems. These skills are essential for navigating the ever-changing world and ultimately pinpointing your niche, your area of expertise, through focused self-assessment.

- Psychological and Neurocognitive Connections: The development of critical thinking skills is closely linked to cognitive development and prefrontal cortex maturation. These skills involve higher-level cognitive functions such as reasoning, problem-solving, and decision-making. Neurobiologically, engaging in critical thinking tasks strengthens neural connections in the prefrontal cortex and other brain regions involved in cognitive processing. Focused analysis, an aspect of selective awareness through disciplined perception, enhances these processes by directing attention to relevant information, filtering out irrelevant details, and promoting objective evaluation. This relates to the concept of cognitive flexibility, the ability to switch between different tasks or mental sets, which is crucial for adapting to new situations and solving complex problems. It also connects to metacognition (thinking about one's thinking), which allows individuals to reflect on their own thought processes and identify areas for improvement.

Transforming Experiences into Insights: The Hands-On Crucible of Focused Learning

Education provides the theoretical framework, but through experience, processed with focused attention (selective awareness through disciplined perception), knowledge becomes truly integrated and transformed into actionable insights. This "hands-on crucible" provides invaluable opportunities for self-discovery and the refinement of one's purpose.

Popular Science: Real-World Adventures in Focused Application

Imagine education as the theoretical map and work experience as the real-world adventure. Just as explorers venturing into uncharted territory gain practical knowledge and adapt their maps based on their discoveries, your early work experiences, even if not your ultimate destination, provide invaluable hands-on learning. As the concept suggests, you "tear through experience," encountering challenges and successes that shape your understanding of different fields and capabilities. When approached with focused application (selective awareness through disciplined action), this process allows you to connect theory with practice, identify areas of strength and weakness, and refine your understanding of your potential.

- **Psychological and Neurocognitive Connections:** This aligns with Kolb's experiential learning cycle, which emphasizes the importance of concrete experience, reflective observation, abstract conceptualization, and active experimentation in the learning process.1 Neurobiologically, engaging in real-world experiences strengthens neural connections through long-term potentiation (LTP), a process that strengthens synaptic connections based on repeated activation. Focused application enhances this process by directing attention to specific aspects of the experience, facilitating deeper processing and encoding of information. This also relates to the concept of embodied cognition, which suggests that our cognitive processes are deeply intertwined with our physical experiences.

Self-Help: Entry-Level Opportunities for Focused Self-Discovery

Do not underestimate the power of entry-level positions. While they might not be your dream job, they offer a crucial opportunity to test the waters, develop new skills, and gain a deeper understanding of your strengths and weaknesses through focused self-discovery. This self-discovery, facilitated by selective awareness through disciplined introspection, is a vital step in refining your career aspirations and setting your sights on your DMP. This is where you can begin to apply the principles of selective awareness in a practical context, focusing your attention on what you learn from each experience and using that information to refine your understanding of your purpose.

- **Psychological and Neurocognitive Connections**: Entry-level positions provide opportunities for skill development and competence building, which contribute to a stronger sense of self-efficacy. Psychologically, these experiences can lead to increased self-awareness and a more realistic understanding of one's abilities. Focused self-discovery enhances this process by encouraging self-reflection and self-assessment, allowing individuals to identify their strengths and weaknesses and to understand how their values and interests align with different career paths. This relates to the concept of self-regulation, the ability to monitor and control one's own behavior, emotions, and thoughts, which is crucial for achieving goals and adapting to new situations.

Liberal Arts: Broadening the Horizon of Focused Perception

While specialized education provides focused expertise, a liberal arts education broadens the horizon of focused perception, offering a diverse intellectual landscape that cultivates critical thinking, adaptability, and a richer understanding of the world. It is about learning how to practice selective awareness across a wider range of subjects, enhancing cognitive flexibility.

Scientific: Mental Conditioning for Focused Perspective-Taking

While specialized education equips you with specific skills, a liberal arts education offers a broader perspective. It is a form of mental conditioning that exposes you to diverse schools of thought, from philosophy and history to literature and science. This intellectual engagement, approached with focused perspective-taking (selective awareness through disciplined intellectual exploration), strengthens your critical thinking muscles and allows you to see the world through a kaleidoscope of lenses. It trains you to consider multiple viewpoints, analyze complex issues from different angles, and develop a more nuanced understanding of human experience.

- **Psychological and Neurocognitive Connections:** Exposure to diverse subjects promotes cognitive flexibility—the ability to switch between different thought processes and perspectives. This is crucial for problem-solving, creativity, and adapting to new situations. Neurobiologically, this type of broad learning strengthens connections between different brain regions, promoting more integrated and flexible thinking. Focused perspective-taking enhances this by encouraging active engagement with different viewpoints, requiring the brain to inhibit habitual ways of thinking and consider alternative perspectives. This relates to the concept of theory of mind, which is the ability to understand that other people have different beliefs, intentions, and perspectives than one's own.

Thriller: Unlocking Uncharted Territories of Focused Discovery

Imagine a hidden door in your mind leading to a chamber filled with uncharted territories. A liberal arts education is the key that unlocks this door, allowing for focused discovery. Suddenly, you are presented with a vast array of possibilities, from the intricacies of social justice to the mind-blowing discoveries of science. When approached with focused discovery (selective awareness through disciplined intellectual curiosity), this exploration might ignite a passion you never knew existed, a hidden talent waiting to be unleashed. It is about using selective awareness to identify what truly resonates with you within this broad knowledge landscape.

- **Psychological and Neurocognitive Connections:** This relates to the psychological concepts of curiosity and exploration, which are driven by intrinsic motivation and a desire for novelty. Neurobiologically, exploring new areas of knowledge activates the brain's reward system, reinforcing learning and promoting further exploration. Focused discovery enhances this process by directing attention to specific areas of interest within the broader field of liberal arts, leading to deeper engagement and more meaningful learning. This also connects to the concept of latent inhibition, the ability to filter out irrelevant stimuli. A broad education can actually reduce latent inhibition, making individuals more receptive to new ideas and connections, which can be beneficial for creativity. However, focused discovery helps balance this by directing attention to relevant information, preventing cognitive overload.

The Road to Selective Awareness: Charting Your Course with Focused Purpose

The key takeaway from these stages is that a DMP is not a sudden, random occurrence; it is the culmination of a thrilling journey of self-discovery fueled by education, real-world experience, and a willingness to explore diverse perspectives, all navigated through selective awareness and disciplined perception. Once you establish your DMP, you can then fully harness the power of selective awareness, focusing your energy, attention, and resources on achieving that desired outcome.

The Synthesis of Experience and Reflection: Building a Focused Vision

The journey to defining your DMP is a process of synthesizing various experiences—educational, professional, and personal—and reflecting on them with focused attention. This synthesis, facilitated by selective awareness through disciplined introspection, allows you to identify recurring themes, values, and interests that contribute to your overall sense of purpose.

- **Psychological and Neurocognitive Connections:** This process aligns with the psychological concept of meaning-making, the human drive to find meaning and purpose in life experiences. Neurobiologically, this involves the integration of information from different brain regions, including the prefrontal cortex (for executive functions and planning), the hippocampus (for memory and learning), and the limbic system (for emotions and motivation). Disciplined introspection enhances this integration by directing attention to relevant experiences, facilitating deeper processing and encoding of information, and promoting self-awareness. This relates to the concept of autobiographical memory, the memory system responsible for storing and retrieving personal experiences.

From Exploration to Focus: Refining Your Purpose Through Selective Attention

Exploring diverse perspectives and experiences through formal education, work experience, or personal pursuits is crucial for refining your DMP. When approached with selective awareness through disciplined exploration, this exploration allows you to narrow your focus, identify your niche, and develop a more specific and actionable vision for your future.

- **Psychological and Neurocognitive Connections:** This relates to cognitive differentiation, the ability to distinguish between different concepts and categories. As you explore different areas, you develop a more nuanced understanding of the world and your place within it. Selective attention, practiced through disciplined exploration, plays a crucial role in this process by filtering out irrelevant information and focusing on relevant details. This strengthens neural connections associated with the chosen area of focus, making it easier to process information and make decisions related to that area.

Harnessing Selective Awareness for Goal Pursuit: Directed by Disciplined Action

Once you have a clear DMP, you can fully harness the power of selective awareness, directed by disciplined action, to pursue your goals with focus and determination. This involves setting specific, measurable, achievable, relevant, and time-bound (SMART) goals, developing action plans, and consistently monitoring your progress.

- **Psychological and Neurocognitive Connections**: This relates to goal-setting theory, which emphasizes the importance of setting specific and challenging goals for motivating behavior and improving performance. Neurobiologically, goal pursuit involves the activation of the prefrontal cortex, which is responsible for planning, decision-making, and working memory. Disciplined action, facilitated by selective awareness through disciplined perception, strengthens these neural connections, making staying focused on your goals and resisting distractions easier. This also connects to the concept of self-efficacy, the belief in one's ability to succeed, which is crucial for maintaining motivation and perseverance in the face of challenges.

The Selective Awareness Advantage: Powered by a Defined Purpose and Disciplined Perception

Having a DMP is not just about personal satisfaction; it is the foundation for harnessing selective awareness's full power through disciplined perception. A clear purpose provides the target, while disciplined perception provides the means to hit that target consistently. Here is how a well-defined purpose transforms your approach to the world:

A Beacon in the Fog: Focused Direction Through Disciplined Navigation

Imagine navigating a dense forest. Without a clear direction, every turn could lead you deeper into confusion. A DMP acts as your compass, a guiding light that cuts through the fog of distractions and keeps you focused on your desired path. Selective awareness, practiced through disciplined navigation, then amplifies this focus, filtering out irrelevant information and propelling you steadily toward your goals. Disciplined navigation involves consciously choosing which paths to take, evaluating progress, and adjusting course as needed, all while keeping the DMP firmly in mind.

- **Psychological and Neurocognitive Connections:** This relates to the psychological concepts of goal-directed behavior and cognitive mapping. A DMP provides a clear goal, while selective awareness through disciplined navigation allows you to create and follow a mental map to achieve that goal. Neurobiologically, this involves the prefrontal cortex responsible for planning, working memory, and decision-making. The act of navigating towards a goal strengthens neural connections in this area, enhancing executive function and cognitive control. The reflection question encourages metacognition (thinking about one's thinking and its effect on behavior), and the exercise promotes goal setting and visualization.

The Energy Catalyst: Focused Motivation Through Disciplined Action

Enthusiasm for your DMP fuels a surge of energy within you. Selective awareness, practiced through disciplined action, acts as a conductor, channeling this energy and directing it toward productive actions. You become less susceptible to procrastination and distractions, finding the motivation to take consistent steps towards achieving your dreams. Disciplined action involves breaking down large goals into smaller, manageable tasks, creating a structured plan, and consistently following through on those actions.

- **Psychological and Neurocognitive Connections:** Enthusiasm and motivation are linked to the release of dopamine, a neurotransmitter associated with reward and pleasure. A clear DMP provides a strong source of intrinsic motivation, making it easier to stay engaged and focused. Selective awareness through disciplined action helps maintain this motivation by focusing attention on progress and positive outcomes. This relates to self-determination theory, which emphasizes the importance of autonomy, competence, and relatedness in promoting motivation and well-being. The reflection question encourages self-awareness about motivational triggers, and the exercise promotes self-regulation and habit formation.

The Architect of Your Reality: Focused Creation Through Disciplined Intention

With a DMP in mind, you begin to shape your environment to support your goals subconsciously. Selective awareness, practiced through disciplined intention, refines this process. You become adept at identifying opportunities that align with your purpose and attracting the right people and resources into your life. It is as if the universe conspires to help you achieve your dreams. Disciplined intention involves consciously setting your mind on achieving your DMP, visualizing success, and taking actions that align with your vision.

- **Psychological and Neurocognitive Connections:** This relates to the psychological concept of self-fulfilling prophecy, where beliefs and expectations can influence behavior and outcomes. By focusing on your DMP and visualizing success, you create a positive feedback loop that increases your likelihood of achieving your goals. Selective awareness through disciplined intention helps you identify and seize opportunities that support your vision, further reinforcing this positive cycle. This also connects to the concept of attentional bias, where attention is selectively drawn to information that is congruent with one's goals and beliefs. The reflection question encourages environmental awareness, and the exercise promotes visualization and affirmation, techniques that can influence subconscious beliefs and motivations.

Embrace the Journey of Focused Discovery and Purposeful Refinement

The journey towards selective awareness, practiced through disciplined perception, is not a straight shot to a predetermined destination; it is an exhilarating quest of continuous learning, adaptation, and refinement. Embrace the inherent uncertainty of youth, viewing it not as a hindrance but as the fertile ground for focused exploration and the initial stages of defining your purpose. Utilize the tools of education and experience, navigated with disciplined perception, to chart your unique path. Remember, the road is paved with discovery, not blind certainty.

1) **Embracing Uncertainty as a Catalyst for Focused Exploration**

    The uncertainty of youth is not a sign of weakness; it is an opportunity for focused exploration. This period of exploration, approached with selective awareness through disciplined curiosity, allows you to try different paths, experiment with different ideas, and discover what truly resonates with you. This process is crucial for developing a strong and authentic DMP.

    o **Psychological and Neurocognitive Connections:** This relates to the psychological concepts of exploration, experimentation, and identity formation. Embracing uncertainty allows for greater exploration and reduces the fear of failure, which can inhibit learning and growth. Neurobiologically, this exploration period strengthens neural connections associated with learning, memory, and adaptability. This also relates to the concept of cognitive flexibility, the ability to switch between different thought processes and adapt to new situations.

2) **The Evolving Nature of the DMP: Refined Through Focused Reflection and Adaptation**

Your DMP isn't a static entity; it's a living document that adapts and grows alongside you as you gain new experiences and insights. This continuous refinement, facilitated by selective awareness through disciplined reflection and adaptation, is essential for maintaining motivation and ensuring that your purpose remains aligned with your evolving values and goals.

o **Psychological and Neurocognitive Connections: This** aligns with the concept of lifelong learning and the idea that personal growth is a continuous process. Psychologically, this involves self-reflection, self-assessment, and a willingness to adapt one's goals and strategies based on new information and experiences. Neurobiologically, this ongoing learning and adaptation strengthens neural connections and promotes cognitive reserve, the brain's ability to resist damage and maintain function. This relates to neuroplasticity, the brain's ability to change and adapt throughout life.

3) **Selective Awareness as the Guiding Force: Navigated by Disciplined Perception**

It is this constant exploration and refinement, navigated by selective awareness through disciplined perception, that ultimately unlocks the full power of focused attention and allows you to pursue your purpose with clarity and determination. Selective awareness, practiced through disciplined perception, helps you filter out distractions, focus on relevant information, and make informed decisions that align with your evolving DMP.

o **Psychological and Neurocognitive Connections:** Selective awareness, maintained through disciplined perception, plays a crucial role in goal pursuit by directing attention to relevant information, filtering out distractions, and promoting focused action. This involves the prefrontal cortex, responsible for executive functions like planning, working memory, and decision-making. By consistently practicing selective awareness, you strengthen these neural connections and improve your ability to stay focused on your goals.

Additional Tips for Navigating the Journey of Focused Purpose Discovery

These additional tips provide practical guidance for navigating the journey of discovering and refining your DMP, all while practicing selective awareness through disciplined perception:

1) **Embrace the Power of Mentorship:** Focused Guidance Through Disciplined Learning: Find mentors who embody the qualities you admire and share similar interests. Their guidance and insights, received with focused attention (selective awareness through disciplined listening), can be invaluable in navigating the complexities of career exploration.

o **Psychological and Neurocognitive Connections:** Mentorship provides a structured environment for social learning, where individuals learn through observation, modeling, and feedback. Disciplined listening enhances this process by directing attention to key insights and advice the mentor provides. This also relates to social cognitive theory, which emphasizes the role of social interaction and observation in learning and development.

2) **Never Stop Learning:** Focused Growth Through Disciplined Acquisition of Knowledge: The world is constantly evolving, and so should your knowledge base. Embrace lifelong learning, whether through taking online courses, attending workshops, or simply reading books in your field of interest. This continuous learning approach with selective awareness through disciplined study keeps your mind engaged, expands your understanding of the world, and opens up new possibilities for your DMP.

   o **Psychological and Neurocognitive Connections:** Lifelong learning promotes cognitive reserve and neuroplasticity, maintaining brain health and cognitive function throughout life. Disciplined acquisition of knowledge ensures that learning is focused and effective, maximizing the benefits for cognitive development. This also connects to the concept of a growth mindset, the belief that abilities and intelligence can be developed through effort and learning.

3) **Listen to Your Gut:** Focused Intuition Through Disciplined Self-Reflection: While logic and reason are important, do not discount your intuition. There is power in gut feelings, a voice within that can guide you towards opportunities that resonate with your deeper desires. When interpreted through focused self-reflection (selective awareness through disciplined introspection), this intuition can provide valuable insights that complement logical analysis.

   o **Psychological and Neurocognitive Connections:** Intuition is often described as a form of implicit learning where knowledge and patterns are acquired unconsciously. While the exact neural mechanisms are still being researched, it is thought to involve integrating information from various brain regions, including the amygdala (for emotional processing) and the basal ganglia (for habit formation). Disciplined self-reflection helps bring these unconscious insights into conscious awareness, allowing for more informed decision-making.

4) **Do not Be Afraid to Experiment: Focused** Exploration Through Disciplined Action: The path to your DMP might not be linear. Embrace the opportunity to experiment with different interests and career paths. You might discover hidden passions or stumble upon unexpected opportunities that set you on a whole new course. This experimentation approached with selective awareness through disciplined action, allows you to gather valuable data about your preferences, strengths, and weaknesses, which can inform your DMP.

   o **Psychological and Neurocognitive Connections:** Experimentation is crucial for self-discovery and identity formation. It allows individuals to test different roles and identities, gaining a clearer understanding of who they are and what they want. Disciplined action ensures that these experiments are purposeful and lead to meaningful learning experiences.

5) **Celebrate Your Achievements (Big and Small):** Focused Reinforcement Through Disciplined Recognition: The journey towards your DMP is a marathon, not a sprint. Take the time to celebrate your achievements, both big and small. Recognizing your progress through focused self-recognition (selective awareness through disciplined self-assessment) will fuel your motivation and keep you moving forward.

   o **Psychological and Neurocognitive Connections:** Celebrating achievements triggers the release of dopamine, reinforcing positive behaviors and promoting motivation. Disciplined recognition ensures that these celebrations are meaningful and contribute to a stronger sense of self-**efficacy**. This relates to reinforcement learning, a learning process where behaviors are strengthened or weakened based on their consequences.

In Conclusion

Cultivating a Definite Major Purpose (DMP) is not a passive waiting game; it is an active and ongoing process of focused exploration guided by selective awareness through disciplined perception. It is about consciously directing your attention towards self-discovery, utilizing the tools of education, experience, and reflection to uncover your unique talents, values, and aspirations.

This thrilling hunt for your life's mission involves several key stages, all enhanced by the practice of selective awareness through disciplined perception:

- **Embracing youthful indecisiveness as a period of focused exploration:** Recognizing that uncertainty is a natural part of development and using it as an opportunity to explore different possibilities with focused curiosity.

- **Harnessing the power of education for focused knowledge acquisition:** Utilizing education to broaden your horizons, develop critical thinking skills, and identify areas of interest that align with your emerging purpose.

- **Transforming experiences into focused insights:** Actively reflecting on your experiences, both positive and negative, to extract valuable lessons and refine your understanding of yourself and the world.

By embracing these stages and nurturing your DMP through selective awareness and disciplined perception, you unlock a powerful synergy that transforms your life approach. You gain:

- **Clarity of direction:** A clear DMP acts as a compass, guiding your decisions and actions.

- **Increased motivation and focus:** Enthusiasm for your purpose fuels your energy and directs your attention.

- **Enhanced ability to attract opportunities and resources:** A strong sense of purpose makes you more magnetic to others who share your vision or can contribute to your goals.

Therefore, embark on this adventure of self-discovery, practicing selective awareness through disciplined perception at every step. By consciously defining your purpose, you gain the unwavering focus and clarity needed to navigate your path and create a fulfilling and impactful future.

The Making of an Executive: Cultivating the Symphony of Leadership Through Focused Orchestration

Successful executives are not born; they are developed through the conscious cultivation of leadership skills honed by selective awareness through disciplined perception. They are the maestros of the organizational world, wielding a unique blend of focused attention, influence, and strategic delegation to orchestrate exceptional results. Let us delve into the key characteristics that elevate them from managers to leaders, transforming their teams into high-performing symphonies of success.

Masters of Directed Attentiveness: Sharpening the Mental Scalpel Through Disciplined Focus

"Directed attentiveness" is not simply about paying attention; it is about consciously directing and sustaining attention to relevant information and tasks while effectively filtering out distractions. This is the essence of selective awareness through disciplined focus, a key characteristic of effective leadership.

Scientific: The Neurocognitive Basis of Focused Executive Function

Neuroscience sheds light on the "directed attentiveness" of successful executives. They have effectively harnessed the power of the prefrontal cortex, the brain's region responsible for executive functions such as working memory, planning, decision-making, and cognitive control. This enables them to hyper-focus and analyze details with surgical precision. However, unlike their micromanaging counterparts, their amygdala, the seat of emotional response, is well-regulated, allowing for balanced and rational decision-making. This emotional control, achieved through selective awareness through disciplined emotional regulation, empowers them to delegate with confidence and trust.

- **Neurocognitive Connections:** This relates to the concept of executive control, which involves the ability to regulate thoughts, emotions, and actions to achieve goals. The prefrontal cortex plays a crucial role in this process, and its effective functioning is essential for directed attentiveness. Disciplined emotional regulation involves the interplay between the prefrontal cortex and the limbic system, allowing for conscious control over emotional responses.

Popular Science Conceptualizing: The High-Powered Computer of Focused Processing

Imagine an executive as a high-powered computer capable of both focused processing and broad overview. They can "zoom in" on specific tasks, analyzing data and identifying potential roadblocks with laser focus (selective awareness through disciplined analysis). However, unlike a basic computer program, they can also "zoom out," maintaining a clear picture of the bigger picture (selective awareness through disciplined perspective-taking). This allows them to delegate with precision, assigning tasks to the most qualified individuals while keeping the overarching goals firmly in sight.

- **Cognitive Concepts:** This relates to the concepts of focused attention and divided attention. Successful executives can effectively switch between these modes of attention, focusing on specific details when necessary while also maintaining awareness of the broader context.

Self-Help: Cultivating Focused Presence Through Disciplined Practice

Developing directed attentiveness is not about superhuman abilities; it is about mindful practice. Techniques like meditation and mindfulness exercises can enhance focus, concentration, and emotional regulation. By strengthening mental control through disciplined practice, you can achieve the clarity and composure needed to make strategic decisions and delegate effectively. This is the practice of selective awareness through disciplined mindfulness.

- **Psychological and Neurocognitive Connections:** Mindfulness and meditation practices have been shown to increase gray matter density in the prefrontal cortex and improve connectivity between different brain regions. This enhances executive function, attention regulation, and emotional control.

Thriller Twist: Thriving Under Pressure Through Focused Action

Imagine a high-stakes situation, a complex problem demanding immediate attention. The successful executive thrives in this environment. Their laser focus, achieved through selective awareness through disciplined action, allows them to analyze every detail, anticipate potential challenges, and formulate a winning strategy. But they are not lone wolves; they delegate tasks with the precision of a seasoned chess player, deploying their team members like skilled pawns on the corporate chessboard.

- **Psychological:** Mastering Internal Focus Through Disciplined Self-Awareness: The ability to maintain directed attentiveness is not just about managing external tasks; it is also about managing internal distractions. Successful executives are masters of self-awareness, practiced through disciplined introspection. They recognize their emotional triggers and develop coping mechanisms to maintain focus under pressure. This emotional intelligence, cultivated through selective awareness through disciplined emotional regulation, allows them to delegate with trust, knowing their team members can handle their assigned tasks with minimal supervision.

The Power of Influence: Beyond Direct Action—Inspiring the Collective Symphony Through Focused Connection

A successful executive does not rely solely on direct action or control to achieve results. They are masters of influence, inspiring and motivating their team members to excel beyond expectations through focused connection and communication. This influence is not manipulative but rather a natural outcome of embodying selective awareness through disciplined perception and fostering a shared vision.

Thriller Twist: Igniting Collective Fire Through Focused Communication

Imagine a charismatic leader delivering a speech, their words igniting a collective fire in the hearts of their team. This is the power of influence—the ability to orchestrate a symphony of peak performance from each individual through focused communication and shared purpose. This "fire" is fueled by shared values, clear communication of the vision, and genuine enthusiasm, all projected through selective awareness and disciplined communication.

- **Psychological and Neurocognitive Connections: This** relates to the psychological concepts of charisma, transformational leadership, and shared identity. Charismatic leaders often possess strong communication skills and the ability to connect with their audience on an emotional level. Neurobiologically, this can trigger mirror neuron activity in the listeners, leading to a sense of shared emotion and understanding. Focused communication ensures that the message is clear and concise and resonates with the audience's values and motivations.

Popular Science Conceptualizing: The Contagious Wave of Focused Enthusiasm

Think of influence as a contagious wave of enthusiasm spread through focused interaction. Successful executives understand the power of nonverbal communication, positive reinforcement, and shared goals. Their words and actions inspire a ripple effect of motivation throughout the team, propelling everyone toward a common objective. This "contagion" is facilitated by selective awareness through disciplined observation of team dynamics and focused communication of positive expectations.

- **Psychological and Neurocognitive Connections:** This relates to the concept of emotional contagion, where emotions are transmitted from one person to another through nonverbal cues and social interaction. Mirror neurons play a role in this process as well. Focused enthusiasm amplifies this effect by directing attention to positive emotions and reinforcing them through verbal and nonverbal communication.

Self-Help: Cultivating Authentic Influence Through Focused Self-Awareness

Developing your influence is a journey of self-discovery enhanced by focused self-awareness. Identify your leadership style, whether it is transformational, servant, or visionary. Authenticity is key; people respond best to leaders who are genuine and passionate about their goals. By fostering a sense of shared purpose and celebrating individual achievements through focused recognition, you create a fertile ground for collective excellence.

- **Psychological and Neurocognitive Connections:** This relates to the concept of emotional intelligence, which involves the ability to understand and manage one's own emotions and the emotions of others. Focused self-awareness is a crucial component of emotional intelligence, allowing individuals to identify their strengths and weaknesses, understand their emotional triggers, and develop effective coping mechanisms.

Psychological: Empathy and Emotional Intelligence Through Focused Connection

The power of influence is rooted in empathy and emotional intelligence, developed through focused connections with team members. Successful executives understand their team members' needs and motivations. They tailor their communication style to resonate with each individual, fostering trust and a sense of psychological safety. This allows them to delegate with confidence, knowing their team feels supported and empowered to contribute their best work.

- **Psychological and Neurocognitive Connections:** Empathy involves the ability to understand and share the feelings of others. This is facilitated by mirror neurons and other brain regions involved in social cognition. Focused connection enhances empathy by directing attention to team members' individual needs and perspectives. This creates a stronger sense of trust and rapport, which are essential for effective leadership and delegation.

Relational Efficiency: Building a Collaborative Masterpiece Through Focused Connection and Communication

Relational efficiency is not simply about having a friendly team; it's about cultivating a collaborative environment where focused connection and communication are guided by selective awareness through disciplined perception, maximizing team performance, and driving exceptional results.

Scientific: The Neurobiology of Collaborative Performance Through Focused Interaction

Studies have shown that strong social connections within a team can significantly enhance productivity. Successful executives cultivate this relational efficiency by fostering a collaborative environment based on trust, open communication, and mutual respect. This psychological safety, achieved through focused interaction and empathetic communication, allows for the free flow of ideas, leading to more innovative solutions and a more engaged workforce.

- **Neurocognitive Connections:** Social connections and positive interactions trigger the release of oxytocin, a hormone associated with bonding, trust, and social connection. This strengthens social bonds and promotes cooperation. Focused interaction enhances this by directing attention to the needs and perspectives of others, fostering empathy and rapport. This relates to the concept of social neuroscience, which studies the neural mechanisms underlying social behavior.

Popular Science Conceptualizing: The Glue of Focused Communication and Shared Purpose

Imagine a team where everyone feels valued, their voices heard, and their contributions appreciated. This essence of relational efficiency is achieved through selective awareness through disciplined communication. Successful executives create this environment by promoting open communication, celebrating diverse perspectives through focused recognition, and fostering a sense of camaraderie. Think of it as the glue that binds the team together, creating a synergy that elevates individual contributions into a masterpiece of collective achievement.

- **Psychological Concepts:** This relates to group cohesion, the sense of unity and belonging within a team. Strong group cohesion is associated with increased motivation, productivity, and job satisfaction. Focused communication ensures that everyone feels heard and understood, strengthening group cohesion. Focused recognition reinforces positive contributions and fosters a sense of shared purpose.

Thriller Twist: Navigating Challenges Through Focused Collaboration

A team riddled with distrust and communication breakdowns can quickly become a breeding ground for chaos and missed opportunities. Successful executives understand this and cultivate relational efficiency through focused collaboration. They foster a collaborative environment where information flows freely, allowing for swift decision-making and rapid responses to unexpected challenges. Imagine a team facing a crisis; their strong relationships and open communication, facilitated by focused collaboration, enable them to strategize effectively, delegate tasks with precision, and emerge from the situation stronger than ever.

- **Psychological and Neurocognitive Connections:** In stressful situations, strong social support can buffer the negative effects of stress and promote resilience. Focused collaboration ensures that team members can effectively communicate and coordinate their efforts, even under pressure. This relates to the concept of collective intelligence, the ability of a group to perform better than any individual member could alone.

Psychological: Psychological Safety Through Focused Empathy

Relational efficiency is not just about creating a feel-good environment; it is about fostering psychological safety through focused empathy. Successful executives create a space where team members feel comfortable taking calculated risks, sharing ideas without fear of judgment, and learning from mistakes. This psychological safety, cultivated through selective awareness and disciplined empathy, allows for the free flow of creativity and innovation, propelling the team toward groundbreaking solutions and exceptional results.

- **Psychological and Neurocognitive Connections:** Psychological safety is crucial to team performance and innovation. It allows individuals to feel comfortable expressing their ideas and taking risks without fear of negative consequences. Focused empathy helps create this environment by fostering trust and understanding between team members. This relates to the concept of trust and its role in social interactions.

Delegation with Expertise: Empowering the Orchestra Through Focused Assignment and Development

Effective delegation is not simply assigning tasks; it's about strategically empowering individuals by aligning tasks with their expertise and fostering their development through focused assignment and support, guided by selective awareness through disciplined perception.

Scientific: Leveraging Expertise Through Focused Task Allocation

Effective delegation is not just about assigning various tasks; rather, it is about strategically tapping into the skills of all individuals within a team. Successful executives understand the strengths and weaknesses of their team members through focused observation and analysis (selective awareness through disciplined assessment). This understanding allows for focused task allocation, ensuring that assigned tasks align with individual expertise, leading to better performance and a stronger sense of ownership.

- **Neurocognitive Connections:** This relates to the concept of cognitive specialization, where different brain regions are specialized for different functions. Executives are leveraging this specialization by assigning tasks that align with individual expertise, maximizing efficiency and performance. This also relates to working memory and cognitive load. By delegating tasks appropriately, executives reduce the cognitive load on individual team members, allowing them to focus more effectively on their assigned responsibilities.

Popular Science Conceptualizing: Conducting the Orchestra of Focused Contributions

Imagine an executive as a conductor and their team members as skilled musicians. Effective delegation is like assigning the right instrument to each player. A successful executive, through focused observation and communication (selective awareness through disciplined interaction), understands the strengths of each team member and assigns tasks that allow them to utilize their individual talents to their fullest potential. This creates a harmonious symphony of productivity, where every individual contributes their unique melody to the team's overall success.

- **Psychological Concepts:** This relates to team roles and the importance of having a diverse team with individuals who possess complementary skills. Effective delegation ensures that each team member has a clear role and understands how their contributions fit into the overall team goals.

Self-Help: Empowering Growth Through Focused Development and Trust

It all begins with self-awareness, practiced through disciplined introspection. As a leader, it is crucial to understand your own strengths and weaknesses. Then, through focused observation and communication, take the time to understand the strengths and weaknesses of your team members. Provide them with growth opportunities that allow them to develop skills in areas where they seek development. Empower your team with knowledge, set clear expectations through focused communication, and then delegate with confidence, knowing they have the capacity for excellence. This is the practice of selective awareness through disciplined trust.

- **Psychological and Neurocognitive Connections:** Providing growth opportunities and empowering team members contributes to their self-efficacy and intrinsic motivation. When individuals feel competent and autonomous, they are more likely to be engaged and perform at their best. Disciplined trust involves setting clear expectations, providing necessary resources and support, and then allowing individuals the autonomy to complete their tasks. This fosters a sense of ownership and responsibility, further enhancing motivation and performance. This relates to self-determination theory, which emphasizes the importance of autonomy, competence, and relatedness in promoting motivation and well-being.

In Conclusion

The essence of executive leadership is not individual brilliance but the ability to orchestrate collective excellence through focused orchestration, guided by selective awareness through disciplined perception. The successful executive is not a soloist but a conductor, drawing upon the diverse talents of their team to create a harmonious symphony of productivity. This orchestration is achieved through the consistent application of selective awareness through disciplined perception in several key areas:

- **Directed Attentiveness (Focused Focus): Using** disciplined focus to analyze details while maintaining a strategic overview, ensuring everyone is "playing the right notes."

- **Power of Influence (Focused Connection):** Inspiring and motivating team members through focused communication and fostering a shared vision.

- **Relational Efficiency (Focused Collaboration):** Building a collaborative environment based on trust, open communication, and mutual respect through focused interaction.

- **Delegation with Expertise (Focused Assignment and Development):** Empower team members by aligning tasks with their expertise and providing opportunities for growth through focused assignments and support.

These qualities, cultivated through selective awareness and disciplined perception, transform a manager into a true leader. By consciously practicing focus, connection, collaboration, assignment, and development, you improve your performance and empower your team to achieve remarkable things together.

Therefore, embrace the role of the conductor, practicing selective awareness through disciplined perception in every interaction and decision. By consciously directing your attention, fostering strong relationships, and empowering your team, you can lead them to a symphony of sustained success and create a lasting positive impact.

SECTION V

LIFE SPECIALIZATION: FUELING SELECTIVE AWARENESS

᠊ᢀᠯᠪᢀᠯᠪᢀᠯᠪ

I n a world overflowing with information and opportunities, the ability to focus—to selectively attend to what truly matters—is more crucial than ever. Life specialization is the strategic application of selective awareness through disciplined focus to achieve a specific, meaningful purpose. It's about consciously choosing where to direct your energy, expertise, and precious time to make the greatest impact, rather than spreading yourself thin across numerous, less impactful endeavors. It's not about limiting yourself, but rather about magnifying your potential by concentrating your efforts.

Imagine a laser beam, a concentrated form of light focused on a single, infinitesimal point. That focused energy can cut through steel, perform delicate surgical procedures, and transmit vast amounts of data across continents. Now, imagine that same amount of light scattered across a broad surface; it would have little to no discernible effect. This analogy perfectly illustrates the power of specialization. Just as the laser's focused beam achieves extraordinary results, specialized knowledge and skills, combined with disciplined perception, can empower you to achieve extraordinary results in your chosen field.

Life specialization, therefore, is not simply about acquiring a particular set of skills; it is about making a conscious commitment to a specific area of focus and then cultivating expertise within that domain through disciplined practice and continuous learning. It is about aligning your talents and passions with a clear purpose, creating a powerful synergy that drives you toward mastery. This disciplined approach to focus, facilitated by selective awareness, allows you to:

- **Filter the noise:** In a world of constant distractions, specialization helps you filter out irrelevant information and focus on what truly matters to your chosen field.

- **Deepen your understanding:** Concentrating your efforts allows you to delve deeper into a subject, developing a nuanced understanding that is impossible to achieve with a superficial approach.

- **Accelerate your skill development:** Focused practice and application within a specific domain lead to faster skill acquisition and mastery.

- **Maximize your impact:** By becoming an expert in a particular area, you can make a more significant contribution to your field and the world.

This chapter explores how specialization enhances selective awareness through disciplined focus, leading not only to mastery and a more fulfilling career but also to a life of purpose, where your unique talents and skills are used to make a real difference. It delves into the practical strategies and mindset shifts necessary to embrace specialization and harness its transformative power.

Focused Energy: The Path to Mastery Through Disciplined Specialization

Imagine a spotlight illuminating a single object, throwing everything else into shadow. This powerful image represents the essence of specialization—the disciplined channeling of your mental and physical energy into mastering a particular skill set or domain. This focused approach ignites selective awareness through disciplined specialization, transforming scattered potential into concentrated power.

Benefits of Specialization

a) **Increased Efficiency Through Focused Resource Allocation:** When you specialize through disciplined focus, you eliminate the cognitive drag of divided attention. No more scattered efforts or wasted mental energy trying to be a jack-of-all-trades. Instead, you develop laser focus, enabling you to accomplish more with less. This increased efficiency stems from reduced cognitive switching costs—the mental effort required to shift attention between different tasks.

- **Neurocognitive Connection:** This relates to the concept of attentional control, the brain's ability to focus on relevant information while ignoring distractions selectively. Disciplined specialization strengthens neural pathways associated with attentional control, leading to improved efficiency in information processing and task completion

b) **Greater Power Through Focused Expertise Development:** Specialization is not just about efficiency; it is about unlocking your full potential through focused expertise development. You develop a deeper understanding of your chosen field through disciplined practice, deliberate learning, and focused feedback. This expertise empowers you to tackle complex challenges, solve problems creatively, and achieve remarkable results. This deep understanding allows for developing schemas—mental frameworks that organize knowledge and facilitate efficient processing of information within the specialized domain.

- **Psychological and Neurocognitive Connections:** This relates to the concept of expertise development, which involves a process of deliberate practice, feedback, and refinement. Neurobiologically, this process leads to structural and functional changes in the brain, including increased gray matter density in relevant cortical areas and stronger connections between different brain regions. This also relates to long-term potentiation (LTP), the strengthening of synaptic connections through repeated activation, which underlies learning and memory

c) **Harmony with Definiteness of Purpose Through Focused Alignment:** Remember the concept of definiteness of purpose—the cornerstone of selective awareness? Disciplined specialization aligns perfectly with this principle. By dedicating yourself to a specific field with focused intent, you move closer to achieving your goals, ensuring your focused energy fuels your journey toward success. This alignment creates a powerful sense of intrinsic motivation, driving you to pursue mastery with passion and dedication.

- **Psychological Connection:** This relates to the concept of self-concordance, the alignment between one's goals and one's values and interests. When goals are self-concordant, individuals are more likely to be motivated and committed to achieving them

Disciplined Specialization: A Multifaceted Approach

Specialization is not about blind pursuit; it is a disciplined approach to learning and development. Imagine a skilled athlete meticulously honing their technique through focused practice. This same dedication, guided by disciplined perception, applies to any field. Disciplined specialization requires:

a) **Disciplined Perception: Focused Information Filtering:** You learn to filter out distractions, prioritizing information and experiences that are directly relevant to your chosen field. This refined selective awareness, practiced through disciplined perception, allows you to maintain a laser focus on your goals and avoid cognitive overload. This relates to the concept of selective attention, the ability to focus on specific stimuli while ignoring others.

- **Neurocognitive Connection:** The prefrontal cortex is responsible for attentional control and filtering irrelevant information. Disciplined perception strengthens these neural circuits, enhancing the ability to maintain focus and avoid distractions

b) **Conserving Mental and Physical Energy Through Focused Effort Allocation:** You conserve precious mental and physical energy by eliminating the mental strain of juggling multiple pursuits. This conserved energy, channeled through disciplined effort allocation, can then be invested in focused learning, practice, and innovation within your chosen field. This reduces cognitive fatigue and allows for more sustained and productive work.

- **Psychological and Neurocognitive Connections:** This relates to the concept of cognitive load theory, which suggests that working memory has limited capacity. Reducing the number of tasks being juggled simultaneously frees up cognitive resources for deeper processing and learning.

Strategies for Disciplined Specialization

a) **Strategic Resource Allocation:** Maximizing Impact Through Focused Investment: Specialization allows for strategically allocating resources—time, money, effort—towards a single, well-defined goal. This focused investment maximizes impact and accelerates progress. Instead of spreading resources thinly across multiple areas, you can concentrate them where they will have the greatest effect.

- **Practical Application:** This involves prioritizing tasks, setting clear budgets, and creating a strategic plan for resource utilization. For example, instead of subscribing to multiple general-interest magazines, a specialist might invest in a few highly specialized journals and attend industry-specific conferences.

- **Psychological and Economic Connections:** This connects to the concept of opportunity cost, the value of the next best alternative forgone when making a decision. By specializing, you are consciously choosing to forgo other opportunities to maximize your potential in a chosen field. This also has connections to return on investment (ROI) in economic terms. By focusing resources, you maximize the return on your investment of time and energy.

b) **Continuous Improvement Through Focused Feedback and Iteration:** Specialization fosters a cycle of continuous improvement through focused feedback and iteration. Concentrating on a specific domain makes it easier to identify areas for improvement, seek targeted feedback, and refine your skills through deliberate practice. This iterative learning, applying, and refining process is essential for achieving mastery.

- **Practical Application:** This involves actively seeking feedback from mentors, peers, and experts in your field, analyzing your performance, and making adjustments to your approach based on this feedback. This could involve keeping a learning journal, tracking your progress, and regularly reviewing your goals and strategies.

- **Psychological and Neurocognitive Connections:** This relates to the concept of deliberate practice, which involves focused, repetitive practice with feedback and reflection. Neurobiologically, this process strengthens neural connections and improves skill acquisition. This also connects to the concept of growth mindset, the belief that abilities can be developed through effort and learning.

c) **Building a Powerful Network Through Focused Engagement:** Specialization allows you to build a powerful network of like-minded individuals and experts in your field. By focusing your attention on a specific domain, you can connect with others who share your passion and expertise, creating opportunities for collaboration, mentorship, and knowledge sharing.

- **Practical Application:** This involves attending industry events, joining professional organizations, participating in online communities, and actively networking with others in your field.

- **Sociological and Psychological Connections:** This relates to the concept of social capital, the value of social networks and relationships. Strong social connections can provide access to resources, information, and opportunities to accelerate career growth and personal development. This also connects to the psychological need for belonging and connection.

In Conclusion

Life specialization, practiced through disciplined specialization, is not about narrowing your world but amplifying your impact within it. You unlock the transformative power of selective awareness by consciously choosing a specific domain and channeling your energy, resources, and attention with focused intent. This disciplined approach to specialization, guided by disciplined perception, is the true path to mastery.

This journey toward mastery involves several key elements, all interwoven with the practice of selective awareness through disciplined perception:

- **Maximizing Efficiency and Power:** By eliminating the distractions of divided attention and focusing on developing deep expertise, you achieve greater efficiency and unlock your full potential within your chosen field.

- **Aligning with Definiteness of Purpose:** Specialization provides a clear direction and purpose, fueling your motivation and driving you toward your goals with focused intent.

- **Cultivating Disciplined Perception:** By consciously filtering information and prioritizing relevant experiences, you sharpen your selective awareness and maintain laser focus.

- **Conserving Mental and Physical Energy:** By streamlining your efforts and avoiding the drain of multitasking, you conserve valuable energy for focused learning, practice, and innovation.

- **Strategically Allocating Resources:** By focusing your investments of time, money, and effort, you maximize your impact and accelerate your progress.

- **Committing to Continuous Improvement:** Through focused feedback and iteration, you constantly refine your skills and deepen your expertise, moving ever closer to mastery.

- **Building a Powerful Network: By** engaging with like-minded individuals and experts in your field, you create opportunities for collaboration, mentorship, and accelerated growth.

When practiced with disciplined perception, these elements create a powerful synergy that propels you towards mastery. Remember, the most brilliant light emanates from a single, focused source. So, embrace disciplined specialization, refine your focus through disciplined perception, and watch as your selective awareness propels you towards extraordinary achievement, a fulfilling career, and a life of purpose.

The Power of United Expertise: Specialization as a Force Multiplier Through Focused Collaboration

Specialization extends beyond individual pursuits, becoming a true force multiplier when diverse specialized units collaborate effectively. This is where selective awareness, practiced through disciplined collaboration and communication, becomes essential. It is about not only being an expert in your own domain but also understanding how your expertise integrates with the expertise of others to achieve a shared goal.

Principles of United Expertise

a) **Synergistic Collaboration Through Focused Communication:** United expertise thrives on effective communication and collaboration between specialized units. When individuals with different areas of expertise work together, they can generate solutions and innovations that would be impossible for any single individual to achieve alone. This synergistic collaboration is facilitated by focused communication and a shared understanding of the overall goals.

- **Psychological and Organizational Connections:** This relates to teamwork and the importance of effective communication, coordination, and cooperation within teams. It also connects to knowledge sharing, where individuals share their expertise and insights with others to improve collective performance.

b) **Emergent Properties Through Focused Integration:** When specialized units are effectively integrated, emergent properties can arise—new capabilities and outcomes that are greater than the sum of their parts. This is because the interaction between different areas of expertise creates new possibilities and perspectives. This focused integration requires a shared vision and a commitment to collaboration.

- **Complex Systems and Biological Connections:** This relates to the concept of emergence in complex systems, where complex patterns and behaviors arise from the interaction of simpler components. This is also seen in biological systems, such as the human body, where different organs work together to maintain life.

c) **Adaptive Capacity Through Focused Diversity:** A network of specialized units is more adaptable to change than a homogenous group. If one area of expertise becomes less relevant or important, the organization can adapt by reallocating resources and focusing on other areas. This focused diversity provides resilience and allows the organization to thrive in a dynamic environment.

- **Evolutionary and Strategic Connections:** This relates to the concept of adaptive evolution, where populations evolve to better adapt to their environment. In a business context, this translates to the ability to adapt to changing market conditions, technological advancements, and other external factors.

Practical Applications of United Expertise:

Department Stores: A Symphony of Focused Selection and Value Creation

The department store analogy effectively illustrates this principle. Each section (clothing, electronics, homeware) functions as a specialized team with highly informed specialists within its product lines. This focused expertise creates a superior customer experience through a wider selection of higher-quality products at competitive prices. Imagine a seasoned detective specializing in criminal behavior entering a department store after a crime. Their specialized knowledge, honed through years of focused observation and analysis (selective awareness through disciplined investigation), allows them to identify subtle clues that a generalist might miss.

- **Psychological and Organizational Connections:** This relates to the concept of distributed cognition, where cognitive processes are distributed across individuals and tools within a system. In a department store, the collective knowledge of the specialists is greater than any individual's knowledge, allowing for more effective problem-solving and decision-making

Beyond Efficiency: The Bargaining Power of Focused Collective Action

The benefits of specialization extend beyond individual expertise to the collective bargaining power of focused collective action. These distinct units, operating under a single organizational structure, gain a significant advantage through increased buying power. This allows for bulk purchasing, cost savings, and greater negotiating leverage with suppliers. This focused collective action is only possible through effective communication and coordination, facilitated by selective awareness through disciplined communication and collaboration.

- **Economic and Strategic Connections:** This relates to the concepts of economies of scale and competitive advantage. Specialization allows organizations to achieve economies of scale by producing or purchasing goods in larger quantities, reducing costs per unit. This cost advantage can then be passed on to consumers, creating a competitive advantage in the marketplace.

Sub-Specialization in Complex Systems: A Well-Oiled Machine

Specialization extends to sub-specialization within complex systems like banks. Each department (loan processing, wealth management) is further divided into specialized roles, ensuring that every step of a complex financial transaction is handled by an expert. Imagine a young professional seeking guidance from a wealth advisor or a specialist in financial planning. The advisor's focused expertise, combined with selective awareness through disciplined analysis of the client's needs, allows them to develop a personalized financial roadmap.

- **Organizational and Psychological Connections:** This relates to the concept of division of labor, which increases efficiency and productivity by assigning specialized tasks to different individuals. It also connects to the concept of job satisfaction, as individuals are more likely to be satisfied when they are able to use their skills and expertise effectively.

From Scattered Efforts to Abundant Harvests Through Focused Cultivation

The concept of specialization extends to agriculture as well. Farmers who focus on specific crops are more likely to achieve surplus production through focused cultivation. Their specialized knowledge of crop science and efficient farming techniques, combined with selective awareness through disciplined observation of their crops, leads to increased yields and profitability.

- **Ecological and Economic Connections:** Specialization in agriculture can lead to increased efficiency and productivity, but it can also have negative ecological consequences, such as monoculture and soil depletion. Sustainable specialization requires careful consideration of ecological factors and the implementation of sustainable farming practices.

Avoiding the Generalist Trap: Focused Effort Breeds Abundance

The passage emphasizes the limitations of a scattered approach. A farmer who dabbles in a variety of crops might struggle to excel in any single one. This aligns with the saying, "Jack of all trades, master of none." Specialization, guided by selective awareness through disciplined focus, allows individuals and organizations to concentrate their efforts, leading to increased productivity, exceptional skills, and greater rewards.

In Conclusion

When combined with focused collaboration, specialization transcends individual expertise and becomes a powerful force multiplier, creating synergistic outcomes far greater than the sum of individual parts. This "united expertise" is not a passive phenomenon; it requires conscious cultivation through selective awareness, disciplined perception, communication, and collaboration.

This chapter has explored how specialization acts as a force multiplier by examining its principles and practical applications:

Principles of United Expertise:

- **Synergistic Collaboration Through Focused Communication:** Effective communication and collaboration between specialized units generate innovative solutions and enhance collective performance.

- **Emergent Properties Through Focused Integration:** The integration of specialized knowledge and skills creates new capabilities and outcomes that are greater than the sum of individual contributions.

- **Adaptive Capacity Through Focused Diversity:** A network of specialized units is more adaptable and resilient to change.

Practical Applications of United Expertise:

- **Department Stores:** Demonstrating how specialized departments create a superior customer experience and leverage collective buying power.

- **Complex Systems (e.g., Banks):** This illustrates how sub-specialization ensures the efficient and effective handling of complex processes.

- **Agriculture:** Showing how specialized farming practices lead to increased yields and a more abundant food supply.

These examples and the principles they embody demonstrate that united expertise is not merely about having specialized individuals; it is about creating a system where those individuals can effectively communicate, collaborate, and integrate their expertise to achieve shared goals. This requires:

- **Focused Communication:** Clear, concise, and targeted communication between specialized units.

- **Focused Integration:** Conscious efforts to connect different areas of expertise and create synergistic outcomes.

- **Focused Diversity:** Recognizing the value of diverse perspectives and expertise in enhancing adaptability and innovation.

By cultivating these elements through selective awareness and disciplined perception, organizations and individuals can unlock the full potential of united expertise. Embrace specialization not as a silo but as a vital component of a thriving ecosystem of collaboration, where focused individual contributions combine to create a truly remarkable collective impact.

Cultivating Selective Awareness: The Journey to Your Niche Through Focused Self-Discovery

Selective awareness, the ability to focus on what truly matters, is not an innate talent; it is a skill cultivated through focused self-discovery and purposeful action guided by disciplined perception. It is a journey of understanding your unique strengths, passions, and values and then strategically applying that knowledge to find your niche.

Unveiling Your Inner Power Through Focused Introspection

The Spark of Self-Discovery: Igniting Focused Self-Reflection:

It all begins with self-discovery—understanding your unique strengths, talents, and passions. It is about finding what truly ignites your sense of purpose. Activities like focused self-reflection (selective awareness through disciplined introspection), exploring diverse interests with focused curiosity, and seeking guidance from mentors through focused listening can illuminate hidden potentials and reveal your inherent aptitudes.

- **Psychological and Neurocognitive Connections:** This relates to the psychological concepts of self-awareness, self-concept, and identity formation. Neurobiologically, self-reflection involves the prefrontal cortex and other brain regions associated with introspection and self-referential processing. Focused introspection enhances this process by directing attention inward and promoting a deeper understanding of one's inner world.

Identifying Your Values: Focusing on Your Core Principles

Self-discovery is not just about identifying your skills and interests but also about clarifying your values—the core principles guiding your decisions and actions. Understanding your values provides a strong foundation for choosing a niche that aligns with your deepest beliefs and motivates you to contribute meaningfully.

- **Practical Application:** This involves reflecting on past experiences, identifying what was most meaningful to you, and considering what kind of impact you want to have on the world. Tools like values clarification exercises and journaling can be helpful.

- **Psychological Connections:** This relates to the concept of values congruence, the alignment between one's personal values and the values of their work or organization. When values are congruent, individuals experience greater job satisfaction, motivation, and well-being.

Specialization: Channeling Your Power Through Focused Application

Once you have unearthed your inner power, it is time to channel it through focused application. This is where specialization comes in. You cultivate disciplined perception by focusing on a specific field that aligns with your strengths and interests. You train your mind to excel within a chosen niche, refining your skills and knowledge through focused practice and deliberate learning to become a true expert.

- **Psychological and Neurocognitive Connections**: This relates to the concept of deliberate practice, which involves focused, repetitive practice with feedback and reflection. Neurobiologically, this process strengthens neural connections and improves skill acquisition. This also connects to self-efficacy, the belief in one's ability to succeed in specific situations

Finding Your Place in the Grand Scheme Through Focused Contribution

A Contribution to Make: Focused Contribution Through Value Alignment:

Everyone has a valuable contribution to make. Just as a well-oiled machine requires specialized parts, society thrives when individuals leverage their unique talents through focused contribution. Self-discovery, guided by selective awareness through disciplined assessment of your values and the world's needs, helps you identify the specific role you were meant to play, the niche where your skills can shine the brightest and make a meaningful impact.

- **Psychological and Sociological Connections:** This relates to the concept of social roles and the importance of individuals finding their place within society. It also connects to the psychological need for purpose and meaning.

Preparation with Purpose: Focused Preparation Through Goal Alignment:

Preparation has the most impact when it is directed towards a specific goal. Self-discovery, practiced with focused intention, helps you define that goal—your chosen niche. With a clear target in mind, your preparation becomes focused and purposeful, accelerating your journey to mastery.

- **Psychological and Neurocognitive Connections:** This relates to goal-setting theory, which emphasizes the importance of setting specific, measurable, achievable, relevant, and time-bound (SMART) goals. Neurobiologically, having a clear goal activates the prefrontal cortex and enhances executive functions like planning and motivation.

Exploring Different Avenues: Focused Experimentation and Learning

Exploring Different Avenues: Focused Experimentation and Learning: Do not be afraid to explore different avenues and experiment with various interests. This focused experimentation, guided by selective awareness through disciplined exploration, allows you to gain firsthand experience, discover hidden talents, and refine your understanding of what truly resonates with you. It is about actively seeking out opportunities to learn and grow, even if they are outside your comfort zone.

- **Practical Application:** This could involve taking online courses, volunteering, shadowing professionals in different fields, or pursuing personal projects.

- **Psychological and Learning Connections:** This relates to the concept of experiential learning, where knowledge and skills are acquired through active engagement and reflection. It also connects to the concept of growth mindset, the belief that abilities can be developed through effort and learning

Refining Your Path Through Focused Analysis and Connection

Analyzing Feedback and Adapting: Focused Refinement Through Disciplined Assessment

As you explore and experiment, it is crucial to analyze feedback from others and reflect on your own experiences. This focused refinement, achieved through selective awareness through disciplined assessment, allows you to identify areas for improvement, adjust your course as needed, and continuously refine your understanding of your niche.

- **Practical Application:** This involves actively seeking feedback from mentors, peers, and supervisors, reflecting on your successes and failures, and making adjustments to your approach based on this feedback.

- **Psychological and Neurocognitive Connections:** This relates to the concept of metacognition, thinking about one's own thinking and learning processes. It also connects to the concept of feedback loops, where information about the results of an action is used to adjust future actions.

Building a Support Network: Focused Connection and Collaboration

Finding your niche is not a solitary endeavor. Building a support network of mentors, peers, and other professionals in your field can provide valuable guidance, support, and opportunities for collaboration. This focused connection, cultivated through selective awareness through disciplined networking, can accelerate your progress and provide a sense of belonging and community.

- **Practical Application:** This involves attending industry events, joining professional organizations, and actively networking with others in your field.

- **Sociological and Psychological Connections:** This relates to the concept of social capital and the importance of social connections for career success and personal well-being.

Concentration Through Self-Knowledge: Focused Effort Through Strategic Alignment

Concentration refers to the ability to focus one's mental and physical resources on a specific task or goal. However, concentration is most effective when it is informed by a deep understanding of oneself—one's strengths, weaknesses, values, interests, and motivations. Self-knowledge provides the compass that directs one's concentration toward the most fruitful areas.

Psychological and Neurocognitive Connections

- **Metacognition:** Self-knowledge is closely tied to metacognition, the ability to think about one's own thinking. You can optimize your concentration strategies by understanding how you learn, process information, and make decisions.

- **Self-regulation:** Self-knowledge allows for better self-regulation—the ability to control impulses, emotions, and behaviors. This is crucial for maintaining concentration in the face of distractions and challenges.

- **Motivation and Engagement:** When you understand what truly motivates you, you are more likely to be engaged and focused on tasks that align with your values and interests. This intrinsic motivation fuels deeper concentration and more sustained effort.

Focused Effort Through Strategic Alignment:

This refers to the practice of directing your energy and actions towards goals and tasks that are congruent with your self-knowledge. Strategic alignment involves making conscious choices about where to invest your time and energy based on your strengths and priorities. It is about maximizing your return on effort by focusing on activities that play to your strengths and contribute to your overall purpose.

Practical Applications

- **Identifying Your Strengths and Weaknesses:** Through self-assessment, feedback from others, and experimentation, identify your core strengths and areas for improvement. Focus your efforts on leveraging your strengths and developing skills that support them.

- **Setting SMART Goals:** Set Specific, Measurable, Achievable, Relevant, and Time-bound goals that align with your values and long-term vision. This provides a clear direction for your efforts.

- **Prioritizing Tasks:** Use prioritization techniques (e.g., the Eisenhower Matrix) to focus on the most important and impactful tasks. This ensures that your efforts are directed towards high-value activities.

- **Creating a Supportive Environment:** Design your environment to minimize distractions and support your concentration. This could involve creating a dedicated workspace, setting clear boundaries with others, and using tools and techniques to manage your time and attention.

Psychological and Organizational Connections

- **Job Crafting:** This involves proactively changing your job's tasks, relationships, and perceptions to better align with your strengths and interests. Strategic alignment with self-knowledge can inform effective job crafting.

- **Organizational Fit:** When your personal values and goals align with the values and goals of an organization, you are more likely to be engaged, productive, and satisfied. Self-knowledge plays a crucial role in finding a good organizational fit.

Example

Imagine two individuals who want to improve their writing skills. One person writes for hours every day without a clear plan or focus. The other, on the other hand, after reflecting on his strengths and weaknesses, realizes he is good at generating ideas but struggles with grammar and structure. They then strategically focus their efforts on improving their writing through targeted exercises and feedback. The second person, through strategic alignment with self-knowledge, is likely to make much faster progress.

In summary, "Concentration Through Self-Knowledge: Focused Effort Through Strategic Alignment" emphasizes that true concentration and effective effort are not about brute force but about aligning your actions with a deep understanding of yourself. By strategically focusing your energy on activities that contribute to your strengths and overall purpose, you maximize your impact and achieve greater fulfillment.

In Conclusion

Cultivating selective awareness and finding your niche is not a passive search; it is an active and ongoing journey of focused self-discovery guided by disciplined perception. It is about consciously directing your attention inward to understand your core values, strengths, and passions and then strategically applying that understanding to find where you can make the greatest contribution.

This journey navigated through selective awareness and disciplined perception, involves several interconnected stages:

- **Unveiling Your Inner Power:** This begins with igniting the spark of self-reflection, identifying your core values, and channeling your energy through focused specialization.

- **Finding Your Place in the Grand Scheme:** Understanding how your unique talents can contribute to the world, preparing with focused intent towards your chosen niche, and exploring different avenues through focused experimentation.

- **Refining Your Path:** This crucial stage involves analyzing feedback with disciplined assessment, building a supportive network through focused connection, and concentrating your efforts through strategic alignment with your evolving self-knowledge.

By embracing these stages and consistently practicing selective awareness through disciplined perception, you unlock the potential to not only find your niche but also to thrive within it. It is about more than just finding a job; it is about discovering your calling, contributing your unique talents to the world, and living a life of purpose and fulfillment. So, embark on this exciting adventure of focused self-discovery, embrace specialization through disciplined application, and watch your selective awareness blossom, guiding you towards a meaningful and impactful life.

The Power of Focus: Climbing the Ladder of Specialization Through Disciplined Expertise Development

Specialization is not merely about mastering a specific skill; it is a potent engine for career advancement, propelling you up the ladder of professional success through focused expertise development. By concentrating your efforts and cultivating deep expertise, you become a valuable asset, highly sought after for your unique abilities.

Sharpening Your Sword: From Novice to Master Through Focused Practice

The journey from novice to master is a testament to the power of focused practice and specialization.

From Novice to Master Through Focused Practice

Imagine an apprentice blacksmith. They might start with learning various metalwork skills—forging tools, making ornaments, or fixing broken pots and pans. However, to become the very best in their craft, they need to laser-focus their concentration on a specific area, such as sword-making. This hyper-focus enables the art of sword-making to reach deep into perfecting the right techniques, such as hardening steel and striking the right balance between strength and flexibility. Years of specialization, guided by selective awareness through disciplined practice, sharpen the craftsman's skills and, in a very real sense, enable the graduation of an apprentice into a master swordsmith whose blades are sought out by both warriors and collectors.

- **Psychological and Neurocognitive Connections:** This relates to the concept of deliberate practice, which involves focused, repetitive practice with feedback and reflection.

Neurobiologically, this process strengthens neural connections and improves skill acquisition through long-term potentiation (LTP).

- **Example:** A novice programmer might learn basic coding in several languages. However, to become a sought-after software engineer, they might specialize in a specific area like AI development, focusing their practice on algorithms, machine learning models, and related technologies.

Mental Discipline Through Focused Cognitive Training

Specialization is not just about acquiring skills but about developing mental discipline through focused cognitive training. By focusing on a specific area, you train your brain to filter out distractions and channel your energy into mastering a particular craft. Imagine a detective specializing in cybercrime. Their years of honing their focus, guided by selective awareness through disciplined analysis of digital evidence, allow them to navigate the intricate digital landscape with laser focus, sifting through mountains of data to identify the tiniest digital footprint left by a perpetrator. This focused cognitive training provides a significant advantage, allowing them to crack cases that might bewilder a generalist investigator.

- **Neurocognitive Connections:** This relates to cognitive control, the ability to regulate thoughts, emotions, and actions to achieve goals. Specialization strengthens neural pathways associated with cognitive control, improving attention, working memory, and decision-making.

- **Example:** A general physician might have a broad understanding of medicine. However, through specialized training and focused experience, a cardiologist develops a deep understanding of the cardiovascular system, allowing them to diagnose and treat complex heart conditions with greater precision.

Thriller Twist: Expertise Under Pressure Through Focused Action

Specialization can also be a significant asset in high-pressure situations. For example, think of a bomb disposal expert working in the midst of a hostage situation. Years of specialized training, combined with selective awareness through disciplined action under pressure, take over as the individual carefully examines the bomb, identifies its components, and proceeds to carry out the defusing process with practiced ease. Their specialist knowledge and focused action stand between a devastating explosion and the successful resolution of a potentially hazardous situation.

- **Psychological Connections:** This relates to the concept of automaticity, where skills become so well-practiced that they can be performed with minimal conscious effort. This allows experts to perform complex tasks under pressure without becoming overwhelmed.

- **Example:** A pilot undergoing emergency training practices specific procedures repeatedly until they become automatic. In a real emergency, this specialized training allows them to react quickly and effectively, even under extreme stress.

Promotions Through Focused Expertise and Strategic Positioning

Specialization is not just about acquiring skills; it is about strategically positioning yourself for career advancement through focused expertise development and targeted skill application. Becoming an indispensable asset in a specific area significantly increases your value to any organization and accelerates your progress up the career ladder.

Advancement Through Focused Contribution and Recognition

The path to promotion is often paved with demonstrable expertise and impactful contributions within a specialized area. As you embark on the journey of specialization, the experience, combined with focused self-reflection (selective awareness through disciplined introspection), allows you to identify an area where you can become indispensable to an organization. For example, a marketing professional might start by handling various tasks, from email campaigns to print advertisements. However, suppose they develop a particular interest in social media and decide to specialize in it. This focused expertise allows them to master ever-changing trends, innovate new marketing strategies through focused analysis, and closely monitor campaign performance through focused observation. This focused contribution and demonstrable expertise set them apart as an ideal candidate for a social media manager position, putting them on the fast track up the corporate ladder.

- **Organizational and Economic Connections:** This relates to the concept of human capital, the skills, knowledge, and experience an individual possesses that contribute to their economic value. By specializing, you increase your human capital in a specific area, making you more valuable to employers. This also connects to the concept of supply and demand. Suppose there is a high demand for a particular skill set and a limited supply of qualified individuals. In that case, those with specialized expertise are more likely to be promoted and command higher salaries.

  Example: A general software developer might know multiple programming languages. However, if they specialize in cybersecurity, they become highly sought after due to the increasing demand for cybersecurity professionals. This specialization makes them a prime candidate for promotions to security architect or lead security engineer roles.

Self-Help: Personal Fulfillment Through Focused Mastery and Ownership

Specialization is not just about external recognition; it is also about personal fulfillment. When you focus on a specific area and develop mastery through focused practice, you cultivate a sense of accomplishment and pride in your work. Imagine a graphic designer who specializes in creating user interfaces (UIs). Through years of honing their skills with focused attention to user experience and design principles, they become adept at crafting intuitive and visually appealing interfaces that enhance user experience. This focused mastery allows them to take ownership of their work and find deep satisfaction in creating products people love using.

- **Psychological Connections:** This relates to the concept of intrinsic motivation, which is driven by internal rewards such as satisfaction, accomplishment, and a sense of purpose. When you are intrinsically motivated, you are more likely to be engaged and persistent and find fulfillment in your work. This also connects to the concept of flow, a state of deep immersion and engagement in an activity that is both challenging and rewarding.

- **Example:** A musician who specializes in a particular instrument, such as the violin, may spend years practicing scales, etudes, and concertos. Through this focused dedication, they develop technical proficiency and a deep appreciation for the instrument and the music they create, leading to a profound sense of personal fulfillment.

Beyond the Grind: Strategic Versatility Through Focused Specialization and Adaptability

Strategic versatility is not about being a "jack-of-all-trades"; it is about building a strong foundation of diverse skills and then strategically specializing in a specific area, allowing for both depth of expertise and adaptability to change. This is achieved through the strategic application of selective awareness through disciplined learning, analysis, and adaptation.

A Well-Rounded Foundation: Building Cognitive Flexibility Through Focused Exploration

A versatile foundation is crucial, especially early in your career. Gaining experience in various areas broadens your perspective and equips you with a well-rounded skillset, fostering cognitive flexibility. The blacksmith apprentice, for instance, might benefit from learning various metalworking techniques—welding, casting, and even basic blacksmithing repairs—before specializing in sword-making. This initial exposure to diverse techniques, approached with focused exploration and learning, allows them to develop a strong understanding of the underlying principles of metalworking, which proves invaluable as they delve deeper into the intricacies of sword crafting.

- **Neurocognitive Connections:** Early exposure to a variety of skills strengthens cognitive flexibility, the ability to switch between different thought processes, and adapt to new situations. This is linked to increased connectivity between different brain regions, particularly the prefrontal cortex.

  Example: A business student might take courses in marketing, finance, accounting, and operations management. This broad exposure gives them a solid understanding of how different business functions interact, preparing them for future specialization in a specific area like financial analysis or marketing strategy.

Scientific Exploration: Enhancing Adaptability Through Focused Learning

Neuroscience tells us that early exposure to a variety of skills can strengthen cognitive flexibility. This allows you to adapt to new situations and approach problems from different angles. Imagine a marketing professional with a background in psychology. Their understanding of human behavior gained through focused study and observation, can inform their social media marketing strategies, allowing them to craft targeted campaigns that resonate with specific demographics. This cognitive flexibility, a product of a well-rounded foundation, gives them a competitive edge in the ever-evolving marketing landscape.

- **Psychological Connections:** This relates to the concept of transfer of learning, where knowledge and skills learned in one context can be applied to other contexts. A broad foundation increases the likelihood of positive transfer of learning.

  Example: A software engineer with experience with both front-end and back-end development is better equipped to understand the complexities of full-stack development and can more easily adapt to projects requiring expertise in both areas.

Strategic Specialization: Navigating the Path to Mastery Through Focused Application

While a broad foundation is valuable, strategic specialization is crucial for true career advancement.

Imagine a climber scaling a mountain. They might start by traversing different terrains—rocky slopes, dense forests, even icy glaciers—building their overall strength and agility. But to reach the summit, they need to focus on a specific path, strategically using their climbing skills, guided by selective awareness through disciplined route planning, to navigate the final, challenging ascent. Similarly, a marketing professional with a strong foundation in various marketing channels can leverage their experience to specialize in social media marketing, propelling them towards higher positions within that field.

- **Strategic Connections:** This relates to the concept of competitive advantage. By specializing in a high-demand area, you differentiate yourself from generalists and increase your competitive advantage in the job market.

  Example: Given the growing demand for skilled IT project managers, a project manager with experience in various industries might choose to specialize in IT project management. This specialization makes them more attractive to technology companies.

Maximizing Long-Term Career Success Through Focused Growth and Adaptation

The combination of a well-rounded foundation and strategic specialization, guided by selective awareness through disciplined learning and adaptation, allows you to excel in your chosen field and adapt to the ever-changing demands of the modern workplace.

Futureproofing Your Skillset Through Focused Learning

Specialization allows you to develop a deep understanding of the latest trends and technologies within your chosen field through focused learning. Imagine a software engineer specializing in artificial intelligence (AI). Their focused attention allows them to stay abreast of cutting-edge AI research and development advancements. This future-proofs their skillset, ensuring they remain relevant and in demand as AI continues transforming various industries.

- **Technological and Economic Connections: This** relates to the concept of continuous learning and the importance of staying up-to-date with technological advancements in your field.

Example: To remain competitive, a financial analyst specializing in fintech needs to continuously learn about new technologies like blockchain, cryptocurrency, and algorithmic trading.

Lifelong Learning: Cultivating a Growth Mindset Through Focused Development

The pursuit of specialization fosters a growth mindset. You cultivate a lifelong love of learning by constantly seeking new knowledge and honing your expertise through focused development. Imagine a data analyst who specializes in financial modeling. Their dedication to specialization compels them to stay updated on the latest statistical techniques and financial data analysis tools. This lifelong learning ensures they can tackle complex financial problems with ever-increasing efficiency and accuracy.

- **Psychological Connections:** This reinforces the concept of a growth mindset, the belief that abilities can be developed through effort and learning.

  Example: A teacher specializing in special education must continually learn about new research and best practices in the field to effectively support their students.

The Power of Networks: Building Strategic Connections Through Focused Engagement

Specialization connects you with a dedicated community of like-minded professionals. Imagine a graphic designer specializing in user experience (UX) design. Their focus on this specific field allows them to connect with other UX designers through online forums, industry conferences, and professional organizations. This focused engagement builds a valuable network that provides invaluable opportunities to share knowledge, collaborate on projects, and stay informed about the latest UX design trends.

- **Sociological and Career Connections:** This reinforces the importance of networking and building professional relationships.

  Example: A lawyer specializing in intellectual property law benefits from connecting with other IP lawyers, patent attorneys, and technology experts

Branching Out from the General: Achieving Greater Impact Through Focused Specialization

Moving beyond general knowledge and embracing specialization is a strategic move that unlocks greater impact, both professionally and personally. By focusing your expertise, you increase your value in the marketplace and discover deeper meaning and fulfillment in your work.

Reaping the Rewards of Focused Expertise

Specialization offers significant advantages that extend beyond simply acquiring skills.

Increased Earning Potential Through Focused Value Creation

The idea emphasizes the financial rewards of specialization. You increase your value in the job market by focusing on a specific area and becoming an expert through focused skill development. Imagine a general mechanic versus a specialist in high-performance engines. The mechanic might rely on a broad toolbox of skills to fix everyday car problems. The engine specialist, however, possesses a deep understanding of complex engine mechanics gained through focused study and hands-on experience, allowing them to diagnose and repair intricate issues that would leave a general mechanic stumped. This specialized expertise makes them a highly sought-after commodity, commanding a higher salary and potentially opening doors to lucrative consulting opportunities.

- **Economic and Market Connections**: This relates to the economic principles of supply and demand and specialized labor markets. When demand for a specific skill exceeds the supply of qualified individuals, those with specialized expertise can command higher wages.

  Example: A general contractor might be able to handle basic home renovations. However, a contractor specializing in green building practices, with expertise in sustainable materials and energy-efficient design, can command higher fees due to the growing demand for eco-friendly construction.

Intensifying Impact Through Focused Energy Application

Think of specialization as a laser beam. A generalist's skills are like a broad light source, illuminating a wide area but lacking intensity. A specialist's focus, however, intensifies their skills, transforming them into a powerful beam that can penetrate even the most complex problems through focused energy application. This allows them to solve issues faster and more precisely, making them invaluable assets within their chosen field.

- **Physics and Engineering Connections:** This analogy relates to energy density and power principles. Concentrating energy into a smaller area increases its intensity and effectiveness.

  Example: A general software developer might be able to create basic websites. However, a specialist in machine learning, with focused expertise in algorithms and statistical modeling, can develop complex AI systems that solve challenging problems in fields like healthcare or finance.

Self-Help: Purpose and Fulfillment Through Focused Community and Contribution

Specialization can also lead to a greater sense of purpose and fulfillment. When you dedicate yourself to mastering a specific skill through focused dedication, you become part of a larger community of experts. Imagine a software developer who specializes in creating artificial intelligence applications. Connecting with other AI specialists through focused engagement allows them to share knowledge, collaborate on projects, and contribute to advancing this rapidly evolving field. This sense of belonging to a community with a shared passion fuels their motivation and fosters a sense of purpose in their work.

- **Psychological and Sociological Connections:** This relates to the psychological needs for belonging, connection, and meaning. Being part of a specialized community provides a sense of belonging and allows individuals to connect with others who share their interests and values.

  Example: A researcher focused on a particular field, such as cancer biology, joins a worldwide consortium of scientists dedicated to discovering novel therapies and cures. This commitment to a broader cause imparts a profound sense of purpose and satisfaction.

Specialization Breeds Opportunity Through Focused Expertise and Strategic Positioning

Specialization enhances your current role and creates new and exciting opportunities for career advancement and impactful contributions. Becoming a recognized expert in a specific domain opens doors to a wider range of possibilities, allowing you to leverage your expertise for greater impact and influence.

Expanding Horizons Through Focused Expertise and Strategic Visibility

Specialization acts as a catalyst for new opportunities by enhancing your visibility and demonstrating your unique value proposition. Specialization can open doors to new opportunities within your field. Through focused skill development and strategic networking (selective awareness through disciplined engagement with the professional community), the social media marketing expert might be offered a position managing social media campaigns for a prestigious brand. Their specialized skillset grants them access to a wider range of career options, allowing them to leverage their expertise to work on high-profile projects and potentially secure leadership positions within the social media marketing domain.

- **Career and Networking Connections:** This relates to the concept of career capital, the skills, knowledge, and experience that make you valuable in the job market. Specialization increases your career capital in a specific area, making you more attractive to potential employers. Strategic networking further enhances your visibility and creates opportunities for career advancement.

- **Example:** A lawyer specializing in environmental law might be offered a position at a leading environmental advocacy organization, or a government agency focused on environmental policy. Their specialized expertise makes them a valuable asset in these settings.

Scientific Advancement Through Focused Research and Innovation

Specialization means you focus on a specific area, get to know the most up-to-date developments in that area through focused research, and stay at the leading edge of your particular industry. This focused research and knowledge acquisition (selective awareness through disciplined study) automatically make you an asset in the eyes of companies that want innovation and prefer to keep ahead of their competition. For example, a medical researcher specializing in gene editing can stay updated on recent breakthroughs, through a focused study of CRISPR technology and other gene-editing tools, leading to life-changing discoveries against diseases.

- **Scientific and Technological Connections:** This relates to the concept of scientific progress, which is often driven by specialized research in specific areas. Specialization allows researchers to delve deeper into complex problems and make significant contributions to their fields.

- **Example:** A materials scientist specializing in nanotechnology might develop new materials with unique properties that can be used in various applications, from electronics to medicine. Their specialized knowledge and focused research drive innovation in their field.

Thriller Twist: Critical Impact in High-Stakes Situations Through Focused Response and Action

Specialization can also be crucial in high-stakes situations. Imagine a cybersecurity specialist responding to a large-scale cyberattack. Their years of focusing on network security protocols and intrusion detection, combined with selective awareness through disciplined analysis of network traffic and system logs, allow them to quickly identify the source of the attack, implement containment measures, and mitigate the damage. This specialized expertise and focused action play a critical role in protecting sensitive data and safeguarding critical infrastructure.

- **Risk Management and Security Connections:** This relates to the importance of specialized expertise in managing and mitigating risks in complex and high-stakes environments.

- **Example:** A pilot specializing in emergency procedures is better equipped to handle unexpected events during a flight, such as engine failure or severe weather. Their specialized training and focused response can prevent a potential disaster

In Conclusion

When channeled through disciplined expertise development and strategic positioning, the power of focus is a powerful catalyst for career advancement and impactful contributions. Specialization is not about limiting your options; it is about maximizing your potential by concentrating your energy and attention on a specific domain, guided by selective awareness through disciplined perception.

This subdivision has explored how focused expertise development propels individuals up the ladder of specialization and creates new opportunities:

- **From Novice to Master Through Focused Practice:** Dedicated practice and refinement within a specific area lead to mastery and recognition as an expert.

- **Promotions Through Focused Contribution and Recognition:** Demonstrating expertise through impactful contributions and strategic networking opens doors to career advancement.

- **Expanding Horizons Through Focused Expertise and Strategic Visibility:** Specialization enhances visibility and creates new opportunities for impactful work and leadership roles.

These pathways to professional growth are all underpinned by the consistent application of selective awareness through disciplined perception, which allows you to:

- **Sharpen Your Skills Through Focused Learning:** Concentrating your learning and practice can help you develop deep expertise and stay at the cutting edge of your field.

- **Navigate Complex Challenges Through Focused Analysis:** Specialization equips you with the tools and knowledge to tackle intricate problems faster and more precisely.

- **Seize New Opportunities Through Focused Engagement:** By strategically positioning yourself and building a strong professional network, you expand your horizons and create new possibilities.

Therefore, embrace the power of focus and embark on the journey of disciplined expertise development. By consciously directing your attention, honing your skills, and strategically positioning yourself within your chosen field, you can unlock your full potential, achieve remarkable career success, and make a lasting impact. Remember, the path to mastery and impactful contributions is paved with focused effort, guided by selective awareness through disciplined perception.

The Path to Purpose: Evolving Through Selective Awareness Through Disciplined Adaptation

Life is a dynamic journey, and our goals, like ourselves, constantly evolve. Selective awareness, practiced through disciplined adaptation, empowers us to navigate these shifts and refine our major purpose when a new and compelling calling emerges. This process of evolution is not about abandoning previous pursuits but about integrating new insights and aligning with a deeper understanding of ourselves and our place in the world.

The Call to Something More: Recognizing and Responding to Focused Inner Guidance

An intense inward urge, a desire for greater fulfillment, frequently indicates the onset of a new purpose.

Aligning with Your True Self Through Focused Introspection

The core principle is the discovery of a true self-call. This is not a fleeting whim or a reaction to temporary setbacks; it is a deep, internal yearning for a new direction, a purpose that resonates with your core values and ignites your passion. This requires focused introspection (selective awareness through disciplined self-reflection) to discern genuine callings from transient desires. Imagine Marie Curie, a brilliant physicist, initially focused on studying magnetism. However, a compelling call emerged when she discovered the phenomenon of radioactivity. This ignited a new passion, leading her to dedicate her life to pioneering the field of nuclear science. Her story exemplifies how selective awareness and the disciplined perception of new information can guide us toward a purpose that aligns with our deepest curiosity and potential.

- **Psychological and Neurocognitive Connections:** From a psychological standpoint, this true self-call can be understood as a form of self-actualization, as described in Abraham Maslow's hierarchy of needs. Once our basic needs are met, we strive to fulfill our potential and achieve a sense of purpose. Neurobiologically, this involves the prefrontal cortex, responsible for higher-level cognitive functions like self-awareness, goal setting, and decision-making. Focused introspection strengthens neural pathways associated with these functions.

  Example: A successful corporate lawyer might experience a growing desire to contribute to social justice. This internal call might lead them to transition to a career in human rights law, aligning their professional life with their deeply held values.

Avoiding the Quicksand of Discouragement Through Focused Self-Assessment

This change should not be a knee-jerk reaction to difficulties. Challenges are inevitable on any path. However, constantly abandoning ship due to temporary setbacks will only lead to frustration and a lack of progress. Through focused self-assessment, it is important to distinguish between passing discouragement and a genuine misalignment with your current purpose. Self-help techniques like journaling, meditation, and focused reflection can help you gain clarity on your true desires and differentiate between temporary frustrations and a fundamental misalignment with your current goals.

- **Psychological Connections:** This relates to the concept of resilience, the ability to bounce back from adversity. It also connects to emotional regulation, the ability to manage and control one's emotions.

  Example: A writer facing writer's block might feel discouraged. However, through focused self-assessment, they might realize that the block is due to a lack of research on a specific topic, not a lack of passion for writing. They can overcome the obstacle by addressing the research gap and continue pursuing their writing goals.

Self-Help: Cultivating Emotional Intelligence Through Focused Self-Awareness

The operative word here is emotional intelligence, developed through focused self-awareness. It is about knowing your feelings, understanding why you feel that way through focused introspection, and developing strategies to manage those emotions effectively. There is nothing inherently wrong with feeling discouraged; rather, stepping back and reflecting on what is discouraging you and relating this to your overall sense of purpose gives you clarity about whether to continue on a path or take another route altogether.

- **Psychological and Neurocognitive Connections:** Emotional intelligence involves several key components, including self-awareness, self-regulation, motivation, empathy, and social skills. Focused self-awareness is the foundation of emotional intelligence, allowing individuals to recognize and understand their own emotions. This involves the prefrontal cortex and the limbic system responsible for emotional processing and regulation.

  Example: A salesperson experiencing a string of rejections might feel discouraged. By practicing focused self-awareness, they might realize their discouragement stems from a fear of failure. By addressing this fear through cognitive reframing techniques, they can regain their confidence and continue pursuing their sales goals.

The Price of Transformation: Embracing Strategic Disengagement for Focused Growth

Transforming your purpose often requires strategic disengagement from previous pursuits to embrace new opportunities fully. This process, guided by selective awareness through disciplined evaluation and acceptance, involves recognizing and accepting "acceptable losses" to pave the way for focused growth in a new direction.

Embracing Acceptable Losses Through Focused Evaluation and Acceptance

Change often necessitates sacrifice. There might be skills you have developed, relationships you have cultivated, or experiences you have accumulated that will not be directly applicable to your new path. The concept acknowledges this "acceptable loss," which can be significant. Be prepared to let go of some aspects of your past through focused evaluation and acceptance to fully embrace your future opportunities. Think of Leonardo da Vinci, a master of multiple disciplines—painting, sculpting, engineering, and anatomy. While his early training focused on traditional painting techniques, his selective awareness and disciplined evaluation of his diverse interests led him to embrace a wider range of scientific and artistic pursuits. He understood that letting go of a singular focus was necessary to fully explore his genius's breadth. This involved accepting the "loss" of potentially becoming a purely traditional painter to achieve a greater, more multifaceted impact.

- **Psychological Connections:** This relates to the concept of cognitive dissonance, the discomfort experienced when holding conflicting beliefs or values. Letting go of past pursuits can create cognitive dissonance, but accepting the "loss" and focusing on the new purpose can resolve this dissonance. This also connects to the concept of loss aversion, the tendency to feel the pain of a loss more strongly than the pleasure of an equivalent gain. Recognizing this bias can help individuals make more rational decisions about letting go.

  Example: A successful sales manager might decide to pursue a career in teaching. This might involve accepting a lower initial salary and giving up the status and perks associated with their previous role. However, they accept these "losses" to pursue a more fulfilling career aligned with their passion for education.

Scientific exploration: Synaptic Pruning for Focused Neural Resource Allocation

Neuroscience tells us that the brain constantly forms new neural connections and prunes unused pathways. Letting go of skills from your previous path can be seen as a form of synaptic pruning. This allows your brain to dedicate more resources—neural connections, energy, and processing power—to learning and mastering the skills required for your new purpose. This process, guided by selective awareness through a disciplined focus on new learning, optimizes neural efficiency and enhances learning capacity.

- **Neurocognitive Connections:** Synaptic pruning is a natural process that occurs throughout life, especially during childhood and adolescence. It involves eliminating less-used synapses, strengthening the remaining connections, and improving neural efficiency. This process is essential for learning and adaptation.

  Example: A musician transitioning from the piano to the guitar may experience initial difficulties. As they concentrate on guitar practice, the brain circuits linked to piano playing may diminish slightly, while those related to guitar playing strengthen. This enables them to enhance their proficiency on the guitar.

Reframing "Loss" as "Investment" Through a Focused Perspective Shift

The concept of "acceptable losses" can be reframed as a strategic investment in your future. By consciously choosing to let go of certain skills, relationships, or opportunities, you are freeing up resources—time, energy, and attention—to invest in your new purpose. This requires a focused perspective shift, viewing these "losses" not as sacrifices but as strategic choices that pave the way for greater gains in the long run.

- **Psychological Connections:** This relates to the concept of cognitive reframing, a technique used in cognitive behavioral therapy (CBT) to change negative thought patterns. By reframing "loss" as "investment," you can reduce negative emotions associated with letting go and increase motivation for pursuing your new purpose.

Example: A project manager who decides to transition to a career as a data scientist might need to give up managing large teams and complex projects. However, they can reframe this "loss" as an investment in developing their data analysis skills, ultimately leading to a more fulfilling and impactful career.

Prioritizing Future Gains Over Past Comforts Through Focused Value Assessment

Accepting "acceptable losses" requires prioritizing future gains over past comforts. It is about recognizing that clinging to familiar but ultimately irrelevant skills or experiences can hinder your progress and prevent you from fully embracing your new purpose. This demands focused value assessment, carefully weighing the potential benefits of the new path against the perceived costs of letting go of the old.

- **Decision-Making and Economic Connections:** This relates to the concept of opportunity cost, the value of the next best alternative forgone when making a decision. Choosing a new path often involves forgoing other opportunities, but by focusing on the potential gains of the new path, you can make more informed and strategic decisions.

  Example: A musician who has spent years performing in local bands might decide to pursue a solo career. This might involve giving up the camaraderie and stability of being in a band. However, they prioritize the potential for greater creative control and artistic expression in a solo career, making the "loss" of the band an acceptable trade-off.

Managing Emotional Attachment Through Focused Emotional Regulation

Letting go of past pursuits can be emotionally challenging, especially if you have invested significant time and effort in developing certain skills or building specific relationships. Managing this emotional attachment through focused emotional regulation is crucial for successfully navigating the transition. This involves acknowledging and processing your emotions while maintaining a clear focus on your new purpose.

- **Psychological and Neurocognitive Connections:** This relates to emotional regulation, the ability to manage and control one's emotions. It involves the prefrontal cortex and the limbic system, which are responsible for emotional processing and regulation. Techniques like mindfulness, meditation, and cognitive reframing can help manage emotional attachment and facilitate the transition.

  Example: An athlete compelled to retire owing to injury may undergo a phase of sadness and loss. By employing targeted emotional regulation, they can effectively process these feelings and channel their energy into new objectives, such as coaching or sports commentary.

The Power of a Growth Mindset: Fueling Transformation Through Focused Learning and Adaptation

Changing your major purpose requires a fundamental shift in mindset—from a fixed mindset to a growth mindset. This transformation, powered by selective awareness through disciplined learning and adaptation, involves embracing challenges as opportunities for growth and recognizing the brain's inherent plasticity.

Cultivating a Growth Mindset Through Focused Learning and Adaptation:

A growth mindset is not simply about positive thinking; it is about actively engaging in learning and adapting to new challenges.

Embracing Challenges Through Focused Learning

Changing your major purpose involves embracing the challenges of learning new skills, acquiring new knowledge, and developing new perspectives. Consider the artist who would like to shift their work from landscapes to abstract. They would need to cultivate a growth mindset by embracing the challenges of learning new techniques, experimenting with different styles, and developing their unique artistic voice. This focused learning and experimentation, guided by selective awareness through disciplined practice, fuels determination and the strength to persevere in their new direction.

- **Psychological Connections:** This relates to the concept of mastery orientation, a motivational pattern characterized by a focus on learning and improving skills rather than demonstrating ability or avoiding failure. Individuals with a growth mindset are more likely to adopt a mastery orientation.

  Example: A marketing professional transitioning to a career in data science would need to embrace the challenge of learning new programming languages, statistical methods, and data analysis tools. A growth mindset would enable them to view these challenges as opportunities to expand their skill sets and become a valuable data scientist.

Scientific exploration: Neuroplasticity and Focused Neural Rewiring

Neuroscience tells us that the brain possesses remarkable neuroplasticity—the ability to create new neural connections and prune away unused pathways throughout life. The growth mindset fosters this plasticity by framing challenges as opportunities for learning and growth, stimulating the formation of new neural connections, and strengthening existing ones through focused neural rewiring. This focused rewiring allows the brain to adapt to new demands and acquire new skills more efficiently.

- **Neurocognitive Connections:** Neuroplasticity is the brain's ability to reorganize itself by forming new neural connections throughout life. This process is driven by experience and learning. A growth mindset promotes neuroplasticity by encouraging individuals to seek out new experiences and challenges, which stimulate the formation of new neural connections.

    Example: Acquiring a new language necessitates the formation of novel neural connections in the brain. A growth mentality fosters perseverance in learners facing the initial difficulties of mastering grammar and vocabulary, ultimately resulting in enhanced fluency and competency over time.

Historical Insight: Embracing New Frontiers Through Focused Exploration

One can think of Marie Curie. Trained as a physicist, she found her true calling in radioactivity. With a growth mindset, embracing the challenges of this new scientific frontier through focused exploration and experimentation came discoveries that changed our understanding of the universe forever. Her willingness to embrace the unknown and persevere through numerous obstacles is a prime example of the power of a growth mindset.

Self-Help: Cultivating Resilience and Perseverance Through Focused Self-Belief

The growth mindset operates on the premise that your abilities can be developed through hard work, dedication, and a focused commitment to learning. It allows you to view challenges as valuable learning and growth opportunities and cultivate the resilience and perseverance needed to overcome the obstacles you will inevitably face on your path to finding and fulfilling your purpose. This focused self-belief in your capacity to learn and grow is crucial for navigating the challenges of transformation.

- **Psychological Connections:** This relates to the concept of self-efficacy, the belief in one's ability to succeed in specific situations. A growth mindset enhances self-efficacy by promoting the belief that abilities can be developed through effort and practice.

  Example: An entrepreneur encountering challenges in their firm might adopt a growth mindset to perceive these obstacles as learning experiences and opportunities to enhance their tactics. This resilience and tenacity are essential for sustained success.

Setting Realistic Goals: Charting a Course for Focused Achievement

Setting realistic goals is essential for navigating the path to a new purpose. This process, guided by selective awareness through disciplined planning and evaluation, involves defining achievable milestones that build upon each other, creating a clear roadmap for focused achievement.

Attainability Through Focused Research and Planning

Attainability is key to maintaining motivation and making consistent progress. The reading indicates that you should ensure the new purpose you have identified in your life is achievable. Setting unrealistic goals often results in disappointment and a lack of motivation. Therefore, conducting focused research on the new field (selective awareness through disciplined investigation) is crucial. Understand what level of skill, experience, and resources are necessary to create a viable pathway to your desired outcome. Take a hypothetical young entrepreneur interested in fashion sustainability. They may have initially envisioned launching their international clothing line. However, through focused research and self-assessment, they might realize that starting with a local boutique specializing in ethically sourced clothing is a more attainable initial goal. This realistic approach allows them to acquire practical experience, build a local customer base, and gradually work towards their larger vision.

- **Strategic and Economic Connections**: This relates to strategic planning, which involves setting clear objectives, defining action steps, and allocating resources to achieve those objectives. It also connects to market analysis, which involves researching market demand, competition, and other factors that can affect the success of a business venture.

  Example: A software developer interested in creating their own video game might start by developing small mobile games or contributing to open-source projects. This allows them to gain experience in game development and build a portfolio before attempting to create a large-scale commercial game.

Education: Acquiring Essential Knowledge and Skills Through Focused Learning

Many institutions offer courses, workshops, and certifications relevant to a wide range of fields. These educational resources, approached with focused learning and disciplined study, can equip you with the knowledge and skills necessary to bridge the gap between your current foundation and your new calling. For instance, artists transitioning to abstract art could enroll in online courses on color theory, explore the works of contemporary abstract artists with focused observation, and even pursue a certificate program in abstract expressionism through disciplined study.

- **Learning and Cognitive Connections:** This relates to the concept of scaffolding in learning, where learners are provided with support and guidance to help them acquire new knowledge and skills. Educational resources provide this scaffolding, helping learners progress from novice to expert.

  Example: A career changer moving into data analytics could take online courses in statistics, data visualization, and programming languages like Python or R. These courses provide the foundational knowledge and skills needed to succeed in a data analytics role.

Breaking Down Large Goals into Smaller, Manageable Steps Through Focused Task Decomposition

Large, ambitious goals can often feel overwhelming. Breaking them down into smaller, more manageable steps through focused task decomposition makes the journey less daunting and more achievable. This involves identifying the key milestones you need to reach and creating a detailed plan with specific action steps and timelines for each milestone.

- **Project Management and Psychological Connections:** This relates to project management, which involves planning, organizing, and managing resources to achieve specific goals. It also connects to the psychological concept of self-efficacy, which is enhanced by achieving smaller successes that build confidence and motivation.

  Example: Someone wanting to write a novel might break down the process into smaller steps, such as outlining the plot, developing characters, writing a certain number of words each day, and revising each chapter. This makes the overall goal of writing a novel feel less overwhelming and more attainable.

The Power of Specialization: Accelerating Progress Through Focused Expertise

This section reinforces the chapter's core message: Specialization is a powerful catalyst for accelerating progress, achieving mastery, and making significant contributions. This is achieved through the focused application of expertise, guided by selective awareness through disciplined practice and analysis.

Focus for Success Through Focused Expertise Development

Focused effort within a specific area is essential for achieving mastery and making a significant impact. The passage concludes by reiterating the importance of specialization. Sooner or later, successful individuals focus their efforts on a specific area within their chosen field. After embracing abstraction, the artist might specialize in a particular style or medium, such as abstract expressionism or digital abstract art, further refining their skills and achieving mastery through focused practice and experimentation. Self-help principles emphasize that focused action is essential for achieving goals. Specialization allows you to channel your energy and resources into a specific area, accelerating your progress and propelling you toward mastery.

- **Psychological and Learning Connections:** This relates to the concept of deep work, which involves focused, uninterrupted work on a single task. Specialization facilitates deep work by providing a clear focus and minimizing distractions. It also connects to the 10,000-hour rule, which suggests that achieving mastery in a skill requires approximately 10,000 hours of deliberate practice.

- **Example:** A writer might initially write in various genres, such as fiction, non-fiction, and poetry. However, by specializing in a specific genre, such as science fiction or historical fiction,

346

they can develop a deeper understanding of that genre's conventions, themes, and target audience, leading to greater success.

Maximizing Impact Through Focused Investigation

Imagine a scientist studying marine biology. Their initial research might encompass a broad range of marine life. However, they might discover a particular fascination with coral reefs as they delve deeper. By specializing in coral reef ecology through focused investigation and data analysis, they can focus their research on this specific ecosystem, contributing valuable insights into coral bleaching, reef conservation, and the impact of climate change. This focused approach allows them to contribute more significantly to the field than would have been possible with a more general approach. Similarly, by specializing in a particular style of abstraction through focused experimentation and critical analysis of their work, the artist can hone their technique, develop a unique voice, and potentially leave a lasting impact on the art world.

- **Scientific and Research Connections: This** relates to the importance of focused research questions in scientific inquiry. Specialization allows researchers to formulate more specific and testable hypotheses, leading to more meaningful discoveries.

  Example: A computer scientist might initially study various areas of computer science. However, by specializing in a specific area like artificial intelligence, they can contribute to the development of new AI algorithms, machine learning models, and other cutting-edge technologies.

Achieving Recognition Through Focused Contribution and Visibility

Specialization accelerates progress toward mastery and increases visibility and recognition within a specific field. By becoming a recognized expert, you can access more opportunities for collaboration, publication, and career advancement.

- **Career and Networking Connections:** This relates to the importance of building a professional reputation within your field. Specialization helps you establish yourself as a thought leader and expert, which can lead to invitations to speak at conferences, publish articles, and collaborate with other experts.

  Example: A chef specializing in a particular cuisine, such as French or Italian, might gain recognition for their culinary expertise and be invited to participate in cooking competitions, write cookbooks, or open a restaurant.

In Conclusion

The path to purpose is not a static destination but a dynamic journey of continuous evolution, guided by selective awareness through disciplined adaptation. It is about recognizing the internal call to something more, navigating the challenges of transformation, and embracing the power of a growth mindset to achieve a fulfilling and impactful life.

This segment has explored how selective awareness empowers us to evolve our purpose through several key stages:

- **Recognizing and Responding to Focused Inner Guidance:** Identifying and responding to a true self-call through focused introspection and self-assessment, distinguishing genuine purposeful shifts from temporary discouragement.

- **Embracing Strategic Disengagement for Focused Growth:** Accepting "acceptable losses" through focused evaluation and reframing them as strategic investments in your future, prioritizing future gains over past comforts.

- **Fueling Transformation Through Focused Learning and Adaptation:** Cultivating a growth mindset through focused learning, embracing challenges as opportunities for growth, and leveraging the brain's neuroplasticity for focused neural rewiring.

- **Charting a Course for Focused Achievement:** Setting realistic goals through focused research, planning, task decomposition, and acquiring essential knowledge and skills through focused learning.

These stages navigated through selective awareness and disciplined perception, are not always linear or sequential. They often involve cycles of reflection, experimentation, and adaptation. The key is to:

- **Maintain Focused Self-Awareness:** Continuously reflect on your values, passions, and evolving goals to stay aligned with your true self.

- **Embrace Focused Learning and Growth:** View challenges as opportunities for learning and development and cultivate a growth mindset that fosters resilience and perseverance.1

- **Adapt with Focused Intention: Be** willing to adjust your course as needed, making strategic decisions about where to invest your time and energy.

By embracing this dynamic process of evolution, guided by selective awareness through disciplined adaptation, you can create a life that is not only successful but also deeply meaningful and fulfilling. Remember, the path to purpose is not about finding a fixed destination; it is about continuously evolving and growing, guided by your inner compass and the focused application of your unique talents and skills.

Choosing Between Career Paths: Unleashing Your Potential Through Focused Specialization and Strategic Alignment

Choosing the right career path—professional or business—is a crucial decision that should be aligned with your unique strengths, values, and aspirations. Specialization, guided by selective awareness through disciplined self-assessment and strategic planning, empowers you to make an informed choice and flourish in your chosen field, transforming your journey into a compelling narrative of self-discovery and impactful contribution.

The Power of Focused Expertise

Professional careers offer unique opportunities for deep expertise development, independent decision-making, and continuous learning.

Mastery and Impact Through Focused Skill Application

Professional careers cultivate deep expertise in a specific domain, akin to a highly skilled detective honing their observational skills to solve complex cases through focused observation and analysis. Imagine a doctor, a lawyer, or an engineer—each a Sherlock Holmes in their domain, wielding their specialized knowledge to make a tangible difference. The doctor unravels the intricate puzzle of a patient's illness through focused diagnosis and treatment planning, the lawyer meticulously builds a case to secure justice through focused legal research and argumentation, and the engineer crafts innovative solutions to real-world problems through focused design and problem-solving.

- **Cognitive and Problem-Solving Connections:** This relates to the concept of expert problem-solving, which involves using specialized knowledge and skills to efficiently and effectively solve complex problems. Experts develop mental models and schemas to identify relevant information and quickly generate effective solutions.

Example: A software engineer specializing in cybersecurity uses their focused expertise to identify and mitigate security vulnerabilities in software systems, protecting sensitive data from cyberattacks.

Independent Decision Making Through Focused Judgment and Action

Many professions offer autonomy, allowing you to exercise independent judgment and directly influence outcomes through focused judgment and action. Picture a surgeon in the operating room, not unlike a skilled bomb disposal expert, making split-second decisions with the weight of a life in their hands based on a focused assessment of the patient's condition and focused execution of surgical procedures. A lawyer, channeling their inner Atticus Finch, passionately argues for their client, their words holding the power to sway a jury based on focused legal analysis and focused presentation of evidence.

- **Decision-Making and Leadership Connections: This** relates to the concept of executive function, which includes skills like decision-making, planning, and problem-solving. Professions that require independent decision-making often demand strong executive function skills.

  Example: A financial analyst making investment recommendations for clients uses their focused expertise in financial modeling and market analysis to make informed decisions that impact their client's financial well-being.

Lifelong Learning Through Focused Knowledge Acquisition and Adaptation

Professional fields demand continuous learning to keep pace with advancements in the field, akin to a seasoned explorer venturing into uncharted territories through focused exploration and discovery. Doctors attend conferences and stay abreast of the latest medical breakthroughs through the focused study of medical journals and research findings. Lawyers follow legal developments, ensuring their strategies remain razor-sharp through focused case law and legislation analysis. Furthermore, engineers embrace new technologies, constantly pushing the boundaries of the known through focused experimentation and innovation.

- **Learning and Adaptability Connections:** This relates to the concept of lifelong learning and the importance of continuous professional development. To remain competitive, professionals must constantly update their knowledge and skills in rapidly evolving fields.

  Example: A data scientist must continuously learn about new machine learning algorithms, data visualization techniques, and big data technologies to stay at the forefront of their field.

The Thrill of Building and Leading in Business Careers: Focused Vision and Strategic Execution

Embracing the Challenges and Rewards of Focused Business Acumen. Business careers offer a unique blend of innovation, leadership, and strategic execution. They provide opportunities to build something new, lead teams, and make a significant impact on the marketplace. This requires selective awareness through disciplined vision, strategic planning, and effective communication.

Entrepreneurial Spirit: Igniting Innovation Through Focused Vision and Strategic Execution

Business careers ignite the flame of innovation and a desire to build something new, much like a pioneering adventurer venturing into the unknown through focused vision and strategic execution. Imagine a young entrepreneur launching a revolutionary tech startup, like Steve Jobs, unveiling the first iPhone, driven by a focused vision of transforming personal communication and a disciplined execution of product development and marketing strategies. Alternatively, a seasoned executive leading a global corporation is akin to a captain navigating the high seas of international commerce through focused strategic planning and disciplined management of resources.

- **Strategic and Innovation Connections:** This relates to entrepreneurship and the importance of innovation in creating new products, services, and markets. It also connects to strategic management, which involves formulating and implementing strategies to achieve organizational goals.

  Example: An entrepreneur developing a new sustainable food packaging solution is driven by a focused vision of reducing plastic waste and a disciplined execution of research, development, and marketing.

Leadership and Communication: Inspiring and Motivating Through Focused Communication and Influence

Businesses thrive on strong leadership and clear communication facilitated by focused communication and influence. Like a charismatic motivational speaker, a CEO inspires their team through a compelling vision and communicates through focused and persuasive messaging, igniting their passion and propelling the company forward. A marketing manager, channeling their inner

Don Draper, crafts a persuasive presentation to propel sales, weaving a narrative that captivates their audience through focused market research and targeted messaging.

- **Leadership and Communication Connections:** This relates to the concept of transformational leadership, which involves inspiring and motivating followers to achieve extraordinary outcomes. Effective communication is a crucial component of transformational leadership.

  Example: A project manager leading a software development team uses focused communication to clearly define project goals, assign tasks, and provide regular feedback, ensuring the team works effectively towards a shared objective.

Versatile Skillset: Adapting to Dynamic Environments Through Focused Skill Development and Application

Business careers require adaptability and a diverse skillset, akin to a Swiss Army Knife—a single tool with a multitude of functions, applied through focused skill development and application. An MBA graduate might leverage finance, marketing, and human resources knowledge depending on their role, demonstrating the versatility demanded in business. This requires focused learning and the ability to apply different skills in different contexts.

- **Management and Organizational Connections:** This relates to the concept of management skills, which include a wide range of abilities such as planning, organizing, leading, and controlling. Effective managers need to be versatile and able to adapt to changing circumstances.

  Example: A startup founder might need to handle tasks ranging from product development and marketing to sales and customer service, requiring a diverse skillset and the ability to learn new skills as needed quickly.

Finding Your Niche: Specialization as a Catalyst for Focused Self-Discovery and Strategic Alignment

Choosing between professional and business careers is a deeply personal decision. There is no single "right" answer. The key lies in understanding yourself through focused self-discovery and strategically aligning your strengths, passions, and values with the demands of each path. Specialization acts as a catalyst in this process, helping you clarify your direction and maximize your potential.

Guiding Questions for Focused Self-Assessment. The following questions, approached with focused introspection and disciplined self-assessment (selective awareness through disciplined self-reflection), can guide you on your journey of self-discovery and help you determine which path—professional or business—is the best fit:

What ignites your passion? Focused Exploration of Intrinsic Motivation

Do you yearn for the intricate problem-solving of a professional field, akin to untangling a complex web through focused analysis and deductive reasoning, or the thrill of building a business empire, like constructing a magnificent castle from the ground up through focused vision and strategic planning? This question delves into your intrinsic motivation and what truly excites and engages you.

- **Psychological Connections:** This relates to the concept of intrinsic motivation, which is driven by internal rewards such as enjoyment, satisfaction, and a sense of purpose. Identifying what ignites your passion is crucial for finding a fulfilling career.

Example: A person driven by an insatiable curiosity for the unknown may find themselves captivated by a research career, delving into intricate scientific enigmas and playing a pivotal role in the advancement of knowledge (Astrophysics): Stephen Hawking's intense obsession with the cosmos and the intricate rules that dictate its existence drove him to delve into theoretical physics, even in the face of his crippling condition. His relentless pursuit of knowledge and commitment to unraveling the mysteries of the universe captivated minds, leaving an indelible mark on the realm of astrophysics.

Example: A person fueled by a fervent desire to craft groundbreaking products and launch them into the market may find themselves irresistibly attracted to a path of entrepreneurship, where they can construct a business empire around their visionary concepts. Social Enterprise: Driven by an intense passion to aid those in need, Blake Mycoskie embarked on a mission that culminated in the creation of TOMS Shoes. The "One for One" business model, where a pair of shoes is donated for every purchase made, has created a profound ripple effect in society.

Where do your strengths lie? Focused Assessment of Core Competencies

Do you excel at independent analysis, a master detective meticulously piecing together clues through focused observation and critical thinking (professional), or inspiring and leading others, a charismatic captain steering their crew towards a shared goal through focused communication and team building (business)? This question encourages you to assess your core competencies and identify where you naturally excel.

- **Psychological Connections:** This relates to the concept of strengths-based development, which focuses on identifying and leveraging individual strengths rather than focusing on weaknesses.

Example: A person possessing keen analytical abilities and adept problem-solving skills could find themselves thriving in the realms of engineering or finance, particularly in structural engineering. Fazlur Rahman Khan, a master of his craft, wielded extraordinary analytical prowess and problem-solving abilities, forging groundbreaking structural systems that would redefine the skyline of skyscrapers. His keen insight into structural engineering birthed the revolutionary "bundled tube" system, paving the way for the rise of towering, efficient skyscrapers such as the John Hancock Center and the Willis Tower, once known as the Sears Tower.

Example (Finance - Investment Analysis): Warren Buffett, a renowned investor and business magnate, possesses exceptional analytical skills and a deep understanding of financial markets. His focused analysis of companies' financial statements and business models has enabled him to make highly successful investment decisions over decades.

Example: A person endowed with exceptional communication, leadership, and interpersonal abilities could thrive in the dynamic realms of sales, marketing, or management, particularly in the intricate world of brand management. Steve Jobs wielded his remarkable communication and leadership abilities like a masterful puppeteer, crafting a vision for Apple that captivated minds and ignited a fervor within his team, driving them to conjure groundbreaking innovations. His meticulous approach to communication and marketing crafted a formidable brand that captivates audiences across the globe.

What kind of work environment excites you? Focused Evaluation of Preferred Work Style

Do you prefer the structured nature of a profession, a well-oiled machine with a defined process and clear hierarchy, or the dynamic pace of the business world, a thrilling rollercoaster ride of constant change, innovation, and ambiguity? This question prompts you to consider your preferred work style and the type of environment where you thrive.

- **Organizational and Psychological Connections:** This relates to organizational culture and the importance of finding a work environment that aligns with one's values and preferences.

  Example: An illustration for those who find comfort in routine and predictability, a meticulously organized professional landscape, where roles and responsibilities are distinctly outlined, can be particularly appealing. (Library Science - Archiving): An archivist navigates a meticulously organized realm, where every document and artifact is ensconced within a web of systems designed for preservation and retrieval, each piece whispering secrets of the past waiting to be uncovered. Their efforts demand an unwavering focus on precision, a commitment to preservation protocols, and navigation through a clearly defined hierarchy.

  Example: Consider an individual who flourishes amid upheaval and relishes the thrill of uncertainty; such a person may find themselves irresistibly attracted to the frenetic energy of a startup or the exhilarating atmosphere of a swiftly expanding enterprise (Investment Banking—Trading Floor). In the heart of an investment bank, the trading floor pulses with intensity, a realm where traders navigate the chaos, making lightning-fast decisions amid the relentless ebb and flow of the market's unpredictable tides. This ever-shifting landscape demands sharp instincts, a willingness to embrace uncertainty, and the capacity to navigate intense pressure.

Embrace Specialization, Fuel Personal Growth Through Focused Expertise Development

Life specialization is not about limiting your horizons but about sharpening your focus to fuel continuous personal growth and maximize your impact. The sculptor chips away at a block of marble with precision, guided by a focused vision, allowing a masterpiece to emerge from the seemingly endless stone. Similarly, specialization empowers you to shape your potential and achieve extraordinary results.

Empowering Growth Through Focused Expertise and Continuous Development: Specialization empowers personal growth in several key ways, all driven by focused effort and disciplined perception.

Selective Awareness Through Focused Information Filtering

Specialization provides a refined lens through which to view the world, sharpening your selective awareness through disciplined information filtering. It allows you to filter out irrelevant information and focus on what is truly relevant to your field. The doctor learns to recognize subtle signs of health and disease through focused observation and analysis of medical data, and the advanced detective traces an almost invisible fingerprint at a crime scene through focused examination of evidence and the application of forensic techniques. At the same time, the entrepreneur identifies a gap in the market—a hidden opportunity to be seized—through focused market research and analysis of consumer trends.

- **Cognitive and Perceptual Connections:** This relates to selective attention, the ability to focus on specific stimuli while ignoring others. Specialization enhances selective attention by training the brain to prioritize relevant information within a specific domain.

Example: Imagine two financial analysts, both tasked with evaluating the potential investment value of a publicly traded technology company.

Analyst A (Lacking Focused Filtering): This analyst approaches the task broadly, overwhelmed by the sheer volume of information available. They spend time reading general news articles about the tech industry, browsing social media discussions about the company, and looking at basic stock charts. They gather much information, but it is unfocused and does not provide a clear picture of the company's true value. They are experiencing information overload.

Analyst B (Using Focused Filtering): This analyst, specializing in stock valuation, uses selective awareness to filter the information effectively. They focus on:

- **Financial Statements (10-K, 10-Q):** They meticulously analyze the company's balance sheet, income statement, and cash flow statement, focusing on key metrics like revenue growth, profit margins, debt levels, and return on equity. They understand that these documents provide the most accurate and reliable information about the company's financial health.

- **Industry Reports and Analyst Research:** They focus on reports from reputable research firms and industry analysts who specialize in the technology sector. They understand that these reports offer valuable insights into market trends, competitive landscape, and future growth prospects.

- **Competitive Analysis:** This type of analysis focuses on understanding a company's competitive advantages and disadvantages compared to its main competitors. It analyzes market share, product differentiation, and pricing strategies.

- **Management Discussion and Analysis (MD&A):** They pay close attention to the MD&A section of the financial reports, where management discusses the company's performance, challenges, and future outlook. They understand that this section provides valuable insights into the company's strategy and management's perspective.

By focusing on these specific areas and filtering out the noise, Analyst B can develop a much clearer and more accurate assessment of the company's intrinsic value. They can then use this focused analysis to make informed investment recommendations.

Deep Dives and Discovery Through Focused Exploration and Learning

Specialization kindles an insatiable curiosity that drives you to delve deeper into your chosen field through focused exploration and learning. The doctor delves deeper into medical research, unraveling the complexities of the human body through focused study of anatomy, physiology, and pathology. At the same time, the entrepreneur explores newer technologies and business models to venture into unexplored territories of innovation through focused market research and analysis of emerging trends. This focused pursuit of knowledge fuels discovery and keeps you engaged and passionate about your area of expertise.

- **Motivational and Learning Connections:** This relates to the concept of intrinsic motivation, which is driven by internal rewards such as curiosity, mastery, and a sense of accomplishment. Specialization fosters intrinsic motivation by providing opportunities for deep exploration and learning.

Example: A software engineer specializing in artificial intelligence might delve into the intricacies of deep learning algorithms and neural networks, constantly exploring new research papers and experimenting with different models.

Confidence and Expertise Through Focused Mastery and Contribution

Mastery breeds confidence—a professional athlete confidently steps onto the field, knowing they can perform at their best due to years of focused training and practice. The doctor confidently makes a diagnosis based on their focused expertise in medical knowledge and clinical experience. The entrepreneur leads with a clear vision and decisive action based on focused market analysis and strategic planning. This focused expertise empowers you to make meaningful contributions to your field, becoming a source of inspiration and guidance for others. This means you can inspire others to follow in your footsteps, becoming a role model for aspiring professionals or entrepreneurs.

- **Psychological and Social Connections:** This relates to the concept of self-efficacy, the belief in one's ability to succeed in specific situations. Mastery increases self-efficacy, which in turn leads to greater confidence and motivation. It also connects to the concept of social influence, where experts can inspire and motivate others through their knowledge and expertise.

  Example: A renowned architect specializing in sustainable design can inspire other architects and builders to adopt more environmentally friendly practices.

Embrace the Journey: A Thrilling Tale of Self-Discovery

Ultimately, specialization is not a static destination but a dynamic and lifelong journey of focused self-discovery, continuous learning, and purposeful evolution. It is a constantly unfolding narrative filled with new challenges, triumphs, and opportunities for growth. By aligning your passions, strengths, and values with a specialized path guided by selective awareness through disciplined perception, you unlock your full potential, significantly impact the world, and cultivate a fulfilling career that fuels continuous personal growth and contributes to a life of purpose.

A Synthesis of Focused Action and Continuous Adaptation

This journey of specialization, driven by selective awareness and disciplined perception, involves several key interconnected elements:

- **Focused Self-Discovery:** Understanding your core values, passions, and strengths through focused introspection and self-assessment, identifying the areas where you can make the greatest contribution.

- **Focused Expertise Development: Honing** your skills and knowledge within a specific domain through focused practice, learning, and experimentation, achieving mastery and becoming a recognized expert.

- **Focused Collaboration and Contribution:** Leveraging your specialized expertise to collaborate with others, contribute to your field, and make a meaningful impact on the world.

- **Focused Adaptation and Growth:** Embrace challenges as opportunities for growth, cultivate a growth mindset, and adapt to the ever-changing demands of your field through focused learning and continuous improvement.

The Power of Selective Awareness Through Disciplined Perception

Throughout this journey, selective awareness through disciplined perception acts as your guiding compass, enabling you to:

- **Filter Information Effectively:** Focus on what is truly relevant to your field, filter out distractions, and prioritize key insights.

- **Make Strategic Decisions:** Align your actions with your values and goals, making informed choices that maximize your impact.

- **Navigate Challenges with Resilience:** View setbacks as learning opportunities, adapt your approach, and persevere toward your goals.

- **Embrace Continuous Evolution:** Recognize that your purpose may evolve over time, and be willing to adapt your path accordingly.

A Call to Action: Embrace the Focused Journey

Thus, specialization emerges not as a constraint but as a powerful enhancement of your capabilities. It revolves around deliberately selecting a journey, cultivating profound knowledge, and leveraging that knowledge to create an impact. Immerse yourself in this captivating journey of intense self-exploration and relentless growth, driven by the force of intentional awareness through meticulous observation. By immersing yourself in the journey, you unlock the door to professional triumph while weaving a tapestry of depth, significance, and influence in your life.

Choose Your Genre: Tailor Your Path to Your Personality Through Focused Self-Alignment

The beauty lies in personalization. Do you crave the psychological thriller of a high-stakes legal battle or the medical drama of a life-saving surgery (professional)? Perhaps the fast-paced world of venture capitalism or the strategic maneuvering of international business negotiations (business) ignites your spirit.

Embrace the Challenge: The Hero's Journey Awaits

The beauty of choosing a career path lies in personalization. There is no one-size-fits-all approach. The key is to understand your personality, values, and preferred work style and then align them with the characteristics of different career paths. This process, guided by selective awareness through disciplined self-reflection and analysis of different career options, allows you to choose a "genre" that truly resonates with you and sets you up for success and fulfillment.

Matching Your Inner World to Your Outer Pursuits Through Focused Self-Analysis and Career Exploration: This section emphasizes the importance of aligning your personality with your chosen career path.

Matching Your Inner World to Your Outer Pursuits Through Focused Self-Analysis and Career Exploration

Do you crave the psychological thriller of a high-stakes legal battle, requiring focused analysis of evidence, strategic argumentation, and the ability to perform under pressure, or the medical drama of life-saving surgery, demanding focused attention to detail, quick decision-making, and the ability to handle high-stress situations (professional)? Perhaps the fast-paced world of venture capitalism requires focused market analysis, risk assessment, and the ability to identify promising investment opportunities, or the strategic maneuvering of international business negotiations, demanding focused communication, cultural sensitivity, and the ability to build relationships across different cultures (business) ignites your spirit? This focused self-analysis, combined with focused exploration of different career paths, allows you to identify the "genre" that best suits your personality and motivations.

- **Psychological and Personality Connections:** This relates to various personality theories, such as the Big Five personality traits (Openness, Conscientiousness, Extraversion, Agreeableness, Neuroticism) and Carl Jung's theory of psychological types. Understanding your personality can help you identify career paths that are a good fit for your natural tendencies and preferences.

  Example (Professional - Law): Someone high in conscientiousness and analytical thinking might thrive in a legal career where attention to detail and logical reasoning are essential.

  Example (Professional - Medicine): Someone high in agreeableness and empathy might be drawn to a career in medicine, where caring for others and building strong patient relationships are important.

  Example (Business - Venture Capital): Someone high in openness to experience and risk tolerance might be drawn to venture capitalism, where they can explore new ideas and invest in innovative startups.

  Example (Business - International Business): Someone high in extraversion and cultural sensitivity might thrive in international business, where they can interact with people from different cultures and build global partnerships.

Beyond the "Thrill": Aligning Values and Work Style Through Focused Value Clarification and Work Environment Analysis

The allure of a specific career can certainly ignite passion, yet it is crucial to reflect on your core beliefs and the way you prefer to engage with your work. Do you cherish the freedom of working alone, or do you find greater strength in the synergy of collaboration? Do you find yourself energized by environments that are meticulously organized, with defined rules and protocols, or do you lean towards more fluid and ever-changing atmospheres? The meticulous examination of various work environments and the deliberate clarification of values are crucial for achieving enduring career fulfillment.

- **Organizational and Values Connections:** This relates to the concept of person-environment fit, which emphasizes the importance of aligning individual characteristics with the characteristics of the work environment. A good fit leads to greater job satisfaction, motivation, and performance.

  Example: Someone who values autonomy and independent work might be drawn to a freelance career or a research-oriented position in academia.

  Example: Someone who values collaboration and teamwork might thrive in a team-based business environment or a collaborative research project.

The Final Chapter: A Legacy of Focused Impact and Enduring Influence

As you progress on your specialized path, guided by selective awareness through disciplined perception and action, the impact you make ripples outwards, influencing the lives of others and shaping the world around you. The doctor who develops a groundbreaking treatment through focused research and clinical practice, the lawyer who fights for social justice through focused legal advocacy and strategic litigation, or the entrepreneur who creates innovative solutions through focused vision and strategic execution all leave a lasting legacy of focused impact and enduring influence.

Building a Legacy Through Focused Expertise and Purposeful Action

This final segment emphasizes the long-term impact of specialization, focusing on the legacy you create through your focused expertise and purposeful action. The impact you make through specialization is not limited to your immediate work; it extends to the broader community and future generations. The doctor's groundbreaking treatment improves the lives of countless patients, the lawyer's fight for social justice creates a more equitable society, and the entrepreneur's innovative solutions address real-world problems and drive progress. This lasting legacy is built through focused expertise, purposeful action, and a commitment to making a positive difference.

- **Social and Philosophical Connections:** This connects to the concept of legacy, the impact you leave on the world after you are gone. It also relates to the philosophical concept of meaning and purpose, which suggests that human beings have a fundamental need to find meaning and purpose in their lives.

  Example (Medicine): Jonas Salk's polio vaccine development has had a lasting impact on global health, preventing countless cases of this debilitating disease.

  Example (Law): Nelson Mandela's fight against apartheid in South Africa has profoundly impacted social justice and human rights worldwide.

Example (Business): Elon Musk's work in electric vehicles and space exploration is driving innovation in sustainable transportation and space technology, potentially shaping humanity's future.

Inspiring Future Generations Through Focused Mentorship and Knowledge Sharing

Your journey of specialization can also inspire future generations to pursue their passions and make their contributions. By sharing your knowledge, mentoring others, and becoming a role model, you can extend your impact beyond your work and empower others to achieve their full potential. This focused mentorship and knowledge sharing creates a ripple effect, multiplying your influence and contributing to the growth and development of your field.

- **Educational and Leadership Connections:** This relates to mentorship, where experienced individuals guide and support less experienced individuals in their professional development. It also connects to leadership, which involves inspiring and motivating others to achieve shared goals.

  Example: A renowned scientist might mentor young researchers, guiding them in their research projects and helping them develop their scientific careers.

  Example: A successful entrepreneur might create a mentorship program for aspiring entrepreneurs, sharing their knowledge and experience to help them launch their businesses.

A Life of Purpose Through Focused Self-Actualization and Contribution

Ultimately, specialization is not just about achieving external success; it is about living a life of purpose and making a meaningful contribution to the world. By aligning your passions, strengths, and values with a specialized path, you embark on a journey of self-actualization, fulfilling your potential and leaving a lasting legacy of focused impact and enduring influence. This focused pursuit of purpose, guided by selective awareness through disciplined action and reflection, leads to a life of deep satisfaction and fulfillment.

- **Psychological and Philosophical Connections: This** connects to the concept of self-actualization, the realization of one's full potential, as described by Abraham Maslow. It also relates to the philosophical concept of eudaimonia, a Greek term for human flourishing, which emphasizes living a life of purpose and meaning.

  Example: Someone who dedicates their life to environmental conservation, through focused expertise in ecology and environmental policy, might contribute significantly to protecting natural resources and preserving the planet for future generations.

The Choice is Yours: Authoring Your Legacy Through Focused Specialization and Purposeful Action

So, take a deep breath, turn the page, and begin authoring the next chapter of your life's story. Specialization is your pen, your chosen field the canvas, and selective awareness through disciplined perception is your guiding hand. With dedication, passion, a thirst for knowledge, and a commitment to focused action, you can transform your career—and your life—into a compelling narrative of self-discovery, impactful contribution, and enduring success.

A Call to Focused Action and Continuous Growth: This concluding message emphasizes your agency in shaping your destiny through focused specialization and purposeful action.

Authoring Your Legacy Through Focused Intention and Action

Your choice of which "genre" your story will be—professional or business—and within that, your chosen specialization—is entirely yours. Specialization is about aligning your inner world with your outer pursuits through focused self-reflection, strategic planning, and consistent action. It provides the tools and the focus to craft a unique and impactful narrative, contributing to a legacy that extends beyond your own individual achievements.

- **Psychological and Narrative Connections:** This relates to the concept of narrative identity, the stories we tell ourselves about who we are and how we fit into the world. Choosing a career path and specializing within it is a way of writing your own narrative and shaping your identity.

  Example: Someone who chooses a career in environmental science and specializes in climate change research is writing a story about their commitment to protecting the planet.

Embracing the Journey of Continuous Evolution Through Focused Learning and Adaptation

This journey of specialization is not a single chapter but an ongoing series of connected stories filled with new challenges, opportunities, and discoveries. Embrace the process of continuous evolution through focused learning, adaptation, and growth. Be open to new possibilities, willing to refine your focus as needed, and committed to making a lasting impact through focused contribution.

- **Growth Mindset and Adaptability Connections:** This reinforces the importance of a growth mindset and the ability to adapt to changing circumstances. The journey of specialization is not a linear path; it involves continuous learning, adaptation, and growth.

Example: A software developer who specializes in mobile app development might need to adapt their skills as new mobile technologies and platforms emerge.

Living a Life of Purpose Through Focused Self-Actualization and Contribution

Ultimately, the power of specialization lies in its ability to empower you to live a life of purpose, fueled by focused self-actualization and meaningful contribution. By aligning your passions, strengths, and values with a specialized path, you create a life that is not only professionally successful but also deeply fulfilling and impactful. This is achieved through focused action, guided by selective awareness through disciplined perception, leading to a legacy that extends far beyond your own individual achievements.

- **Philosophical and Existential Connections:** This relates to life's search for meaning and purpose. Specialization can provide a sense of purpose by allowing individuals to make a meaningful contribution to the world.

  Example: A teacher who specializes in special education teaches academic skills and empowers students with disabilities to reach their full potential, contributing to a more inclusive and equitable society.

A Final Invitation: Begin Your Focused Story Today

The choice is yours. Embrace the power of specialization, guided by selective awareness through disciplined perception, and begin writing your own unique and impactful story today.

In Conclusion

Choosing between professional and business career paths is a pivotal decision that should be guided by a deep understanding of yourself and a strategic alignment with your aspirations.

Specialization, empowered by selective awareness through disciplined perception, is not just about acquiring skills; it is about strategically positioning yourself for a fulfilling and impactful career, regardless of which path you choose.

This section has explored how focused expertise and strategic alignment play out in both professional and business contexts:

- **The Power of Focused Expertise in Professional Careers:** Professionals cultivate deep expertise, exercise independent judgment, and engage in lifelong learning within a structured environment driven by focused skill application, judgment, and knowledge acquisition.

- **The Thrill of Building and Leading in Business Careers:** Business careers offer opportunities for innovation, leadership, and strategic execution in a dynamic environment driven by focused vision, communication, and skill development.

The key to making the right choice lies in focused self-analysis, guided by selective awareness through disciplined self-reflection:

- **Identifying Your Passions and Strengths: What** truly motivates you? Where do your natural talents lie? These questions, approached with focused introspection, will guide you toward a path that resonates with your core being.

- **Evaluating Your Preferred Work Style:** Do you thrive in structured environments or dynamic, fast-paced settings? Understanding your preferred work style through a focused analysis of your work habits and preferences will help you find a career that aligns with your natural tendencies.

- **Considering the Long-Term Impact:** What kind of legacy do you want to create? How do you want to contribute to the world? These questions, considered through focused reflection on your values and goals, will help you choose a path that is not only professionally rewarding but also personally meaningful.

Ultimately, whether you choose the focused mastery of a professional career or the dynamic leadership of a business career, specialization, combined with strategic alignment and guided by selective awareness through disciplined perception, is the key to unlocking your full potential. Embrace the journey of self-discovery, explore your options with focused intention, and choose the path that allows you to make your unique mark on the world.

Selective Awareness: Weaving the Tapestry of Benefits for Your Destiny

Envision a world where your focus becomes a piercing light, slicing through the chaos of thought and revealing the route to your triumph. This transcends mere fiction; it embodies the formidable strength of selective awareness, honed through rigorous perception and intentional action. It revolves around nurturing a vibrant inner realm that produces a bounty of self-control, unwavering well-being, and the capacity to tackle challenges with pinpoint precision, ultimately crafting a rich fabric of advantages for your future. Harnessing the power of selective awareness transforms you into the master of your own destiny, steering through the complexities of life with razor-sharp focus and deliberate intent.

Inner Power & Clarity:
From Scattered Thoughts to Focused Willpower Through Disciplined Attention

Neuroscientists reveal that our minds are relentlessly assaulted by a barrage of stimuli every single second. This relentless onslaught can leave us feeling fragmented, inundated, and grappling with mental exhaustion. By honing your ability to focus and filter information with precision selectively, you can turn your mind into an extraordinary filter, wielding control over what you perceive. You take the helm of your vessel, navigating through the storm of distractions and charting a course toward your ambitions. This awakening brings forth a formidable strength and piercing insight. You cultivate an acute awareness of your deepest yearnings and craft a meticulously detailed strategy to realize them, executed with unwavering determination.

- **Neurocognitive and Psychological Connections**: This relates to attention regulation, the ability to control and direct one's attention. Mastering selective awareness strengthens neural pathways associated with attention regulation, particularly in the prefrontal cortex, which is responsible for executive functions like planning, decision-making, and working memory.

  Example: A student preparing for an important exam can use selective awareness to filter out distractions like social media and focus their attention on studying relevant material, leading to improved concentration and better exam performance.

Surrounded by Support: Building Your Dream Team Through Focused Relationship Cultivation

Just like a captain does not sail alone, a master of selective awareness surrounds themselves with a trusted crew through focused relationship cultivation. These positive influences, mentors, and collaborators act as your "trustworthy aids." They provide encouragement, offer valuable insights through focused communication and feedback, and hold you accountable on your journey through focused collaboration. Imagine a young entrepreneur building a tech startup. By surrounding themselves with experienced mentors and collaborators, they gain invaluable knowledge and foster a network of support that propels them toward success.

- **Social and Psychological Connections:** This relates to the concept of social support, which is crucial for well-being and success. Having a strong support network provides emotional support, practical assistance, and valuable feedback.

  Example: An artist seeking to improve their skills might join a local art group or seek mentorship from an established artist, gaining valuable feedback and support from their peers

The Thrill of Purpose: Setting Sail with a Clear Destination Through Focused Goal Setting and Visioning

Have you ever experienced the exhilarating feeling of setting a goal and taking the first step towards achieving it? Mastering selective awareness replicates that feeling on a continuous basis through focused goal-setting and disciplined visioning. You identify your true north star—your most cherished desires—and chart a course to get there through focused planning and strategic action. This unwavering focus fuels a constant sense of purpose and direction. It is like a sailor setting sail on a vast ocean, the compass guiding them towards a clear destination. Every action you take becomes imbued with meaning, propelling you forward with the electrifying thrill of working towards a purpose that aligns with your deepest values.

- **Motivational and Goal-Setting Connections:** This relates to the concept of goal-setting theory, which emphasizes the importance of setting specific, measurable, achievable, relevant, and time-bound (SMART) goals. Having a clear purpose and well-defined goals provides motivation and direction.

  Example: A writer setting out to write a novel can use selective awareness to focus on specific writing goals, such as completing a certain number of words each day or finishing a draft of a chapter each week, maintaining their focus and motivation throughout the writing process.

Wielding Power Wisely: From Focused Awareness to a Force for Good Through Disciplined Ethical Application

With great power comes an equally profound obligation. The idea underscores the critical role of "self-discipline" in mastering this newfound power. Mastering selective awareness does not transform you into a dictator issuing commands. Instead, it fosters an intense awareness of duty through concentrated moral contemplation. You grasp the profound influence of your concentrated thoughts and deliberate actions, and you consciously decide to channel them toward meaningful outcomes. Envision a practitioner meticulously sharpening their insight through relentless years of rigorous training. Their keen perception enables them to unravel intricate ailments with astonishing clarity, ultimately serving not only their own interests but also the well-being of the patients under their care.

- **Ethical and Social Responsibility Connections:** This relates to the importance of ethical decision-making and the responsibility that comes with expertise and influence.

  Example: A software engineer developing artificial intelligence systems has a responsibility to consider the ethical implications of their work and ensure that AI is used for beneficial purposes and not for harmful ones.

Inner Peace Through Resilience: Building Your Emotional Fortress Through Focused Emotional Regulation and Adaptive Capacity

Mastering selective awareness empowers you to build an inner fortress of resilience, shielding you from external pressures and fostering inner peace. This is achieved through focused emotional regulation, adaptive capacity, and the cultivation of healthy relationships.

Protecting Your Freedom: Shielding Yourself from Mental Manipulators Through Focused Attention and Critical Thinking

The world is full of distractions and external pressures that can easily derail you from your path. However, by mastering selective awareness through focused attention and critical thinking, you build an inner fortress, shielding yourself from these subtle manipulations. By filtering out irrelevant or harmful information through focused analysis, you become less susceptible to social media rabbit holes, manipulative advertising, and the negativity of others. Your focused attention acts as a mental filter, allowing only what serves your goals and well-being to pass through.

- **Cognitive and Psychological Connections**: This relates to cognitive biases, systematic patterns of deviation from norm, or rationality in judgment. Selective awareness helps you become aware of these biases and mitigate their influence. It also connects to the concept of psychological reactance, the tendency to resist attempts to control or manipulate your behavior.

  Example: Someone aware of the persuasive techniques used in advertising can use selective awareness to critically evaluate marketing messages and make informed purchasing decisions rather than being swayed by emotional appeals.

Mutually Beneficial Relationships: Building Bridges, Not Walls Through Focused Empathy and Collaboration

Mastery fosters the ability to acquire your needs without harming others through focused empathy and collaboration. It is not about ruthless competition but about creating win-win situations through focused communication and negotiation. You develop the emotional intelligence to navigate complex relationships and build bridges of trust with others. Imagine a seasoned negotiator who uses their focused attention to understand the needs of all parties involved. Through "peaceful and harmonious negotiation," facilitated by focused listening and empathetic communication, they craft solutions that benefit everyone at the table, fostering a sense of camaraderie and respect.

- **Social and Emotional Intelligence Connections:** This relates to emotional intelligence, the ability to understand and manage one's own emotions and those of others. It also connects to social skills, the ability to interact effectively with others.

  Example: A team leader using focused empathy can understand their team members' different perspectives and needs, fostering a collaborative and supportive work environment.

Developing Emotional Intelligence Through Focused Self-Awareness, Empathy, Regulation, Social Skills, and Motivation

Developing emotional intelligence is crucial for building resilience and navigating relationships effectively. This is achieved through focused self-awareness, empathy, regulation, social skills, and motivation.

1) **Self-awareness:** The first step is to understand your emotions through focused introspection. Regularly reflect on your feelings and reactions. Journaling, mindfulness, and focused self-reflection can be powerful tools for this.

- **What it is:** Self-awareness is the foundation of EQ. It is the ability to recognize and understand one's emotions, their triggers, and their impact on one's thoughts and behavior. It is about being honest with oneself about one's strengths and weaknesses.

- **How to develop it through focused practice:**

  a) **Focused Introspection/Self-Reflection:** Regularly take time to reflect on your experiences and identify the emotions you felt. Ask yourself: What emotions did I experience in this situation? Why did I feel this way? How did this emotion influence my actions?

  b) **Journaling:** Writing down your thoughts and feelings can help you identify patterns and gain deeper insights into your emotional landscape. Focus on describing the emotions you experienced, the situations that triggered them, and your reactions.

  c) **Mindfulness:** Practices like meditation and mindfulness exercises help you become more present and aware of your emotions in the moment. Focus your attention on your breath, bodily sensations, and thoughts without judgment.

  Example: After a challenging meeting, instead of simply feeling stressed, you might use focused introspection to identify that you felt frustrated because your ideas were not heard. This self-awareness allows you to address the underlying issue more constructively in future meetings.

2) **Empathy:** Through focused perspective-taking, put yourself in others' shoes. Practice active listening by giving your full attention to the speaker, acknowledging their feelings, and responding thoughtfully.

- **What it is:** Empathy is the ability to understand and share the feelings of others. It involves putting yourself in their shoes and seeing the world from their perspective. It is not just about understanding their words but also their underlying emotions.

- **How to develop it through focused practice:**

  a) **Focused Perspective-Taking:** Consciously try to see situations from the other person's point of view. Ask yourself: How might this person be feeling? What are their needs and concerns?

  b) **Active Listening:** Give the speaker your full attention verbally and nonverbally. Acknowledge their feelings by summarizing their points and asking clarifying questions. Focus on understanding their message rather than formulating your response.

  Example: During a disagreement with a colleague, instead of getting defensive, you might use focused perspective-taking to understand their concerns and find a mutually agreeable solution.

3) **Self-Regulation:** Manage your emotions effectively through focused emotional regulation techniques. Techniques such as deep breathing, mindfulness, and pausing before responding can help.

- **What it is:** Self-regulation is the ability to manage your own emotions effectively. It is about controlling impulsive reactions, handling stress, and adapting to changing

SECTION V: LIFE SPECIALIZATION

circumstances. It is not about suppressing emotions but about expressing them appropriately.

- **How to develop it through focused practice:**

    a) **Focused Emotional Regulation Techniques:** Practice techniques like deep breathing, mindfulness, and pausing before responding to emotionally charged situations. Focus on controlling your immediate reactions and responding thoughtfully.

    b) **Cognitive Reframing:** Challenge negative or unhelpful thoughts and replace them with more positive and realistic ones. Focus on changing your interpretation of events rather than the events themselves.

    Example: If you feel anger rising during a discussion, take a few deep breaths and count to ten before speaking. This focused pause helps you respond calmly rather than reacting impulsively.

4) **Social Skills:** Build strong relationships by being approachable and maintaining open communication through focused interpersonal engagement. Practice positive body language, show appreciation, and give constructive feedback.

- **What it is:** Social skills are the ability to interact effectively with others. It involves clear communication, active listening, empathy, and the ability to build and maintain positive relationships.

- **How to develop it through focused practice:**

    a) **Focused Interpersonal Engagement:** Practice positive body language (eye contact, smiling), active listening, and clear communication. Focus on building rapport and showing genuine interest in others.

b) **Giving and Receiving Feedback: Learn** to give constructive feedback in a supportive way and be open to receiving feedback from others. Focus on specific behaviors and their impact.

Example: During a team meeting, use positive body language and actively listen to each member's perspective. Offer constructive feedback on their ideas and show appreciation for their contributions

5) **Motivation:** Stay driven by your internal values and goals through focused value clarification and goal setting. Reflect on what motivates you and align your actions with these drivers.

• **What it is:** In the context of EQ, motivation is driven by internal values and goals rather than external rewards or pressures. It is about having a clear sense of purpose and aligning your actions with your values.

• **How to develop it through focused practice:**

a) **Focused Value Clarification:** Reflect on your core values and identify what is truly important to you. Focus on understanding what drives you and what gives your life meaning.

b) **Focused Goal Setting:** Set personal and professional goals that align with your values and provide a sense of direction. Focus on setting SMART goals (Specific, Measurable, Achievable, Relevant, Time-bound).

Example: Set personal goals that are meaningful to you, such as learning a new skill or contributing to a cause you care about. Regularly review your progress and celebrate small victories to stay motivated

Navigating Complex Relationships Through Focused Communication, Conflict Resolution, Trust Building, Networking, and Collaboration

Building and maintaining healthy relationships requires focused communication, conflict-resolution skills, trust-building strategies, effective networking, and a collaborative mindset.

1) **Conflict Resolution:** Approach conflicts with a problem-solving mindset through focused analysis of the situation and empathetic communication. Use "I" statements to express your feelings without blaming others and seek to understand the other person's perspective.

   - **What it is:** Conflict is inevitable in any relationship. Conflict resolution is the ability to address disagreements constructively and find mutually acceptable solutions. It is about focusing on the problem, not the person.

   - **How to develop it through focused practice:**

     a) **Focused Analysis of the Situation:** Before reacting, take time to understand the root cause of the conflict. What are the different perspectives involved? What are the underlying needs and concerns? Focus on gathering information and understanding the context.

     b) **Empathetic Communication:** Use "I" statements to express your feelings and needs without blaming or accusing the other person. For example, instead of saying, "You always miss deadlines," say, "I feel concerned when deadlines are missed because it affects our project timeline." This focused communication helps de-escalate the situation and promotes understanding.

c) **Active Listening:** Give the other person your full attention, listen carefully to their perspective, and acknowledge their feelings. Focus on understanding their point of view rather than preparing your rebuttal.

d) **Finding Common Ground:** Focus on identifying areas of agreement and building upon them. Look for solutions that address the needs of all parties involved.

Example: Two team members disagree about the best approach to a project. Using focused analysis, they realize the disagreement stems from different priorities (speed vs. quality). Through empathetic communication, they express their concerns and find a compromise that balances both priorities.

2) **Building Trust:** Trust is the foundation of any strong relationship. Be consistent, reliable, and transparent in your actions through focused integrity and open communication.

- **What it is:** Trust is the cornerstone of any strong relationship. It is the belief that others are reliable, honest, and have your best interests at heart.

- **How to develop it through focused practice:**

    a) **Focused Integrity:** Be consistent in your words and actions. Follow through on your commitments and be honest in your dealings with others. This focused integrity builds a reputation of reliability and trustworthiness.

b) **Open Communication:** Communicate clearly and transparently. Share information openly and be willing to listen to feedback. Focus on creating a safe and open communication environment.

c) **Vulnerability (Appropriate):** Showing appropriate vulnerability can foster deeper connections and build trust. This might involve admitting mistakes or sharing personal experiences (within appropriate boundaries). Focus on being genuine and authentic in your interactions.

Example: A manager consistently follows through on their promises to their team, communicates openly about company changes, and admits when they make mistakes. This focused integrity and open communication build trust within the team.

3) **Networking:** Expand your network by building genuine connections through focused engagement with professional communities. Show genuine interest in others and offer help and support.

- **What it is:** Networking is about building and maintaining professional relationships with people in your field or related fields. It is not just about collecting contacts; it is about building genuine connections.

- **How to develop it through focused practice:**

  a) **Focused Engagement:** Attend industry events, join professional organizations, and participate in online communities related to your field. Focus on actively engaging with others and contributing to the conversation.

b) **Genuine Interest:** Show genuine interest in others by asking about their experiences, work, and perspectives. Focus on listening more than talking and building rapport.

c) **Offering Help and Support:** Be willing to offer help and support to others without expecting immediate returns. This focused generosity builds goodwill and strengthens relationships.

d) **Follow-up:** Follow up with a personalized message or email after meeting someone new. This focused follow-up demonstrates your interest and strengthens the connection.

Example: A graphic designer attends a design conference, actively participates in workshops, and connects with other designers. They offer feedback on others' work and share their insights, building valuable connections within the design community.

4) **Collaboration:** Foster a collaborative environment by encouraging teamwork and valuing diverse perspectives through focused communication and inclusive leadership.

- **What it is:** Collaboration is the ability to work effectively with others towards a shared goal. It involves teamwork, communication, and mutual respect.

- **How to develop it through focused practice:**

  a) **Focused Communication:** Communicate clearly and effectively with team members. Ensure everyone is on the same page and that information is shared openly and transparently.

  b) **Inclusive Leadership:** Create an inclusive environment where everyone feels valued and respected. Encourage diverse perspectives and create opportunities for team members to contribute. Focus on building a sense of shared ownership and responsibility.

c) **Active Participation:** Actively participate in team meetings and projects. Contribute your ideas, listen to others, and be willing to compromise. Focus on working together towards a common goal.

d) **Recognizing Contributions:** Acknowledge and appreciate the contributions of others. This focused recognition strengthens team morale and fosters a positive collaborative environment.

Example: A marketing team working on a new campaign uses focused communication to brainstorm ideas, assign tasks, and track progress. They create an inclusive environment where everyone feels comfortable sharing their perspectives, leading to a more creative and effective campaign.

Inner Peace and Acceptance: Finding Serenity in the Storm Through Focused Acceptance and Adaptive Coping

Life presents unexpected twists. It is unavoidable. Yet, by honing your ability to focus and embrace adaptive coping mechanisms selectively, you nurture a profound inner landscape of resilience. You cultivate a keen awareness of life's unpredictable nature, channeling your energy into transforming challenges into opportunities.

Picture a lone hiker caught off guard by an unexpected deluge, the sky darkening ominously as nature unleashes its fury. They might find themselves disheartened and ready to surrender. Yet, a true connoisseur of perception would embrace the rain, recalibrate their intentions if needed, and forge ahead on their path with an unwavering resolve. Embracing this understanding, along with targeted solutions, cultivates profound tranquility and emotional strength, empowering you to maneuver through life's tumultuous challenges with poise and tenacity.

- **Psychological Connections:** This relates to the concept of acceptance and commitment therapy (ACT), which emphasizes accepting difficult thoughts and feelings rather than trying to avoid them. It also connects to the concept of cognitive flexibility, the ability to adapt your thinking and behavior to changing circumstances.

Problem-Solving Powerhouse: Sharpening Your Mental Axe Through Focused Analysis and Persistent Effort

Mastering selective awareness transforms you into a problem-solving powerhouse, sharpening your mental axe through focused analysis and persistent effort. It empowers you to dissect complex challenges, identify their core elements, and develop effective solutions with precision and unwavering determination.

Laser Focus, Burning Through Obstacles: Precision Strikes Against Challenges Through Focused Analysis and Strategic Thinking

The passage beautifully describes focused attention as a powerful tool: "It burns a hole straight through the heart of the knottiest of problems." This "laser focus," cultivated through selective awareness and disciplined analysis, allows you to cut through distractions and concentrate on the essential elements of a challenge. Imagine a detective meticulously examining a crime scene through focused observation and application of forensic techniques. Their keen eye, honed through years of selective awareness practice, allows them to identify seemingly insignificant details that others might miss. A single fingerprint, a subtle fiber snagged on a garment—these become crucial pieces of the puzzle, all brought to light by the detective's laser focus. This same approach empowers you to tackle challenges in your own life. By directing your mental energy with unwavering concentration through focused analysis and strategic thinking, you can dissect complex problems, identify their core elements, and develop solutions with surgical precision.

- **Cognitive and Problem-Solving Connections:** This relates to the concept of focused problem-solving, which involves breaking down complex problems into smaller, more manageable parts, analyzing each part individually, and then synthesizing the findings to develop a solution. It also connects to the concept of critical thinking, which involves evaluating information objectively and identifying underlying assumptions and biases.

  Example: A software developer facing a complex coding bug can use focused analysis to isolate the problem, systematically test different solutions, and eventually identify and fix the bug.

Relentless Determination: From Persistence to Perseverance Through Focused Effort and Adaptive Problem-Solving

Mastery does not stop at the initial hurdle. The passage emphasizes that focused attention "keeps on until it liquidates what is left around the hole." This relentless determination, driven by focused effort and adaptive problem-solving, is not blind stubbornness; it is a conscious choice to persist in the face of obstacles, adapting your approach as needed. Imagine a scientist on the verge of a breakthrough discovery. They encounter a series of setbacks, experiments that fail to yield the desired results. But a master of selective awareness would not be deterred. They would analyze their failures through focused reflection, learn from them, and refine their approach through focused experimentation. Their unwavering focus, combined with focused adaptation, fuels their perseverance, pushing them to keep chipping away at the problem until they achieve their desired outcome.

- **Motivational and Psychological Connections:** This relates to grit, defined as perseverance and passion for long-term goals. Grit is associated with higher levels of achievement and success. It also connects to the concept of resilience, the ability to bounce back from adversity.

  Example: Consider the journey of an entrepreneur embarking on a new venture; they are likely to encounter a labyrinth of obstacles, from the elusive quest for funding to the unpredictable tides of marketing and the relentless competition lurking in the shadows. With relentless determination and a keen ability to navigate challenges, they can dismantle barriers and forge a thriving enterprise. They would dissect every detail, evolve with each twist, and relentlessly forge ahead.

Strategic Adaptation: Refining Your Approach Through Focused Reflection and Learning from Feedback

True problem-solving mastery involves persistence and the ability to adapt one's approach based on feedback and new information. This requires focused reflection on one's progress, a willingness to learn from one's mistakes, and the flexibility to adjust one's strategies as needed.

- **Learning and Adaptability Connections:** This relates to the concept of iterative problem-solving, which involves repeatedly testing and refining solutions based on feedback. It also connects to the concept of learning from failure, which involves viewing mistakes as opportunities for growth and development.

Example: A writer receiving feedback on their manuscript might use focused reflection to identify areas for improvement and revise their work accordingly. This iterative process of writing, feedback, and revision leads to a stronger final product.

In Conclusion

Cultivating a Life of Purpose and Impact Through Focused Selective Awareness!

Selective awareness mastery is not a mere skill; it is a transformative journey of focused self-discovery, continuous growth, and purposeful impact. It empowers you to become the architect of your own destiny, cultivating a flourishing inner landscape that yields a bountiful harvest of self-mastery, resilient well-being, and the ability to navigate life's challenges with laser focus and unwavering determination. It is about consciously choosing where to direct your mental energy, cultivating the ability to discern the essential from the trivial, and acting with focused intention to create a life of meaning and purpose.

This chapter has explored how selective awareness weaves a tapestry of benefits for your destiny through several key areas:

- **Blooming with Self-Mastery:** Navigating Your Life with Focused Intention and Direction: Master your inner world through focused attention, build a supportive network through focused relationship cultivation, set clear goals through focused visioning, and wield your influence responsibly through focused ethical application.

- **Inner Peace Through Resilience:** Building Your Emotional Fortress Through Focused Emotional Regulation and Adaptive Capacity: Shielding yourself from negative influences through focused attention and critical thinking, building mutually beneficial relationships through focused empathy and collaboration, developing emotional intelligence through focused self-awareness, regulation, social skills, and motivation, and finding inner peace through focused acceptance and adaptive coping.

- **Problem-Solving Powerhouse:** Sharpening Your Mental Axe Through Focused Analysis and Persistent Effort: Tackling complex challenges with precision through focused analysis and strategic thinking, maintaining relentless determination through focused effort and adaptive problem-solving, and refining your approach through focused reflection and learning from feedback.

These interconnected elements, cultivated through focused practice and guided by selective awareness through disciplined perception, empower you to:

- **Live with Greater Clarity and Purpose:** By focusing on your core values and goals, you create a life that is aligned with your true self.

- **Build Stronger and More Meaningful Relationships:** By practicing empathy and focused communication, you foster deeper connections with others.

- **Overcome Challenges with Resilience and Determination:** By developing focused problem-solving skills and a growth mindset, you navigate life's obstacles with greater ease and confidence.

- **Make a Lasting Impact on the World:** By focusing your expertise and contributing meaningfully to your chosen field, you leave a legacy that extends beyond your own individual achievements.

A Final Reflection: The Potential Within Us All

While some may seem to possess an almost preternatural ability to focus and achieve extraordinary results, the truth is that the power of selective awareness resides within us all. It is a skill that can be cultivated and honed through focused practice and disciplined perception. By consciously choosing where to direct our attention, we can unlock our own potential and create lives of purpose, impact, and enduring fulfillment.

Thriller Twist

Imagine the potential of a world where more individuals have mastered the principles of focused selective awareness, not as shadowy manipulators but as focused problem-solvers, compassionate leaders, and innovative thinkers working collaboratively to address the world's most pressing challenges. This is not a fantasy; it is a future we can actively create by embracing the power of focused selective awareness in our own lives and sharing these principles with others. Perhaps this is the most compelling story of all – the story of a world transformed by the focused potential within each of us.

DISCIPLINED DEVOTION: SHAPING REALITY WITH PRAYER AND LOVE

ᏧᏫᏧᏫᏧᏫ

Selective awareness, the ability to focus on specific information while filtering out distractions, isn't just a cognitive skill; it's a potent tool for enriching our experience of the world. This concept finds remarkable application in two fundamental aspects of human life: prayer and love. Through these practices, we cultivate exceptional power utilization, transforming our inner landscape and forging profound connections with the external world.

Prayer: A Symphony of Intention and Focus

Prayer, in its many forms, transcends religious boundaries. It's the act of directing our focused attention towards a specific intention– a silent conversation with something greater than ourselves, an expression of gratitude, or a heartfelt petition for guidance. Neuroscientists have begun to explore the neurological basis of prayer, revealing its potential to activate brain regions associated with positive emotions, self-reflection, and a sense of belonging. By harnessing the power of selective awareness, prayer allows us to:

- **Cultivate Inner Strength:** When we focus on our hopes and aspirations during prayer, we activate neural pathways associated with motivation and resilience. This focused intention strengthens our resolve and empowers us to navigate life's challenges with greater fortitude.

- **Connect with Something Greater:** Prayer transcends the limitations of the self. Whether directed towards a deity, a universal force, or simply a higher purpose, it fosters a sense of connection that reduces feelings of isolation and fosters a sense of belonging to something larger than ourselves.

- **Foster Gratitude:** Prayer, when used to express thankfulness, activates brain regions associated with positive emotions. By focusing on blessings received, we cultivate an attitude of gratitude, a powerful tool for boosting overall well-being.

Love: A Tapestry of Selective Attention and Empathy

Love, in all its multifaceted forms, thrives on selective awareness. When we focus our attention on a loved one, we become attuned to their subtle cues, emotions, and needs. This focused empathy allows us to build strong, supportive relationships. Selective awareness empowers love by fostering:

- **Deep Connection:** By focusing our attention on a loved one, we create a sense of intimacy and shared understanding. We become more attuned to their emotions and needs, fostering a deeper connection.

- **Compassion and Forgiveness:** Selective awareness allows us to recognize and understand the perspectives and experiences of others. This fosters compassion and forgiveness within relationships, strengthening the bonds of love.

- **Joy and Gratitude:** When we focus on the positive aspects of a loved one and the joy they bring to our lives, we activate brain regions associated with positive emotions. This fosters a sense of gratitude and appreciation for the love we share.

Selective Awareness: Cultivating a Tapestry of Meaning

Prayer and love, when practiced with intention and focused attention, become powerful tools for shaping our reality. By directing our selective awareness towards these practices, we cultivate exceptional power utilization, enriching our inner lives and forging meaningful connections with the world around us. They become a testament to the transformative potential of human intention and a powerful reminder of the profound impact we can have on ourselves and those around us.

Unveiling the Hidden Power: Prayer as a Portal to Perception and Reality

We journey into the enigmatic realm of prayer, a practice that transcends mere supplication. Here, it becomes a potent weapon in the arsenal of selective awareness, a key that unlocks the hidden chambers of perception and, some whisper, reality itself. Let us dissect the mechanics of this enigmatic ritual and unveil the psychological landscapes it cultivates within the mind.

1. The Art of Directed Attentiveness: Crafting the Perfect Plea

Unveiling the Hidden Power: Prayer as a Portal to Perception and Reality

The Art of Directed Attentiveness: Crafting the Laser-Focused Plea

Has your mind wandered during prayer as if your mind is juggling thoughts that will only truly reside with you for fleeting moments and with ambiguous yearning? Great prayer transcends this noisome mental din. The directed attentiveness is a strong laser that cuts through the veil of the commonplace.

Imagine a sculptor meticulously shaping a masterpiece from a block of marble. Each word in your prayer is a precise chisel stroke, crafting a coherent and articulate message. Superfluous language falls away, leaving only the essence of your plea, rich in adoration and devoid of empty embellishments. This coherence strengthens your "Disciplined Perception," ensuring your message resonates with unwavering clarity.

Scientifically, studies suggest that focused attention during prayer may enhance cognitive function by reducing distractions and promoting clarity. This "laser beam" focus may be linked to increased activation in brain regions associated with language processing and emotional regulation. **Always Remember, Prayer is not a rigid formula!**

Improvisation in Prayer: A Symphony of the Soul

At its core, prayer is a deeply personal expression. The passage compares it to the improvisation of skilled artists. Just as musicians pour their souls into a unique melody, each heartfelt prayer is a spontaneous creation. No two invocations are exactly alike, for they are born from the individual's raw emotions and genuine yearnings.

This improvisation underscores the power of authenticity in prayer. The most potent pleas are not scripted or rehearsed; they are the unfiltered expressions of a yearning heart.

Human psychology echoes this sentiment—prayer is not about rambling wishes. It is like a mental workout, honing your focus into a powerful beam. Imagine sculpting a masterpiece—each word a precise chisel stroke, crafting a clear and concise message. Ditch the fluff and focus on the essence of your plea, packing it with genuine emotions. This laser-sharp focus ensures your message lands with unwavering impact.

Psychologically, studies suggest that focused attention during prayer may enhance cognitive function and emotional regulation.

This "disciplined perception" allows you to craft clear and authentic pleas, free from distractions and anxieties.

The power of improvisation in prayer does not mean abandoning structure entirely. It is about allowing your heart to guide your words, creating a prayer that's uniquely yours. Embrace the power of focused attention to hone your message and unleash your inner voice in a symphony of the soul.

2. The Impact of Prayer on Destiny: A Tapestry of Connection

Strengthening Bonds: Weaving the Threads of Faith

Imagine two threads, initially loose and unconnected. One represents your individual self, the other, a higher power, the divine. Prayer, then, becomes the weaver's hands, meticulously interlacing these threads. With each heartfelt plea, each whispered gratitude, the bond between these threads strengthens.

Psychologically, this consistent prayer practice fosters a sense of closeness and belonging to something larger than oneself. As your faith deepens, so too does the strength of this connection. It is not a blind dependence but a source of unwavering support that allows you to navigate life's challenges with newfound courage and resilience.

Additionally, studies suggest that prayer can lead to increased feelings of hope and optimism. This positive outlook can empower you to take action and persevere through difficulties.

Manifestations of Divine Love: A Shower of Blessings

The passage emphasizes that even the simplest prayers hold immense power. Imagine a thirsty traveler lost in the desert. A single, whispered plea for water carries immense weight. Similarly, even the most basic prayers, uttered with genuine yearning, are acknowledged by the divine.

The Self-Help approach emphasizes that these prayers are not met with mere silence but with a "shower of strengthening manifestations of divine love." This does not necessarily mean the fulfillment of every wish but rather the bestowing of spiritual fortitude and emotional resilience to navigate life's challenges. It is a testament to the unwavering love and support that lies at the heart of the divine connection fostered through prayer.

Scientifically, the concept of "manifestations of divine love" might translate to the physiological and psychological benefits associated with prayer. Studies have shown that prayer can lower stress hormones, improve emotional regulation, and strengthen a sense of purpose.

In essence, prayer strengthens the connection between the individual and the divine, fostering a sense of belonging, hope, and inner strength. Whether you view it as a spiritual connection or a self-improvement tool, prayer offers a powerful tool for navigating the complexities of life.

3. Universality of Prayer: A Whisper Heard Across the Void

Prayer Without Borders: Transcending Space and Time

Prayer requires no specific space or time, unlike a symphony, which would need a concert hall or a painting that would demand a canvas. An illicit message can reveal the substance of prayer whispered in a marketplace just as much as one formally declared from a throne room. You can pray alone in the stillness of your room, with the multitudes in a crowded church, or along busy streets. There are no set postures, no set times, and no fixed places.

Scientifically, this universality aligns with the concept of neuroplasticity–the brain's ability to change and adapt throughout life. Regardless of form or location, prayer can activate neural pathways associated with emotional regulation, hope, and even pain management.

Human cognitive psychology provides an easier analogy. Imagine prayer as mental gymnastics. You do not need fancy machinery or a specific place to benefit from an exercise—similarly, prayer tempers your inner resilience irrespective of where or when you utilize it.

The Posture of the Mind: A Symphony of the Soul

It shows that prayer, since it is basically an act of the mind, has to rise from the intention and consciousness of the soul, not so much from the physical positions that one assumes in prayer. Think of a sculptor's work of art: the true beauty it represents is not derived from the chisel or the stone it has been carved from but from the vision within the artist's mind. So, too, the deepest, most powerful prayers emerge not from a knee or other specific posture but from ardent longings and trust that pour out on behalf of the soul.

Psychologically, this concept aligns with the idea of "focused attention." A simple thought imbued with genuine emotion and a clear intention can be just as potent as an elaborate ritual. It is the "posture of the mind," the unwavering focus of your "Disciplined Perception," that truly matters.

The realm of self-help underscores the notion of accessibility, inviting individuals to explore their potential with ease. Prayer stands as an accessible instrument, poised for use by anyone, in any place, at any moment. The essence of prayer transcends the confines of posture, location, or even the articulation of words; it resides within, waiting to be awakened. What one truly requires is an authentic desire coupled with a concentrated intellect.

In essence, prayer transcends the limitations of the physical world. It is a practice that flourishes in the fertile ground of the human mind, offering a powerful and universally accessible tool for navigating life's complexities.

4. The Continuum of Prayer: A Tapestry Woven Throughout Life

Breathing Spirituality: An Unceasing Conversation with the Divine

Prayer transcends the idea of a one-time event. It is not a chore to be checked off a daily to-do list. The passage likens prayer to breathing–a continuous and essential function that sustains life. Imagine a person gasping for air; shallow breaths would not suffice. Similarly, effective prayer is not a series of isolated pleas but an unceasing conversation with the divine.

Self-Help emphasizes this concept. Prayer is a lifelong habit, a continuous thread woven into the tapestry of your existence. This "lifelong, continuous, unceasing habit" transforms even the most mundane aspects of your life into a form of prayer. Every action and thought becomes imbued with a sense of purpose and connection to something larger than yourself. Washing the dishes becomes an act of mindful gratitude; a student hitting the books is infused with a desire to learn and contribute to the world.

Scientifically speaking, that fits right into what we call mindfulness. Infusing one's day with prayer helps one become more aware of each present moment and one's place in it. This can translate into increased focus, less stress, and more peace in one's life.

The Stoic's Whisper: A Philosophy of Constant Connection

The passage quotes Epictetus, a Stoic philosopher who emphasizes the importance of integrating prayer into the very fabric of one's being. He urges us to "think of God more often than you breathe." This is not about blind devotion but about cultivating a constant awareness of the interconnectedness of all things.

Psychologically, this fits with how to live a values-driven life. In this sense, adding prayer into the fabric of your life constructs a character and molds a life to keep up with the most important values and desires. It does not make much sense to pray for patience in the morning and then spend the rest of the day in a rage. As Epictetus says, "True prayer is the way of life philosophy of perpetual connectivity manifesting in every minute detail of your life."

The thriller injects a touch of suspense. Imagine prayer as a secret code, a constant dialogue with a higher power that shapes your actions and decisions. By living a life guided by this "code," you could unknowingly unravel a grand mystery or fulfill a preordained destiny.

The Truest Life: A Symphony of Purpose

And then, in this rousing sentence, the passage ends: "The truest life is literally a way of prayer." As prayer keeps on being part of your every wakeful minute, it imbues your life with, perhaps, an unseen depth in living. Every action now, every thought, becomes an expression of your innermost longings and a reflection of your relatedness to God. This is not blind obedience; this is a life lived to the letter with your highest values, trying to live with intention and purpose.

Human cognitive psychology provides an interesting analogy. Think of prayer as your internal compass. By keeping it constantly engaged, you ensure your actions and decisions are aligned with your true north. Ultimately, this is the essence of the "truest life"–a life lived in constant conversation with the divine, where every breath becomes a prayer, and every action expresses your deepest purpose.

5. The Timing of Divine Response: An Unfolding Mystery

The Nature of the Prayer: Planting Seeds for the Future

This idea delves into the intriguing question of response times to prayer. Unlike a text message with an immediate (almost guaranteed) reply, prayer operates on a different timescale. Sometimes, the answer manifests within seconds, a tangible response to a heartfelt plea. Other times, the wait can stretch for hours, days, or even years. This variability can be a source of frustration and doubt. Let us explore the factors that influence this enigmatic waiting period.

- **The Brain's Response Time:** While the concept of a "divine response" may not translate directly through scientific notions, studies suggest that prayer can release endorphins and other neurochemicals associated with feelings of well-being. This "response" may not be immediate but can manifest over time with consistent prayer practice. Research on mindfulness meditation, which shares similarities with prayer, has shown that it can change brain structures and functions, particularly in areas related to emotion regulation and stress reduction. For instance, mindfulness practices have been found to reduce symptoms of depression by altering brain activity patterns. Similarly, meditation and yoga have been shown to modulate brain mechanisms that affect behavior and anxiety, suggesting that these practices can lead to long-term changes in brain function.

- **Planting Seeds for the Future:** Imagine planting a seed. The time it takes for that seed to blossom into a flower depends on the seed type, the soil quality, and the nurturing it receives. Similarly, the nature of your prayer influences the response time. A simple request for guidance might find a swift answer, while a more complex plea, one that requires significant personal growth or a shift in circumstances, may necessitate a longer period of "unfolding." This does not mean your prayer is unheard. It simply suggests that the answer is unfolding in a way that best serves your growth and ultimate well-being. Just as mindfulness and meditation practices require time and consistency to produce noticeable changes in the brain and behavior, prayer requires patience and persistence, too. The gradual unfolding of answers to prayer can be seen as a process of personal and spiritual growth, akin to how mindfulness practices cultivate a deeper sense of awareness and emotional resilience over time.

- **The Unfolding Mystery:** The timing of a divine response adds an element of suspense. Imagine praying for a specific outcome, then witnessing seemingly unrelated events unfold. Could these be the first pieces of a grand puzzle, a divine response slowly taking shape? For example, a study from Duke University found that individuals who maintained a regular prayer practice reported experiencing a series of positive life changes over time, which they attributed to their prayers. These changes often appeared as small, incremental shifts that eventually led to significant personal transformation.

Human cognitive psychology offers an interesting explanation. At the Duke Clinical Research Institute, specifically through the MANTRA project, the research investigated the healing power of prayer among heart patients and found some interesting results. The Center for Spirituality, Theology, and Health at Duke University further publishes literature discussing how prayer benefits one's mind and body. These studies indeed show that frequent prayer may result in improvements in well-being, reductions in stress, and greater life satisfaction, thereby supporting the idea that the relatively small, cumulative changes noted by the individual are part of a greater transformation process.

Further supporting this, research consistently shows that prayer can have numerous benefits, such as self-soothing, coping with loss, and dealing with traumatic circumstances. Prayer can also serve as a form of concentrated mental motivation for achieving personal goals and focusing on the well-being of others. However, there is no empirical evidence that such mental messaging works when it comes to prayer as a form of asking for something from a divine source and then getting it.

What is Necessary for Fulfillment: A Grand Design Beyond Our Perception

Here, prayer introduces the concept of a "grand design," a divine plan that may extend far beyond our limited human understanding. Our prayers may not always be answered in the way we expect because the ultimate fulfillment might lie in a path we have not foreseen.

Imagine a skilled chess player; their moves on the board may seem nonsensical to an observer, but they are part of a larger strategy leading to victory. Similarly, the divine response to one prayer might not be immediate or obvious, but it could be setting the stage for a more profound and lasting fulfillment in the grand scheme of things.

Reframing Expectations

The idea of the "grand design" is a helpful reframing, putting a slightly different twist on what we perhaps expect to get from prayer. It is not necessarily what we want, but trusting a process that may unfold in other ways alleviates frustration and fosters acceptance.

Faith as a Guiding Light

This concept insists that prayer is not a one-time transaction. "The prayer must continue until it produces the desired results." In other words, this is not an act of badgering the divine but of being in constant relation- a conversation in time. Think of a long-distance relationship; it takes trust and communication if it is going to work out. In the same way, prayer, if given steadfastness by faith, builds trust, enabling you to wait patiently and understandingly.

The Power of Consistent Practice: Just like building muscles or learning any new skill, the benefits prayed for might be amplified through practice over time. Thus, a sustained prayerful disposition in daily life, even in waiting times, will further reinforce one's inner resilience and help generate calm acceptance.

In Conclusion

The enigma of when the divine chooses to respond lingers in the shadows, yet the act of prayer endures as a formidable instrument of connection. By delving into the myriad factors that shape response times, we can nurture a profound sense of trust and acceptance, enabling the outcomes of our prayers to unfold in their own exquisite timing.

6. Unveiling the Hidden Arsenal: Prayer's Tangible Effects in a World of Doubt

The influence of prayer can feel like an intangible whisper in the vast cosmos. Yet, its impact is demonstrably real, leaving a trail of evidence as undeniable as a spy's coded message. Once a skeptical observer, science is now peering into the dimly lit corridors of prayer, uncovering a hidden arsenal with the potential to reshape our reality experience.

Measurable Outcomes: Cracking the Code of the Unseen

Envision a clandestine organization harnessing an enigmatic power, one that possesses the ability to transform your very essence of condition. Explorations into this previously uncharted domain are revealing a connection between prayer and:

- **Enhanced Physical Resilience:** Research suggests prayer can act like a covert agent, lowering blood pressure and reducing stress hormones–the body's harbingers of chaos. This translates to a heightened sense of physical buoyancy, a fortification against the relentless assault of daily stress.

- **Sharpened Mental Acuity:** Focused prayer may be a clandestine training ground for the mind. Studies hint that it fosters mental clarity by silencing the incessant chatter of distractions, leading to a sharper intellect, better equipped to tackle life's challenges.

- **Fortified Moral Compass:** Prayer can be a beacon in the murky waters of ethical dilemmas. Strengthening your connection to a higher purpose potentially steers you towards more principled decisions, turning you into a champion for justice in the grand moral play of life.

- **Deeper Connections Unveiled:** Prayer can cultivate empathy and compassion like a secret society, fostering a sense of camaraderie amongst its members. This can lead to stronger, more meaningful relationships, weaving a tapestry of understanding where there once was isolation.

These are just a few whispers from the vast network of benefits. Science, the quintessential skeptic, is beginning to acknowledge the tangible effects of prayer, leaving a trail of evidence as undeniable as a spy's coded message.

Awakening the Self: A Descent into the Hidden Chambers

But the impact of prayer extends far beyond the physical. It is a psychological thriller, a descent into the labyrinthine chambers of your own mind. Prayer can be the spark that ignites a flame within the depths of consciousness, illuminating:

- **Self-Awareness:** Prayer creates a sanctuary for quiet contemplation, a space where you can confront your reflection without the distorting filters of self-deception. This brutally honest self-assessment reveals your strengths and weaknesses, your desires and fears–a crucial first step on the path to genuine self-improvement.

- **Moral Evolution:** As prayer forces you to confront your shortcomings, it can act as a catalyst for moral growth. It becomes a crucible where your ego is tempered, fostering intellectual humility and a heightened sense of moral responsibility. You emerge not as a self-righteous victor but a student forever striving to improve.

- **The Path to Grace:** Confronting your flaws might seem like a harrowing psychological thriller, but it ultimately paves the way for a more compassionate and understanding self. Prayer allows you to embrace your humanity with all its imperfections, fostering the acceptance and grace that eluded you before.

Remember! Prayer is not a one-time event! It is a lifelong practice with the potential to transform our perception of reality. By understanding its measurable benefits and profound impact on the inner self, we unlock the true power of this hidden arsenal.

Revelation Through Thought: A Message from the Enigma

There is an undeniable allure to the notion that prayer can facilitate a connection with a higher intelligence, a hidden benefactor whispering solutions in your ear. This "directed attentiveness," as some scholars call it, can lead to:

- **Inspired Solutions:** Focused prayer can be a breeding ground for creative solutions. Imagine a message encoded in a dream or a sudden flash of insight, sparking innovative approaches to seemingly insurmountable problems. Prayer can be the secret decoder ring that unlocks the hidden language of inspiration.

- **Actionable Strategies:** The insights gained from prayer are not abstract philosophies but translated into actionable strategies. You emerge from your contemplation not just with a new understanding but with a clear-cut strategy for sailing through life's intricacies and reaching your objectives.

- **Revelation Through Introspection:** The very act of prayer itself, even without the whisper of a divine voice, can be a powerful catalyst for introspection. By delving into the depths of your own being, you gain a deeper understanding of yourself and the world around you, a revelation that unfolds like a thrilling narrative, chapter by chapter.

In Conclusion

The Fabric of Existence: An Ode to Inner Strength! Prayer's impact unfolds across various dimensions, resonating within the mind, body, and spirit. Through the lens of self-awareness and moments of profound clarity, prayer emerges as a vital instrument for traversing the intricate maze of existence. It lies in wait, a concealed arsenal yearning for revelation.

7. The Worshiping Spirit: A Journey of Self-Discovery

Prayer as the Emanation of the Worshiping Spirit

The passage delves into the core essence of prayer, defining it as the "emanation of man's worshiping spirit." This is not simply about uttering words or adhering to rituals. It is about a fundamental human yearning for connection, a deep-seated desire to commune with something larger than oneself. Let us explore how prayer facilitates this connection and fosters self-discovery.

- **Intrinsic Motivation:** Prayer can be understood as an expression of our inherent need for meaning and purpose in life. It is a way to connect with something larger than ourselves, which can be a powerful motivator for positive growth.

- **The Spark of Divinity Within:** Envision a diminutive ember radiating warmth within your being, a flicker of the transcendent essence. Prayer serves as the catalyst that transforms this ember into a vibrant flame. This intrinsic "worshiping spirit" reflects a fundamental aspect of humanity, a deep-seated longing to connect with the very essence of existence itself. In the act of prayer, you cultivate this essence, permitting it to cast light upon the journey of self-exploration.

Moral Apex: A Climb Upward

The passage suggests that prayer can help us reach the "apex of moral identity." Moral growth is not a destination; it is a continuous journey. Prayer acts as a guide on this journey, a tool for introspection and self-reflection. As you engage in heartfelt prayer, you confront your flaws and limitations. This self-awareness becomes the catalyst for moral growth, motivating you to strive toward a more compassionate, ethical, and principled way of living.

The Climber's Rope

Imagine a mountain climber scaling a peak. Prayer is the rope that secures them, the fuel that propels them forward. With each heartfelt plea, each moment of introspection fostered by prayer, you ascend the slopes of your own morality. Prayer can:

- **Cultivate Compassion:** In the act of reaching beyond the confines of the self, one may discover that prayer cultivates a profound empathy and a deeper understanding of the human experience shared with others.

- **Strengthen Your Resolve:** Praying can fortify one's inner resolve, facilitate resistance against temptation, and guide decisions that resonate with one's core values.

- **Provide Moral Clarity:** In the quiet moments of contemplation, the act of prayer emerges as a beacon, illuminating the intricate dance between morality and choice, steering one toward a more principled existence.

The Invisible Energy of Devotion

This idea describes the emanation of the "worshiping spirit" as the "most powerful form of energy one can generate." This energy is not a physical force but a potent surge of devotion, gratitude, and love that radiates outward. This invisible energy has the power to transform your inner landscape, fostering a sense of peace, purpose, and connection to all things.

The Power of Positive Emotions

Research suggests that feelings of gratitude, compassion, and love can positively impact mental and physical well-being. By nurturing these emotions, prayer can contribute to a more positive outlook and inner peace.

Prayer: A Catalyst for Transformation

By nurturing the worshiping spirit through prayer, you embark on a profound journey of self-discovery. This journey is not just about uncovering your flaws; it is about revealing the immense potential for moral growth and spiritual evolution that resides within you. Prayer becomes the catalyst for a transformation, guiding you toward becoming the best version of yourself.

Unveiling Your Potential: Prayer is a tool for self-discovery that helps you shed light on your strengths, weaknesses, and aspirations. By confronting your shadow and embracing your potential, you pave the way for significant personal growth.

In Conclusion

At its core, prayer embodies a complex interplay of dimensions, offering the possibility to deepen our existence in profound and varied ways. It serves as a refuge, a fountain of creativity, and a beacon illuminating the journey toward ethical and spiritual evolution.

8. A Force Beyond Nature: The Mystery of Miracles[6]

This concept explores the fascinating idea of prayer as a powerful agent that can shape reality in ways that challenge our traditional

---

[6] **The "blurring of lines"** is not about science proving or disproving the existence of the spiritual. It is about recognizing the limitations of each domain and exploring the potential for dialogue and mutual enrichment. It acknowledges that human experience encompasses both the measurable and the immeasurable, the physical and the metaphysical. While science focuses on the natural world, philosophy, and theology provide frameworks for exploring the deeper questions of meaning, purpose, and the nature of reality that often lie beyond the scope of scientific inquiry. It is about recognizing the validity of different ways of knowing and seeking a more holistic understanding of human existence.

John Polkinghorne: Polkinghorne, a physicist turned theologian, advocates for a "critical realism" approach. He suggests that both science and religion offer insights into reality, albeit through different methodologies. He emphasizes the importance of empirical evidence and rational reflection in understanding the world.

- **Experiences that seem to defy scientific explanation:** Some experiences, such as near-death experiences, spontaneous healings, or powerful spiritual experiences, can be difficult to explain perceptions. It posits that prayer may serve as a catalyst for results frequently characterized as "miraculous."

Observable Power: Blurring the Lines Between Science and Spirit

Note: It is important to be very careful when discussing prayer and its effects on health within a " science framework." While personal experiences and anecdotal evidence can be meaningful, they do not constitute scientific proof. Rigorous scientific studies on prayer and healing are complex and often yield mixed results. It is crucial to avoid presenting prayer as a scientifically proven medical intervention.

The prayer's magnificent unpredictable outcomes, as written by a physician, highlight the observable power of prayer. They have witnessed firsthand individuals overcoming seemingly insurmountable challenges through prayer. This phenomenon blurs the lines between the realm of science and the realm of the spirit.

- **Research on mindfulness and meditation,** while not directly investigating prayer, offers valuable insights into the potential psychological benefits of focused attention and reflection practices. These practices share commonalities with prayer, such as quiet contemplation, focused awareness of the present moment, and a sense of connection to something

---

solely through scientific means. These experiences can lead some to believe that there are forces or realities beyond the scope of current scientific understanding. However, science typically seeks natural explanations first and continues to investigate these phenomena.

- **The search for meaning and purpose:** Science can explain how the universe works but does not necessarily address the why. Questions of meaning, purpose, and values are often addressed by religion and philosophy. Some argue that a complete understanding of human existence requires integrating both scientific and spiritual perspectives.

- **The impact of beliefs on health and well-being:** As discussed previously with the placebo effect, beliefs, and expectations can have a measurable impact on physical and mental health. This can lead to discussions about the role of faith and spirituality in healing, although it is crucial to distinguish between correlation and causation.

- **The exploration of consciousness:** The nature of consciousness is a complex problem that both science (neuroscience, cognitive science) and philosophy/spirituality grapple with. Some argue that consciousness cannot be fully explained by purely physical processes and that there may be a spiritual or non-physical dimension to it.

larger than oneself. Studies have consistently demonstrated the positive effects of mindfulness and meditation on stress reduction, anxiety management, and overall well-being. Jon Kabat-Zinn's foundational work, Full Catastrophe Living: Using the Wisdom of Your Body and Mind to Face Stress, Pain, and Illness (Kabat-Zinn, 1990), provides a comprehensive introduction to mindfulness-based stress reduction (MBSR) and its applications in managing stress, pain, and illness. Furthermore, a meta-analysis by Grossman et al. (2004), titled "Mindfulness-based stress reduction and health benefits," examined numerous studies on MBSR and confirmed its efficacy in improving various health outcomes, including psychological well-being. These findings suggest that the focused attention and reflective nature of practices like mindfulness and meditation can positively impact mental and emotional health, which may have parallels with the experience of prayer.

- **The placebo effect is another important factor to consider when exploring the potential influence of belief** and expectation on health outcomes. The placebo effect highlights the powerful influence of the mind-body connection, where positive expectations and beliefs about treatment can lead to measurable improvements in symptoms, even if the treatment itself is inert. This phenomenon suggests that the belief in the power of prayer, or any other healing modality, can contribute to a positive placebo response. While the exact mechanisms underlying the placebo effect are still being investigated, the research emphasizes the importance of context and the patient-practitioner relationship in shaping treatment outcomes. Miller and Kaptchuk (2008), in their article "The power of context: reconceptualizing the placebo effect," discuss the complexities of the placebo effect and argue that it is not simply a matter of "trickery" or "suggestion" but a complex psychobiological response influenced by various contextual factors. This research suggests that the belief and expectation associated with prayer could contribute to perceived or actual improvements in well-being, even if there is no direct causal link between prayer and physical outcome.[118]

- **Anecdotal Evidence and Personal Narratives:**[7] This is the most common form of evidence cited in discussions of prayer and healing. Countless books and personal testimonies recount individuals' experiences with prayer and perceived positive outcomes. However, these are subjective and do not control for other factors that might have contributed to the outcome.

Sustainable Practice: Cultivating the Wellspring of Power

The concept underscores the significance of a steadfast commitment to prayer as a means of channeling this latent power. It posits that prayer's potency "originates from and radiates through those individuals who maintain a sustainable practice of prayer."

Envision a source of vitality, its currents surging with vigor and steadiness, nourished by an unending cycle of renewal. In a manner akin to the unfolding of a profound truth, the potency of prayer appears to deepen and expand through the steadfastness of its practice. The deeper you delve into this "serene effort" of prayer, the more you access a profound reservoir of transformative potential.

---

[7] **Important Considerations:**

- **Correlation vs. Causation:** It is crucial to distinguish between correlation and causation. Just because someone experiences a positive outcome after prayer does not mean that the prayer directly caused the outcome.

- **Scientific Rigor:** Conducting scientifically rigorous studies on prayer is challenging due to the difficulty of controlling for confounding variables and the subjective nature of prayer.

- **Respect for Different Perspectives:** It is important to approach this topic with sensitivity and respect for different beliefs and perspectives.

Miracles and the Quieter Magic

In this realm, one may contemplate the striking occurrences of outcomes that defy logic, often ascribed to the power of prayer and commonly termed "miracles." Yet, this also unveils a more nuanced yet profoundly significant influence of prayer. This "constant, quieter miracle" alludes to the unwavering stream of strength and resilience that prayer bestows upon the fabric of daily existence.

Envision athletes in pursuit of excellence—while relentless preparation may not ensure a place in the annals of history, it fortifies their resolve to transcend limits and embrace the journey of speed and endurance. In much the same way, the act of persistent prayer may not ensure miraculous outcomes. Yet, it cultivates within you a profound strength, enabling you to traverse the complexities of existence with enhanced grace and unwavering resilience.

The Unknown Identity: A Force Yet to be Fully Understood

The source and nature of prayer's power remain, for many, a mystery. It can be described as a "force of unknown identity," not to diminish its potential impact but to acknowledge the vastness of what we do not yet fully understand about the universe and the human spirit's connection to it. This "unknown identity" does not necessarily imply a supernatural force; it simply represents the limits of our current scientific understanding. It opens the door to exploring the interplay between belief, subjective experience, and the potential for phenomena that current scientific paradigms may not fully explain.

The Power of Belief and its Impact on Experience: Regardless of the ultimate source, the power of belief itself can be a transformative force. Prayer, as an expression of faith, hope, intention, or deep reflection, can shape our perception of reality and influence how we respond to challenges. This aligns with research on the placebo effect, which demonstrates the powerful influence of belief and expectation on health and well-being. Belief can influence physiological processes, impacting stress levels, immune function, and even pain perception. This suggests that prayer, as a focused act of belief and intention, can have real effects on individuals, even if the underlying mechanisms are not fully understood.

In Conclusion

Prayer: An Instrument of Metamorphosis! Regardless of whether you perceive prayer as a profound manifestation of devotion or a mechanism that can reshape the very essence of existence, its ability to catalyze change in your life is inarguable. Through nurturing a steadfast prayer ritual, one embarks on a journey toward a profound connection with the vastness beyond the self, tapping into an inexhaustible source of inner fortitude and embracing the potential for the extraordinary in all its myriad forms, both grand and subtle.

9. Prayer as a Sign of Maturity and Strength: A Symphony of Body, Mind, and Spirit

Here, we explore the concept of prayer as a hallmark of personal growth and maturity. It suggests that prayer is not merely a childish petition but a potent tool for achieving "unshakable strength." Let us delve into this profound idea:

Maturity in Prayer: A Sign of Growth

This idea challenges the notion that prayer is a simple activity for the immature or helpless. Instead, it argues that "properly understood" prayer is a "mature activity."

Imagine a child throwing a tantrum to get what they want. This is not prayer. True prayer, born from self-reflection and a growing awareness of your place in the universe, signifies a step toward personal maturity. As you confront your vulnerabilities and yearn for connection with something larger than yourself, you engage in a form of "conscious and personal maturity" that prayer fosters.

Harmonious Assembly: A Unification of Being

This notion describes how prayer facilitates a powerful "harmonious assembly" of body, mind, and spirit.

Imagine an orchestra—each instrument, on its own, may create sound, but the harmonious interplay of all elements creates a symphony. Similarly, prayer brings together the various aspects of your being. The physical act of kneeling or meditating calms your body. Your mind quiets as repetitive chants or heartfelt pleas focus your attention. And your spirit soars as you connect with something beyond yourself. This unification fosters a sense of wholeness and inner strength.

The Frail Reed Finds Strength: A Reservoir of Resilience

One can use a metaphor to describe the impact of prayer. It compares a human being to a "frail human reed."

Imagine a single reed, easily bent by the wind. Through prayer, however, this reed acquires "unshakeable strength." This strength does not come from arrogance or physical prowess but from the deep wellspring of peace, purpose, and connection cultivated through prayer. It equips you with the emotional resilience to face life's challenges and the unwavering determination to keep moving forward.

A Symphony of Transformation

Prayer, then, is more than just words whispered into the void. It is a multifaceted practice that fosters personal growth, inner peace, and a powerful sense of connection. By unifying body, mind, and spirit, prayer empowers you to navigate the complexities of life with newfound strength and resilience. As you mature in your prayer practice, you discover a wellspring of inner power that allows you to weather any storm and emerge stronger on the other side.

In Conclusion

Prayer, therefore, is far more than words spoken into the void; it is a symphony of transformation. It is a multifaceted practice that fosters personal growth, inner peace, and a profound sense of connection to something larger than oneself. By unifying body, mind, and spirit, prayer empowers individuals to navigate life's complexities with newfound strength and resilience. As one matures in their prayer practice, they discover a wellspring of inner power that allows them not only to withstand adversity but also to emerge from it stronger and more grounded. It becomes a source of enduring strength and a testament to the power of the human spirit to connect with the divine, the universe, or a deeper sense of self.

10. Prayer as a Source of Luminous Energy

This section delves into the idea of prayer as a source of radiant energy, capable of illuminating the inner core and empowering us to navigate challenging times.

Radium of the Spirit

The passage uses a powerful metaphor, comparing prayer to radium. Radium is a naturally occurring radioactive element known for its luminescence and ability to generate heat. Similarly, prayer is described as a source of "luminous, self-generating energy" that radiates from within. This "radium of the spirit" illuminates the depths of our being, fostering strength, resilience, and a sense of inner peace.

Overcoming Adversity: A Light in the Dark

The passage acknowledges that prayer does not always change external circumstances. It may not bring back a lost loved one or alleviate physical pain. However, prayer offers a powerful source of strength and comfort even in the face of adversity.

Imagine yourself lost in a dark forest. While prayer may not magically transport you out, it can be the source of light that helps you navigate the darkness with greater courage and resilience.

True Power: Inner Strength and Acceptance

The key takeaway is that prayer's power lies not in altering external reality but in transforming our inner landscape. It equips us with the emotional fortitude to endure hardship, the wisdom to find acceptance, and the unwavering spirit to keep moving forward.

Remark

True, prayer may not restore a dead child to life or bring immediate relief from physical pain. But prayer, like radium, is a source of luminous, self-generating energy that can illuminate our path in times of darkness, fostering the strength and resilience to navigate even the most challenging circumstances.

Imagine a candle flame flickering in the darkness. The flame itself may not dispel the darkness entirely, but it provides a source of light and warmth, guiding you through difficult moments. Similarly, prayer offers a beacon of hope and inner strength that illuminates your path during challenging times.

11. Prayer as a Dynamic Cosmic Force

This section dives into the uncharted territory where science and spirituality converge, exploring the concept of prayer as a way to connect with a vast and limitless source of energy that permeates the cosmos.

The Infinite Source: A Bridge Between Worlds

Modern physics explores the concept of a unified field, a theoretical underlying structure of the universe where all fundamental forces are interconnected. From this perspective, prayer could be seen as a way to tap into this interconnectedness, a bridge between the known and the unknown.

- Imagine the universe as a giant symphony, with all its elements playing a harmonious role. In this analogy, prayer could be the conductor's baton, a way to connect with the universal flow of energy and align ourselves with its rhythm.

We all have moments where we feel depleted, like a battery running low. From this perspective, prayer can be a powerful tool for recharging our inner reserves. By connecting with something larger than ourselves, we access a wellspring of strength and inspiration that can revitalize our spirit.

Throughout history, whispers of a hidden dimension have echoed in spiritual traditions. In this context, prayer becomes a thrilling act of reaching out, a tentative touch into the unknown, hoping for a response from beyond the veil.

The act of prayer, regardless of the object of devotion, has been shown to have a measurable impact on brain activity. Areas associated with hope, peace, and focus become more active during prayer, suggesting a potential neurological basis for its benefits.

The Energy Transformation: From Finite to Limitless

Quantum mechanics introduces the concept of wave-particle duality, suggesting that energy and matter are two sides of the same coin. From this perspective, prayer could be a way to influence the energetic field around us, potentially impacting our physical and mental well-being.

- Envision a flickering campfire, casting its gentle glow and offering a comforting embrace against the encroaching darkness. In this metaphor, prayer serves as the bellows, intensifying the flickering flames of our finite energy while harnessing the boundless fire of the universe.

We all have moments of self-doubt and limitation. From this perspective, prayer can be a way to transcend our perceived limitations and tap into a reservoir of universal potential. By connecting with something larger, we access a sense of empowerment and possibility.

- Imagine a hidden doorway within the human psyche. In this context, prayer becomes the key that unlocks this doorway, granting us access to a realm of boundless energy and hidden potential.

Research suggests that prayer can foster a sense of coherence, a feeling that our lives have meaning and purpose. This sense of coherence has been linked to increased resilience and improved mental health.

The Power of the Humble Plea

The placebo effect demonstrates the power of belief to influence our perception of reality. From this perspective, prayer could be a way to harness this power for positive change.

- Imagine a tuning fork struck against a resonant object. In this analogy, prayer acts like the tuning fork, its vibrations resonating with the universe and potentially influencing the energy around us.

In all its varied manifestations, prayer serves as a conduit for articulating our most profound needs and aspirations. In recognizing our inherent vulnerabilities and extending a hand for support, we invite the potential for assistance to flow into our lives, both from within and from the world around us.

- Envision a long-lost tongue, a cipher imbued with the ability to reveal concealed realms of existence. In this realm, prayer emerges as the neglected utterance, a fervent invocation articulated in the dialect of existence, yearning for comprehension.

Prayer can be a powerful tool for self-reflection. By expressing our thoughts and feelings in prayer, we gain clarity and perspective on our own situations.

Aligning with the Universe: A Place Within the Grand Design

The concept of biocentrism suggests that consciousness shapes the universe. From this perspective, prayer could be a way to align our own consciousness with the universal flow of energy, potentially influencing outcomes in subtle ways.

- Imagine a vast ocean teeming with life. In this analogy, prayer acts like a bioluminescent creature, sending out a beacon into the cosmic ocean, a message of connection and a plea for harmony.

Feeling lost and alone is a universal human experience. From this perspective, prayer can be a way to reconnect with the grand scheme of things, reminding us that we are not isolated but part of a vast and interconnected whole.

- Imagine a hidden map leading to a forgotten treasure. Prayer, in this context, becomes the act of following the map, a thrilling quest to navigate the unknown in search of a deeper connection with the universe

Criticisms and Counterarguments

Prayer gives many a sense of comfort and meaning, yet some criticisms and counterpoints carry as much credit. According to some, the positive outcomes experienced by an individual from praying are very much because of the working psychological processes rather than because of any God. For instance, praying allows one to feel in control or at ease in a vague occurrence, thus decreasing stress and anxiety levels. Other critics also point to the meager quantity of empirical evidence supporting the efficacy of prayer in influencing external outcomes and how usually such evidence is inconclusive.

Skeptics maintain, however, that the presence of personal effort, social support, and natural resilience may better account for such life changes. According to them, the benefits of prayer are best described as individual mindsets and placebo effects rather than divine interventions.

With these criticisms in mind, one can give a better-balanced view of prayer's role in aligning with the universe. While it may not guarantee specific outcomes, the value of prayer may lie in cultivating a sense of connection, purpose, and inner peace- all so crucial for well-being.

12. Prayer as a Continuous Divine Accompaniment

Presence of the Divine: A Constant Companion

Imagine life as a grand adventure. In its truest form, prayer is not just a fleeting request whispered in a quiet moment. It is the constant presence of a trusted companion by your side, a divine friend journeying with you through every twist and turn. This companionship is not confined to designated prayer times or specific locations. It is a continuous awareness, a state of receptivity that allows you to feel the divine presence woven into the fabric of your everyday existence. Notice the warmth of the sun on your skin, the breathtaking beauty of a blooming flower–these moments become opportunities to acknowledge the divine spark that animates the universe.

Delve into the concept of panpsychism, the theory that consciousness is a fundamental property of the universe. From this perspective, prayer becomes a way to tune into universal consciousness, a subtle dialogue with the very essence of reality.

- Imagine the universe as a vast symphony, with every element playing its part. Prayer becomes your instrument, a way to harmonize with the cosmic melody. As you navigate life's challenges, your prayers become notes in the grand symphony, adding your unique voice to the ongoing composition of the universe.

We all experience moments of feeling lost or alone. Prayer, as a continuous state of companionship with the divine, offers a powerful antidote to isolation. It reminds you that you are never truly alone and that a source of love and guidance is always present, offering support and strength on your journey.

- Imagine the universe as a vast, hidden city teeming with unseen life. In this context, prayer becomes your way of navigating the unseen streets, a whispered conversation with a benevolent guide who helps you navigate the hidden currents and unseen forces that shape your reality.

Psychologically, research suggests that mindfulness practices, like meditation, can reduce stress and anxiety. Prayer, as a form of continuous awareness and connection with the divine, cultivates a similar state of mindfulness. By remaining present and attuned to the divine presence, you foster a sense of inner peace and calm that spill over into all aspects of your life.

Reciprocal Gaze: A Two-Way Street

Forget the transactional model of prayer–the idea of bartering with God or making deals for favors. At its core, prayer is a reciprocal gaze, a heartfelt acknowledgment of the divine presence. It is not just about seeking God's attention but also about cultivating a deep awareness that you are seen and heard by a higher power.

- Imagine a child gazing up at a loving parent. In this analogy, prayer becomes your way of looking up at the divine with love and trust. It is a way of acknowledging your dependence on a higher power and expressing your gratitude for the blessings in your life.

Imagine a forgotten language, a code with the power to unlock hidden dimensions. In this context, prayer becomes the forgotten phrase, a heartfelt murmur in the language of the universe, hoping to be understood and acknowledged by the unseen forces that shape reality.

Psychologically, researchers suggest that gratitude practices can lead to increased happiness and well-being. Prayer, as a form of continuous appreciation for the divine presence, fosters a similar sense of gratitude. By acknowledging the blessings in your life, you cultivate an optimistic outlook and a deeper sense of connection with the universe.

Beyond Requests: Cultivating Character

Prayer is not just about getting things from God. It is about becoming more like God. Do not use prayer as a celestial vending machine, dispensing favors based on your desires. True power comes from aligning yourself with the divine, striving to embody the qualities you associate with a higher power–love, compassion, forgiveness, and service.

- Imagine a mirror reflecting your true self. In this sense, prayer becomes the act of holding yourself up to the divine mirror, striving to reflect the positive qualities you admire in a higher power. As you pray, use it as an opportunity to reflect on your actions and intentions, aligning yourself with the highest version of yourself.

- Imagine a hidden map leading to a forgotten treasure. In this context, prayer becomes the act of following the map, a thrilling quest to discover the divine spark within yourself, and a deeper connection with the source of all existence.

Practical Exercises for Daily Life

Incorporating practical exercises into your daily routine can help cultivate a continuous state of prayerful awareness and align your actions with the qualities you admire in a higher power. Begin each day with a few minutes of quiet reflection, considering your actions and intentions. During this time, ask yourself how they align with the divine qualities you strive to embody. This practice can help you maintain a sense of connection and purpose throughout your day.

- **Gratitude journaling** is another powerful tool. By keeping a journal and writing down things you are grateful for each day, you can cultivate a sense of appreciation and align your thoughts with positive qualities such as love and compassion. This simple act can transform your mindset and enhance your overall well-being.

- **Engaging in small acts of kindness** and service to others is also essential. Whether it is helping a neighbor, volunteering, or simply offering a kind word, these actions can help you embody the qualities of compassion and service. Each act of kindness reinforces your connection to the broader community and the divine.

- **Mindful breathing exercises** can further center yourself and connect you with the present moment. This practice serves as a form of prayerful meditation, helping you to align your mind and spirit with a sense of peace and divine presence. Focusing on your breath can cultivate a deeper awareness of the here and now.

- **Finally, using positive affirmations** that reflect the qualities you wish to embody can reinforce your intentions. Repeat these affirmations during your prayer time to align your mindset with your higher self. This practice can help you internalize the divine qualities you seek to manifest in your life.

13. Prayer: The Intangible Bridge

This section delves into the enigmatic nature of prayer, exploring it as an invisible yet potent bridge connecting humanity to the divine. It acknowledges the mystery inherent in this connection, a yearning that transcends the limitations of human understanding.

Defining the Divine Contact: A Whispered Conversation

The passage describes prayer as an "intangible form of contact" between creation and its creator. This contact is elusive, defying easy explanation. Imagine a whispered conversation across a vast distance, a yearning that reaches out towards something unseen yet deeply felt. The essence of prayer lies in this intangible connection, a bridge built not of physical materials but of faith, hope, and devotion.

Simplifying Complex Concepts

Before delving deeper, let us briefly explain some philosophical concepts that might be complex for some readers.

- **Biocentrism** is the theory that consciousness plays a fundamental role in shaping the universe. It suggests that life and consciousness are central to the existence and structure of the universe.

- **Panpsychism** is the idea that consciousness is a universal feature of all things, not just humans. It proposes that even inanimate objects possess some form of consciousness.

Applying These Concepts to Prayer

From the perspective of biocentrism, prayer becomes an attempt to connect with the universal consciousness, a subtle dialogue with the very fabric of reality. Imagine the universe as a vast ocean teeming with unseen life forms. Prayer, in this analogy, becomes a bioluminescent signal sent out into the cosmic ocean, a beacon of our existence and a yearning for connection with something greater than ourselves.

We all experience moments of loneliness or a yearning for something beyond ourselves. Prayer, in this context, becomes a way to bridge that gap, a whispered message sent out into the unknown, offering solace and a sense of connection in the face of our human limitations.

- Imagine a forgotten language, a code with the power to unlock hidden dimensions. In this context, prayer becomes an attempt to speak this forgotten language, a series of hopeful whispers reaching out toward a potentially unseen and unknown realm.

Psychologically, Research suggests that social connection is vital for mental and emotional well-being. As a form of reaching out to a higher power, prayer can fulfill this need for connection, fostering a sense of belonging and purpose.

Redemption Through Prayer: A Rekindled Spark

The passage suggests that prayer can lead to the "redemption" of the soul and the enrichment of one's purpose in life. This redemption is not a literal transaction but rather a metaphorical rekindling of the divine spark within us.

- Imagine a dusty mirror reflecting a distorted image. In this analogy, prayer becomes the act of cleaning the mirror, allowing us to see ourselves more clearly and reconnect with our inherent goodness and potential. As we engage in prayer, we may find a renewed sense of purpose and direction in life.

Many spiritual traditions view prayer as a way to purify the soul and align oneself with a higher purpose. Through prayer, we may experience a sense of forgiveness, inner peace, and a renewed connection with the divine essence that resides within all of us.

In Conclusion

The enigma endures! The true purpose of prayer lies shrouded in the mysteries beyond human comprehension. Though the intricacies of this connection may elude our understanding, the essence of prayer resides in the profound experience it offers. The endeavor to connect, the deep-seated longing for communion, and the tranquility that emerges from prayer serve as powerful reflections of its significant influence on the essence of humanity.

14. The Powerhouse of Prayer: Fueling Humanity's Journey

This section looks at how prayer pervasively touches upon the levels of individual and social welfare; hence, it attempts to argue that it forms the inexhaustible source of strength and guidance in the unstoppable quest of humanity.

The Binding Necessity: A Source of Strength

Prayer is here referred to as an individual and national "binding necessity." To abandon it could lead humanity toward the "edge of destruction." This is one way of pointing out an understanding that strength and resiliency come through prayer.

- **Individual Level:** Imagine a long and arduous journey. In this context, prayer becomes the fuel that keeps you going. Through prayer, individuals draw upon a wellspring of inner strength, finding solace, guidance, and the resolve to face life's challenges.

- **Societal Level:** Consider a society in chaos. In such a situation, prayer becomes like cement in the people's lives, holding them together and drawing strength from a common sense of direction and relationship to something greater than oneself.

The Wellspring of Perfection: Refining Our Spirit

The passage suggests that prayer is not just about seeking help but also about a "way of perfection derived from exercising their spirit willpower." In this sense, prayer is seen as a tool for self-cultivation, a way to refine our character and align ourselves with higher ideals.

- **Spiritual Growth:** Imagine a sculptor meticulously shaping a piece of raw marble. Prayer, in this analogy, becomes the chisel and hammer, the tools we use to sculpt our own spiritual development. We strive to become better versions of ourselves through prayerful reflection and introspection.

- **Beyond Material Needs:** While prayer can be a source of comfort and support in times of need, it goes beyond simply fulfilling material desires. It is about nurturing the human spirit, fostering compassion, forgiveness, and a sense of connection to something larger than ourselves.

The Power of Evidence

While the impact of prayer is often a matter of personal experience, a growing body of research is exploring its potential benefits. Studies suggest that prayer can lead to reduced stress, increased feelings of hope and well-being, and a stronger sense of purpose in life.

In Conclusion

A Call to Action! This concept does not dictate a specific form of prayer or religious belief. Instead, it highlights the potential of prayer as a universal human practice that can contribute to individual and societal well-being. It is a call to consider the role that prayer might play in our own lives and the lives of those around us.

15. The Peril of Neglecting the Spiritual: The Hollow Drum – A World Without Spirit

Imagine a once vibrant drum, now reduced to a dull thud. This is the world in which the spirit has been amputated, and the link with everything else beyond ourselves is severed. The passage warns of the dangers involved with disregarding the spiritual dimension of life and that when humanity becomes disconnected from that realm, it takes them down a perilous path.

The Binding Necessity: A Call for Wholeness

The idea argues that the lack of a "religious sense" has brought the world to the "edge of destruction." This strong statement highlights the perceived importance of spirituality as a foundation for a healthy and thriving society. In this context, prayer becomes a "binding necessity" for individuals and nations. It is a call for wholeness, a reminder that true well-being encompasses not just our physical and material needs but also our spiritual yearning.

A Hollow Shell: The Individual Without Spirit

Consider a person who neglects their physical health. Their body weakens, leaving them susceptible to illness. A lack of spirituality, in this analogy, becomes a similar neglect. Just as our bodies need nourishment to function, our spirits crave connection and meaning. Without nurturing our spiritual aspect, we risk becoming hollow shells that are susceptible to various forms of suffering. We lose a sense of purpose, and our capacity for compassion and love diminishes.

A Fractured Society: The World Without Spirit

Imagine a society consumed by materialism and self-interest. In this context, a lack of spirituality leads to a breakdown of social cohesion and a loss of shared values. The spiritual dimension often provides a foundation for empathy, compassion, and a sense of collective purpose. Without it, societies become fractured and self-serving, with the pursuit of personal gain eclipsing the needs of the greater good.

The Untapped Wellspring: A Neglected Power Source

The passage suggests that neglecting prayer leaves our "deepest source of power and perfection" undeveloped. In this context, prayer becomes an "exercise of the spirit," a way to cultivate our inner strength and potential. Imagine a vast, untapped reservoir of energy. A lack of prayer, in this analogy, is like neglecting this reservoir, leaving a potentially powerful source of strength unused. We tap into this wellspring through prayer and spiritual practices, nurturing our inner resources and resilience. We cultivate a sense of peace, purpose, and a connection to something larger than ourselves, drawing upon this strength to navigate life's challenges.

Beyond Materialism: True Perfection

The passage warns against the dangers of focusing solely on the material world. It argues that true "perfection" lies not in accumulating possessions but in cultivating our character and spirit. Material possessions are fleeting, but the growth fostered through spiritual practices has a lasting impact. It shapes our values, strengthens our resolve, and guides us on a path toward a more fulfilling existence.

In Conclusion

A Call to Rejuvenation, A World Rekindled! The passage does not dictate a specific religious belief system. Instead, it emphasizes the potential importance of the spiritual dimension in human life. It is a call to action, urging individuals and societies to consider the role that prayer and spiritual practices might play in creating a better world. It is a call to listen for the faint, forgotten rhythm of the spirit and to work towards rekindling the vibrant sound that can guide us all.

16. Unveiling the True Prayer: Beyond Ritual and Misconception

Unveiling the True Power of Prayer: Beyond Misconceptions

Prayer is often misunderstood—reduced to a rote ritual or dismissed as a last-ditch plea for material gain. These misconceptions, like a fog obscuring a hidden city, prevent us from grasping prayer's true power. Prayer transcends simple requests; it is an avenue for gratitude, hope, and connection.

Research shows that repetitive behaviors can create neural pathways in the brain. From this perspective, prayer strengthens pathways for well-being and resilience, much like a mental exercise in hope and gratitude.

- Imagine the universe as a vast symphony. Prayer becomes your unique contribution, not about following a script but about expressing authentic emotions—your hopes and fears— harmonizing with the grand melody of existence.

Prayer can also help break negative thought patterns. By releasing anxieties and vulnerabilities in prayer, we create space for hope and renewal. It is not about a genie granting wishes but about establishing a connection with unseen forces shaping reality.

Prayer also fulfills our need for connection. Whether to a higher power or a deeper part of ourselves, expressing thoughts and feelings, even in silence, fosters belonging and purpose.

A Symphony of the Soul: Beyond Ritualistic Words:

Like a street musician captivating an audience with raw emotion, prayer's power lies in its sincerity, not in complex words or formal scripts. It is a heartfelt conversation with the universe—a symphony of your soul.

True connection isn't about the perfect words but about authenticity. Prayer lets you express your deepest self without the pressure of perfection. It is a conversation with a higher power or your own inner wisdom, allowing your soul to sing its unique song.

Like a forgotten language, prayer is your attempt to communicate with the mysteries beyond. It's not about memorized phrases but about expressing raw emotions and desires that resonate with unseen forces shaping reality.

Nonverbal communication often speaks louder than words—a smile, a tear, a touch. Similarly, prayer is the nonverbal expression of your soul's deepest desires and hopes, carried by the emotions that give it power.

This version simplifies the structure while keeping the depth and imagery of your original message. Does this better align with what you were aiming for?

A Source of Strength: Beyond Refuge for the Weak

Prayer is often seen as a crutch, a desperate plea during life's storms. While it can bring comfort, prayer is much more than a temporary escape. Picture a soldier facing a daunting enemy—not seeking prayer to avoid the battle, but to find the courage to face it head-on. Prayer becomes a wellspring of strength, offering guidance and emotional fortitude to navigate life's toughest challenges. It helps us conquer, not by avoiding hardship but by meeting it with grace and resilience.

Studies suggest that mindfulness practices, like meditation, can reduce stress and anxiety. Prayer, as a form of focused attention and connection with a higher power, cultivates a similar state of mindfulness. Prayer can bolster emotional resilience by quieting external noise and tuning into inner strength.

- Imagine a vast ocean where a storm rages, violently tossing ships. Prayer becomes your anchor, connecting you to deeper currents of stability and guidance amidst the chaos and reminding you that you are not alone.

Prayer taps into an inner wellspring of courage in moments of doubt and fear. You build confidence and resilience by acknowledging your fears and seeking strength from a higher power or within.

Now, imagine following a hidden map toward a forgotten treasure. Prayer guides you on this treacherous path, leading you to discover hidden reserves of strength and courage within yourself—a quest for self-discovery fueled by faith and determination.

Research suggests that a sense of purpose in life contributes to greater well-being. Prayer, as a way to connect with something larger than yourself and explore your values, can foster a sense of purpose. By aligning your actions with your core beliefs, you cultivate a sense of meaning and direction in life, which fuels your inner strength.

A Higher Purpose: Beyond Material Gains

Finally, the notion of prayer as a "childish petition for material things" needs to be dispelled. While there is nothing wrong with seeking material blessings, prayer serves a far grander purpose. Imagine a farmer diligently sowing seeds in the fertile soil. Their goal is not just to harvest a single flower for fleeting beauty but to cultivate a thriving garden that nourishes them for years to come. Similarly, prayer is about cultivating a deeper connection with something larger than ourselves, fostering personal growth, and aligning our lives with our core values. Material possessions may be fleeting, but the spiritual growth fostered through prayer can have a lasting and transformative impact. It shapes our character, strengthens our resolve, and guides us on a path toward a more fulfilling existence.

Studies suggest that gratitude practices can lead to increased happiness and well-being. Prayer, as a form of expressing appreciation for the blessings in life, can cultivate a similar sense of gratitude. By focusing on the positive aspects of your life, you shift your mindset and cultivate a more optimistic outlook.

- Imagine the universe as a vast garden teeming with diverse life forms. Prayer, in this analogy, becomes the act of tending to your own unique corner of the garden. It is not about growing the biggest or flashiest flower but about cultivating a space that reflects your values and brings beauty to the world.

We all yearn for growth and self-improvement. Prayer, in this context, becomes a tool for reflection and introspection. By expressing your hopes and dreams in prayer, you gain clarity on your life's direction and identify areas for personal growth.

Imagine a forgotten language, a code with the power to unlock hidden dimensions of your own potential. Prayer, in this context, becomes your attempt to speak this language. It is a thrilling quest for self-discovery, a way to tap into hidden reserves of creativity, compassion, and strength within yourself.

Research suggests that forgiveness can be a powerful tool for healing and moving on from past hurts. Prayer, as a form of expressing gratitude and forgiveness, can foster a sense of peace and acceptance. You create space for inner growth and a more fulfilling life by letting go of resentment and negativity.

17. A Cautious Approach to Prayer: When Good Intentions Go Astray

Prayer, a cornerstone of many belief systems, transcends mere supplication. It is a complex neuropsychological phenomenon with the potential to influence our well-being and shape our reality. However, like any potent tool, prayer requires careful handling to ensure its effectiveness and avoid unintended consequences. Let us explore three potential pitfalls associated with prayer through various lenses: scientific, philosophical, self-help, thriller, and psychological.

The Powerlessness of Fear-Driven Prayers

Fear is a primal response that hijacks the amygdala, our brain's emotional center. This hijacking disrupts the prefrontal cortex, which is responsible for higher-order thinking and faith. Studies by Newberg and d'Aquili suggest that focused prayer activates the prefrontal cortex, potentially explaining why fear-filled pleas might struggle to resonate.

- Think of prayer as a radio signal. Fear, like static, disrupts the clarity of your message. Cultivate a sense of calm amidst the storm. Meditation or deep breathing exercises can help quiet the amygdala, allowing faith to emerge and amplify your prayer.

- Imagine a frantic call for help during a hostage situation. The kidnappers can easily distinguish between a desperate plea and a well-coordinated plan. Similarly, a prayer fueled by pure terror might be easily dismissed by a higher power or the universe itself if such a force exists.

Fear can manifest as negativity bias, focusing on the worst-case scenario. This negativity can become a self-fulfilling prophecy, hindering the positive outcomes prayer seeks to achieve.

Respecting the Laws of Nature

The laws of physics and nature are immutable. Prayer cannot defy gravity or rewrite the laws of thermodynamics. However, the placebo effect, a well-documented phenomenon in medicine, demonstrates the mind's ability to influence our perception of reality. Perhaps prayer's effectiveness lies not in bending the universe to our will but in fostering an internal state conducive to healing or positive outcomes.

- Imagine a river flowing relentlessly towards the sea. Prayer is not about damming the river but about finding the right boat to navigate its current. Seek harmony with the natural order, not control over it. Pray for the strength and wisdom to navigate life's currents, not to alter their course entirely.

- Imagine a high-stakes heist where the criminals attempt to use a mystical artifact to manipulate the laws of physics. While such a scenario might make for a thrilling movie, it highlights the potential danger of viewing prayer as a tool for controlling the universe's fundamental laws.

Unanswered prayers for impossible outcomes can frustrate people and lead to feelings of helplessness and despair. Setting realistic expectations and focusing on areas where prayer can genuinely make a difference can help maintain a positive psychological state.

The Ethics of Prayer

Prayer should be a force for good, not a weapon. Consider the karmic implications of negativity. The universe, or whatever force you believe in, might simply reject prayers born of malice.

- Imagine a villain praying for the downfall of the protagonist. This trope is a staple of the genre. However, the narrative tension often hinges on the potential for the hero's good intentions to triumph over the villain's malice. Perhaps the universe itself conspires against those who wield prayer for nefarious purposes.

Harboring negative emotions like hatred or revenge can be psychologically corrosive. Focusing on the misfortune of others can breed resentment and hinder your own well-being. Prayer, when used for forgiveness and compassion, can have a cathartic effect, promoting inner peace and emotional healing.

In Conclusion

Prayer is a powerful tool for cultivating connection, seeking guidance, and finding inner peace. Regardless of your beliefs, approaching prayer with a clear mind, respect for the natural order, and a focus on positive intentions is key to maximizing its effectiveness. Understanding the potential pitfalls and harnessing the power of focused attention can ensure your prayers resonate deeply and contribute to a more positive and meaningful existence.

18. Rekindling the Flame: A Call to Active Prayer

In a world increasingly dominated by noise and distraction, the power of prayer can feel lost, a forgotten melody amidst the cacophony. Yet, the human spirit still yearns for connection, for a wellspring of strength beyond the material realm. This section is a call to rekindle the flame of prayer to rediscover its transformative potential for the individual and for society as a whole.

A Wellspring of Strength

Imagine a weary traveler crossing a vast desert. In this analogy, prayer becomes the hidden oasis, a source of refreshment and renewal that allows them to press on with renewed vigor. It is not a magic shortcut but a deep well from which we can draw strength, courage, and clarity in the face of life's challenges.

Scientifically, Studies suggest that mindfulness practices like meditation can reduce stress and anxiety. Prayer, as a form of focused attention and connection with a higher power or your inner wisdom, cultivates a similar state of mindfulness. Prayer can bolster your emotional resilience by quieting the external noise and tuning into your inner strength.

Self-Help: We all face moments of self-doubt and struggle. In this context, prayer becomes a way to tap into your inner wellspring of courage. By acknowledging your fears and seeking guidance from a higher power or your own inner wisdom, you build your confidence and resilience.

A Collection of Connection

Imagine humanity as a vast tapestry woven from countless threads. In this analogy, prayer becomes the act of weaving these threads together, fostering a sense of connection that transcends differences. Through shared moments of reflection and gratitude, prayer strengthens the bonds that hold us together as a community.

Psychologically, research suggests that social connection is vital for mental and emotional well-being. Prayer can fulfill this need for connection as a form of reaching out to a higher power or even a deeper part of yourself. The act of expressing your thoughts and feelings, even in silence, can foster a sense of belonging and purpose.

- Imagine the universe as a vast ocean teeming with diverse life forms. In this analogy, prayer becomes a bridge that connects you to the greater whole. It allows you to recognize the interconnectedness of all things and fosters a sense of belonging within the grand tapestry of existence.

A Force for Good

Imagine a world where compassion and kindness ripple outward, creating a wave of positive change. In this analogy, prayer becomes the pebble tossed into the pond, the initial act that sets this positive transformation in motion. By cultivating our own inner peace and well-being through prayer, we contribute to the creation of a more peaceful and harmonious world.

We all have the potential to be a source of light in the world. In this context, prayer becomes a way to cultivate kindness, compassion, and forgiveness within ourselves. By focusing on these positive qualities in prayer, we not only uplift ourselves but also radiate these qualities outward, inspiring others to do the same.

- Imagine a hidden force for good, a dormant power waiting to be awakened. Prayer, in this analogy, becomes the key that unlocks this potential. By aligning ourselves with a higher purpose and actively engaging in prayer, we contribute to the awakening of a force for positive change in the world.

In Conclusion

An Invitation to Engage! This section does not champion a particular religious tradition but rather emphasizes the significance of prayer itself, the profound act of reaching out to something greater than our individual existence. It beckons us to unearth the profound potential of prayer, a force that lies dormant within, yearning for the moment of awakening. May prayer serve as the luminous spark that revives the essence of humanity, intricately intertwining bonds of connection, resilience, and empathy crafted through each sincere invocation.

Beyond the Veil: Love's Journey of Discovery Through Insight and Focus

Laying the Foundation of Love

For millennia, humanity has chased the elusive key to strong, lasting relationships. Theories abound, from social contracts to complex psychological models. Yet, there is a fundamental principle, an emotion so potent it transcends all others—Love.

Love's Essence: Beyond Fleeting Feelings

Love, in its purest form, is not a fleeting infatuation or a hormonal surge. It is a state of being, a way of approaching the world with an open heart and a heightened sense of connection. Some might say it is of divine origin, a spark of the very force that binds the universe.

Love's Tapestry: Philosophical and Cultural Threads

The ancient Greeks viewed love philosophically and defined it as a fabric made of many different strands. "Agape" is the unconditional and universal love-the fountain of empathy and compassion that binds people together. "Philia" constitutes deep friendship and steadfast loyalty in profound relationships that create shared community and belonging. Such an insight into love from them steps out of the fleeting passions to a complex, multistranded force.

But love is even richer when analyzed from historical and cultural perspectives. Different societies have formed the history of their very existence around love. Much as the Greeks defined love in terms of many kinds, which happened to set the social framework, the Japanese use the term "Wabi-sabi," indicating the beauty of imperfection. If this is applied to love and relationships, it would, therefore, mean embracing flaws and frailties, thus making love true and sustainable. In understanding these different ways of viewing, the mosaic about love is complete, showing its power in connecting not only to people but also to the world that comprises us.

Love has also been the ulcerative part of philosophy throughout history. Consider the medieval concept of "courtly love": a way in which love was supposed to ennoble and inspire the individual, influencing art, literature, and social mores. The more we take into consideration the philosophical conceptions and understandings of love, the more we realize just how complex and important love is to human experience.

Scientific Insights: Love's Journey Within

This exploration of love is not a battle between science and spirituality. Instead, it is a harmonious dance between the two. Science sheds light on the neurological mechanisms of love, while spirituality offers a framework for understanding its deeper meaning and purpose. By integrating both perspectives, we gain a comprehensive understanding of the power of love in human life.

Imagine the human connection as a vast, intricate network. In this analogy, love becomes the invisible force that strengthens the connections within this network. This metaphor aligns with a scientific understanding of the brain's neural connections, which form complex networks that facilitate communication and information processing.

Scientifically, Cognitive neuroscience research suggests that the brain releases a cocktail of hormones during love, including dopamine (reward), oxytocin (bonding), and serotonin (well-being). This neurochemical symphony fosters connection and attachment, aligning with self-help principles emphasizing the importance of nurturing relationships and building trust. For example, the release of oxytocin during physical touch and acts of kindness supports the self-help practice of expressing affection and compassion.

Psychologically, Research suggests that secure attachment styles, often formed in early childhood, contribute to healthy adult relationships. In this context, love becomes the foundation for secure attachment, fostering trust, communication, and a sense of emotional safety within relationships.

Spiritually, while science can provide valuable insights into the biological underpinnings of love, it cannot fully capture the subjective and personal nature of the experience. The spiritual dimensions of love, such as its ability to transcend time and space or its connection to a higher power, often remain beyond the scope of scientific inquiry. However, scientific findings can support spiritual beliefs. For instance, releasing oxytocin during acts of kindness or compassion can be seen as a biological manifestation of the spiritual principle of love.

By integrating these perspectives, we gain a deeper understanding of the power of love in human life. Love is not merely a biological phenomenon but a complex interplay of scientific, spiritual, and personal factors.

Thriller Twist: Imagine love as a hidden code, a language that transcends words. It allows for a deep understanding and connection that goes beyond the surface. Love, in this thriller context, becomes the key to unlocking another person's deepest desires and motivations, fostering a powerful and sometimes even mysterious bond.

Love: The Quintessential Human Connection

Love, a word whispered in sonnets and screamed from rooftops, transcends mere emotion. It is the very fountain of life, the animating force that propels us towards connection, growth, and a deeper understanding of ourselves and the world around us. This section delves into the multifaceted nature of love, exploring it as both a Disciplined Perception and a guiding principle for human relationships.

A Deep Dive into Love's Qualities

i.   **The Philosophical Tapestry of Love**

Love transcends the realm of mere emotions. It is the ultimate form of human connection, a tapestry woven from philosophical understanding and the richness of lived experience. It surpasses fleeting infatuation, reaching a depth of shared understanding and experience that surpasses all other bonds. Imagine, as the ancient Greeks might have, two rivers converging, their distinct waters mingling and flowing as one. True love creates a similar unity, a profound sense of "we" that dissolves the limitations of "me" and "you." This interconnectedness transcends the physical and emotional, creating a connection that nourishes the very essence of our being.

ii.   **Universality and Crossing Boundaries**

Love's beauty lies in its universality, mirroring the concept of "Philia"–the deep friendship and loyalty that transcends differences. It bridges cultural divides, religious beliefs, and societal norms, acting as a language understood by hearts across the globe. Imagine a symphony where instruments from all corners of the world come together to create a harmonious melody. Love acts as the conductor, uniting diverse individuals into a beautiful and powerful chorus.

iii. The Universal Language of Love

The beauty of love lies in its universality. It transcends cultural differences, religious beliefs, and societal norms. It is a language understood by hearts across the globe. Imagine a symphony where instruments from all corners of the world come together to create a harmonious melody. Love acts as the conductor, uniting diverse individuals into a beautiful and powerful chorus. Love acts as the bridge, fostering understanding, connection, and a sense of shared humanity.

iv. Ultimate form of Human Connection

Love is not just an emotion; it is the ultimate form of human connection. It transcends fleeting infatuation or physical attraction, reaching a depth of understanding and shared experience that surpasses all other bonds. Imagine two rivers converging, their waters mingling and flowing as one. True love creates a similar unity, a sense of "we" that transcends the limitations of "me" and "you."

v. Love as the Antidote to Vice

Love is not merely a warm fuzzy feeling; it is a potent force for good. Imagine a garden choked by weeds. True love acts like a gentle yet persistent gardener, weeding out negativity and fostering a flourishing garden of virtue. Envy, greed, and revenge shrivel under the warmth of genuine love. The desire for something for nothing melts away when replaced by the joy of giving and receiving within a loving relationship.

vi.   **Aligning with the Infinite**

Love, in its purest form, transcends the boundaries of the ego. It connects us to something larger than ourselves, be it another person, a cause, or a higher power. Some believe this connection aligns us with the infinite intelligence that governs the universe. Imagine a vast ocean teeming with life. Each drop of water, while unique, is ultimately part of the greater whole. Love allows us to recognize the interconnectedness of all things, fostering a sense of belonging and purpose within the grand tapestry of existence.

vii.   **The Power of Love in Relationships**

Love is the cornerstone of healthy, fulfilling relationships. It fosters trust, intimacy, and a sense of security. Imagine a garden where each plant flourishes thanks to the careful tending of a gardener. Love acts as the nurturing touch in our relationships, allowing individuals to blossom and reach their full potential. It motivates us to see the best in others, to offer support during challenging times, and to celebrate each other's triumphs.

Understanding these profound characteristics of love can cultivate this powerful force in our lives. Love has the potential to bring us mental clarity, eradicate negativity, foster spiritual connection, and create a sense of shared purpose. Let love be the guiding light in our relationships, illuminating the path toward a more harmonious and fulfilling existence.

Love's Spiritual Tapestry: Weaving Oneness from Duality

Love, at its core, transcends the physical and emotional. It reaches into a deeper, spiritual dimension, fostering a connection that transcends the boundaries of the self. Imagine two flames, not extinguishing each other but merging into a single, unified light.

This luminous embrace exemplifies the essence of spiritual love—a sense of oneness where the separation between self and other dissolves.

This connection is not merely emotional but a profound recognition of our interconnectedness, a shared existence woven into the fabric of reality. It aligns beautifully with the Greek concept of "Agape" love - a universal, unconditional love that extends far beyond romantic relationships. Agape fuels empathy and compassion for all beings, fostering a sense of belonging within the grand tapestry of life.

This spiritual dimension of love is not a fleeting feeling; it is a wellspring of strength and resilience. It allows us to see beyond the limitations of the ego and connect with something larger than ourselves. In the face of adversity, this shared light can offer solace and support, reminding us that we are not alone on this journey.

Furthermore, love's spiritual dimension inspires a sense of responsibility toward the world around us. When we recognize the interconnectedness of all things, we become more mindful of our actions and their impact. This awareness fosters a desire to contribute positively, nurture and protect the environment, and build a more harmonious world for all.

Love, in its spiritual essence, is not just a feeling; it is a transformative force. It illuminates the path towards deeper connection, empathy, and a sense of belonging. It is a luminous embrace that reminds us of our shared existence and inspires us to be better versions of ourselves, not just for our loved ones but for all beings.

The Journey of Love

Love is not a destination but rather a journey through which ups and downs are expected to take place. Love is a voyage of entangled and ever-changing phases. There will be times of intense passion, silent companionship, and even disagreements at times. It is all about navigating these complications with comprehension, empathy, and a desire to learn and grow with our partners. In this sense, love will be able to keep on creating newer possibilities of continuance in our lives through a deeper connectedness, meaning, and placement within the universe.

Imagine love as a beautiful garden. It requires constant care and attention to flourish. There will be times when weeds need to be pulled, harsh weather needs to be endured, and delicate blooms need to be nurtured. Like a garden, love requires consistent effort and dedication to maintain beauty and strength.

Thriller Twist: Envision a captivating odyssey, a path woven with unforeseen complexities and profound revelations. In this metaphor, love transforms into the compass that steers you through the labyrinthine journey of existence. Though the journey may be fraught with obstacles, it is love that illuminates the way, offering both the impetus to confront adversity and the joy of shared triumphs.

Love in All Its Forms: Love is not confined to romantic relationships. It manifests in the tender bond between parent and child, the unwavering loyalty of friends, the love for a cherished pet, and the universal love some feel for all beings. Each form of love serves a unique purpose, enriching our lives and shaping who we become.

Love, The Foundation for Harmony: By embracing love as the highest principle of human connection, we create fertile ground for harmony and growth. It is the foundation upon which strong families, supportive communities, and even a more peaceful world can be built. Let us cultivate this divine spark within ourselves, allowing it to guide our interactions and illuminate the path toward a future filled with love, understanding, and connection.

Soulmates, Shared Purpose, and the Impact of Love: The profound connection that is nurtured with love does not necessarily have to be emotionally intimate; it can also stir within someone a sense of shared purpose. Consider the numerous couples who have devoted their lives to social justice movements or creative projects stirred into action by their love and a will to impact one another for good. Attachment Theory, for example, postulates that it is a secure and loving relationship that acts like a safe haven for us to make our voyage into the world with confidence and courage. This feeling of "we" created by the unity of love empowers us to go into the world, knowing we have a strong base to return to for support and connection.

The Sacred Flame: Love vs. Desire

Love and desire are powerful emotions that are often intertwined yet fundamentally different. While both can draw people together, their destinations lie on separate paths. Let us delve into the essence of each, distinguishing the fleeting flame of desire from the enduring fire of love.

Desire: The Yearning for Fulfillment

Desire is a primal force, a yearning for something we perceive as lacking. Imagine a person parched in the desert, desperately craving a cool drink. Desire is like thirst, driving us to seek out what we believe will satisfy our needs. Desire is regarded as a powerful force that fuels our motivations, guides our actions, and compels us to seek what brings us pleasure, security, or a sense of completion. It can be a powerful motivator, driving us towards goals and achievements.

Love: A Spiritual Oneness

Love, in its truest form, transcends the limitations of desire. It is a spiritual power, a connection that transcends the boundaries of the ego. You describe it as a state of "oneness," where two souls become interwoven, each a part of the other. Imagine two flames merging into a single, radiant light—this is the essence of love. It fosters a deep sense of connection, empathy, and a willingness to see the world through another's eyes.

The Ephemeral Nature of Desire vs. The Enduring Power of Love

Desire, by its very nature, is often fleeting. Once the object of desire is attained, the initial spark can fade. Imagine someone who desperately desires a new gadget, only to find themselves bored with it a few weeks later. Love, on the other hand, is an enduring force that deepens and strengthens over time. It weathers challenges and grows with shared experiences.[8]

Beyond Sentimentality and Infatuation

You rightly distinguish this love from mere sentimentality or infatuation, often referred to as "puppy love." These fleeting feelings are fueled by desire, a yearning for the excitement and novelty of a new connection. These experiences can be intense and exhilarating, but they often lack the depth and commitment of true love. Puppy love is often fueled by infatuation and the excitement of newness. True love, however, endures beyond the initial spark. It weathers challenges, deepens with time, and fosters a sense of unwavering commitment.

---

[8] **Love: A Force for Connection and Growth**

Love, however, transcends mere desire. It is a state of being that fosters a deep connection with another person, a spiritual union that goes beyond physical attraction or the need to fulfill a personal void. It's about seeing the inherent value in another individual, appreciating their unique qualities, and desiring their well-being as much as your own.

Key Differences:

- **Focus:** Desire focuses on what we lack, while love focuses on the abundance already present.
- **Motivation:** Desire is driven by a need for fulfillment, while love is driven by a desire for connection and shared existence.
- **Sustainability:** Desire can be fleeting and dependent on external factors, while love has the potential for enduring strength and resilience.
- **Transformation:** Desire can be self-serving, while love has the power to transform both individuals involved.

Love vs. Sex: A Distinction, not a Separation

You separate love from the emotion of sex, which is often mistakenly equated with love. While physical intimacy can be a beautiful and powerful expression of love, it is not the defining factor; it is just one facet of a multifaceted relationship. Love can exist without physical intimacy, and sex without love can be a purely physical experience.

- **Love: A Bridge, not a Possession**

  Love does not seek to possess another person; it seeks to connect with them on a deeper level. Imagine two islands separated by a vast ocean. Love builds a bridge between these islands, allowing for a two-way flow of connection, support, and shared experiences. It is not about controlling the other island but about creating a space where both can flourish.

- **Love: A Compass for Relationships**

  Understanding the distinction between love and desire can help us build stronger, more meaningful relationships. Love acts as a compass, guiding us toward connection, compassion, and a shared growth journey. It allows us to see beyond the superficial and connect with the essence of another person, fostering a spiritual union that enriches both partners.

- **Love: A Transformative Force**

  Love, in its purest form, has the power to transform us. It compels us to be better versions of ourselves, to be more compassionate, understanding, and supportive. Imagine a rough stone being polished into a gleaming gem–this is the transformative power of love. It refines our character and allows us to see the beauty and potential in ourselves and others.

In Conclusion

Love and desire are profound energies that mold the tapestry of our connections. Desire ignites the first flicker that unites our paths, while love transforms into an everlasting blaze, weaving us together in a profound spiritual connection. Through the exploration of these nuances, we may nurture connections that resonate with profound significance in our existence. Let us endeavor to cultivate the profound spark of love, for it is within this bond that we encounter the authentic nature of human connection and the essence of fulfillment.

Purposeful Love: The Power of Focus in Love

Imagine a bustling marketplace, sights and sounds bombarding your senses. Now, imagine the presence of someone you deeply love. Their voice cuts through the noise; their gaze draws your focus like a lighthouse beam. This focused attention is precisely what love does in the realm of human connection.

Love is not passive; it is a Disciplined Perception, a focused awareness directed towards a shared goal. Imagine two climbers scaling a mountain, their focus unwavering as they support and motivate each other. True love fosters a similar sense of shared purpose and responsibility. Partners become each other's "keepers," working together towards a common vision.

Love involves selective awareness, a conscious choice to direct our attention and energy towards the well-being of our loved one and the relationship itself. Imagine an artist working on a masterpiece, meticulously focusing on each detail. True love requires a similar dedication and a willingness to nurture and grow the bond over time.

Love as a Disciplined Perception

Science is beginning to unveil the profound impact of love on our brains. Studies suggest that love activates reward pathways, flooding us with feel-good chemicals like oxytocin and dopamine. But love goes beyond mere pleasure. It acts as a Disciplined Perception, sharpening our focus and directing our attention. Imagine a botanist meticulously examining a rare flower, their gaze intent on capturing its intricate details. Love allows us to do the same with human experience, attuning us to the subtle nuances of emotions, needs, and desires in ourselves and others. This heightened perception fosters empathy, compassion, and a deeper understanding of the human condition.

For instance, a parent's love allows them to decipher their child's unspoken needs through a simple whimper or a fleeting change in expression. Similarly, love between partners can lead to a kind of nonverbal communication, where unspoken thoughts and feelings are understood through a shared glance or a gentle touch.

Mental Clarity Through Love, imagine a room filled with flickering candles, each casting dancing shadows on the walls. With its laser focus, true love acts like a spotlight in this room. It quiets the incessant chatter of the mind, allowing us to concentrate on what truly matters–the connection with our beloved. Studies suggest that deep love activates brain regions associated with focus and attention, promoting a state of mental clarity. Distracting thoughts fade away, replaced by an intense presence in the moment.

Love as Selective Awareness

A Spotlight on Connection, imagine a spotlight in a vast theater, its beam illuminating a single performer on stage. This focused attention is precisely what love does in human connection. It allows us to filter out distractions and direct our entire being towards another. Observe a couple deeply in love–their conversations flow effortlessly, their eyes locked in a silent dialogue. This is not mere coincidence; it has controlled attention at its finest, a testament to love's power in shaping our interactions.

Evolutionary Perspective: From an evolutionary standpoint, this intense focus served a critical purpose. It fostered strong bonds between parents and offspring, increasing the chances of survival for both. Over time, this focus evolved into the foundation for romantic love, allowing us to create secure and nurturing relationships.

Vulnerability and Perseverance – The Strength of True Love: Love is not always sunshine and rainbows. There will be times when misunderstandings arise, and patience wears thin. However, acknowledging these challenges adds a layer of vulnerability and authenticity to the relationship. Just as a sculptor patiently chisels away at a block of marble, love requires dedication and effort to reach its full potential. Through perseverance and a commitment to nurturing the bond, love can weather any storm, leaving behind a legacy of connection and understanding.

Love: A Bridge Between Selves

Love, in this context, transcends mere affection. It becomes a bridge connecting two souls across the vast ocean of existence. Different cultures may express this connection uniquely, with some emphasizing passionate devotion while others focus on a deep sense of companionship. Yet, the core principle remains the same– love allows partners to share experiences, support each other's growth, and create a shared reality far richer than the sum of its parts.

Thriller Twist: Imagine two people trapped on separate sides of a vast chasm. In this context, love becomes the bridge that allows them to cross over and connect. It requires courage, trust, and a willingness to meet halfway, but ultimately, love provides the means to overcome the obstacles that separate individuals and forge a lasting bond.

Self-Help: Imagine yourself building a strong and supportive relationship. Love, in this analogy, becomes the foundation upon which you build. Without a strong foundation, the relationship will struggle to weather the storms of life. Love provides the stability and support needed to create a safe and nurturing space for both partners to grow and thrive.

Love's Transformative Power

The transformative power of love is undeniable. It has the ability to soften hardened hearts, heal past wounds, and inspire acts of immense kindness and compassion. Witness a couple who has weathered the storms of life together, their love not only enduring but deepening with each challenge. This enduring strength is a testament to love's ability to transform individuals and relationships alike. However, love is not a passive force. It requires effort, communication, and a willingness to grow alongside your partner.

Scientifically, Studies suggest that social connection and positive emotions can have a positive impact on physical and mental health. Love, fostering both connection and positive emotions, can be a powerful tool for healing and transformation.

Imagine a barren wasteland slowly being transformed into a flourishing garden. In this metaphor, love becomes the life-giving water that nourishes the soil and allows love and compassion to blossom. It has the power to heal past wounds, cultivate kindness, and inspire positive change in both individuals and the world around them.

Love – The Foundation for Harmony

By embracing love as the highest principle of human connection, we create a fertile ground for harmony and growth. It's the foundation upon which strong families, supportive communities, and even a more peaceful world can be built. Love transcends cultural differences, fostering empathy, understanding, and a sense of shared humanity. Let us strive to cultivate this divine spark within ourselves, allowing it to guide our interactions and illuminate the path toward a future filled with love, understanding, and connection.

- **Cultural Diversity – Love's Many Expressions**

  Love is expressed in a myriad of ways across the globe. In some cultures, passionate declarations of love are prized, while others value quiet acts of devotion. For example, in Western cultures, romantic love is often celebrated through public displays of affection. In contrast, in some Eastern cultures, love may be expressed more subtly through acts of service and self-sacrifice.

- **Inspiring Change – Love's Transformative Power**

  Love's impact extends far beyond individual relationships. Consider Mahatma Gandhi, whose unwavering love and commitment to non-violent resistance sparked a movement for social change in India. In South Africa, Nelson Mandela's unwavering belief in the power of love and forgiveness helped to heal the deep wounds of apartheid and build a more united nation.

- **Mother Teresa – A Beacon of Compassion**

  Mother Teresa, fueled by love and compassion, dedicated her life to serving the poorest of the poor in India and Albania. Her unwavering commitment to helping those in need inspired countless individuals to follow her example and make a difference in the world. Mother Teresa's work serves as a powerful reminder of the transformative power of love and its positive impact on society.

- **Examples from Various Cultures**

    To further illustrate the cultural specificity of love, consider these examples:

    o **Japan:** The concept of "omotenashi," which translates to "wholehearted hospitality," is deeply rooted in Japanese culture. This practice reflects a love of others and a desire to make them feel welcome and valued.

    o **India:** The Hindu tradition of ahimsa, which means "non-violence," is a cornerstone of Indian culture. This principle emphasizes the importance of love, compassion, and respect for all living beings.

    o **Latin America:** In many Latin American cultures, love is often expressed through passionate music, dance, and poetry. This reflects the region's vibrant and expressive culture.

In Conclusion

Love is the cornerstone of meaningful human connection. By recognizing its multifaceted nature, nurturing it with care, and harnessing its transformative power, we can build stronger relationships, foster a more compassionate world, and illuminate the path toward a brighter future.

Love: The Embodiment of Shared Faith

Love, in its truest form, transcends mere emotion. It becomes a powerful expression of applied faith, a shared belief system that conquers selfishness and fear, propelling us toward a higher purpose.

Imagine two climbers scaling a treacherous mountain. Their shared faith in each other's abilities and their unwavering belief in the ultimate summit conquer any fear of heights or doubts about their individual strengths. This is the essence of love as applied faith.

Overcoming Selfishness and Fear

Love, in this context, acts as an antidote to selfishness. Imagine a room filled with treasures. True love does not focus on grabbing the biggest piece for oneself; it celebrates the joy of sharing the bounty with your beloved. It fosters a sense of "we" that transcends the limitations of "me." Fear, too, withers under the warmth of genuine love. Imagine a child lost in the dark, trembling with fear. A parent's embrace acts as a shield, dispelling the darkness and replacing it with a sense of security and trust. True love offers a similar refuge, a safe haven from the storms of life.

A Vision Towards a Shared Cause

Love ignites a vision within us, a shared belief in a cause greater than ourselves. Imagine a group of artists collaborating on a magnificent mural. Their love for their craft and shared vision fuel their dedication, pushing them to create something remarkable. This collaborative spirit exemplifies the power of love as applied faith.

Disciplined Perception and Infinite Intelligence

This shared faith is driven by Disciplined Perception, a focused awareness directed towards the shared goal. Imagine a scientist conducting a groundbreaking experiment. Their unwavering belief in the potential of their work fuels their meticulous attention to detail. True love operates similarly, directing our energy and attention towards nurturing and strengthening the bond with our partner.

Harmony with the Infinite Intelligence

Love, in its highest form, aligns with an infinite intelligence, a force that governs the universe (or a higher purpose you believe in).

Imagine a vast ocean teeming with life; each drop is unique yet connected to the whole. True love fosters a similar sense of interconnectedness, a belief that our actions, guided by love, contribute to a greater good.

Balancing Faith and Reality

The journey of love is not always easy. There will be moments when doubts creep in and challenges test the strength of the bond. However, couples who cultivate love as applied faith possess a deeper strength. Their shared belief in the relationship and their commitment to working through difficulties together allows them to emerge stronger. For example, Helen Keller and Anne Sullivan's extraordinary bond is a testament to the power of love and unwavering faith in each other's potential.

Challenges and Growth

Even the strongest shared faith can be tested. Arguments, misunderstandings, and external pressures can strain even the most loving relationships. However, love as applied faith equips us to navigate these challenges. It allows us to approach conflict with empathy and a willingness to understand each other's perspectives. It fosters forgiveness and a commitment to working through difficulties together. Through these challenges, love can grow even stronger, emerging from the fire more resilient and enduring.

Maintaining Shared Faith Through Challenges

The journey of love is not always smooth sailing. There will be disagreements, misunderstandings, and moments of doubt. Yet, couples who cultivate love as applied faith possess the tools to navigate these challenges. They can emerge stronger and more connected through open communication, a commitment to forgiveness, and a shared belief in the enduring strength of their love.

Real-Life Examples of Applied Love

Throughout history, countless couples have exemplified the power of love as applied faith. Consider Marie and Pierre Curie, whose unwavering love for science fueled their groundbreaking discoveries in radioactivity. Their shared passion and belief in each other's abilities propelled them to achieve scientific breakthroughs that continue to benefit humanity. Closer to home, countless couples dedicate their lives to causes they deeply care about, from environmental activism to social justice movements. Their love serves as a wellspring of strength and motivation, inspiring positive change in the world.

In Conclusion

Love, as applied faith, transcends fleeting emotions. It becomes a powerful force for good, conquering selfishness and fear and propelling us towards a shared vision and a higher purpose. By cultivating this type of love in our relationships, we create a foundation for strength and resilience. We can start by actively nurturing our shared faith through open communication, mutual respect, and a commitment to working together. As we cultivate love as applied faith in our own lives, we contribute to a world where collaboration, trust, and a sense of shared humanity prevail.

The Constructive Nature of Love

Beyond the Whirlwind – Love as the Architect, Not the Wrecker! Love. Often painted as a tempestuous storm of emotions, it can feel all-consuming and unpredictable. Nevertheless, beneath the surface lies a deeper truth: love is a force for construction, not destruction. It is the architect, not the wrecker, the cornerstone that binds us together and fosters growth. This section delves into the transformative power of true love, distinguishing it from fleeting infatuation and manipulative tactics. We will explore how love acts as a powerful tool, building stronger connections, fostering personal growth, and ultimately creating a more harmonious world.

Building with Love's Sacred Power

Imagine a magnificent cathedral rising from the ground, each stone meticulously placed to create a haven of peace and beauty. True love operates with this same focused dedication. It is a spiritual power that directs our attention toward a shared purpose—the betterment of the relationship and those involved. This force is not about dominance or tearing down but about building a foundation of trust, respect, and mutual understanding, like a skilled gardener cultivating a fertile garden. Despots, fueled by ego and a thirst for power, are incapable of harnessing this power. Their actions stem from a place of fear and control, the antithesis of true love.

Love's Discerning Power – Growth, Not Manipulation! True love, like a master gardener, cultivates a space for growth and prosperity. Its spiritual force is not available to those driven by negativity. Only those "willingly accepting good deeds" can harness this power. It becomes a test, revealing the true intentions of the heart. Those seeking manipulation or control are left empty-handed, for love's power thrives on genuine connection and the desire to build something beautiful together. Unlike fleeting infatuation or manipulative tactics, true love acts as a discriminator, separating genuine connection from negativity.

Unveiling the Heart: Love's Discerning Power

True love acts as a prism, refracting the light of a relationship and revealing its true nature. Like a beam of light split into its component colors, love exposes the genuineness of affection. Hate, with its destructive core, cannot hide behind a facade of love in the face of this powerful force. Love's focus on building a shared future, a flourishing garden from a barren landscape, unveils the emptiness of negativity.

The Gardener's Touch – Nurturing vs. Manipulation: True love, the skilled gardener cultivates a space for empathy, compassion, and genuine desire for the other's growth. False affection, often a weed disguised as a flower, harbors destructive tendencies. It can be manipulative, controlling, or fueled by selfish desires. Here, love acts as the discriminator, separating genuine hearts from those filled with hate. The spiritual power of love simply cannot be wielded for destruction. It fosters growth, not desolation.

Focused Attention for a Definite End

Love is not passive; it requires controlled attention, a Disciplined Perception directed towards a common goal. Imagine a team of architects meticulously planning a magnificent building. True love fosters a similar focus. Partners, united by their affection, work together towards a shared vision, their efforts strengthening the bond they share. This "definite end," as you describe it, is not about domination or control; it is about creating something beautiful and lasting together.

Love's Boundless Power: Building Beyond Romance

Love, in its purest form, transcends the realm of romantic relationships. It flourishes within families, where parents nurture their children with unwavering support, and siblings forge lifelong bonds of loyalty. It kindles enduring friendships, providing a safe haven of understanding and acceptance. But love's reach extends far beyond these personal connections, weaving itself into the very fabric of our communities and artistic expressions.

- **Love in Community**

  Within communities, love binds individuals together by a common purpose. Consider the work of organizations like Habitat for Humanity, driven by a love for their fellow humans and a desire to provide affordable housing. The volunteers who dedicate their time and energy to building homes for those in need are motivated by a deep sense of compassion and a belief in the power of love to make a difference. Their efforts are not just acts of charity but manifestations of a profound love for humanity and a desire to uplift and empower others.

Another example is the global response to natural disasters. When calamities strike communities, people from all walks of life come together to provide aid and support. This collective effort, fueled by love and empathy, showcases the boundless power of love to unite and heal.

- **Love in Artistic Expression**

  Love can also be a catalyst for artistic expression. A musician pours their heart into composing a symphony, their love for music driving their creativity. A painter, inspired by the love for nature, captures its essence on canvas. Love inspires artists to create meaningful, impactful, and inspiring work. Through their art, they communicate emotions and ideas that resonate deeply with others, spreading love and beauty in ways that words alone cannot.

  Consider the works of Vincent van Gogh, whose love for the natural world and human experience is vividly expressed in his paintings. His art continues to touch hearts and inspire countless individuals, demonstrating how love can transcend time and space through artistic expression.

- **Love in Cultural Practices**

  Love practices vary greatly across cultures, influencing customs related to marriage, family dynamics, and expressions of affection. In many cultures, love is celebrated through festivals and rituals that strengthen communal bonds. For instance, in India, the festival of Raksha Bandhan honors the love between siblings, symbolizing protection and care.[119]

In Japan, the concept of "amae" reflects a deep sense of dependency and love within relationships, emphasizing the importance of mutual care and support. These cultural practices highlight how love shapes social structures and interpersonal relationships, fostering a sense of belonging and unity.

- **The Ripple Effect of Love**

  Love is the invisible thread woven through acts of kindness, big or small—a neighbor offering a helping hand to an elderly person struggling with groceries, a stranger giving up their seat on the bus for someone in need. Fueled by love and compassion, these seemingly insignificant gestures create a ripple effect of positivity throughout society. Each act of love, no matter how small, contributes to a larger tapestry of kindness and connection, fostering a sense of community and shared humanity.

Remember, Love manifests as a profound energy that transcends the boundaries of individual connections, reaching into the very fabric of existence. It serves as the bedrock of resilient communities, igniting the flames of artistic creativity and propelling the momentum for transformative progress. By embracing love as our guiding principle, we hold the potential to shape a world that is more compassionate, just, and harmonious. The essence of love extends beyond mere personal bonds, igniting a shared impetus that propels humanity toward collective endeavors. It emerges as a transformative force capable of reshaping both individual destinies and the fabric of society itself.

Despots and the Mirage of Love: A Force for Unity, Not Division

Love, in its essence, is a force for unity and connection. It seeks to build bridges of understanding, not walls of division. This is why the actions of despots, who thrive on control and fear, can never be fueled by true love. Their tyrannical rule, seeking to demolish and subjugate, stands in stark contrast to the constructive nature of love.

The essence of spiritual power, nourished by love, emerges as an abundant source of uplifting energy. It cultivates a spirit of collaboration, ignites empathy, and propels individuals toward benevolent actions. A leader motivated by compassion endeavors to forge a cohesive and harmonious community rather than cultivate division and chaos. Their choices reveal a profound concern for the welfare of their community, cultivating an atmosphere of unity and mutual advancement.

We can illuminate the distinction between manipulation and authentic love in this space. Though a despot may cloak their deeds in the guise of patriotism, the underlying intentions frequently reveal a pursuit of personal gain. They may assert they aim to "unite" the populace, yet their tactics are steeped in fear and domination, rather than nurturing authentic bonds among individuals. Genuine love, in contrast, serves as a catalyst for empowerment and inspiration, fostering a community in which each person is cherished and held in esteem.

Love's Enduring Legacy: Building Harmony Across Generations

Love's legacy is far grander than the fleeting emotions of a single moment. It is a magnificent cathedral, a testament to the collective effort of countless individuals bound by love. True love fosters a spirit of collaboration, where partners, families, and communities work together to create something beautiful and enduring. This legacy stretches across generations like a precious family heirloom passed down with care.

- **Generations Spanning Impact:** Parents who raise their children with unwavering love create a ripple effect. Their kindness and compassion become the foundation upon which future generations are built. Grandparents who share stories and traditions with their grandchildren weave a tapestry of love that binds families together, ensuring these values continue to flourish. Through love, families become a wellspring of strength and support, shaping individuals who contribute positively to the world around them.

- **Ripples of Positivity:** Love's influence transcends the boundaries of individual relationships. A simple act of kindness, fueled by love, can spark a chain reaction of positivity. Imagine someone holding the door open for another person, who, in turn, performs a good deed for someone else. Motivated by love and compassion, these seemingly small gestures contribute to a more harmonious society. A smile is offered to a stranger, a helping hand to a neighbor–these ripples of love create a more positive and supportive environment for everyone.

- **Leaving the World a Better Place:** Ultimately, love's legacy is about leaving the world a better place than we found it. Through acts of love, big or small, we contribute to a world filled with compassion, understanding, and cooperation. Whether it is a parent tirelessly advocating for their child's education or a group of volunteers planting trees to combat climate change, love inspires us to work toward a brighter future for all. The Taj Mahal, a breathtaking monument to love, stands as a testament to this enduring power. Great works of art, literature, and music, often inspired by love, leave a lasting legacy that continues to touch hearts for centuries.

The legacy of love unfolds not merely through monumental acts but in the subtle tapestry woven from daily kindness, unwavering support, and the quiet strength of collaboration. It is a powerful current that connects the threads of time, nurturing a vision of a brighter future and urging us to create a meaningful legacy for the generations yet to unfold.

In Conclusion

We frequently perceive love through a lens that softens reality, honing in on the euphoria and fervor while overlooking the complexities that lie beneath. Discipline, in contrast, may evoke a sense of severity, a requisite force that starkly counters the unrestrained essence of love. Yet, genuine love, akin to a skilled gardener, demands both elements in harmony. True love, akin to a master sculptor, employs both discipline and insight to forge a profound masterpiece. It perceives the imperfections intertwined with the allure, providing subtle guidance and steadfast encouragement. It demands a profound insight, an acute sensitivity to the needs of others, and the steadfast resolve to elevate their welfare, even amidst the challenges that arise.

Through the lens of discipline, we can meticulously remove the weeds of toxic habits, nurturing instead the rich soil where love may take root and thrive. It is the firm resolve that steers us through challenging dialogues, the steadfast dedication that enables us to endure the tempests of existence in unison. It is the deliberate decision to elevate our partner's joy above our own, even when such an act demands a relinquishment of personal desires.

Love, in its essence, refines our understanding of existence. It invites us to delve deeper, to grasp and cherish the essence of the one we hold dear. We grow increasingly sensitive to their needs and desires, nurturing a profound bond through empathy and insight. This intentional focus, steered by affection, enables us to cultivate the finest aspects of each other, forging a bond that is both fervent and lasting.

In the grand tapestry of existence, love and discipline intertwine, not as foes, but as harmonious companions engaged in a profound and intricate dance. Structure and focus emerge from discipline, while passion and commitment are ignited by love. In unison, they craft a rich fabric of interrelation, evolution, and steadfast encouragement. The intricate dance of existence reveals how love etches its deepest and most lasting imprint—a realm where empathy and insight steer our choices, nurturing the growth of love's essence for countless generations ahead.

SHAPING THE COLLECTIVE MIND AND BUILDING A BETTER WORLD

৬ৡ ৬ৡ ৬ৡ

Beyond the Labyrinth of the Mind

W e've delved into the transformative power of disciplined perception on an individual level. But this ability to direct our attention is not just about personal empowerment. It holds the key to shaping the very fabric of our reality, our communities, and our future.

From Personal Growth to Global Harmony

Throughout history, those who have achieved great feats, from scientific breakthroughs to social movements, have harnessed the power of selective attention. They honed their focus on a specific goal, filtering out distractions and directing their energy with laser-like intensity. By understanding these processes, we can cultivate a similar focus on a global scale.

Learning from the Masters of Harmony

Contemplate the civilizations celebrated for their harmony and collaborative spirit. What insights might we glean from their unique perspective on existence? Is there a focus on fostering empathy and understanding within their educational frameworks? Do their cultural narratives emphasize the importance of unity and the welfare of the community as a whole? Through deliberate observation and the embrace of these practices, we may begin to transform the shared perspective into a more harmonious existence.

A Call to Disciplined Awareness

The future of humanity hinges on our ability to cultivate disciplined perception. We must move beyond the constant bombardment of information and cultivate the ability to focus on what truly matters. This requires a conscious effort, a commitment to learning from those who have achieved peace and prosperity, and a willingness to shift our collective focus toward a brighter future.

A Thrilling Prospect: Rewiring Our Social Fabric

The idea of rewiring the very fabric of human perception might seem like something out of a thriller novel. But the reality is far more compelling. By understanding the power of disciplined attention, we hold the key to fostering cooperation, understanding, and a more peaceful world.

A Scientific Imperative: Factoring in the Human Element

While scientific advancements continue to propel us forward, true progress necessitates a deeper understanding of human behavior. Disciplined perception bridges this gap. By factoring in the power of collective focus, we can ensure that our scientific advancements serve the greater good and contribute to a world where humanity thrives.

Leaving a Lasting Legacy: Shaping Our Destiny

The choices we make today regarding our collective awareness will have a profound impact on generations to come. By cultivating disciplined perception and fostering a global focus on peace and understanding, we can leave a lasting legacy—a world shaped not by chaos and distraction but by intention and collaboration.

Harnessing Awareness to Conquer Economic Challenges: Lessons from FDR[9]

Overcoming Adversity Through Collective Focus – Lessons from the Great Depression! History is replete with many such examples of disciplined perception-witness to the grand scale. The Great Depression, otherwise known as the period when economic ruin firmly gripped the United States and much of the rest of the world, still serves as a jolting reminder of the fragile nature of human life. It was within this darkness, though, that a beacon of optimism could be found. President Franklin D. Roosevelt's administration marshaled the collective will of a nation in its struggle to regain its footing.

Stages to initiate and activate mass selective awareness

Stage 1: A Unified Purpose–The Wellspring of Collective Action

Fostering a unified purpose was the bedrock of Roosevelt's approach. He intuitively understood that social betterment- the advancement of society- rests on the capacity of leadership to put aside its differences in favor of a common purpose. This was not a form of ideological amnesia but rather an attempt to find a grand purpose that went beyond the limited interests of partisan politics. Picture a group of climbers working to conquer the most hazardous peak. Each has his own different strengths and sets of skills: one is a master in navigation, another in using ropes and anchors. But that, again, does not matter how good each of them is at his or her

---

[9] FDR: Franklin D. Roosevelt is the 32nd U.S. President

particular skill- the team will not make it without a common goal, a common purpose forcing them to work in coordination as one force, one entity. It is this sense of unity of effort that the Great Depression asked of the citizens of America.

- **Roosevelt's Masterstroke: A Crucible for Shared Focus**

  Roosevelt's first move exemplified the power of this approach. He summoned leaders from both houses of Congress to the White House, a symbolic act that bridged the political chasm. His message was a potent cocktail of psychology and pragmatism. He urged them to set aside the partisan bickering that had become commonplace temporarily and instead focus all their efforts on a singular, unifying objective–restoring confidence in the American people. This was not just about economic recovery; it was about rekindling the spirit of a nation and the belief in a brighter future.

- **The Power of Shared Focus: A Psychological Tug-of-War**

  This act of convening was not merely symbolic. Roosevelt fostered a sense of shared responsibility by bringing together leaders from opposing sides. Imagine a team of detectives working on a complex case. Despite their differing investigative styles and personalities, they are all united in their pursuit of the truth. In a similar vein, Roosevelt's leadership created a shared mental framework, a disciplined perception on a national scale. This psychological shift was crucial for economic recovery. By fostering a sense of collective purpose, Roosevelt tapped into a potent wellspring of human resilience, a psychological force that could propel the nation forward.

Stage 2: Orchestrating the Message–Media as the Amplifier

Having established a unified purpose, Roosevelt understood the critical role of disseminating that message across the nation. This required the strategic engagement of various media channels to amplify the call to action and foster a sense of national unity.

- **The Power of the Press: Shaping Public Perception**

  The first group Roosevelt targeted was the news industry. He summoned representatives of major newspapers, acutely aware of their immense influence in shaping public perception. Imagine a sculptor meticulously shaping a block of marble. In this analogy, Roosevelt is the sculptor, and the news media represents the chisel and hammer. Through carefully crafted messaging and editorials, the press could help shape a national narrative focused on hope, resilience, and the pursuit of the newly established common goal.

- **Engagement, Not Coercion: Building Trust with the Fourth Estate**

  Roosevelt did not resort to coercion or censorship. Instead, he engaged with the press, seeking their partnership in a national endeavor. This strategy, rooted in mutual respect and a shared sense of purpose, proved highly effective. The press, recognizing the gravity of the situation, readily committed to amplifying Roosevelt's message of unity and hope.

- **Beyond the Headlines: Reaching Hearts and Minds Through Faith**

  Roosevelt's outreach extended beyond the secular sphere. He also understood the profound influence of religious leaders. He invited them, regardless of denomination, to participate in this national effort. Imagine a conductor leading a vast orchestra, each instrument contributing its unique voice to create a harmonious symphony. Similarly, religious leaders, with their established congregations and moral authority, could play a pivotal role in unifying the nation.

- **A Call to Shared Values: Inspiring Action Through Faith**

  There was no attempt to dictate specific religious beliefs. The focus was on core values–compassion, perseverance, and a belief in a brighter future. By appealing to these shared values, Roosevelt sought to inspire religious leaders to champion the national cause. Their enthusiastic compliance underscored the power of faith to unite people in times of crisis.

Stage 3: A President Speaks to a Nation–The Power of Direct Communication

Having established a unified purpose and harnessed the media apparatus, Roosevelt understood the importance of direct communication with the American people. This was not just about disseminating information; it was about inspiring confidence, fostering solidarity, and creating a sense of shared struggle.

- **The Fireside Chats: Intimacy and Inspiration in a Time of Crisis**

  One of Roosevelt's most enduring legacies is his now-famous series of "fireside chats." These radio broadcasts served as a powerful tool for direct communication with the American people. Imagine a lone sailor navigating a treacherous storm. A reassuring voice from a distant lighthouse, offering guidance and hope, can make all the difference. In a similar vein, Roosevelt's fireside chats provided a beacon of hope and reassurance in a time of immense national anxiety. He spoke directly to the American people, not as a distant politician, but as a trusted leader, a neighbor sharing the burdens and promising a brighter future.

- **Beyond Information: Cultivating a Shared Narrative**

  These broadcasts transcended mere pronouncements of policy or economic updates. Roosevelt wove a compelling national narrative that emphasized American resilience, the power of collective action, and the unwavering pursuit of the established common goal. He spoke of sacrifice, yes, but also of hope and a shared destiny. By cultivating this narrative, Roosevelt fostered a sense of disciplined perception on a national scale. The American people, united in their focus on overcoming adversity, became a formidable force for economic recovery.

- **A Symphony of Voices: Enlisting the Power of Communication**

  Roosevelt's direct communication efforts extended beyond his fireside chats. He understood the importance of a unified message across all communication channels. Radio announcers, for instance, were enlisted to promote the national cause. Imagine a vast orchestra, each instrument contributing its unique voice to a harmonious symphony. Similarly, Roosevelt ensured that all communication channels–newspapers, radio broadcasts, and even public speeches–echoed the message of unity and perseverance.

Stage 4: Mobilizing Action–The Alphabet Soup Agencies Take Center Stage

Having established a unified purpose, harnessed the media apparatus, and fostered direct communication, Roosevelt understood the need to translate rhetoric into action. This gave rise to the now-iconic "Alphabet Soup" agencies–the Civilian Conservation Corps (CCC), the Works Progress Administration (WPA), the Tennessee Valley Authority (TVA), and countless

others. These agencies served as powerful tools for mobilizing the
nation's collective focus toward economic recovery.

- **Beyond Relief: Restoring Dignity Through Work**

  The immediate impacts of these Alphabet Soup agencies
  cannot be denied. They provided jobs to millions of the
  unemployed, returned food to the table, and salvaged the lost
  dignity of the workers. Think of a large, rich field gone to
  fallow. The CCC- and its attendant projects in the realm of
  conservation- was like an expert team of farmers tilling the soil,
  planting the seeds, and nurturing life anew. These agencies not
  only addressed the immediate crisis of unemployment but also
  provided further prosperity. For instance, construction
  projects led by the WPA serve communities around the
  country to this day.

- **A Symphony of Action: Disciplined Perception in
  Practice**

  The very act of establishing these agencies served a crucial
  psychological purpose. It reinforced the message of unity and
  collective action. Imagine a team of firefighters battling a
  massive blaze. Each firefighter plays a crucial role, but it is their
  coordinated effort, their disciplined perception focused on a
  single objective, that ultimately extinguishes the flames.
  Similarly, while addressing specific needs, the Alphabet Soup
  agencies fostered a sense of shared responsibility and a unified
  national focus on recovery. By putting millions of Americans
  back to work on projects that benefited the entire nation,
  Roosevelt harnessed the power of disciplined perception on a
  massive scale.

- **Beyond Jobs: Symbols of Hope for a Brighter Future**

  The consequences of these Alphabet Soup agencies were not all economic in nature. They also had the power to act as icons for the instillation of hope and renewal within the nation. The CCC, for one, merely put young men to work in planting trees, building parks, and conserving natural resources. These projects would then create jobs and stimulate economic activity while offering an almost tangible symbol of progress. This indeed spoke volumes about planting trees for a future to be better than the ravaged Depression time, when the nation would begin to bloom again. Similarly, Roosevelt used the agencies as symbols of hope and national renewal, manipulating disciplined perception's power to ensure that the mass gaze remained affixed on a future replete with promise.

Stage 5: Symbols of Hope–Cultivating Optimism Through Action

Beyond the crucial role of the Alphabet Soup agencies, Roosevelt understood the importance of fostering optimism during a time of immense despair. He achieved this by promoting potent symbols of hope, as well as visual and narrative reminders of a brighter future waiting to be realized.

- **A Nation Rebuilds: The Power of Tangible Progress**

  One such symbol was the construction of infrastructure projects like dams, bridges, and public buildings. Imagine a weary traveler traversing a vast desert, their hope dwindling with every step. The sight of a glistening oasis, a symbol of new life and renewed possibility, can rejuvenate the spirit. Similarly, the construction of these projects offered a tangible reminder of the nation's collective strength and resilience. The very act of building, of creating something new and lasting from the

ashes of despair, instilled a sense of optimism in the American
people.

- **Beyond Infrastructure: The Civilian Conservation Corps
  and Nature's Renewal**

The Civilian Conservation Corps (CCC) served as another
powerful symbol of hope. By putting young men to work
planting trees, building parks, and conserving natural
resources, the CCC offered a glimpse of a future where the
environment was not ravaged but cherished and protected.
Imagine a barren landscape slowly being transformed into a
lush, vibrant ecosystem. This process mirrored the nation's
own journey towards recovery—a journey from devastation to
renewal. Through its focus on environmental stewardship, the
CCC offered a powerful symbol of hope and a shared vision
for a sustainable future.

- **The Power of Narrative: Weaving a Story of Resilience**

Beyond tangible projects, Roosevelt also cultivated hope
through a carefully crafted narrative. His "fireside chats" spoke
not only of the challenges at hand but also of the unwavering
spirit of the American people. He emphasized the nation's
history of overcoming adversity, its inherent strength, and
creativity. By weaving a compelling story of resilience,
Roosevelt instilled a sense of collective optimism, a belief that
the nation could and would emerge stronger from the crisis.

These stages showcase how Roosevelt went beyond rhetoric
to create a national environment conducive to economic
recovery. By harnessing disciplined perception, he mobilized
the nation's collective focus towards a shared goal, fostering a
sense of unity and hope that ultimately paved the way for a
brighter future.

The Power of Collective Focus: Results of Disciplined Perception

Outcome 1: Overcoming Divisions–A Nation Reunited

The Great Depression exposed deep societal divisions, but Roosevelt understood the transformative power of a unified citizenry. This stage focused on fostering a sense of national unity through a suspension of personal differences and a shift in media narratives.

- **Suspension of Prejudices: A Time for Unity**

  In times of crisis, a fascinating phenomenon occurs. People tend to set aside personal differences and unite towards a common goal. Roosevelt recognized this and actively fostered a spirit of national unity. Spurred on by the gravity of the situation, Americans temporarily put aside their "personal prejudices of race, creed, and political leaning." This was not about erasing identities but recognizing a higher purpose, a shared struggle transcending individual differences.

- **Shifting the Narrative: Optimism Replaces Despair**

  The media, influenced by Roosevelt's leadership, stopped dwelling on negativity. The "scare headlines about 'Business Depression'" were replaced with narratives of "Business Recovery." This shift in focus was not about denying the challenges but about fostering a more optimistic outlook, which is essential for an economic turnaround. By replacing despair with hope, the media played a crucial role in uniting the nation behind a shared vision of a brighter future.

Outcome 2: Confidence Restoration–A Nation Believes Again

The collective focus on a positive outcome had a profound impact on the nation's economic picture. This stage centered on restoring confidence in the American people and the American economy.

- **Harnessing the Power of Belief**

  The citizenry, encouraged by Roosevelt's message, "concentrated their minds upon the one task of restoring confidence." This was not just about blind optimism but about recognizing the nation's inherent strength and resilience. Roosevelt's leadership, fireside chats, and the various programs implemented fostered a sense of collective agency, a belief that the American people could overcome adversity.

- **Shifting the Economic Mindset**

  With a renewed sense of optimism, the "whole economic picture began to swing back from failure to success." It was not just about government programs; it was about a collective shift in perception, a belief that the nation could overcome adversity. This newfound confidence spurred innovation, investment, and a return to economic growth.

Outcome 3: Establishing Collective Mind Power–A Nation Reimagines Its Future

The Power of Collective Focus: Results of Disciplined Perception

Perhaps the most significant outcome of Roosevelt's approach was harnessing a collective "Disciplined Perception." This stage focuses on creating a powerful mental force through the alignment of individual focus toward a shared goal.

- **Adapting Strategies Over Time: Sustaining Collective Focus**

  While the crisis was on a roll, Roosevelt constantly readjusted his moves to ensure the people's collective interest would be strengthened continuously. These more radical reforms were reflected in legislation such as the Social Security Act and the Wagner Act during the Second New Deal. With this proactive mentality of policymaking, the collective effort would stay relevant and effective through the active interest of the public.

- **A Symphony of Minds: Sustaining Collective Effort**

  His leadership, the media involvement, and the Alphabet Soup agencies were all interrelated. Yet, for a continuous group effort, Roosevelt adjusted his methods to the cycle of crisis. For instance:

  o **Early New Deal:** Initially, Roosevelt focused on providing immediate relief through programs like the New Deal. By addressing the American people's most pressing needs, he helped restore confidence and maintain public support.

  o **Later New Deal:** As the crisis deepened, Roosevelt shifted his focus to long-term economic recovery. Programs like the Social Security Act and the Wagner Act aimed to create a more stable and equitable economic system.

  o **Wartime Economy:** When World War II broke out, Roosevelt's policy makings were adjusted further to meet wartime needs. The government took the lead in mobilization and directed resources toward meeting the war.

- **A Masterstroke in Directed Attention: Sustaining Collective Focus**

    Roosevelt's use of "Directed Attentiveness" was a masterstroke. By strategically focusing the nation's attention on a shared goal, he unleashed the power of collective perception, paving the way for a brighter future. This was not about manipulation but about harnessing the immense potential that arises when a nation unites behind a common vision.

- **Sustaining Focus Through Storytelling and Symbolism**

    Roosevelt was a master storyteller who used powerful rhetoric and symbolism to maintain the nation's focus. His fireside chats, for example, helped to humanize the presidency and build a sense of trust with the American people. By framing the crisis as a shared challenge, Roosevelt encouraged a sense of national unity and purpose.

In Conclusion

These stages showcase the transformative power of disciplined perception. Roosevelt led the United States out of economic despair and towards a brighter future by strategically directing collective attention, fostering optimism, and harnessing a sense of national unity. The lessons learned from the Great Depression offer valuable insights that can be applied to address societal challenges today.

Forging Unity from the Ashes: The Birth of the United Nations

The abhorrence of World War II had left a world in ruins-a vivid reminder of how the divisive spirit of nations could go totally berserk. It was in the wake of this unparalleled global war that a strong desire to live in peace and cooperation sprouted. It was not a case of blind optimism but the realization of a joint destiny-that all nations shared a common future.

The United Nations' founders understood the transformative power of collective consciousness. They conceived an organization whose indispensable underpinning was "selected awareness": a shared concentration on a single purpose, which would transcend personal differences and nationalist contests. Imagine a mountain range-sized mass of water churned by violent storms into a frenzy of clashing waves, finally coming to a state of comparative calm: It was a wish for the newly formed UN, much like this ocean, to afford a platform wherein nations can tide over their differences to forge a way toward a more peaceful future.

Though still bearing fresh persecution and oppression scars, the founders of the UN did not fail to perceive that it is often from adversity so created that good change may be effectuated. An "adversity bringing with it the seed of an equivalent benefit." Just as the shared experience of suffering can bind a people together, so the shared experience of devastation could, they hoped, unite the nations in a common purpose—the pursuit of lasting peace and international cooperation.

The UN was not formed to create a monolithic world government but to bring about a sense of "harmonized group-selective awareness" on a global scale. But nations, each with their separate identities, would all be jointly concerned with peace among nations, human rights, and problems all over the world. This "mysterious aiding power" –collaboration and coming together– held the promise of a better future, one in which nations could hold hands to avoid a repetition of the horrors of yet another world war.

Stage 1: From Devastation to Unity—The Seeds of the United Nations

The world in 1945 was a desolate landscape. The horrors of World War II had left a trail of destruction and shattered the illusion of national isolationism. In the face of this unprecedented global crisis, a powerful yearning for peace and cooperation took root. This was not mere optimism but a recognition of a shared fate—the realization that the future of all nations was inextricably linked.

The very concept of the United Nations emerged from this crucible of collective awareness. The founders envisioned an organization built on the "Harmonized Group Awareness" principle—a shared focus on a common goal that transcended national rivalries. Imagine a vast forest, once ravaged by fire, slowly beginning to regenerate. Similarly, the UN aimed to provide a platform for nations to heal the wounds of war and cultivate a sense of global cooperation.

The scars of persecution and oppression were still fresh, but the UN founders believed that adversity could be a catalyst for positive change. The notion of "adversity bringing the seed of an equivalent benefit" became a guiding principle. Just as shared suffering can unite a people, the shared experience of global devastation could, they hoped, unite nations in a common purpose—the pursuit of lasting peace and international cooperation.

The formation of the UN was not about creating a monolithic world government. Instead, it aimed to foster a sense of "Disciplined Perception" on a global scale. While retaining their unique identities, nations would collectively focus on maintaining international peace, promoting human rights, and addressing global challenges. This "mysterious aiding power"—the power of collaboration and collective action—offered the hope of a brighter future, a future where nations could work together to prevent the horrors of another world war.

This stage sets the scene for the birth of the UN, highlighting the transformative potential of shared awareness in the face of immense adversity. It establishes the core principle of "Harmonized Group Awareness" as the foundation for the organization's mission.

Stage 2: Necessity Breeds Unity–The Power of Shared Focus

Imagine a world ravaged by war, a planet teetering on the brink of annihilation. In the ashes of World War II, a new hope emerged– the United Nations. Born from the crucible of conflict, the UN was not just a bold experiment in global cooperation but a testament to the incredible power of human ingenuity when faced with overwhelming adversity, inspiring us all to strive for a better world.

From Imposition to Choice

The experience of the world people post-World War II serves as a template for understanding the power of shared focus. Facing persecution and oppression, they were initially forced to "concentrate their attention upon a Guiding Ambition"–survival. Imagine a lone ship battling a raging storm. The crew, initially focused on immediate survival, must work in perfect unison to weather the tempest. Similarly, the Mormons, united by a common threat, developed a powerful sense of shared focus.

Forging Unity from the Ashes: The Birth of the United Nations

As the world lay in ruins after the cataclysm of World War II, the necessity for a unified global effort became glaringly apparent. The birth of the United Nations in 1945 was not just a diplomatic maneuver but a monumental leap toward a new world order.

Nations, scarred by the horrors of war, recognized the profound
need for a platform that could foster peace and, importantly,
prevent future conflicts, providing a beacon of hope for a more
peaceful future.

Necessity Transforms into Strength: The UN as a Force for Good

Unlike the Mormons, the United Nations wasn't born out of a
singular necessity but from a collective realization. The devastation
of the war provided a powerful impetus for nations to choose
cooperation over confrontation. The UN became a beacon of
"Disciplined Perception," where nations could focus on shared
goals like peace, human rights, and sustainable development,
demonstrating the strength that comes from global unity.[10]

The UN and the Power of Choice

Concrete examples of this disciplined focus can be seen in various
UN initiatives. For instance, the UN Peacekeeping missions, which
deploy over 100,000 personnel globally, embody the principles of
"Disciplined Perception." These missions require meticulous
coordination and a shared vision of maintaining peace and security
in volatile regions, often in the face of significant challenges and
risks.

This stage underscores the transformative potential of shared focus.
While external pressures may initiate it, the ultimate power lies in
the conscious choice of nations to utilize "Disciplined Perception"
for the betterment of humanity.

---

[10] **Case Study: The Marshall Plan**
A prime example of the UN's role in fostering collective focus is the Marshall Plan, a massive economic
aid program launched in 1948 to rebuild Europe after World War II. By providing financial assistance and
technical expertise, the Marshall Plan helped to stabilize the continent and prevent the spread of
communism. This initiative demonstrated the power of nations working together towards a common goal,
a testament to the principles of "Disciplined Perception."

Stage 3: A Spark from the Ashes—The UN and the Legacy of Oppression

The horrors of World War II were a stark reminder of the devastating consequences of unchecked nationalism and the oppression of people by their own governments. Millions were forced to fight and die in conflicts fueled by tyrants, serving as mere pawns in a deadly game of power. This collective experience of suffering was not simply a byproduct of war; it was a spark that ignited the flames of global outrage and the yearning for a different future.

The Power of Shared Suffering: Reinforcing Collective Focus

The unprecedented scale of human sacrifice during World War II forged a powerful bond between nations, reinforcing the collective focus established in Stage 2. Imagine a vast forest ravaged by a wildfire, slowly beginning to regenerate. Similarly, a shared sense of responsibility emerged from the ashes of war to prevent such tragedies from ever happening again. The bereaved families, the war veterans, and the countless individuals who witnessed the atrocities all shared a deep-seated desire for peace and a world where people were not forced to die for the ambitions of tyrants. This shared experience of suffering became a potent force for change.

Breaking the Chains of Oppression: From Shared Suffering to Collective Action

This shared purpose fueled the creation of the United Nations. The UN was not just about establishing peace treaties or drawing borders; it was about dismantling the very systems that led to such widespread oppression. The organization aimed to create a global platform where nations could work together to address the root causes of conflict—poverty, inequality, and the denial of fundamental human rights.

The UN as a Catalyst for Change: Building on Collective Focus

The architects of the United Nations understood that lasting peace could not be built on a foundation of oppression. Their vision was an organization dedicated to liberating people from the clutches of tyranny and preventing them from becoming pawns in the games of power-hungry leaders. Imagine a vast prison, its iron gates finally crumbling. The UN, much like the fall of these gates, aimed to liberate oppressed people and offer them a future free from the threat of war.[11]

Leveraging Collective Focus for Positive Change

The United Nations emerged not from a singular, cataclysmic moment of shared suffering but rather as a complex tapestry woven from diverse threads of human experience and aspiration. Yet, it found its power in the collective recollections of the conflict and the mutual aspiration to avert the recurrence of such a scenario. The organization stands as a crucible for nations to harness their "Disciplined Perception," united in pursuing a noble aspiration: to shield humanity from the shackles of oppression and uphold the sanctity of life and liberty for every individual. Through the cultivation of global collaboration and the imposition of accountability for violations of human dignity, the UN endeavors to create a world where no community is condemned to become a mere pawn in the relentless quest for oppressive authority.

---

[11] **Specific Examples of Disciplined Perception**
To illustrate the power of disciplined perception within the UN framework, consider the following examples:

- Human Rights Council: The UN Human Rights Council investigates and addresses human rights abuses worldwide. Through its mechanisms, the Council promotes accountability and seeks to prevent future violations.
- International Criminal Court: The ICC prosecutes individuals accused of war crimes, crimes against humanity, genocide, and the crime of aggression. By holding perpetrators accountable, the ICC contributes to a more just and equitable global order.
- UN peacekeeping missions: UN peacekeepers work in conflict-ridden areas to maintain peace and security. Through their presence and mediation efforts, they help to prevent violence and promote dialogue between warring parties.

In Conclusion

The United Nations, emerging from the remnants of World War II, serves as a profound symbol of humanity's capacity for unity and shared purpose. Through the collective understanding of hardship and the insights gleaned from history, the UN has emerged as a transformative force, striving to confront the fundamental sources of injustice and foster a more fair and balanced global society.

Stage 4: From Cooperation to Self-Determination–The EU and the UN's Legacy

The European Union (EU) journey offers valuable insights into the power of "Disciplined Perception" and its impact on achieving self-determination. While the UN initially focused on preventing global conflict, the EU demonstrates how shared goals can evolve into a powerful force for economic and political integration.

Learning from the UN Playbook: A Legacy of Cooperation and Challenges

The formation of the EU was not a coincidence. It followed in the footsteps of the UN's success in fostering international cooperation. The devastation of World War II served as a stark reminder of the dangers of national rivalries. Imagine a vast, fertile field left barren by years of conflict. Much like the UN, the EU aimed to create a platform for nations to heal the wounds of war and cultivate a spirit of collaboration.

UN's Impact: A Mixed Bag of Achievements and Failures

Throughout its history, the UN has recorded great successes in peacekeeping, humanitarian aid, and human rights promotion. However, criticism continues to emanate from some quarters over the UN's failures to avoid or participate in conflict resolution processes. In this respect, for example, the UN's inability to prevent both the Rwandan genocide and the Bosnian War.

The UN's successes also include its great contribution to the collapse of apartheid in South Africa, its fight against climate change through the Paris Agreement, and its humanitarian assistance for war-torn parts of the world. These successes have proven that the United Nations is able to consolidate international cooperation to solve global problems.[12]

The EU's Journey: A Model of Regional Integration

The EU has demonstrated the power of regional integration to achieve shared goals. By gradually deepening economic and political cooperation, the EU has created a single market, established common policies, and promoted democratic values. This journey has not been without challenges, such as the Brexit referendum and the ongoing debate over the eurozone crisis.

The Interconnectedness of the UN and the EU: A Shared Legacy

The UN and the EU have common interests in promoting peace, security, and human rights. The UN has provided the structural framework for international cooperation, while the EU has acted as a test case of how regional integration can effectively be used to realize common goals. Both organizations have influenced each other: the EU has picked up where the UN enunciated principles

---

[12] **Case Study: The Rwandan Genocide**
- The Rwandan Genocide in 1994 is a stark example of the UN's limitations. Despite warnings and the presence of UN peacekeepers, the international community failed to act decisively, resulting in the massacre of approximately 800,000 people. This tragedy underscored the need for more robust mechanisms to prevent and respond to such atrocities.

Case Study: The Paris Agreement
- On the other hand, the Paris Agreement of 2015 showcases the UN's ability to unite nations in the fight against climate change. This landmark accord brought together 196 countries to commit to reducing greenhouse gas emissions and limiting global warming. It exemplifies how the UN can foster global cooperation on critical issues.

of respect for sovereignty, while the UN has benefited from the EU's experience in regional cooperation.

In Conclusion

The experiences of both the UN and the EU illuminate the profound impact of "Disciplined Perception" and underscore the significance of collective aspirations. Though the UN has encountered numerous obstacles in its quest to fulfill its aims, the enduring impact of its efforts to foster peace and collaboration is undeniably profound. The evolution of the EU serves as a compelling narrative, illustrating how the intricate dance of regional integration can cultivate not only economic flourishing but also a profound sense of political equilibrium. Through the examination of the triumphs and missteps of these entities, we may delve deeper into the potential of unified efforts, seeking to forge a more enlightened and harmonious existence for all.

Stage 5: A United Front—Globalization and the Power of Collective Action

The rise of globalization serves as a powerful testament to the importance of "unity of purpose" and the incredible potential that arises when nations combine their resources and efforts to address global challenges. This stage explores how globalization complements the UN's mission by fostering international collaboration in the face of shared threats.

Learning from the UN Playbook: A Global Perspective

The growth of globalization was not a coincidence. It followed in the footsteps of the UN's success in fostering international cooperation. The modern world's interconnectedness has made it increasingly clear that challenges like pandemics, climate change, and economic instability transcend national borders. Imagine a vast ocean, its currents and tides affecting every vessel sailing its waters. Similarly, nations in today's globalized world are all interconnected, and their well-being depends on a collective effort to address shared challenges.

Comparing the EU with Other Regional Organizations

The EU stands as a testament to the intricate dance of regional integration and economic collaboration. Yet, it beckons a deeper inquiry into how its journey aligns with the narratives of other regional entities. Consider the African Union (AU), which has encountered obstacles on its path to achieving comparable levels of integration. Yet, it has forged ahead, making strides in the vital realms of peace and security across the continent of Africa. The Association of Southeast Asian Nations (ASEAN) reveals the profound advantages of regional collaboration, especially in the realms of economic advancement and societal progress.

The Dark Side of Globalization: Balancing Benefits and Costs

Globalization has brought many benefits, including increased trade, economic growth, and cultural exchange. However, it has also led to challenges such as inequality, job losses, and cultural homogenization. It is important to acknowledge the dark side of globalization and work to address its negative consequences.

Building a More Resilient Future: The Power of Collective Action

Despite globalization's challenges, it creates an opportunity for nations to come together in search of solving world problems. The COVID-19 pandemic that recently swept the world was a great example of how "unity of purpose" works in a globalizing world. Faced with a previously unknown and highly contagious virus, nations around the world poured their intellectual and financial resources into vaccine development and advances in global health AI. It was not just a question of individual nations looking after their own citizens; it was an awareness that the only way to defeat the virus would be through a coordinated, genuinely global effort. What this unified determination in the face of one common enemy underlined was an important potential catalyst for change: the power of collaboration. On everything from climate change and sustainable development to poverty reduction, collaboration can help nations create a more resilient and equitable future for everyone.

Building a More Resilient Future

The power of "unity of purpose" is not limited to crisis response. Globalization fosters ongoing collaboration on issues like climate change, sustainable development, and poverty reduction. By working together and sharing resources, nations can develop more effective strategies for building a more resilient and sustainable future for all. Imagine a team of architects, each with a unique specialty, collaborating to design a building that can withstand any storm. Similarly, globalization allows nations to combine their strengths to address complex challenges that require a global approach.

In Conclusion

In the face of its complexities, globalization unveils a vast landscape of possibilities waiting to be explored. Through the lens of collective endeavor and the intricate dynamics of a globalized world, we can forge pathways toward a future that is not only resilient but also sustainable for every inhabitant of our shared planet. The United Nations, the European Union, and various regional entities illuminate the profound implications of unified endeavors and the intricacies of shared understanding. The intricate web of these institutions, coupled with the increasing interconnectedness of our contemporary existence, underscores the necessity of wielding selective awareness as a means to forge a more promising future. Through the lens of our collective aspirations and

collaborative efforts, we may navigate the intricate challenges posed
by globalization, forging a path toward a world that embodies
prosperity and equity for every individual.

Uniting for Prosperity: Lessons from Economic Challenges and Global Cooperation

Imagine a world fracturing! The Great Depression's monstrous
tremor left America desolate, while World War II's smoldering
embers cast a long shadow. Humanity teetered on the brink.

But within the human psyche lies a hidden power—disciplined
Perception. A group can transcend individual anxieties and traumas
by focusing on a unifying goal.

President Franklin D. Roosevelt, a conductor of sorts, recognized
this potential. Through radio addresses, he became a focal point,
directing the nation's attention towards economic recovery, a
unifying melody. The New Deal, a series of orchestrated programs,
channeled this collective focus into infrastructure projects, job
creation, and safety nets. It was like a vast neural network, its
neurons firing in unison toward a singular objective.

The story does not end there. The horrific aftermath of World War
II birthed a similar global "Disciplined Perception." The United
Nations emerged as a fledgling counterpoint to the discord. Its core
principle–a powerful counterpoint to the discord of the previous
years–was this same "Disciplined Perception." It was not just about
maintaining peace but about composing a new symphony for
humanity, one where nations played in harmony towards a
transcendent goal–a world free from war.

Both the New Deal and the UN serve as potent self-help guides.
They demonstrate the power of shared purpose. When individuals
channel their anxieties and frustrations into a collective vision, a

sense of empowerment arises. Imagine a group stranded in the wilderness; fear and despair cripple. But by focusing on building shelter and finding food, their collective energy becomes a potent tool for survival.

However, this human capacity is a double-edged sword! While it can forge nations and propel progress, it can also be weaponized. Cult leaders manipulate followers into obedience, and totalitarian regimes control information through a warped "Disciplined Perception," herding the masses towards destructive goals. Vigilance is key. A healthy dose of skepticism and the courage to question authority are essential safeguards.

The story of human progress is a testament to the power of "Disciplined Perception." Leaders and societies rise from the ashes, united by a shared vision and a relentless focus on a brighter future. Whether through scientific exploration, grassroots movements, or individual determination, the ability to harness collective awareness remains humanity's greatest asset.

So, the next time you feel lost or overwhelmed, remember the captain at the helm, his unwavering focus a beacon of hope in the storm. Together, with a shared purpose and a laser-sharp vision, we can navigate any sea. This shared focus, this symphony of purpose, is the tapestry weave in unity.

Conclusion: A Call to Collective Harmony: A Warning and a Hope

The world finds itself at a pivotal juncture, where choices echo through the corridors of time. The grand orchestration of humanity appears to have fallen into disarray, supplanted by a tumultuous clash of conflicting ideas and behaviors. This chaos looms, urging us ever closer to the brink of our own undoing. We must engage actively in the unfolding narrative of existence. It is imperative that we take action, and that we do so in unison.

Fractured Relationships, Fragile Future: The cracks in our personal and international connections are widening. Broken trust, rising animosity, and a growing sense of "us vs. them" threaten the very fabric of civilization. Imagine a grand tapestry, its vibrant threads once interwoven in a masterpiece. Now, the threads fray and unravel, threatening to leave behind a tattered mess. If we fail to mend the tears in our social fabric, this is the future.

Seeking the Harmony Keepers: But there is hope. We must turn our gaze towards those who have, against all odds, found a way to live in harmony. Individuals, communities, and even nations who, despite their differences, have chosen cooperation over conflict, understanding over animosity. Let us study their methods, their philosophies, and their guiding principles. Perhaps within their stories lies the key to unlocking a future of collective well-being.

A Call to Action! Reharmonize Our Thoughts: The solution lies not in grand pronouncements or sweeping reforms but in a quiet revolution within each of us. We must cultivate a sense of "reharmonization of thoughts." This means actively choosing empathy over judgment, understanding over prejudice, and collaboration over competition. It means recognizing our shared humanity, the invisible threads that bind us together.

Imagine a world where respectful dialogue replaces shouting matches, cooperation replaces competition, and the pursuit of a common good takes precedence over individual gain. This future is within our grasp, but it requires a conscious effort from each and every one of us. Let us become the harmony keepers, the weavers who mend the fraying threads of our world. Let us rewrite the narrative, not with violence and discord, but with compassion, understanding, and a shared vision of a brighter future.

Section VIII

THE ORCHESTRA WITHIN EXCEPTIONAL ACHIEVERS

❧ ❧ ❧

I magine gazing upon the pyramids of Giza, their colossal forms a testament to the focused vision of civilization. Alternatively, picture the soaring melody of a Beethoven symphony, each note meticulously placed to create a masterpiece. These achievements, seemingly born from magic, are actually the result of something far more potent–Disciplined Perception.

This final chapter revisits the lives of some of the most formidable pioneers in harnessing the power of selective awareness to realize fantastic achievements. These remarkable individuals, who have lived from Ancient Times through the Modern Age, have shown exactly how focused attention and a clear vision can result in the most unimaginable discoveries and transformative innovations.

This section, titled The Orchestra within Exceptional Achievers, delves into the minds of history's most remarkable individuals. Inspired by Napoleon Hill's How to Own Your Mind, we will dissect the common threads that bind these trailblazers–the architects, the artists, the innovators who dared to dream and, more importantly, dared to act.

We begin with **Fatima Al-Fihri**, whose dedication to education laid the foundation for one of the world's oldest universities, setting a precedent for pursuing knowledge. **Marie Curie** and **Barbara McClintock** exemplify resilience and passion in scientific research,

breaking barriers and expanding our understanding of the natural
world.

Chien-Shiung Wu, James Watson, and Francis Crick, the Double
Helix Duo, highlight the importance of collaboration and precision
in scientific endeavors. Alan Turing and Nikola Tesla showcase the
power of visionary thinking in computing and electrical
engineering, respectively.

Coming into the modern era, **Roger Penrose** and **Stephen
Hawking** unravel the mysteries of the universe through
mathematical and theoretical physics. **Elon Musk** is the
indefatigable architect of the future, bridging the gap between
theoretical innovation and practical application in the relentless
pursuit of leading-edge technology and pioneering the exploration
of space. **Bill Gates** and **Steve Jobs** reshaped the world of
technology with their futuristic leadership, while Larry Page and
Sergey Brin (Founders of Google) brought curiosity and teamwork
to the digital age.

Finally, we conclude with **Henry Ford**, whose focused action and
innovative spirit transformed the automotive industry and set new
standards for manufacturing and productivity.

These are extraordinary life stories, actually being immersive
explorations into the minds. We will tear apart inventors' thought
processes, such as Marie Curie, dig deep into the relentless focus of
leaders and pioneers like Bill Gates, and learn about the
collaborative brilliance that sent humanity onto the moon. Prepare
to be shocked by how icons struggled in many relatable ways,
including the doubt each wrestled with and the ultimate laser beam-
like focus that flew them to greatness.

Think of yourself as a conductor, leading an orchestra of your own
thoughts and desires. Through focused attention, you, too, can
harmonize these internal instruments, composing a symphony of

success. The science behind disciplined perception will be your guide, while captivating anecdotes serve as the sheet music, bringing these principles to life.

Our hope is that these stories will not just entertain you but ignite a fire within. Perhaps you will discover a hidden talent, unearth a long-forgotten dream, or simply gain the tools to tackle that nagging project with renewed vigor. After all, you, too, have the potential to contribute your verse to the ongoing saga of human achievement. Are you ready to unlock the conductor within?

The Legacy of Fatima al-Fihri: A Symphony of Education and Vision

A. Visionary Philanthropy: The Architect of Opportunity

Fatima al-Fihri was not just a wealthy heiress; she was an architect of opportunity. Imagine a visionary philanthropist using her inheritance to build a bridge to a brighter future. Driven by a passion for education, she dedicated her wealth to creating the al-Qarawiyyin Mosque, a place where knowledge could flourish and minds could be empowered. Her legacy extends far beyond commerce, reminding us of the transformative power of education.

Think of Fatima al-Fihri as the ultimate knowledge investor. She saw the potential for education to unlock a brighter future, not just for herself but for generations to come. Her investment in the al-Qarawiyyin Mosque was not just about bricks and mortar; it was about building a powerhouse of learning that would leave a lasting impact on the world.

Self-Help: Feeling lost or uninspired? Look at Fatima al-Fihri's example. She identified a need–access to education–and took action to address it. Consider how you can leverage your resources, not just for material gain, but to impact the world around you positively.

Thriller Twist: Fatima al-Fihri's philanthropy was a calculated move, a strategic investment in the future. She understood that education was the key to unlocking potential and empowering individuals. Her foresight allowed her to create a powerful institution that would shape the intellectual landscape for centuries to come.

Psychologically, Fatima al-Fihri's story reflects the power of purpose-driven action. Her unwavering commitment to education fueled her vision, allowing her to create a lasting impact on the world. When we align our actions with our deepest values, we experience a sense of flow and focused motivation that can lead to extraordinary achievements.

B. Architectural Acumen: The Symphony in Stone

Fatima al-Fihri was not just a philanthropist; she was an architectural maestro. Imagine an artist composing a symphony in stone. The al-Qarawiyyin Mosque, a masterpiece blending Islamic and Andalusian styles, stands as a testament to her vision and architectural acumen. Its enduring presence as a center of learning reflects the foresight and meticulous planning that went into its creation.

Think of Fatima al-Fihri as the Steve Jobs of mosque design. She did not just build a place of worship; she crafted a beautiful and functional space that fostered learning and intellectual exchange. The al-Qarawiyyin Mosque is a testament to the power of marrying aesthetics with functionality.

Self-Help: When embarking on a project, big or small, take inspiration from Fatima al-Fihri. Do not settle for mediocrity; strive for excellence in both form and function. Consider how thoughtful design can enhance the purpose and impact of your endeavors.

Thriller Twist: The al-Qarawiyyin Mosque was not just a place of worship; it was a symbol of Fatima al-Fihri's ambition. Her architectural masterpiece served as a beacon of knowledge, a powerful testament to her vision and unwavering dedication to education.

Psychologically, Fatima al-Fihri's architectural achievements reflect the power of focused creativity. Her vision for the al-Qarawiyyin Mosque was a clear goal, and her architectural expertise allowed her to translate that vision into a magnificent reality. This state of focused flow, where passion meets skill, is a recipe for extraordinary results.

We will continue to explore the remaining characteristics of Fatima al-Fihri's legacy in the next section.

C. Passion for Interdisciplinary Teaching: The Conductor of Knowledge

Fatima al-Fihri was not just a builder; she was a conductor of knowledge. Imagine a maestro leading an orchestra, but instead of instruments, the musicians are scholars from diverse disciplines. Under her vision, the al-Qarawiyyin Mosque became a haven for the study of Islamic studies, Arabic grammar, medicine, mathematics, and astronomy. This holistic approach fostered a vibrant intellectual exchange, creating a fertile ground cultivating well-rounded scholars and thinkers.

Think of Fatima al-Fihri as the inventor of the ultimate learning app. The al-Qarawiyyin Mosque was not just a school; it was a one-stop shop for knowledge. Students could delve into religious studies, hone their language skills, explore the mysteries of the human body, and unravel the secrets of the cosmos—all under one roof. This interdisciplinary approach allowed students to connect the dots between seemingly disparate subjects, fostering a more comprehensive understanding of the world.

Self-Help: Feeling stuck in a rut? Consider Fatima al-Fihri's approach to education. Do not limit yourself to narrow fields of study. Embrace the power of interdisciplinary learning. Explore seemingly unrelated subjects; you might be surprised at the connections you discover. This well-rounded approach can spark creativity and innovation in your own endeavors.

Thriller Twist: Fatima al-Fihri's diverse curriculum was a strategic move, fostering intellectual agility in her students. By exposing them to a wide range of disciplines, she empowered them to think critically, solve problems creatively, and become well-equipped to tackle the world's complexities. This emphasis on interdisciplinary learning created a generation of scholars who were a force to be reckoned with.

Psychologically, Fatima al-Fihri's vision for the al-Qarawiyyin Mosque reflects the power of intrinsic motivation. By offering a diverse curriculum, she catered to the natural human curiosity to explore and understand the world in all its complexity. This intrinsic motivation fueled a love of learning in her students, propelling them toward a state of flow and intellectual achievement.

Marie Curie: A Pioneer Forged in Resilience and Passion

Marie Curie, the legendary scientist who unlocked the secrets of radioactivity, was not just a scientific genius; she was a Pioneer Forged in Resilience and Passion. Innovation and Creativity, a groundbreaking path for Women in Science, unwavering Resilience in Adversity, and an Unquenchable Passion for Discovery marked her life and work.

A. The Radium Alchemist: Innovation and Creativity Reshape Science

Imagine a historical fiction novel or a captivating science documentary in which a brilliant scientist pushes the boundaries of knowledge. Curie embodied this spirit of Innovation and Creativity. She not only founded the new science of radioactivity (even coining the term itself!), but her discoveries laid the groundwork for cancer treatment. Her groundbreaking work changed the world not once but twice.

B. Shattering Glass Ceilings: A Pioneer for Women in Science

As Patricia Fara, president of the British Society for the History of Science, states, "*Curie boasts an extraordinary array of achievements... the first woman to win a Nobel Prize, the first female professor at the University of Paris...*" Curie's accomplishments transcended scientific breakthroughs; she became a Pioneer for Women in Science. Imagine a powerful social justice documentary highlighting the struggles and triumphs of female pioneers. By excelling in a male-dominated field, Curie shattered glass ceilings and paved the way for generations of women scientists.

C. An Unbreakable Spirit: Resilience in Adversity Fuels Determination

Fara further emphasizes, "*The odds were always stacked against her.*" Curie faced relentless adversity–political oppression in her native Poland, suspicion as a foreigner in France, and gender discrimination throughout her career. Imagine a captivating biography or a suspenseful thriller where the protagonist overcomes seemingly insurmountable obstacles. Curie, much like such a character, possessed an unbreakable spirit. These challenges

fueled her determination, leading her to even greater scientific
achievements.

D. A Relentless Pursuit: Passion and Discovery Drive a Legacy

Despite the dangers of radiation exposure that ultimately led to her
illness, Curie never lost her passion for scientific discovery. Imagine
a biography or a science documentary chronicling the life of a
scientist driven by an insatiable curiosity. Curie exemplifies this
relentless pursuit. Her dedication to her field and the positive
impact of cancer treatment inspired by her work continue to benefit
terminally ill patients worldwide. Her legacy is a testament to the
power of unyielding passion and a life dedicated to discovery.

We gain a richer understanding of the extraordinary Marie Curie by
delving into these diverse perspectives. She was not just a scientist;
she was a symbol of innovation, a champion for gender equality in
science, an embodiment of resilience, and a testament to the
enduring power of passionate scientific exploration. Her life and
work continue to inspire generations to push boundaries, challenge
norms, and relentlessly pursue knowledge for the betterment of
humanity.

The Enigma of Barbara McClintock: A Symphony of Scientific Traits

A. Dedication to Research: The Scientific Detective

McClintock's dedication to corn research was not blind faith; it was a meticulous investigation. Imagine a detective relentlessly pursuing a single case, sifting through every kernel of evidence (literally!). This unwavering focus, fueled by a passion for the scientific truth, led her to groundbreaking discoveries about the corn genome.

Think of McClintock as a plant whisperer. She wasn't just studying corn; she was having a lifelong conversation with it. This dedication allowed her to uncover secrets hidden within the very DNA of these seemingly ordinary plants.

Self-Help: Feeling stuck in a rut? McClintock's dedication is a masterclass in focus. She achieved remarkable results by choosing a subject and relentlessly pursuing its mysteries. Find your own area of fascination and delve deep—you never know what hidden gems you might uncover.

Thriller Twist: McClintock's research was not just about plants but a high-stakes chase after the truth. The scientific establishment scoffed, but she persisted, driven by an unshakeable belief in her observations. Ultimately, her relentless pursuit cracked the code of genetics, forever changing our understanding of life itself.

Psychologically, McClintock's dedication reflects the power of sustained focus. By devoting her life to corn research, she achieved a level of expertise that allowed her to see patterns invisible to others. This unwavering commitment is a key ingredient in achieving mastery in any field.

B. Scientific Unending Curiosity: The Explorer of the Gene Frontier

McClintock's discovery of transposons was not a stroke of luck but a testament to her boundless curiosity. Imagine a fearless explorer venturing into uncharted genetic territory. Her meticulous observations of "jumping genes" revolutionized our understanding of how genes work.

Consider McClintock as a genetic Indiana Jones, unearthing hidden treasures within the corn genome. Her discovery of transposons shattered the idea of genes as static entities, revealing a dynamic dance within our DNA.

Self-Help: Curiosity is the spark that ignites learning. Like McClintock, cultivate a questioning mind. Do not accept things at face value; delve deeper, ask questions, and explore the unknown. You never know what fascinating discoveries await.

Thriller Twist: McClintock's curiosity was a double-edged sword. Her exploration of the unconventional challenged the established order, making her an outsider in the scientific community. But her unwavering pursuit of truth ultimately exposed a hidden mechanism within the code of life.

Psychologically, McClintock's work highlights the importance of open-mindedness in scientific exploration. She was unafraid to challenge the status quo, and her willingness to consider unorthodox possibilities led to a paradigm shift in genetics.

C. Confidence and Fearless Pursuit of Knowledge: The Maverick Geneticist

McClintock's confidence emanated not from arrogance but from a steadfast conviction in the validity of her observations. Imagine a solitary researcher steadfast in the face of skepticism, her unwavering belief ignited by undeniable proof. Her audacious quest for understanding, undeterred by doubt, ushered in revolutionary insights into the realms of telomeres, centromeres, and homologous recombination.

McClintock was a rockstar in the science world, defying convention with her groundbreaking research. Her confidence was not ego-based; it was based on her unwavering belief in the power of her observations.

Self-Help: Do not be afraid to stand up for what you believe in, even if it is unpopular. McClintock's story is a testament to the power of self-belief. If you have evidence to support your ideas, dare to share them, even if they challenge the status quo.

Thriller Twist: McClintock's work was a daring heist, stealing scientific truths from the clutches of conventional thinking. Despite initial rejection, her unwavering confidence in her research ultimately led to a revolution in genetics.

Psychologically, McClintock's story demonstrates the importance of intellectual courage. She dared to challenge established beliefs, paving the way for a new understanding of the genetic code.

D. Continuous Learning: The Lifelong Student of Genetics

McClintock's approach to learning was not about proving herself right; it was about a relentless pursuit of knowledge. Imagine a lifelong learner constantly seeking new information and revising their understanding based on evidence. Her openness to new ideas allowed her to continuously refine her work and make groundbreaking discoveries throughout her career.

McClintock was not just a scientist but a time traveler of genetics. Her work was not confined to a single era; she revisited her own findings with fresh eyes, incorporating new discoveries to refine her understanding of the corn genome continuously. This iterative process and this willingness to learn and adapt allowed her to stay at the forefront of genetic research for decades.

Self-Help: Learning is a lifelong journey, not a destination. Embrace McClintock's spirit of continuous learning. Never stop asking questions, seeking new information, and revising your understanding of the world around you. This growth mindset is the key to unlocking your full potential.

Thriller Twist: McClintock's learning was akin to cracking a complex genetic code, each new discovery revealing a deeper layer of understanding. She was not afraid to revisit old assumptions, her mind constantly evolving as she incorporated new evidence. This relentless pursuit of knowledge allowed her to stay ahead of the curve, a constant threat to the established order with her groundbreaking revelations.

Psychologically, McClintock's work highlights the importance of intellectual humility in scientific exploration. She was not afraid to admit when she was wrong and adjust her theories based on new evidence. This openness to new information is a crucial aspect of the scientific process and a key ingredient in achieving true mastery in any field.

Chien-Shiung Wu: The Conductor of the Exceptional Mind

Chien-Shiung Wu, the physicist whose brilliance helped shape the course of World War II, was not just a scientific mind; she was the Conductor of the Exceptional Mind. Her life and work were a testament to Resilience in the face of adversity, a Love of Education that fueled her discoveries, and a scientific mind that thrived on Discovery, Innovation, and Work Dedication.

A. The Fission Maestro: Scientific Discovery Shapes History

Imagine a historical fiction novel or a captivating science documentary where a brilliant scientist changes the course of history. Wu embodied this spirit of scientific discovery. Her work on the Manhattan Project, particularly solving Fermi's plutonium problem and separating uranium isotopes, directly contributed to ending World War II. Her discoveries not only shaped the outcome of the war but also laid the groundwork for the field of nuclear physics.

B. Beyond the Spotlight: A Champion for Women in Science

Wu's achievements were often overshadowed by her male counterparts despite her groundbreaking contributions. Imagine a powerful social justice documentary highlighting the experiences of women in science. Wu's story exemplifies the challenges faced by women in a male-dominated field. However, her exceptional mind and unwavering dedication paved the way for future generations of female scientists.

C. The Unrelenting Mind: Resilience Fuels Groundbreaking Work

As a woman in science and an immigrant, Wu faced numerous obstacles throughout her career. Yet, she possessed an Unrelenting Mind. Imagine a captivating biography or a suspenseful thriller where the protagonist overcomes seemingly insurmountable challenges. Wu's resilience in the face of adversity fueled her determination, leading her to make groundbreaking discoveries despite her challenges.

D. A Life of Dedication: Work Ethic Shapes a Legacy

Wu's dedication to her work was legendary. Imagine a biography or a self-help book chronicling the life of a highly successful individual. Wu's unwavering Work Ethic serves as a powerful example. Her relentless pursuit of knowledge and meticulous attention to detail are qualities anyone striving for excellence can emulate.

By exploring these diverse perspectives, we gain a richer understanding of the remarkable Chien-Shiung Wu. She was not just a physicist; she was a testament to the power of resilience, a champion for women in science, and a role model for anyone who dares to push the boundaries of their field. Her life and work inspire generations to relentlessly pursue knowledge and innovation.

James Watson and Francis Crick: Unraveling the Secrets of Scientific Collaboration

The discovery of the DNA double helix by James Watson and Francis Crick (The Double Helix Duo) was not just a scientific breakthrough; it was a testament to the power of intellectual synergy and selective awareness in the face of obstacles. By examining their characteristics, we can glean valuable insights into the collaborative spirit that fuels groundbreaking scientific discoveries.

A. The Dance of Ideas: A Symphony of Minds

Watson's quote, "*But I guess I owe most of all to Francis, who really did look after me, and who often tried to keep me from being silly.*" highlights the remarkable intellectual synergy group they formed. Their dynamic was a fascinating dance of contrasting personalities—Watson's boundless enthusiasm balanced by Crick's sharp focus. Yet, it was this very difference that fueled their creativity. They challenged and complemented each other's ideas, creating a fertile ground for scientific discovery.

The Network Effect in Action–Amplifying Scientific Progress! Neuroscience is beginning to shed light on the benefits of collaboration in scientific research. Studies have shown that teams with diverse perspectives are better at problem-solving and generating novel ideas. Watson and Crick exemplify the network effect in action. By combining their unique skillsets and relentlessly critiquing each other's work, they achieved a breakthrough that had eluded others working in isolation.

Self-Help: The Power of Informed Critique–Sharpening Your Ideas! Watson's emphasis on informed criticism is a valuable lesson for anyone engaged in collaborative pursuits. His quote, "*Constantly exposing your ideas to informed criticism is very important,*" underscores the importance of surrounding yourself with colleagues who can challenge your assumptions and offer constructive feedback. This selective awareness, the ability to identify and benefit from valuable criticism, is crucial for refining ideas and achieving breakthroughs.

B. Navigating the Maze: Selective Awareness and Overcoming Obstacles

Watson's statement, "*Francis Crick and I were both in trouble at various times in our careers, but that never really stopped us, because we always found someone to save us,*" highlights their remarkable selective awareness in the face of obstacles. They possessed an uncanny ability to identify and leverage the support systems they needed to navigate the challenges inherent in scientific research. This ability to focus on the resources and collaborations that would propel them forward while filtering out distractions and setbacks was essential for their success.

Psychologically, The Power of Social Support and Growth Mindset. Watson and Crick's collaborative spirit aligns with the concept of social support. Studies have shown that strong support networks can improve our resilience, creativity, and problem-solving abilities. Their ability to overcome obstacles also reflects a growth mindset. They viewed challenges not as roadblocks but as opportunities to learn and adapt.

C. Mentorship Matters: The Power of Collaborative Learning

Watson's critique of his contemporaries highlights the importance of mentorship and collaboration. His quote, "*Give me a dozen healthy infants, well-formed, and my own specified world to bring them up in and I'll guarantee to take any one at random and train him to become any type of specialist I might select—doctor, lawyer, artist, merchant-chief, and, yes, even beggar-man and thief, regardless of his talents, penchants, tendencies, abilities, vocations, and race of his ancestors.*"[120] underscores his emphasis on behaviorism and the idea that environmental factors and conditioning play a crucial role in shaping individuals. This also underscores the value of open communication and a collaborative learning environment. Mentorship provides guidance and support, while collaboration fosters the exchange of ideas and the collective pursuit of knowledge.

By delving into these diverse perspectives, we gain a deeper understanding of the Watson-Crick Model for scientific collaboration. Their success was not just about individual brilliance; it was about the synergy created by two minds working in concert. By embracing the lessons gleaned from their journey, we too can cultivate the collaborative spirit, informed critique, and growth mindset necessary to unlock the potential of groundbreaking discoveries and propelling scientific progress to new heights.

Alan Turing: The Enigma with a Vision

Alan Turing, the brilliant mathematician and computer scientist who cracked the Enigma code during World War II, was not just a wartime hero; he was a visionary who defied expectations. By examining his characteristics, we delve into the enigmatic mind behind the groundbreaking work, revealing a man of Quiet Humility, Boundless Creativity, and a firm belief in Collaborative Power.

A. The Unassuming Genius: Quiet Humility in the Face of Achievement

Turing's quote, "*Sometimes it is the people no one can imagine anything of who do the things no one can imagine*," speaks volumes about his quiet humility. Imagine a self-help hero who accomplishes extraordinary feats while shunning the spotlight. Much like an unassuming hero in a historical thriller, Turing embodied this quality. His work, which arguably shortened the war and saved countless lives, was done behind the scenes, without fanfare.

Psychologically, The Power of Intrinsic Motivation. Turing's dedication was not driven by external validation; it stemmed from a deeper source–intrinsic motivation. He was driven by the thrill of discovery and the challenge of pushing the boundaries of what was thought possible.

B. The Imagination Machine: Boundless Creativity Fuels Innovation

His quote, "*Those who can imagine anything, can create the impossible*," highlights his boundless creativity. Imagine a world where scientists are like inventors in a popular science documentary, constantly pushing the boundaries of imagination. Turing, a pioneer in the field of artificial intelligence, possessed this very quality. He envisioned a future where machines could perform calculations and think creatively, a concept that remains a topic of exploration in modern-day thrillers.

Scientifically, The Importance of Conjecture in Scientific Progress. Turing's belief in the importance of conjecture is evident in his statement: "*The popular view that scientists proceed inexorably from well-established fact to well-established fact, never being influenced by any unproved conjecture, is quite mistaken.*" Science thrives on untested ideas and the courage to explore the unknown. Turing understood that bold conjectures, even if unproven, can spark innovation and lead to groundbreaking discoveries.

C. The Symphony of Minds: Collaborative Power Breeds Progress

Turing quotes, "I believe that at the end of the century, *the use of words and general educated opinion will have altered so much that one will be able to speak of machines thinking without expecting to be contradicted.*" and "*The isolated man does not develop any intellectual power. It is necessary for him to be immersed in an environment of other men, whose techniques he absorbs during the first twenty years of his life.*" this underscores his belief in the collaborative power of intellectual synergy groups.

Psychologically, Social Learning Theory and the Power of Collaboration. Turing's emphasis on the importance of collaboration aligns with social learning theory. We learn and grow through interaction with others, absorbing their knowledge and refining our own ideas. He recognized that true intellectual development flourishes within a supportive community, a message that resonates with the self-help notion of building a strong network.

By exploring these varied viewpoints, we uncover a deeper comprehension of the intricate and captivating figure that is Alan

Turing. He transcended the role of a mere scientist; he embodied a visionary spirit, daring to confront the established norms and forging the path that would ultimately give rise to the digital age. Through the insights drawn from his experiences, we can nurture a profound humility, expansive creativity, and a spirit of collaboration essential for confronting the complexities and revealing the possibilities that lie ahead.

The Tesla Enigma: Unraveling the Secrets of the Wardenclyffe Wizard

Nikola Tesla, the enigmatic visionary behind alternating current (AC) electricity, was more than just an inventor. He was a Disciplined Perceiver, wielding his mental energy like a sculptor meticulously shaping a masterpiece. We can illuminate the hidden pathways to boundless innovation by delving into his life.

Science: Shattering the Myth of the Lone Genius

Neuroscience sheds light on the collaborative nature of invention. While Tesla's brilliance is undeniable, his achievements stemmed from a unique synergy. He possessed an extraordinary ability to visualize complex systems in his mind's eye, a process enhanced by his detailed drawings. However, he also drew inspiration and collaboration from a network of scientists and engineers like George Westinghouse. This collaborative spirit, coupled with his own "disciplined perception," fueled his groundbreaking discoveries.

The AC/DC of Innovation: Inspiration and Experimentation

Self Help: Imagine Tesla's inventions not as isolated moments of genius but as the culmination of a dynamic dance–an alternating current of inspiration and experimentation. Tesla was not afraid to take calculated risks. His notebooks overflowed with ideas, each one meticulously documented and experimented upon. His famous quote, "*My brain is so good at visualizing things that I can actually see them physically in space*," highlights his unique ability to bridge the gap between imagination and reality. This relentless pursuit of innovation, fueled by a thirst for knowledge, is the hallmark of a true inventor.

The Symphony of the Mind: Harmonizing Intuition and Logic

The modern world often pits logic against intuition. However, Tesla's genius stemmed from his ability to harmonize these seemingly disparate forces. He possessed a strong foundation in scientific principles, yet he also embraced his intuition and his vivid visualizations. This symphony of the mind allowed him to think outside the box and develop revolutionary concepts like the Tesla coil. By nurturing both logic and intuition, we too can unlock the full potential of our minds.

Thriller Twist:

The Wardenclyffe Enigma: Unmasking the Secrets of a Visionary Mind

Imagine a world where inventors are not just dreamers but a breed apart, possessing an extraordinary mental focus. With his unwavering vision and relentless pursuit of wireless power transmission, Tesla could be seen as a member of this secret society. His ability to filter out distractions and channel his mental energy into a singular vision becomes almost superhuman. Perhaps the true "invention" was not the AC motor but his mastery over his own mind—a technology far more powerful than any copper coil.

The Wardenclyffe Conspiracy: A Race Against Time

Imagine a world where inventors aren't just eccentric geniuses but strategic minds engaged in a high-stakes game of innovation. With his unwavering focus on wireless power and global connectivity, Tesla could be seen as a protagonist in this thrilling narrative. His dedication to a vision deemed "unrealistic" by his peers becomes his driving force. Every experiment and every setback becomes a calculated move in a grand scheme to revolutionize the world. The race is on to unlock the future, one invention at a time.

The Power of Belief: Fueling Innovation with Unwavering Conviction

Psychologically, Tesla's unwavering belief in his ideas was a cornerstone of his success. While some scoffed at his theories, he remained steadfast in his conviction. This unshakeable belief fueled his relentless pursuit of innovation. However, it is important to acknowledge the potential pitfalls of dogmatic thinking. Tesla's focus on AC electricity may have blinded him to the potential of other technologies like direct current (DC). The key lies in achieving a balance—maintaining a strong belief in one's vision while remaining open to new ideas and alternative perspectives.

Through the examination of these varied viewpoints, we uncover a richer comprehension of the "Tesla Enigma." He was more than a brilliant inventor; he embodied the mastery of his own consciousness, a living proof of the profound potential that lies within disciplined perception. Through the insights drawn from his experiences, we can also shed light on our journey toward creativity, nurture partnerships, and engage with the vibrant dance of inspiration and trial. In doing so, we can direct our concentrated efforts as maestro guiding the orchestra of our own possibilities.

The Penrose Enigma: Unraveling the Mysteries of a Mathematical Maverick

Roger Penrose, the brilliant mathematician and physicist who delves into the mysteries of consciousness, is not just an intellectual giant; he is an enigma wrapped in a paradox. His life's work offers valuable insights into the power of the Subconscious Symphony, the Willpower Challenge, and Relentless Refinement. By unraveling the Penrose Enigma, we embark on a journey to unlock the secrets behind his groundbreaking discoveries.

A. The Unseen Orchestra: Harnessing the Power of the Subconscious

Penrose acknowledges the limitations of current knowledge about the brain, hinting at the possibility of an untapped sixth sense. His quote, *"It may well be there is something else going on in the brain that we do not have an inkling of at the moment,"* resonates with the intrigue of a scientific thriller. His unique approach—*"to ponder long and I hope deeply on problems and for a long time which I keep away for years and years, and I never really let them go"* suggests a deliberate cultivation of the Subconscious Symphony. He allows ideas to simmer in unseen depths, potentially leading to unexpected breakthroughs, like a detective coaxing out a confession from the subconscious mind.

The Quantum Leap–Unconscious Processing and Eureka Moments

Neuroscience is beginning to shed light on the power of the subconscious mind. Studies have shown that even when we are not consciously working on a problem, the subconscious processes information and makes connections. Penrose, perhaps intuitively, understood this phenomenon. He describes microtubules in cells as a source of quantum computing mechanism within the human brain, which he proposes could be a way to find the source of human conscious awareness. He created space for his subconscious to work its magic, trusting that seemingly dormant ideas would eventually surface and coalesce into groundbreaking discoveries, not unlike the sudden insights of a quantum leap.

B. The Tenacious Pathfinder: Unearthing Solutions Through Persistence

Penrose's journey was not a race to the finish line but a relentless trek through uncharted territory. His quote, "*People think of these eureka moments, and my feeling is that they tend to be little things, a little realization and then a little realization built on that*," underscores the importance of the willpower challenge. Imagine yourself as a tenacious pathfinder on a self-help quest for knowledge. Penrose, like a determined investigator in a thriller, championed this approach. He viewed scientific progress as a gradual process of "little realizations"–incremental discoveries built upon one another, step by step. His words capture his tenacity: "*I am pretty tenacious when it comes to problems.*" This unwavering perseverance is a quality that any self-help advocate would endorse.

The Growth Mindset and the Power of Delayed Gratification

Psychologically, Penrose's characteristic tenacity aligns with the concept of a growth mindset. He viewed challenges not as roadblocks but as opportunities for further exploration. In our fast-paced world, where instant gratification reigns supreme, Penrose's message is a powerful reminder of the importance of delayed gratification. He encourages us to resist the allure of quick fixes and embrace the power of patience, meticulously chipping away at challenges until we reach our destination.

C. The Sculptor's Touch: The Art of Relentless Refinement

Penrose was not just a seeker of knowledge but a sculptor of ideas. His quote, "*We have a closed circle of consistency here: the laws of physics produce complex systems, and these complex systems lead to consciousness, which then produces mathematics, which can then encode in a succinct and inspiring way the very underlying laws of physics that gave rise to it,*" demonstrates his meticulous approach. Imagine the brain as a vast studio filled with the potential for groundbreaking theories. Like a sculptor, Penrose meticulously chipped away at his ideas, constantly revisiting, reinterpreting, and refining them for precision and elegance. This relentless refinement resonates with the meticulous nature of a scientific thriller, where every detail matters. Popular science also recognizes the iterative nature of scientific progress, where ideas are constantly revisited and refined.

By exploring these diverse perspectives, we gain a richer understanding of the Penrose Enigma. He was not just a scientist but a pioneer who dared to explore the fringes of human understanding. By embracing the lessons gleaned from his life, we too can cultivate the Subconscious Symphony, the unwavering Willpower Challenge, and the meticulous, Relentless Refinement necessary to push the boundaries of knowledge and unlock our own intellectual potential.

D. The Focused Lens: Acknowledging the Power of Specialization

Penrose's quote, "*Well, I do not know if I can comment on Kant or Hegel because I am no real philosopher in the sense of knowing what these people have said in any detail, so let me not comment on that too much,*" exemplifies his remarkable intellectual humility. Imagine yourself on a self-help journey of intellectual exploration. A true scholar, like Penrose, acknowledges knowledge's vastness and specialization's importance. By dedicating himself to a specific field–mathematics and physics–he was able to delve deeply and make groundbreaking contributions. This focus and humility align with the concept of selective attention in psychology. We are bombarded with information, and focusing our attention on a specific area allows us to process information more effectively and achieve expertise.

The Butterfly Effect and the Interconnectedness of Knowledge

Penrose's focus on specialization should not be misconstrued as isolation. Chaos theory, explored in popular science, reminds us of the Butterfly Effect–how seemingly insignificant events in one system can have profound consequences in another. While Penrose may not have been a philosopher in the traditional sense, his work in physics undoubtedly has implications for our understanding of consciousness, a topic that bridges the gap between science and philosophy. In essence, Penrose's deep knowledge within his chosen field allowed him to make connections and contribute to a broader conversation.

Thriller Twist: The Mastermind and the Specialist Network

Imagine a world of intellectual thrillers where brilliant minds collaborate to solve complex problems. While Penrose himself may not have been a philosopher, his work likely sparked the curiosity of philosophers who, in turn, used his theories to explore the mysteries of consciousness. In this sense, Penrose can be seen as the mastermind, laying the groundwork for a collaborative effort that pushes the boundaries of knowledge. His specialization becomes a strength, allowing him to contribute a vital piece to the larger puzzle.

By incorporating these diverse perspectives, we gain a well-rounded understanding of Penrose's intellectual humility and the power of specialization. He was not just a scientist but a testament to the importance of focused exploration within a chosen field while still acknowledging the interconnectedness of knowledge. By embracing this approach, we, too, can cultivate the focus and humility necessary to excel in our own endeavors while remaining open to the potential for collaboration and the exchange of ideas across disciplines.

The Unfettered Mind: Stephen Hawking's Symphony of Focus

Stephen Hawking, the brilliant physicist who defied his body's limitations to explore the vastness of the cosmos, wasn't just a scientific mind; he was a testament to the transformative power of Disciplined Perception. His life story offers invaluable insights into overcoming physical limitations and achieving remarkable feats through sheer mental focus and strategic collaboration.

A. Transcending the Physical: A Symphony of Mind and Machine

Hawking's ALS diagnosis presented a seemingly insurmountable challenge. Yet, he defied the odds, embracing Disciplined Perception as a tool to transcend his physical limitations. His quote, "However difficult life may seem, there is always something you can do and succeed at," exemplifies this unwavering spirit. He did not allow his physical constraints to define him. Instead, he harnessed the power of selective awareness, focusing his mental energy on areas where he could excel. In essence, Hawking became a conductor, leading an orchestra of his intellect, his assistive technologies, and his collaborative network to achieve groundbreaking discoveries. He became a living embodiment of his own advice: "*Do not be disabled in spirit as well as physically.*"

B. The Unwavering Gaze: A Single-Minded Pursuit of Knowledge

Hawking's dedication to physics was not driven by accolades; it stemmed from a much deeper wellspring–the joy of discovery. His quote, "*No one undertakes research in physics with the intention of winning a prize. It is the joy of discovering something no one knew before*," underscores this intrinsic motivation. He possessed a single-minded focus, a laser-like intensity directed towards unraveling the mysteries of the universe. This unwavering focus, a hallmark of Disciplined Perception, allowed him to delve into the cosmos with unparalleled depth and clarity.

The Power of Neuroplasticity–Rewiring the Brain for Success

While Hawking's ALS limited his physical movement, neuroscience reveals a fascinating counterpoint–neuroplasticity. The brain possesses a remarkable ability to adapt and rewire itself throughout life. Hawking's relentless mental engagement likely strengthened the neural pathways crucial for scientific reasoning and complex problem-solving. In essence, his focused attention became a tool for rewiring his own brain, creating new pathways for intellectual exploration.

The Phoenix Rising–Finding Strength in Adversity

Self-Help: Hawking's story serves as a potent message for anyone facing adversity. It demonstrates that limitations, however severe, need not define us. By harnessing the power of Disciplined Perception, we can cultivate a growth mindset, focusing on the possibilities within our reach rather than the limitations that may seem to confine us. We can learn to channel our energies, collaborate with others, and ultimately rise like a phoenix from the ashes of adversity.

The Hawking Enigma–Unmasking the Secrets of a Focused Mind

Thriller Twist: Imagine a world where brilliant minds possess an almost superhuman ability to focus, shut out distractions, and delve into the universe's deepest mysteries. With his unwavering focus and relentless pursuit of knowledge, Stephen Hawking could be seen as a member of this elite group. His ability to transcend physical limitations through sheer mental power is almost superhuman. Perhaps the true marvel was not the elegance of his theories but the Hawking Enigma–the unwavering mental focus that allowed him to crack the cosmic code.

The Flow State and the Power of Intrinsic Motivation

Psychologically, Hawking's passion for physics aligns with the concept of the flow state. This state of optimal experience occurs when we are fully immersed in a challenging but enjoyable task, losing track of time and self-consciousness. His quote about the "joy of discovery" suggests that he frequently entered this state fueled by intrinsic motivation. By cultivating this state of focused engagement, we, too, can unlock our full potential and experience the profound satisfaction of intellectual pursuits.

By exploring these diverse perspectives, we gain a deeper understanding of the "Hawking Phenomenon." He was not just a physicist; he was a testament to the power of the human mind to overcome limitations and achieve remarkable feats. By embracing the lessons gleaned from his life, we too can cultivate the unwavering focus and collaborative spirit necessary to pursue our own intellectual journeys.

Elon Musk: The Relentless Architect of the Future

Elon Musk, the visionary entrepreneur behind Tesla, SpaceX, and many other audacious businesses, is not just a CEO but rather a force of nature. The qualities that have made him relentless perfectionism, single-minded focus, willingness to take risks and innovate, and involvement right at the grassroots level form the basis of this chapter.

Elon Musk is nothing less than a force of nature in business. He is a far-sighted entrepreneur at the helm of Tesla and SpaceX, among other daring ventures. This chapter explores the dimensions of his personality that so sharply define him: relentless perfectionism, single-mindedness, innovating and risk-taking, and bottom-line involvement.

Two Faces to a Single Coine

While Nikola Tesla and Elon Musk are both dreamers in their own right, their contributions and manners are dissimilar yet intertwined. Tesla, a mystifying inventor, actually bracketed the basics for most modern technologies with his work on electricity and magnetism. His doggedness to keep ahead was a man out of time, so he came to be called "The Wardenclyffe Wizard."

In that respect, Elon Musk represents an insatiable drive to make those ideas plausible, from the realm of the mind into tangible reality. With Tesla, SpaceX, and Neuralink, among others, Musk has stretched the limits of technology and space exploration, making fantastical concepts tangible. He builds upon pioneering work done by people such as Tesla and shows how visionary thinking adjusts and changes with new challenges and opportunities.

A. The Flawlessness Forge: Perfectionism as a Catalyst for Innovation

Imagine a captivating biography or documentary exploring the relentless pursuit of excellence. Musk embodies Unyielding Perfectionism. His unwavering focus on detail, evident in his refusal to accept anything less than a perfect score, translates into a relentless drive for innovation. He understands true progress often lies in relentlessly pushing boundaries and refusing to settle for mediocrity. This pursuit of flawlessness becomes a forge where groundbreaking ideas are born.

B. The Man in the Machine: Singular Focus Fuels Visionary Achievements

Musk's Singular Focus is legendary. Imagine a biography or a suspenseful thriller where the protagonist dedicates themself entirely to a mission. During Tesla's early days, he was not just the CEO; he was deeply embedded in the process. His willingness to work grueling hours, even sleeping at the office, exemplifies his unwavering commitment. This singular focus allows him to delve into complex problems, envisioning solutions that revolutionize entire industries.

C. The Moonshot Maestro: Risk-Taking and Innovation Redefine the Possible

Musk is not afraid to take risks. He is a champion of Risk-Taking and Innovation, a quality that sets him apart from conventional leaders. Whether revolutionizing electric vehicles with the Tesla cars concept or colonizing Mars with SpaceX, he pushes the boundaries of what is considered possible. His audacity and willingness to challenge the status quo inspire others to dream big and strive for the seemingly impossible. His resilience serves as a testament to the power of calculated risk-taking in achieving groundbreaking change.

D. The Hands-On Hero: Ground-Level Involvement for Sustainable Success

Despite leading large companies, Musk prioritizes Ground-Level Involvement. Imagine a biography or a business book highlighting the importance of practical involvement. He dives deep into the technical details of his ventures, understanding the intricacies of the processes he oversees. This hands-on approach allows him to not only lead from the front but also make informed decisions based on a thorough understanding of the challenges and opportunities at play. His commitment to practical involvement serves as a valuable lesson for leaders of all stripes.

By examining these characteristics, we gain a richer understanding of Elon Musk, the relentless architect of the future. He is not just a businessman but a visionary leader who demonstrates the transformative power of unwavering focus, a relentless pursuit of excellence, and a willingness to challenge the status quo. His story serves as an inspiration to anyone who dares to dream big and create a better tomorrow.

The Gates Code: Unlocking the Secrets of a Visionary Leader

Bill Gates, the co-founder of Microsoft and a renowned philanthropist, is more than just a tech titan. He is a master strategist who built his success on a unique blend of collaboration, focus, and a growth mindset. By examining his characteristics, we can unlock the Gates Code, a blueprint for achieving excellence in any field.

A. The Orchestra of Ideas: Building Synergy Through Collaboration

Gates famously stated, "We all need people who will give us feedback. That's how we improve." This quote highlights his deep understanding of the power of collaboration. He recognized that true innovation rarely happens in isolation. By fostering an intellectual synergy group–a team of talented individuals who challenge and complement each other's ideas–Gates created the fertile ground for Microsoft's groundbreaking products.

The Network Effect–Amplifying Intelligence

Neuroscience is beginning to shed light on the benefits of collaboration. Studies have shown that working in teams can lead to increased creativity and problem-solving abilities. When diverse minds come together, they create a network effect, where the collective intelligence is greater than the sum of its parts. Gates, perhaps intuitively, understood this principle. He built Microsoft not just as a company but as a collaborative ecosystem where ideas could flourish.

The Feedback Loop–Sharpening Your Skills

Self-Help: In today's world, surrounded by self-promotion, Gates' emphasis on feedback is a refreshing reminder of its importance. We can create a feedback loop that fuels continuous improvement by surrounding ourselves with trusted advisors and colleagues who offer honest, constructive feedback. This aligns with the concept of a growth mindset, where we view challenges and setbacks as opportunities to learn and evolve.

The Gates Code–Cracking the Innovation Enigma

Thriller Twist: Imagine a world where entrepreneurs possess a secret weapon–the ability to assemble a team of brilliant minds, each one a master of their domain. With his emphasis on collaboration and intellectual synergy, Bill Gates could be seen as a leader in this elite group. His ability to cultivate a focused and growth-oriented environment is the key to unlocking the true potential of his team. Perhaps the true innovation was not just Microsoft software but the Gates Code—a unique approach to leadership that cracked the enigma of innovation.

B. The Focused Lens: Avoiding Distractions and Embracing Your Uniqueness

Gates' quote, "*Do not compare yourself with anyone in this world ... if you do so, you are insulting yourself,*" underscores his unwavering focus. He understood that chasing after someone else's success is a recipe for mediocrity. True fulfillment lies in identifying your own unique strengths and talents and channeling your energy into pursuits that align with your vision. This focus allows you to develop a laser-like intensity, filtering out distractions and directing your efforts toward achieving your goals.

Self-Awareness and the Power of Intrinsic Motivation

Psychologically, Gates' emphasis on self-discovery aligns with the concept of self-awareness. We can chart a course toward a fulfilling life by understanding our strengths, weaknesses, and passions. His focus on individuality resonates with the concept of intrinsic motivation, the internal drive to pursue activities that we find inherently rewarding. When we focus on our own unique path fueled by intrinsic motivation, we are less likely to be swayed by the allure of external validation.

C. The Resilience Furnace: Learning from Failure and Embracing Growth

Gates' advice, "*It is fine to celebrate success, but it is more important to heed the lessons of failure,*" highlights his resilience. He viewed setbacks not as roadblocks but as stepping stones on the path to success. By embracing a growth mindset, we cultivate the ability to learn from our mistakes and emerge stronger from each challenge. This enthusiasm for learning, even from failures, fuels our perseverance and propels us towards achieving our goals.

Delving into these diverse perspectives helps us gain a richer understanding of the Gates Code. Bill Gates was not just a businessman but a visionary leader who understood the power of collaboration, focus, and a growth mindset. By embracing the lessons gleaned from his life, we can, too, cultivate the collaborative spirit, unwavering focus, and growth mindset necessary to achieve our own unique brand of success.

D. The Startup Alchemist: Fueling Innovation with an Entrepreneurial Spirit (Self-Help/Thriller)

Self-Help: His quotes, "*Your most unhappy customers are your greatest source of learning.*" and "*The way to be successful in the software world is to come up with breakthrough software... surprising the marketplace,*" showcase his entrepreneurial spirit. Imagine yourself as a budding entrepreneur on a self-help quest for success. Much like a determined protagonist in a business thriller, Gates exemplifies this quality. He was unafraid to take risks, leaving Harvard to pursue his vision for Microsoft. This decision, fueled by a high level of risk tolerance and a belief in one's abilities, became the catalyst for a technological revolution.

The Growth Mindset and Embracing Failure

Psychologically, Gates' emphasis on learning from unhappy customers aligns with the concept of a growth mindset. He saw challenges and setbacks as opportunities for improvement, constantly seeking feedback to refine his ideas. His quote, "*It is fine *to celebrate success, but it is more important to heed the lessons of failure,"* further underscores this belief.

E. The Evolving Billionaire: From Tech Titan to Global Citizen

Thriller Twist: Gates' transition from Microsoft to philanthropy with the Bill & Melinda Gates Foundation reflects a significant shift in focus toward Philanthropy and Social Responsibility. Imagine a powerful leader in a psychological thriller who undergoes a personal transformation. Gates embodies this evolution, demonstrating a deep sense of social responsibility and a desire to contribute to global health. This shift highlights a complex character with a strong, empathetic side, willing to adapt and prioritize the greater good.

F. The Insatiable Learner: A Journey of Continuous Curiosity

Gates' voracious reading habits and interest in diverse topics like science and education showcase his Intellectual Curiosity and Continuous Learning. Imagine a world of popular science documentaries where brilliant minds constantly expand their knowledge. Gates is a prime example. He has an open-minded approach and a thirst for knowledge fueling his ongoing intellectual growth. This curiosity is likely a key driver of his success, allowing him to innovate in technology and philanthropy.

By exploring these diverse perspectives, we gain a richer understanding of Bill Gates's multifaceted nature. He isn't just a businessman or a philanthropist; he's a testament to the power of entrepreneurial spirit, compassionate leadership, and a lifelong commitment to learning. By embracing these qualities, we, too, can embark on a journey of innovation, social responsibility, and continuous intellectual growth.

Steve Jobs: The Iconoclast with a Vision

Steve Jobs, the co-founder of Apple and a transformative technological figure, was not just a businessman but an Iconoclast with a Vision. By examining his characteristics, we delve into the mind that shaped iconic products and revolutionized user experience. He embodied a relentless focus on Attention to Detail and Design, unwavering Perseverance and Resilience, a visionary approach with Visionary Thinking, and a contagious sense of Confidence.

A. The Design Maestro: Crafting Beauty with Attention to Detail

Jobs' quote, "*Be a yardstick of quality. Some people are not used to an environment where excellence is expected.*" highlights his meticulous approach to Attention to Detail and Design. Imagine a popular science documentary showcasing the meticulous process behind creating a masterpiece. Like a design maestro, Jobs was obsessed with every aspect of his products, from aesthetics to user experience. This relentless focus on quality became a hallmark of Apple and a source of inspiration for aspiring designers and entrepreneurs alike.

The Power of Intrinsic Motivation

Psychologically, Jobs' dedication to design was not driven by market trends; it stemmed from a deeper wellspring–intrinsic motivation. He was driven by a passion for creating beautiful and user-friendly products, a passion that resonated with users and propelled Apple to the forefront of innovation.

B. The Relentless Dreamer: Perseverance and Resilience Fuel Innovation (Thriller/Self-Help)

Jobs quotes, *"You cannot connect the dots looking forward; you can only connect them looking backward. So, you have to trust that the dots will somehow connect in your future. You have to trust in something - your gut, destiny, life, karma, whatever. This approach has never let me down, and it has made all the difference in my life."* speaks volumes about his Perseverance and Resilience. Imagine a character in a self-help thriller facing setbacks but never giving up on their dream. Despite facing challenges and even being ousted from Apple, Jobs persisted in his vision. His unwavering belief is captured in his quote, *"That has been one of my mantras - focus, and simplicity. Simple can be harder than complex... But it is worth it in the end because once you get there, you can move mountains,"* became a guiding light for him and his team.

C. The Tech Oracle: Visionary Thinking Shapes the Future

Thriller Twist: Jobs' quote, *"Innovation distinguishes between a leader and a follower,"* underscores his Visionary Thinking. He was not just building computers; he was envisioning the future of technology. Imagine a world of science documentaries where brilliant minds forecast the future. Jobs, like a tech oracle, possessed this foresight, identifying client needs and predicting trends that would change the way we interact with technology.

D. The Instilling Leader: Confidence Breeds Confidence

Jobs' confidence is evident in his quote, *"You can deliver; do not be afraid."* He was not just a leader but an Instilling Leader, inspiring confidence in his team. Imagine a powerful leader in a psychological thriller who rallies the troops with unwavering belief. Jobs possessed a similar charisma, motivating his team to achieve seemingly impossible feats by believing in himself and inspiring others with his unwavering confidence. His quote, "*Your time is limited, so do not waste it living someone else's life... Do not let the noise of others' opinions drown out your own inner voice. And most importantly, have the courage to follow your heart and intuition.*" This quality exemplifies this quality and is a message that continues to resonate with entrepreneurs and dreamers worldwide.

By exploring these diverse perspectives, we gain a richer understanding of Steve Jobs's complex and captivating Nature. He wasn't just a businessman or a tech guru; he was a testament to the power of meticulous attention to detail, unwavering perseverance, visionary thinking, and infectious confidence. By embracing these qualities, we, too, can push the boundaries of innovation and inspire others to pursue their dreams.

Google Genesis: Visionaries Fueled by Curiosity and Collaboration

Larry Page and Sergey Brin, Google's co-founders, weren't just tech titans; they were the embodiment of a powerful partnership. By examining their characteristics, we delve into the minds that built a search engine empire, unveiling a shared passion for Visionary Thinking, an insatiable Intellectual Curiosity, a commitment to a Collaborative Approach, and a fearless spirit of Risk-Taking.

A. Revolutionaries with a Cause: Visionary Thinking Paves the Way

Their quote, "*If you are changing the world, you are working on important things. You are excited to get up in the morning.*" (Larry Page) and "Lots of companies do not succeed over time. What do they fundamentally do wrong? They usually miss the future." (Larry

Page) exemplifies their Visionary Thinking. Imagine a captivating biography or business documentary where two young entrepreneurs dream of changing the world. With their audacious vision of organizing the world's information, Page and Brin embodied this spirit. Their unwavering commitment to this mission fueled Google's meteoric rise.

B. The Insatiable Mind: Intellectual Curiosity Drives Innovation

Thriller Twist: Their expertise in mathematical algorithms and data mining reflects their Intellectual Curiosity. Imagine a world of science documentaries where brilliant minds constantly push the boundaries of knowledge. Much like relentless investigators in a science thriller, Page and Brin were constantly seeking better answers and pushing technological boundaries. Their quote, *"Always work hard on something uncomfortably exciting."* (Larry Page) further underscores their dedication to unconventional thinking and unrelenting innovation.

C. The Innovation Powerhouse: Collaboration Breeds Success

Their quote, *"Small groups of people can have a really huge impact."* (Larry Page) demonstrates their belief in a Collaborative Approach. Imagine a world of psychology documentaries exploring the power of teamwork. Page and Brin fostered a culture where creativity thrived, and employees were inspired to think outside the box. They energized the workforce with ambitious goals, creating an innovation powerhouse.

D. Daring to Dream Big: The Risk-Takers Who Changed the World

Their unconventional methods, from the Lego server in the early days to the famous "*Do not be evil*" motto, reflect their willingness to take risks. Their quotes, "*If you are not some things that are crazy, then you are doing the wrong things*" (Larry Page) and "*It is very hard to fail completely if you aim high enough.*" (Larry Page) showcase their risk-taking spirit.

Thriller Twist: Imagine a business thriller in which audacious entrepreneurs challenge the status quo. Page and Brin, like the protagonists in such a story, embrace calculated risks and learn from failures (as Sergey Brin suggests, "The only way you are going to have success is to have lots of failures first."), ultimately changing the world with their innovation.

By exploring these diverse perspectives, we gain a richer understanding of Larry Page and Sergey Brin's visionary partnership. Their story is a testament to the power of thinking big, collaborating effectively, and embracing the unknown. By harnessing these qualities, we, too, can embark on a journey of innovation and leave our own mark on the world.

Henry Ford: The Titan of Focused Action

Henry Ford, the man who revolutionized transportation with the Model T, was not just an industrialist; he was a champion of Service and Concentrated Action. His unwavering focus on a single goal–providing affordable transportation for the masses–transformed the automobile industry.

A. The Model-Maker: Service Through Focused Action

Imagine a historical fiction novel or a biography chronicling the rise of an industry titan. Ford embodied the power of service through focused action. His unwavering commitment to providing "the greatest transportation service at the lowest cost" was not just a slogan; it was his guiding principle. By relentlessly pursuing this singular goal, he made automobiles accessible to the average American, forever changing the landscape of transportation.

B. The Master of Efficiency: Selective Awareness in Action

Ford's dedication to service is also manifested in his Selective Awareness. Imagine a biography or a self-help book exploring the power of focus. He understood the importance of filtering out distractions and prioritizing his core business policy. This laser focus allowed him to streamline production with the assembly line, making the Model T affordable and efficient. His approach serves as a reminder of the power of selective awareness in achieving ambitious goals.

C. A Legacy of Innovation: The Enduring Impact of Focused Action

Henry Ford's legacy extends far beyond the Model T. His philosophy of concentrated action continues to influence businesses worldwide. Imagine a documentary exploring the history of innovation. Ford revolutionized an entire industry by focusing on a single, well-defined goal and eliminating distractions. His story is a testament to the enduring impact of focused action and unwavering commitment to service.

Epilogue

ECHOES OF THE MIND

᭔᭔᭔

As you tend to the flourishing realm of discerning insight (Selective Awareness), a remarkable metamorphosis takes shape. In the quiet dawn, a stirring truth unfolds before you: You are the master craftsman of your own fate. No longer tossed about by the tempests of fate, you rise as the steward of your own spirit, commanding the strength of unwavering focus like a skilled artisan nurturing their most cherished creations.

In this verdant realm of discerning insight, the shadows of uncertainty and despair are cast aside, their hold weakened. You have discovered the elixir that dispels the insidious poisons that once imperiled your quest for freedom of choice. Like a wise sage deciphering the riddles of fate, you have unveiled the shadowy powers that endeavored to ensnare your spirit.

This newfound freedom is not a call to indulge in selfish desires. It is a hallowed duty that calls forth the strength of the heart and the courage of the spirit. Thou hast acquired the wisdom to traverse the realm with a keen gaze, ensuring that thy desires are fulfilled with a gentle grace. Vanished is the hasty clutch for ephemeral yearnings, supplanted by the sagacity of a steadfast steward nurturing a fruitful yield.

Within the bounteous world of your thoughts, a deep tranquility begins to flourish. In the grand tapestry of existence, what once appeared as insurmountable barriers transform into pathways for noble ascendance. You have embraced the noble craft of acceptance, not through surrender but with a steadfast assurance in your capacity to endure and flourish amidst the trials of life.

The Flourishing Realm of Discerning Insight is not merely a sanctuary for the soul; it serves as a passage to a realm of greater fulfillment. Through the noble craft of harmonious discourse, you spin a rich tapestry of comprehension, nurturing bonds that serve the good of all. The garden thrives not in solitude but in lively communion with the realm that surrounds it.

Thus, nurture your garden with utmost diligence. For within its flourishing depths lies not merely personal fulfillment but the promise to nurture a realm teeming with harmony, purpose, and the limitless potential of the human spirit.

PRELUDE

FIFTH AND THE FINAL BOOK: ARCHITECTS OF A FUTURE DAWN

❧ ❧ ❧

I n the twilight of our current era, as the stars begin to fade and the first light of a new dawn approaches, we stand on the precipice of an extraordinary transformation. Imagine a world where the boundaries of possibility are constantly being redefined, where the echoes of ancient wisdom harmonize with the whispers of futuristic visions. This is the realm we are about to enter, a realm where the architects of tomorrow are called to rise and shape the future.

As we embark on this journey, we must first acknowledge the ashes from which we rise. The resilience and vision required to rebuild and craft a sustainable future are embodied in the stories of those who have faced adversity and emerged stronger. From Ashes to Ascendancy explores the foundational steps of rebuilding, sustainability, and personal legacy.

Next, we delve into the attributes that define a civilized nation system. The Vanguard of a New Order examines the synthesis of individual potential, the empowerment of communities, and the equilibrium of governance. It is a symphony of checks and balances, where economic ascendancy and the alchemy of inspiration drive progress.

In The Siren's Call, we navigate the misguided ideas that threaten to derail our progress. These are the siren songs of stagnation, sameness, instant gratification, and isolation. Recognizing and overcoming these pitfalls is crucial to maintaining our forward momentum.

Whispers from the Future offers a guide to an enlightened tomorrow. Here, we explore the instruments of progress, foundational principles, and the call to action that will guide us toward a brighter dawn. The guardians of progress who champion humanity's triumph are the torchbearers of this new era.

Finally, in A Tapestry Woven with Starlight, we call upon the guardians of tomorrow to weave a future filled with hope, innovation and shared success. This is a call to action for all who dare to dream and strive for a better world.

As you turn the final pages of this book, envision the pyramids of Giza, their colossal forms a testament to a civilization's focused vision. Picture the soaring melody of a Beethoven symphony, each note meticulously placed to create a masterpiece. These achievements, seemingly born from magic, are actually the result of something far more potent–Disciplined Perception.

Think of yourself as a conductor, leading an orchestra of your own thoughts and desires. Through focused attention, you, too, can harmonize these internal instruments, composing a symphony of success. The science behind disciplined perception will be your guide, while captivating anecdotes serve as sheet music, bringing these principles to life.

I hope is that these stories will not just entertain you but ignite a fire within. Perhaps you will discover a hidden talent, unearth a long-forgotten dream, or gain the tools to tackle that nagging project with renewed vigor. After all, you, too, have the potential to contribute your verse to the ongoing saga of human achievement. Are you ready to unlock the conductor within?

REFERENCES

[1] How We Use Selective Attention to Filter Information and Focus - https://www.verywellmind.com/what-is-selective-attention-2795022

[2] Reticular formation - https://en.wikipedia.org/wiki/Reticular_formation?form=MG0AV3

[3] References – adopted from Copilot AI: Collective Focus and Synergy

- Woolley, A. W., et al. (2010). "Evidence for a Collective Intelligence Factor in the Performance of Human Groups." Science. This study demonstrates how group performance can exceed the sum of individual members' capabilities.

- Senge, P. M. (1990). "The Fifth Discipline: The Art and Practice of the Learning Organization." This book explains how organizations can harness collective learning and focus to achieve extraordinary results.

[4] References – adopted from Copilot AI: Mirror Neurons and Their Function:

- Iacoboni, M. (2009). "Imitation, Empathy, and Mirror Neurons." Annual Review of Psychology. This article explores the role of mirror neurons in social behavior and group dynamics.

- Rizzolatti, G., & Craighero, L. (2004). "The Mirror-Neuron System." Annual Review of Neuroscience. It discusses how mirror neurons contribute to understanding others' actions and intentions.

[5] References – adopted from Copilot AI: Disciplined Perception

- Kabat-Zinn, J. (1990). "Full Catastrophe Living: Using the Wisdom of Your Body and Mind to Face Stress, Pain, and Illness." This book discusses the importance of mindfulness and attention to detail in daily tasks.

- Csikszentmihalyi, M. (1990). "Flow: The Psychology of Optimal Experience." This work explores how complete immersion in activities can enhance focus and satisfaction.

[6] References – adopted from Copilot AI: Metaphor of Building Muscle

- Duhigg, C. (2012). "The Power of Habit: Why We Do What We Do in Life and Business." This book emphasizes the power of small, consistent actions in creating significant changes over time.

[7] Executive Functions - https://papers.ssrn.com/sol3/papers.cfm?abstract_id=2198231&form=MG0AV3

[8] The power of habit: Why we do what we do in life and business. - https://psycnet.apa.org/record/2012-09134-000?form=MG0AV3

[9] Nakamura, J., & Csikszentmihalyi, M. (2009). Flow Theory and Research. In S. W. Driscoll (Ed.), Oxford Handbook of Human Motivation (pp. 195-206). Oxford University Press.

[10] Alterations of neural activity in the prefrontal cortex associated with deficits in working memory performance - https://www.frontiersin.org/journals/behavioral-neuroscience/articles/10.3389/fnbeh.2023.1213435/full?form=MG0AV3

[11] The prefrontal cortex: from monkey to man - https://academic.oup.com/brain/article/147/3/794/7424860?form=MG0AV3

[12] Neurobiological Changes Induced by Mindfulness and Meditation: A Systematic Review - https://www.mdpi.com/2227-9059/12/11/2613?form=MG0AV3

[13] 4 Ways How Meditation Changes Your Prefrontal Cortex (And How It Benefits You) - https://www.outofstress.com/meditation-prefrontal-cortex/?form=MG0AV3

[14] 13 Brain Exercises to Help Keep You Mentally Sharp - https://www.healthline.com/health/mental-health/brain-exercises?form=MG0AV3

[15] Exercise and the Brain: The Neuroscience of Fitness Explored - https://neurosciencenews.com/fitness-neuroscience-23228/?form=MG0AV3

[16] SMART Goals - https://www.projectsmart.co.uk/smart-goals/index.php?form=MG0AV3

[17] "Atomic Habits" by James Clear - https://jamesclear.com/atomic-habits?form=MG0AV3

[18] The Role of the Amygdala in Human Behavior and Emotion - https://www.verywellmind.com/the-role-of-the-amygdala-in-human-behavior-and-emotion-7499223

[19] The Neuroscience of Emotion and Intrinsic Motivation - https://link.springer.com/chapter/10.1007/978-981-99-5378-3_4?form=MG0AV3

[20] CHAPTER 23 From Stimulus Control to Self-Control: Toward an Integrative Understanding of the Processes Underlying Willpower Get access Arrow - https://academic.oup.com/book/32883/chapter-abstract/276400264?redirectedFrom=fulltext

[21] A Review on the Role of the Neuroscience of Flow States in the Modern World - https://www.mdpi.com/2076-328X/10/9/137?form=MG0AV3

[22] The Neuroscience of the Flow State: Involvement of the Locus Coeruleus Norepinephrine System - https://www.frontiersin.org/journals/psychology/articles/10.3389/fpsyg.2021.645498/full?form=MG0AV3

[23] A Review on the Role of the Neuroscience of Flow States in the Modern World - https://www.mdpi.com/2076-328X/10/9/137?form=MG0AV3

[24] Attention in Psychology, Neuroscience, and Machine Learning - https://www.frontiersin.org/journals/computational-neuroscience/articles/10.3389/fncom.2020.00029/full?form=MG0AV3

[25] A comprehensive review of attention tests: can we assess what we exactly do not understand? - https://ejnpn.springeropen.com/articles/10.1186/s41983-023-00628-4?form=MG0AV3

[26] A comprehensive review of attention tests: can we assess what we exactly do not understand? - https://ejnpn.springeropen.com/articles/10.1186/s41983-023-00628-4?form=MG0AV3

[27] Reticular Activating System: Brain Function and Importance - https://neurolaunch.com/ras-brain/

[28] The reticular activating system: a narrative review of discovery, evolving understanding, and relevance to current formulations of brain death - https://link.springer.com/article/10.1007/s12630-023-02421-6?form=MG0AV3

[29] Identifying Risk and Resilience Factors in the Intergenerational Cycle of Maltreatment: Results From the TRANS-GEN Study Investigating the Effects of Maternal Attachment and Social Support on Child Attachment and Cardiovascular Stress Physiology - https://www.frontiersin.org/journals/human-neuroscience/articles/10.3389/fnhum.2022.890262/full?form=MG0AV3

[30] Intrinsically Motivated - How to foster authentic student motivation and build a classroom of engaged, tenacious learners - https://www.gse.harvard.edu/ideas/usable-knowledge/16/09/intrinsically-motivated?form=MG0AV3

[31] Transformational Leadership Style: How to Inspire and Motivate - https://www.simplypsychology.org/what-is-transformational-leadership.html?form=MG0AV3

[32] How Transformational Leadership Can Inspire Others - https://www.verywellmind.com/what-is-transformational-leadership-2795313

[33] The role of passion in sustainable psychological well-being - https://psywb.springeropen.com/articles/10.1186/2211-1522-2-1?form=MG0AV3

[34] Mental Imagery Skills in Competitive Young Athletes and Non-athletes - https://www.frontiersin.org/journals/psychology/articles/10.3389/fpsyg.2020.00633/full?form=MG0AV3

[35] On what motivates us: a detailed review of intrinsic v. extrinsic motivation - https://www.cambridge.org/core/journals/psychological-medicine/article/on-what-motivates-us-a-detailed-review-of-intrinsic-v-extrinsic-motivation/3FC35CD80D991744CD764AF2FBCD3BBB?form=MG0AV3

[36] Intrinsic Motivation Explained: 10 Examples & Key Factors - https://positivepsychology.com/intrinsic-motivation-examples/

[37] Psychological Well-Being and Intrinsic Motivation: Relationship in Students Who Begin University Studies at the School of Education in Ciudad Real - https://www.frontiersin.org/journals/psychology/articles/10.3389/fpsyg.2020.02054/full

[38] What Is Cognitive Behavioral Therapy (CBT) and How Does It Work? - https://www.verywellmind.com/what-is-cognitive-behavior-therapy-2795747

[39] How We Use Selective Attention to Filter Information and Focus - https://www.verywellmind.com/what-is-selective-attention-2795022

[40] How We Use Selective Attention to Filter Information and Focus - https://www.verywellmind.com/what-is-selective-attention-2795022

[41] What Is Cognitive Behavioral Therapy (CBT) and How Does It Work? - https://www.verywellmind.com/what-is-cognitive-behavior-therapy-2795747

[42] Collective Intelligence: Concepts and Reasons to Choose It - https://atlan.com/collective-intelligence/?form=MG0AV3

[43] The Psychology of Teamwork: 7 Habits of Highly Effective Teams - https://positivepsychology.com/psychology-teamwork/?form=MG0AV3

[44] The Power of Buddhist Meditation: A Guide to Inner Peace and Happiness - https://mindfulnessexercises.com/meditation/buddhist/?form=MG0AV3

[45] What is biblical discernment and why is it important? - https://www.gty.org/library/questions/QA138/what-is-biblical-discernment-and-why-is-it-important?form=MG0AV3

[46] Tawakkul (Trust in God): Its Meaning, Importance & Benefits - https://blog.muslimandquran.com/tawakkul-trust-in-god-its-meaning-importance-benefits/?form=MG0AV3

[47] Napoleon Bonaparte: The reckless genius behind the French Empire - https://www.historyskills.com/classroom/year-9/napoleon-bonaparte/?form=MG0AV3

[48] What We Can Learn From Leonardo - https://www.ecoliteracy.org/article/what-we-can-learn-leonardo?form=MG0AV3

[49] Socratic method - https://en.wikipedia.org/wiki/Socratic_method?form=MG0AV3

[50] Stoicism - https://en.wikipedia.org/wiki/Stoicism?form=MG0AV3

[51] Mindsets to Help Athletes Perform in the Zone - https://www.peaksports.com/sports-psychology-blog/mindsets-to-help-athletes-perform-in-the-zone/?form=MG0AV3

[52] What Is Visionary Leadership? 7 Traits of a Visionary Leader - https://status.net/articles/visionary-leadership/?form=MG0AV3

[53] The science of willpower - https://scopeblog.stanford.edu/2011/12/29/a-conversation-about-the-science-of-willpower/

[54] Behaviors, Emotions, And Feelings: How They Work Together - https://www.betterhelp.com/advice/behavior/behaviors-emotions-and-feelings-how-they-work-together/

[55] Analytical Skills Vs Critical Thinking - https://primeast.com/insights/analytical-skills-vs-critical-thinking/

[56] Leadership, Ethics, and Decision-Making - https://www.researchgate.net/publication/369844271_Leadership_Ethics_and_Decision-Making

[57] How Memory Works - https://bokcenter.harvard.edu/how-memory-works

[58] Unleashing Your Creativity: Exploring the Power of Imagination - https://medium.com/@positiveaffirmations91/unleashing-your-creativity-exploring-the-power-of-imagination-16ee354a021a

[59] Exploring Intuition and its Role in Managerial Decision Making - https://www.researchgate.net/publication/254412101_Exploring_Intuition_and_its_Role_in_Managerial_Decision_Making

[60] The Power of the Subconscious Mind - https://www.researchgate.net/publication/365211107_The_Power_of_the_Subconscious_Mind

[61] The Brain That Changes Itself: Stories of Personal Triumph from the Frontiers of Brain Science - https://www.amazon.com/Brain-That-Changes-Itself-Frontiers/dp/0143113100?form=MG0AV3

[62] Flow: The Psychology of Optimal Experience (Harper Perennial Modern - https://www.amazon.com/Flow-Psychology-Experience-Perennial-Classics/dp/0061339202?form=MG0AV3

[63] Kabat-Zinn, J. (1990). Full Catastrophe Living.

[64] Newport, C. (2016). Deep Work: Rules for Focused Success in a Distracted World.

[65] Goleman, D. (2013). Focus: The Hidden Driver of Excellence.

[66] Livio, M. (2017). Why?: What Makes Us Curious.

[67] Taylor, S. E., & Pham, L. B. (1996). Why thinking about goals and dreams enhances performance. Psychological Bulletin.

[68] Berger, W. (2014). A More Beautiful Question: The Power of Inquiry to Spark Breakthrough Ideas.

[69] Emotions Revealed, Second Edition: Recognizing Faces and Feelings to Improve Communication and Emotional Life - https://www.amazon.com/Emotions-Revealed-Second-Recognizing-Communication/dp/0805083391

[70] Detecting Lies and Deceit - Pitfalls and Opportunities 2e - https://www.amazon.sa/-/en/Detecting-Lies-Deceit-Pitfalls-Opportunities/dp/0470516259

[71] The Influence of Experience and Deliberate Practice on the Development of Superior Expert Performance - https://www.cambridge.org/core/books/abs/cambridge-handbook-of-expertise-and-expert-performance/influence-of-experience-and-deliberate-practice-on-the-development-of-superior-expert-performance/C56EDDE9E57B259825916E061B025A72

[72] Understanding expertise: A multidisciplinary approach - https://www.researchgate.net/publication/291521499_Understanding_expertise_A_multidisciplinary_approach

[73] Emotional Intelligence: Why It Can Matter More Than IQ - https://www.amazon.com/Emotional-Intelligence-Matter-More-Than/dp/055338371X

[74] The Functional Architecture of Human Empathy - https://www.researchgate.net/publication/51369194_The_Functional_Architecture_of_Human_Empathy

[75] Executive Functions - https://www.annualreviews.org/content/journals/10.1146/annurev-psych-113011-143750

[76] Full Catastrophe Living (Revised Edition): Using the Wisdom of Your Body and Mind to Face Stress, Pain, and Illness - https://www.amazon.com/Full-Catastrophe-Living-Revised-Illness/dp/0345536932

[77] The Act of Creation - https://en.wikipedia.org/wiki/The_Act_of_Creation

[78] Executive Functions - https://www.annualreviews.org/content/journals/10.1146/annurev-psych-113011-143750

[79] Executive Functions - https://www.annualreviews.org/content/journals/10.1146/annurev-psych-113011-143750

[80] Working Memory: Theories, Models, and Controversies - https://www.annualreviews.org/content/journals/10.1146/annurev-psych-120710-100422

[81] Executive Functions - https://www.annualreviews.org/content/journals/10.1146/annurev-psych-113011-143750

[82] Building a Practically Useful Theory of Goal Setting and Task Motivation: A 35Year Odyssey - https://www.researchgate.net/publication/254734316_Building_a_Practically_Useful_Theory_of_Goal_Setting_and_Task_Motivation_A_35Year_Odyssey

[83] Executive Functions - https://pmc.ncbi.nlm.nih.gov/articles/PMC4084861/

[84] Flow: The Psychology of Optimal Experience - https://www.researchgate.net/publication/224927532_Flow_The_Psychology_of_Optimal_Experience

[85] Behavioral activation - https://en.wikipedia.org/wiki/Behavioral_activation

[86] Behavioral Activation for Depression: A Clinician's Guide - https://www.tandfonline.com/doi/full/10.1080/16506073.2010.514119

[87] References adopted from Google Gemini AI:

- Self-Efficacy: The Exercise of Control - https://edisciplinas.usp.br/pluginfile.php/7953477/mod_resource/content/1/Self-Efficacy_%20The%20Exercise%20of%20Control.pdf

- https://en.wikipedia.org/wiki/Self-Efficacy_(book)

[88] Vroom's Expectancy Models and Work-Related Criteria: A Meta-Analysis - https://www.researchgate.net/publication/232565056_Vroom's_expectancy_models_and_work-related_criteria_A_meta-analysis

[89] Expectancy theory - https://en.wikipedia.org/wiki/Expectancy_theory

[90] Executive Functions - https://www.annualreviews.org/content/journals/10.1146/annurev-psych-113011-143750

[91] The Dual Pathway to Creativity Model: Creative Ideation as a Function of Flexibility and Persistence - https://www.researchgate.net/publication/233301112_The_Dual_Pathway_to_Creativity_Model_Creative_Ideation_as_a_Function_of_Flexibility_and_Persistence

[92] The impact of intergroup idea exposure on group creative problem-solving - https://journals.sagepub.com/doi/10.1177/13684302231216047?icid=int.sj-abstract.similar-articles.4

[93] The effects of emotion on attention: A review of attentional processing of emotional information - https://www.researchgate.net/publication/233893892_The_effects_of_emotion_on_attention_A_review_of_attentional_processing_of_emotional_information

[94] Implementation Intentions: Strong Effects of Simple Plans - https://www.researchgate.net/publication/232586066_Implementation_Intentions_Strong_Effects_of_Simple_Plans

[95] Theory of Cognitive Pattern Recognition - https://cdn.intechopen.com/pdfs/5795/intech-theory_of_cognitive_pattern_recognition.pdf

[96] Mental Models in Cognitive Science - https://www.researchgate.net/publication/228040206_Mental_Models_in_Cognitive_Science

[97] The behavior of organisms - Skinner, BF - https://www.researchgate.net/publication/313181463_The_behavior_of_organisms_-_Skinner_BF

[98] The "What" and "Why" of Goal Pursuits: Human Needs and the Self-Determination of Behavior -

https://selfdeterminationtheory.org/SDT/documents/2000_DeciRyan_PIWhatW
hy.pdf

[99] Building a Practically Useful Theory of Goal Setting and Task Motivation: A
35Year Odyssey -
https://www.researchgate.net/publication/254734316_Building_a_Practically_U
seful_Theory_of_Goal_Setting_and_Task_Motivation_A_35Year_Odyssey

[100] Self-efficacy: The exercise of control - https://en.wikipedia.org/wiki/Self-
Efficacy_(book)

[101] The Role of Deliberate Practice in the Acquisition of Expert Performance -
https://www.researchgate.net/publication/224827585_The_Role_of_Deliberate_
Practice_in_the_Acquisition_of_Expert_Performance

[102] The Role of Positive Emotions in Positive Psychology -
https://pmc.ncbi.nlm.nih.gov/articles/PMC3122271/

[103] Cognitive Behavior Therapy: Basics and Beyond -
https://img3.reoveme.com/m/be38edbbfc79330a.pdf

[104] The Power of Habit: Why We Do What We Do in Life and Business -
https://en.wikipedia.org/wiki/The_Power_of_Habit

[105] Self-efficacy: The exercise of control -
https://edisciplinas.usp.br/pluginfile.php/7953477/mod_resource/content/1/Self-
Efficacy_%20The%20Exercise%20of%20Control.pdf

[106] Building a Practically Useful Theory of Goal Setting and Task Motivation: A
35Year Odyssey -
https://www.researchgate.net/publication/254734316_Building_a_Practically_U
seful_Theory_of_Goal_Setting_and_Task_Motivation_A_35Year_Odyssey

[107] Flow: The Psychology of Optimal Experience -
https://www.amazon.com/Flow-Psychology-Experience-Perennial-
Classics/dp/0061339202

[108] Flow: The Psychology of Optimal Experience -
https://www.researchgate.net/publication/224927532_Flow_The_Psychology_o
f_Optimal_Experience

[109] Willpower: Rediscovering the Greatest Human Strength -
https://en.wikipedia.org/wiki/Willpower:_Rediscovering_the_Greatest_Human_
Strength

[110] Emotion regulation: affective, cognitive, and social consequences -
https://onlinelibrary.wiley.com/doi/pdf/10.1017/S0048577201393198

[111] Flourish: A Visionary New Understanding of Happiness and well-being by
Martin E.P. Seligman - A Book Review -
https://www.researchgate.net/publication/329938839_Flourish_A_Visionary_N

ew_Understanding_of_Happiness_and_well-being_by_Martin_EP_Seligman_-_A_Book_Review

[112] Six views of embodied cognition - https://link.springer.com/article/10.3758/BF03196322

[113] Full catastrophe living: Using the wisdom of your body and mind to face stress, pain, and illness - https://en.wikipedia.org/wiki/Full_Catastrophe_Living

[114] Counting Blessings Versus Burdens: An Experimental Investigation of Gratitude and Subjective Well-Being in Daily Life - https://greatergood.berkeley.edu/pdfs/GratitudePDFs/6Emmons-BlessingsBurdens.pdf

[115] Building a Practically Useful Theory of Goal Setting and Task Motivation: A 35Year Odyssey - https://www.researchgate.net/publication/254734316_Building_a_Practically_Useful_Theory_of_Goal_Setting_and_Task_Motivation_A_35Year_Odyssey

[116] Advances in the Study of Mirror Neurons and Their Impact on Neuroscience: An Editorial - https://pmc.ncbi.nlm.nih.gov/articles/PMC11212500/#:~:text=The%20mirror%20neurons%20constitute%20a,understanding%20of%20social%20cognition%20and

[117] Neuroplasticity - https://gemini.google.com/app/d3e87e747dcdaa56

[118] References adopted from Google Gemini AI:
- Grossman, P., Niemann, L., Schmidt-Wilk, J., & Walach, H. (2004). Mindfulness-based stress reduction and health benefits. Journal of psychosomatic research, 57(1), 35-43.
- Kabat-Zinn, J. (1990). Full catastrophe living: Using the wisdom of your body and mind to face stress, pain, and illness. Delacorte Press.
- Miller, F. G., & Kaptchuk, T. J. (2008). The power of context: reconceptualizing the placebo effect. Journal of the Royal Society of Medicine, 101(5), 222-225.

[119] A Cultural Perspective on Romantic Love https://scholarworks.gvsu.edu/cgi/viewcontent.cgi?article=1135&context=orpc

[120] https://www.simplypsychology.org/john-b-watson.html?form=MG0AV3

www.ingramcontent.com/pod-product-compliance
Lightning Source LLC
Chambersburg PA
CBHW061129120626
46546CB00005B/1716